John Macgregor

The Rob Roy on the Jordan, Nile, Red sea, and Gennesareth

John Macgregor

The Rob Roy on the Jordan, Nile, Red sea, and Gennesareth

ISBN/EAN: 9783337142926

Printed in Europe, USA, Canada, Australia, Japan

Cover: Foto ©Andreas Hilbeck / pixelio.de

More available books at **www.hansebooks.com**

THE

ROB ROY ON THE JORDAN,

NILE, RED SEA, AND GENNESARETH, &c.

A CANOE CRUISE IN PALESTINE AND EGYPT, AND THE
WATERS OF DAMASCUS.

By J. MACGREGOR, M.A.

WITH MAPS AND ILLUSTRATIONS.

NEW YORK:
HARPER & BROTHERS, PUBLISHERS,
FRANKLIN SQUARE.
1870.

TO,

HIS ROYAL HIGHNESS,

THE COMMODORE OF THE CANOE CLUB,

IS DEDICATED

THIS RECORD OF THE 'ROB ROY'S' CRUISE ON ANCIENT RIVERS, LAKES, AND SEAS, IN BIBLE LANDS,

BY

HIS MOST DUTIFUL HUMBLE SERVANT,

THE CAPTAIN.

CONTENTS.

CHAPTER I.

Suez Canal.—Port Said.—Lake Menzaleh.—The Start.—Rogues.—Sandstorm.—Bears.—Ismailia.—Crocodile Lake.—Murders.—Guy Fawkes.—Jackal.—The Canoe.—My Bed..Page 17

CHAPTER II.

Rameses.—Sweet Canal.—Bitter Lakes.—Strange Leap.—Red Sea.—Pharaoh.—Camel Wading.—Wells of Moses.—Mirage.—Suez.—How to lose Money.—Shame!—Cairo Ragged Schools.—On the Nile.—Worship.—Paddle to the Pyramids.—Wild Boars.. 33

CHAPTER III.

The Nile.—Inundation.—Raising Water.—Watering with the Foot.—Rob Roy the Robber.—Catching the Canoe.—Livingstone.—The Delta.—The Seven Streams.—Delight of the Natives.—Fog.—Pigeons.—Potters.—Pumpkin Raft.—Fiddle and Drum.. 48

CHAPTER IV.

Nile and Severn.—Nile and Thames.—Bab el Hagar.—Misery.—Compass-card.—Mansourah.—King Cotton.—Shoeblacks.—The Zrier River.—A Water-puzzle.—A Run on the Bank.—Land of Goshen.—Wonderment.—Admirers.—Finding the Way.—The Makalolo.—The Governor.—Start on Lake Menzaleh.—Living Clouds.—Mataryeh.—Legs of Ingleez.—Egyptian Lock.. 62

CHAPTER V.

River Mushra.—"Field of Zoan."—Strange Creatures.—A Lost Needle.—"Fire in Zoan."—Qualms.—Flamingoes.—Rigs.—A Yarn.—Lubbers.—By Moonlight.—Fort Said.—Parting Shot.—Squall.. 83

CHAPTER VI.

Beyrout.—Massacre.—Good News.—Schools.—Bustle.—Blind.—American Mission.—Moslems.—Prince of Wales.—Agrippa.—Our Flag.—French Lake.—"Gratias." .... Page 97

CHAPTER VII.

Over Lebanon.—Canoe on Wheels.—The Rob Roy in Snow.—Odd Quarters.—"The Young Lady."—Generous.—Zahleh School.—River Litany.—Hanged.—An Eagle.—The Fiji.—Source of Abana.—In-doors.—Cats 111

CHAPTER VIII.

The Abana.—Sources.—Abana and Pharpar.—Their Names.—Canalettes.—Start on Abana.—Change to the Taura.—How to do it.—Pleasant Toil.—Procession 125

CHAPTER IX.

Damascus Dock.—Pretty Girls.—Eastern Desert.—Reconnoitre.—The Rob Roy on Horseback.—Latoof.—On Abana.—Celebrated Canoeists.—Brave Guards.—Tent-life.—Harran.—Mirage.—"Abraham's Well."—Plunging.—Ateibeh Morass.—"Ko-ax Ko-ax." 136

CHAPTER X.

Ateibeh Morass.—Drowned in the Lake.—Menagerie.—Embarking.—Dangerous Day.—A lonely Wold.—End of the Abana.—Retreating.—Christmas on the Abana.—Thoughts.—Northern Lake.—Mouths of the Abana.—Tell Dekweh.—Tell Hijaneh.—Hijaneh Lake.—Paddling to Bashan.—The Giant Cities.—Nimrim.—The Island.—In a Boar-track.—Channel 150

CHAPTER XI.

Hijaneh Lake.—Jungle.—Plain of Pharpar.—Maps.—Bearings.—Off to Bashan.—Brak.—Stone every thing.—Cut-throat.—Stone Gate and Shutter.—Mr. Bright.—King Og.—Paddle on the Pharpar.—Sources.—Adalyeh.—The winding Pharpar.—Damascus.—Spur of Hermon.—Ice 169

CHAPTER XII.

Ruklch.—Bust of Baal.—Mount Hermon.—Kefr Kuk.—Rasheya.—Search for Jordan.—Earliest Spring.—Jordan's Eye.—Sad Loss.—Leeches.—The Hasbany.—Wady et Teim.—Hasbany Source.—First Bridge.—Start on Jordan.—Colored Cascade.—Pitch-pits.—Jordan Vale.—The Litany.—Storm.—Dripping Bedroom..Page 187

CHAPTER XIII.

Across Jordan.—Bloody Fray.—British Officers.—Our Ignorance.—Jordan's Streams.—Tell El Kady.—Dan.—Laish.—The Golden Image.—Sounding the Source.—Justice and Mercy.—Name of Jordan.—El Ghujar.—Hazor.. 208

CHAPTER XIV.

Banias.—Cæsarea Philippi.—Cavern.—Josephus.—Three Streams of Jordan.—Phiale.—Our Saviour's Visit.—The Great Question.—Peter.—Crusaders' Keep.—View from Subeibeh.—Anxious.—Mansoura.—Parliament.—Catechism.—Costumes.—Nose-rings.—Water-ways.—Bright Eyes.—Enter Arabs.. 223

CHAPTER XV.

River Banias.—Strange Rock.—Afloat alone.—Riding.—"Waltzing."—Meeting of the Waters.—Pursued.—At bay.—Fired at.—Caught.—Captive's Appeal.—Carried to Captivity.—Before the Court.—Sentence.—Taunts.—Revenge.—Escape.. 247

CHAPTER XVI.

Chase resumed.—A Rascal.—The River.—Buffaloes.—Snakes.—The Barrier.—How to eat.—Prison Fare.—The Rascal again.—Voice of the Night.—Hurrah.—Riding high-horse.—Free.—Duty.—Cheap......... 262

CHAPTER XVII.

Mellaha.—Waters of Merom.—The Lake.—Raft of Bulrushes.—From above.—Puzzle.—Kedesh.—Start.—Arabs again.—Pelican-hunt.—Grand Discovery.—New Mouth.—Thunder.—Inner Lake.—Lilies.—Royal Salute.—Breadth of Barrier.—Sixteen Swans.—Papyrus.—Its Use.—How it grows.—Bent by Current..Page 277

CHAPTER XVIII.

On Hooleh. — Cutting a Cape. — Canoe Chase. — Hooleh Lake. — Jacob's Bridge.—Who crossed it.—Templars' Keep.—Grand View.—Jew's Lament.—Ten Miles of Torrent.—Hard Times.—A Set of Ruffians.—The Worst.—At last.—All right.—Note on the Rivers 298

CHAPTER XIX.

"On deep Galilee."—Bank.—Names of the Lake.—Shores.—Submerged Ruin.—Naked Stranger.—Lagoons.—Ports.—Bethsaida Julias.—Oozing Streams.—River Semakh.—Gergesa.—A Pause.—Tell Hoom.—Keraseh. —Fête.— Search for Piers.— Submerged Remains.— Breeze.—Storm.— Searching below.—Curious Stones.—No Port.—Tabiga.—Bethsaida Bay. —Flocks and Shoals.—Genesareth... 315

CHAPTER XX.

Bethsaida Beach.—Of old.—Evidence.—Bias.—Sermon afloat.—Stones.— Fishermen.—Ships and Boats.—Distinction.—An Explanation.—Present Boats.—The "Pillow."—Sailing-boat.—Fish.—Nets. — Hooks.—Cliff.— "Scorpion Rock."—"Capharnaonm" Ain et Tin.—Other Streams.—The Coracinus.—Other Fish.—The hot Springs.—The Aqueduct.—Josephus's Fountain.—At Tabiga... 338

CHAPTER XXI.

The Apostles' Voyage.—The "Desert Place."—The Embarkation.—Direction.—Position of the Ship.—The Weather and Waves.—Approach of Christ.—Action of Peter.—Arrival of the Ship.—Other Incidents.—Other Evidence.—"Exalted to Heaven."—Josephus.—Wounded.—Dimensions. —Testimony.—Thanks.—Maps... 362

CHAPTER XXII.

Sea of Galilee.—Magdala.—Dalmanutha.—Ain Bareideh.—Tiberias.—The Jews.—Fast Travellers.—American Confessions.—How to see England.— A rainy Day.—Earthquake.—Shore south of Tiberias.—Hot Swimmers.— South-west Shore.—Night.—Joyous.—Size of the Lake.—Kerak.—Ruins. —Exit of Jordan.—Down Stream.—Molyneux and Lynch.—Farewell to Jordan 381

CHAPTER XXIII.

In the Lake.—Strange Swell.—A Storm.—Submerged Ruins.—The "Herd of Swine."—Semakh Village.—Hippos.—High Sea.—Vale of Doves.—Long last Look.—Cana.—Nazareth.—Old Sights.—Sights unseen.—Plain Words..Page 407

CHAPTER XXIV.

Source of Kishon.—Megiddo.—Fords of Kishon.—Kishon's Banks.—Sisera's Steeds.—Launch in a Storm.—Up the Melchi.—Meeting a Crocodile.—What to do.—Feeling a Crocodile.—Flight.—Evidence.—Start on the Belus.—River Aujeh.—Farewell to the Jordan.—Across the Bay of Acre.—"Ariadne."—Praise.. 429

APPENDIX 451

THE TEMPLE, *London, November* 5, 1869.

ILLUSTRATIONS.

MAPS.

I. The Delta and the Suez Canal	To face Page	93
II. The Morass of Ateibeh, near Damascus	"	142
III. The Abana and Pharpar }	"	171
IV. The Lake of Hijaneh }		
V. The Three Streams of Jordan	"	220
VI. The Waters of Merom	"	305
VII. The Lake of Genesareth	"	372
VIII. Palestine (outline and route)	"	443

WOOD-CUTS.

[The Illustrations marked * are introduced into this edition from Thomson's "The Land and the Book."]

Capture of the Rob Roy on the Jordan	Frontispiece.
The Shallows of Lake Menzaleh	Page 21
Night-Visitor on Crocodile Lake	29
Dinner in the Sweet Canal	35
Camel in the Red Sea	39
Slave Children at Cairo	43
The Barrage of the Nile	52
Fisherman's Raft of Gourds	59
Common Compass-card and Compass-card of the Rob Roy	66
The Land of Gosein from the Banks of the Zrier River	71
Start on Lake Menzaleh in Egypt	78
The "Field of Zoan"	84
Flamingoes taking Wing	88
Night on Lake Menzaleh	92
Beyrout*	96
Street in Beyrout*	98
Fountain at Beyrout*	101
Blind Reading to the Lame	103
Joppa*	108
Crossing Mount Lebanon	113

ILLUSTRATIONS.

New School-house at Zahleh	*Page* 116
Bridge over the Litany*	117
Eagle's Nest*	120
Fiji Source of the Abana	122
Gorge of the Abana near Damascus	132
Pole Frame for the Canoe on Horseback	139
A Plunge in Ateibeh Marsh	148
Christmas Night on a Mouth of the Abana	157
Bird's-eye View of the Lake of Hijaneh (outline)	162
The Rob Roy in the Wild Boar's Haunt	167
Hermon and Plain of the Pharpar	171
Stone Door in Bashan	177
Stone Shutter in Bashan	178
Half a Mile of the Pharpar (outline)	183
"Ain Rob Roy," under Mount Hermon	192
Wady et Teim (outline)	196
Jordan Source near Hasbeya (plan)	197
General View of the Hasbeya Source of the Jordan	199
The Vale of Jordan	204
A Fish from the Hasbany	208
Ard el Hooleh*	213
Jordan Source at Dan (plan)	215
Cave at Banias*	226
Jordan Source at Banias (plan)	228
Lake Phiale*	230
Neby Seid Yuda*	233
Hooleh Morass, from the Castle of Subeibeh	237
Heads of Three Hooleh Arabs	243
Strange Rock in the Jordan (plan)	248
"Waltzing" (plan)	250
Capture by the Arabs of Hooleh	255
Huts and Bull of Bashan	264
Prison Fare in the Waters of Merom	269
Raft of Reeds	279
The New-found Mouth of the Jordan	287
Papyrus Stems and Roots	295
Growth of Papyrus	297
Bridge of Jacob's Sons*	302
Ten Miles of " the Descender" (outline)	307
Jordan Month, Sea of Galilee	317
Lagoon and Port, Butaia Plain—Lagoon	320
Semakh River, near Gergesa	324

ILLUSTRATIONS.

Submerged Ruins near Tell Hoom (plan)	Page 330
Storm on the Sea of Galilee	331
Coast at Tell Hoom, and Curious Stone in the Water	333
Fish-traps near Bethsaida	343
Galilee Fishing-boat	349
The "Scorpion Rock" (plans)	353
Ruins of Tel Hoom*	373
Lake of Tiberias, from the Baths*	380
Mijdel and Plain of Genesareth*	383
Structure in Water near Bareideh (plan)	385
Covered Passage in Sea-wall	386
Tiberias and the Lake, looking to the North-east*	388
Submerged Ruins along the Shore south of Tiberias	397
Exit of the Jordan, and Kerak (plan)	402
Country of the Gergesenes, Sea of Galilee	413
Last View of the Lake of Genesareth	417
Kefr Cana*	420
The New Protestant Church at Nazareth	422
The Vale of Nazareth*	424
The Crocodile on the Kishon	436
Haifa and Carmel*	441
Acre*	446
The "Ariadne's" Farewell	448

APPENDIX.

The Rob Roy Cabin	453
Bed—Bag—Bottle	455
Canoe-wheels	456

THE ROB ROY ON THE JORDAN,

Etc., Etc.

CHAPTER I.

Suez Canal.—Port Said.—Lake Menzaleh.—The Start.—Rogues.—Sandstorm.—Bears.—Ismailia.—Crocodile Lake.—Murders.—Guy Fawkes.—Jackal.—The Canoe.—My Bed.

AT Alexandria we took off the carpet that had covered the "Rob Roy" during her long voyage from England in the good ship "Tanjore."

Her polished cedar deck glittered in the African sun, and the waves of a new sea played on her smooth oak sides.

I stepped in light-hearted for a six months' cruise, and the first half-hour round the crowded harbor showed that the Moslems would be as kind in their welcome of the little craft as the Norsemen had been, and the Swiss, and the Indians of Ottawa in my other journeys.

The dock-yard workmen ran to see the canoe, shouting in their scant attire. The sailors of a hundred vessels peered over their bulwarks to gaze at her dark blue sails and gilded silken flag; even the lone sentry on the walls was aroused from his stare into nothing by the sight of the little English "merkeb" that skimmed over the sea so near to the breakers.

A few days more, and the Rob Roy came to Port Said. the bustling town of wooden shanties, new sprung from the sand at the mouth of the Suez Canal. No place so small as this has so large a variety of inhabitants. It is like a slice of great Nijni fair.

B

When the canoe touched the beach, the red man and the white ran to see her, and gabbled loud; then she was borne on two negroes' shoulders to the "Grand Hôtel de France." Great interest was shown in the arrival of the smallest boat that ever journeyed in the East, and it will be entirely the fault of the narrator if her delightful voyage does not fulfill the expectations of what has to be told. But, the first part of our journey being in Egypt, it has few of the dangers, the adventures, and the discoveries which will be found in her cruise over Syria. It was novel, indeed, to paddle an English canoe upon the Red Sea and the Nile, but what was seen there could be met with in other modes of travel. When, however, the Rob' Roy essayed the Syrian lakes and the rivers and seas of Palestine, she entered on scenes never opened before to the traveller's gaze, and which were entirely inaccessible except in a canoe. These we are to meet farther on. Meanwhile the Rob Roy will be content to start at a slower pace and in easier navigation.

The quick-witted officials of the Suez Canal Company are all day busy here about dredges and barges, and steamers and dusty coal-brigs, and no wonder they hailed with joy our new and dainty craft. They overwhelmed me with hospitality, explaining in voluble accents the wonders of the place, and barely concealing a suspicion that their guest was at least half crazy. A thorough examination of the Suez Canal was the first part of my long programme for this Eastern voyage, and the results of ten days' careful observation were given in a letter to the "Times," which soon revived the question whether it is most difficult to cut a canal, to keep it open, or to make it pay. Two subsequent visits to this gigantic undertaking enabled me to gauge its progress after months of interval; but it would be tedious to refer to what is *passé*, now that the canal is opened, and bishops can come through it to settle the new creed at Rome.

A hole in the sand is an excellent place for sinking capital. You can always dig it deep if people will pay the diggers. You can even keep it clear if you pay dredges rather than dividends. When Europe or Asia or Africa is at war, of course the canal is closed, and the expenses go on, and the earnings stop; but so far as concerns England, we have always got, at Aden, the cork of the other end of the bottle.

The Suez Canal is open, and every body is pleased. President Lesseps has made Africa an island. For him and his shareholders our wishes are much better than our expectations.

Whatever is to come, at any rate there has been brain and muscle hard worked here, and an iron will has ruled, and untiring energy has won great victory. Six years ago there was nothing at Port Said but sand, and even now the streets are nothing else. Men fire at seagulls among the shops; pelicans toss upon the waves, and flamingoes fly above, and porpoises tumble in the harbor. Among these new friends the Rob Roy sailed over the water, and at the *table d'hôte* all the visitors talked the whole time about her intended voyage from the sea of Europe to that of Asia and Africa. One gentleman was very positive in his description of her build and of her crew, for he had "actually *seen* the canoe and the man inside it;" yet he did not recognize me sitting opposite to him all the time. Another, a Belgian, was earnest in his praise of England, and said how hospitably he had been received, with other Belgian riflemen, at the Wimbledon shooting; and the argument was closed by a general confession that "Les Anglais sont plus *chic* que nous." A Frenchman came to thank me for a little paper, "The British Workman" (in French), which I had given* to him at Havre last summer, just before leaving that port in my yawl for a voyage alone over the broad Channel to Portsmouth.

* Good and harm may be done in this, as in other ways; good by giving as a present; harm by giving as a rebuke. Critics were rather hard once upon this ready way of addressing strangers; now their own clever thoughts are daily proffered to each of us, everywhere.

Out of the café to pace the sand, and to ruminate on the rise of nations, we are challenged even here by little ink-faced urchins, who rush at the new traveller with "Black shoes, sare!"

From Map I., at page 93, it will be seen that the canal at first goes through Lake Menzaleh, a vast expanse of shallow water, the accumulation of what trickles through the soft dikes along the Damietta branch of the Nile. The lake, being now full (in October), had advanced its margin close to the town of Port Said. About six weeks afterwards, it was at nearly the same level, when I walked to see the "Gemileh mouth" of the Nile, some six miles west of the town, and where a fitful stream only sometimes overflows seaward. At my visit to Menzaleh a third time (in March), the lake had receded half a mile from the swampy flats, and at that dry season the fulfillment of the prophecy seemed most complete which tells us that the seven streams of the Nile shall fail.

Later in the cruise we shall spend a pleasant week upon Menzaleh.

Meanwhile, in search of adventure, we soon dragged the Rob Roy over the sand-bank which separates the lake from the sea, and launched her upon the calm wide water that reaches away to a far-off horizon.

The sun was hot, the water unruffled by the lightest air or any current, and there was nothing to betray the shallows round us even to a practised eye. Very soon, therefore, the canoe got entangled in mud-banks, and the sharp little ragamuffins of an Arab village gladly perceived there was a new victim come for them to tease.

They scampered out to me, naked and black, and a score of them were splashing and tumbling round the canoe, now helpless to run away.

"Backshish!" was the first cry I heard in the East, and the last I heard there, after wandering long, was "Backshish!" Their lithe limbs revelled in the tepid water, and their feet in the oozy mud. Their heads were like little cocoa-nuts, with only one hair-lock left at the top, for

THE SHALLOWS OF LAKE MENZALEH.

Mohammed to hold them by at last. Their frolics were very forward, to say the least, but boys, black or white, must be humored to be ruled; so I appointed the noisiest of them a "policeman," and paid him a month's salary in advance—one penny—for which he made the rest drag the canoe, with me in it, a long way cheerfully. At last I got out of the boat, and, wading in the soft mud, spoiled forever a pair of chamois shoes twenty years old, but never meant for use in water-work like this. Trudging through the black slush, I dragged the Rob Roy over a wall into deep water, but with a sad loss of dignity, and then launched once more upon the old salt sea. It was charming to be danced on the swell of real ocean waves, and to shoot at the pelicans lifted on the foam, and to scud back under sail with a reef in my lug, and to race with the swarthy Nubians tugging at their oars.

But, after a day or two here of this amphibiouslife, the

sights of Port Said had all been seen, the workshops inspected, and the huge machines of the canal. The last news from England had been read at the "cercle," and a farewell dinner finished with my new French friends. Then my heavy baggage was sent on by water, and my "sea-stores" were embarked by the Rob Roy for our lonely cruise. The exulting delight of freedom possessed me once more with an access of joy which had always come soon in my voyages, and never ceased to the end.

And yet I can not say that it would be wise to begin one's canoeing in the East, or to begin in the East by canoeing.

Over and over I felt the great advantage of having made already three tours in these hot latitudes; and often there was full need for the shifts and plans for safety, speed, or comfort, which had been shaped by the experience of three former journeys afloat entirely alone.*

The wind to-day is from the north, and thus right in my favor. The French officers crowd around as the canoe is launched, now heavy with provisions for four days. Her topsail swells with the breeze as we glide from the shore, and the Egyptian sailors shout, "All right!" in English, nodding their shaven polls. Nothing could be a happier start, and we were soon skimming swiftly on the smooth canal, which here runs perfectly straight for nearly thirty

* The first of these Eastern tours was in 1849, through Palestine, Greece, and Egypt, etc., of which some account was published in "Three Days in the East," and in "Eastern Music." The solitary cruises were described in "A Thousand Miles in the Rob Roy Canoe" through Central Europe; "The Rob Roy in the Baltic" through Northern Europe; and "The Voyage Alone in the Yawl Rob Roy" to Paris, and in the English Channel. When a man has to tell by the pencil and pen what he has done with the paddle, it is impossible to be otherwise than individual and personal in the narration, or even egotistical in style. It would be affectation not to avow that one is sensible of this; but it would be pedantic to try an escape from the inevitable by using the word "we" instead of "I" in the story. Those who write anonymously, and can abide by the good custom of using the impersonal "we," will be best aware of the double protection they enjoy from any such tendency to become naïve in their expression, and they can understand how it may be better for an author to be open to the charge of simplicity than to that of unnatural reserve.

miles, while its banks vanish on the horizon in dim and trembling perspective. It is but a short voyage to-day, and begun in the evening, with no work to do but to steer and to look at the high banks on both sides, like two railway viaducts, five hundred feet apart; at the steam dredges rattling their wheels and chains, and the coal-boats lazily towed in a line, and the pretty fleet of small craft all pressing on with me, crowding white-bosomed sails, and laden with merry songs.

The sky glows softly as the sun sets in red, and the white moon rises full. By its bright shining on the waters of cold Lake Menzaleh, we draw up the Rob Roy ashore, on the bank, in the loneliest spot to be found, near Ras el Esh, and soon my "canoe cuisine" is boiling Liebig's soup, and bread and wine fill up the *carte* of dinner.

The fish are leaping in the moonbeams now. They often jump into the little steamers on the canal, and a fish had leaped right across my boat as she started; but there is no other noise. Wrapped in my great brown cloak for the night, I now take a last look about me to see that nobody is near. For sleeping quietly, the main thing is to be quite alone, and on this Suez Canal all strangers may safely be distrusted as rogues, for the number of murders in its neighborhood is altogether unreasonable.

Under the moon, then, we could see only long rows of water-fowl on the silent lake in regiments gleaming white, so I wrapped my thick cloak around me and turned in, then lighted a beautiful little oil lamp[*] (presented by Colonel Staunton, the Consul-General at Alexandria), and opened a page of the "Times."

With all these comforts about me I passed a miserable night. The place I had chosen so carefully turned out to be only a heap of refuse, and it is swarmed with angry flies,

---

[*] With much trouble I had devised a "canoe candle-lamp," weighing only five ounces; but the oil lamp mentioned above answered far better for many reasons, at least in countries where oil can always be had. This lamp had been obtained at the Paris Exhibition, and its extremely clever construction made it useful on a hundred occasions afterwards in the voyage.

so very minute, and so inquisitive or hungry, that the mosquito-curtains of my cabin were no bar whatever to their entrance.

The moon is, indeed, very pretty to look at, and proper to sing to in rhyme or blank verse; but its pale light shows no color in objects, and so, for selecting night quarters, give me in future the truth-telling rays of honest Father Sol.

Next morning at four it was not cheerful to breakfast only on a cigar, until I could catch a boat and buy bread from a funny little Greek. But a Frenchman hailed me, and his wife brought out some excellent coffee, and both were intensely polite and conversational as they handed the sugar-tongs into the canoe.

At Kantara the canal cuts through the old Arab track over the desert, and by which I had travelled years ago on camel's back, and the name of the place—meaning "bridge" —reminds us that here was once some wet lagoon simmering its tepid fever in the reeking sand.[*]

There I stopped Sunday, and slept in a little wooden shed. A furious storm whirled up the arid plain, and dishevelled the face of nature and dimmed the sun in heaven. The landscape, to look upon, was now one vast yellow sand-cloud, with men and camels faintly floating in a fog of dust, without any horizon. To paddle against this hurricane next day was impossible, but I towed the canoe by a long cord girt round my waist. Even the mosquito-net, double-folded over my face, quite failed to keep out the drifting sand ; and the few wayworn travellers who passed when the Rob Roy was made up for the night under the sheltering bank might well look amazed. A wholesome fear of the strange creature they saw was all in my favor, and often in this journey I traded on the belief that the coward and the superstitious are not seldom the same person.

---

[*] When our Saviour, as a child, was taken into Egypt, the road would, no doubt, pass this place. From Josephus we learn how numerous were the Jews in Egypt then, and that their worship was more pure in Egypt than in Palestine ("Antiquities of the Jews," book xiv. chap. vii. sec. ii.).

Wild dogs, not exactly jackals, for their tails were erect, generally chose the night hours to call upon me, and sometimes travellers belated did the same. The white-robed Rob Roy, whiter under the moonlight, must have puzzled them greatly, and so long as they argued in whispers outside I let them alone, but there was a pistol ready all the time in my bedroom, and I always had the (unfortunate) capacity of instantly waking at the slightest noise.

For several days a curious group of beings had exactly kept pace with the Rob Roy—three brown men leading three brown bears. One bear was old, another was blind, the third was very frisky, but the men insisted upon all of them bathing in the water exactly at noon, about the very last thing a bear would like to do, and it was great amusement to watch their struggles, remembering the gross indignities offered by the bathing-woman to every one of us when he was a British baby.

One pitch-dark night, when I ought to have reached El Gisr,* the sand-hills were high, and I could not find the place. At length, after paddling back and forward a mile or two, I went to a barge, where loud singing told of inmates. When my paddle tapped on the window a man came out, and offered to find me lodging, but, after some parley, he seemed so drunk, and evidently such a villain when sober, that it would never do to leave my canoe with him; so I paddled on, and slept in my cabin as usual, but with no dinner or supper, and frequent visits at midnight from very strange folks. This place is noted for ruffianism.†

There was ample variety in the scenery or circumstances of each day to make it extremely interesting to voyage thus here *once*, and it was an excellent preparation in many ways for the more difficult times and places that were to come. Among other things, I was able to make numerous

---

* "The bridge." Another bridge must have been here to give it this name.

† The Greeks had the worst character by universal consent—including their own. The best men in the canal I found were Austrians.

experiments with my boat, and all her multifarious fittings, of which a full list and description will be found in the Appendix. Her pace I tried repeatedly in calm water, without current, and where all the *kilomètres* were marked by posts on the bank; and this trial was extremely useful afterwards when we (the Rob Roy and I) had to measure the lakes and rivers where no man had been before.

Thus it was found that the canoe, being in heavy sea-trim, and going at the pace one can easily keep up for eight hours a day, would paddle 542 yards, with 100 double strokes (right and left), in five minutes. This pace, it will be seen, is not four miles an hour, but then it can be kept up for months, carrying both food and lodging and comforts all the way. Current and wind are to be so used as to add to the speed and diminish the work.*

In the midday hours the heat was excessive, and I rested then in some shady nook under a mud-barge, or, hauling the canoe ashore, I reclined by its side on the sand, with the sun behind the blue sail. The cooler hours were spent in progress or in visits aboard the numerous steam-dredges which kept dragging, scraping, and shovelling the mud of the desert on each side over the new bank, and this by such very ingenious contrivances, and on so gigantic a scale, that there was enough every hour to study and to admire.

The Rob Roy was next housed at Ismailia, the half-way town of the Suez Canal. All the men here, and animals, and the shrubs and pretty flowers, depend for life upon the fresh water brought from the river Nile along the "Sweet Canal." Another branch of this gives water to Port Said by an iron tube,† with open troughs at intervals to drink from, as the traveller rides or walks a weary fifty miles along the bank, or sails in the salt water of this enormous cut.

---

* This is, of course, for a travelling canoe, which bears the same relation to a fast canoe as a hunter does to a race-horse. Our fast canoes can go a good pace, also, for a long journey. The last "twelve-mile race" of the Canoe Club was accomplished with the tide in eighty-five minutes. No man in a row-boat could keep up with a canoe in strange rivers for a week.

† If this tube were once possessed by an enemy, Port Said would be without fresh water, and the sternest garrison in it would be forced to yield.

A railway from Ismailia to the west had been opened only a few weeks. The station is the largest in the world —the desert. The rails themselves end on the bare sand, and the "station-master" occupies a little bell-tent. Passengers waited for the next train, which was to start "about four o'clock," that is any thing up to six. There was no platform, so they placed their bundles on the sand, and friends took leave of one another as if they could not expect to meet again alive. Certainly it was a strange sound, the guard crying "Now, then, for Rameses!" Then he looked at each man's ticket, a long paper crowded with Arabic writing, and all of them lay down in a row under the bales of goods—guard, engineer, ticket-man and passengers, and most of them were soon fast asleep in the shade.

Ismailia is like a hot-house without the glass, and all the life in it is exotic. The sun's heat and the Nile's fresh water fructify the arid sand itself into a beautiful tropical verdure. Embosomed in this are French *cafés* and *billards*, with Arabs' huts and camels—the sign-boards on booths in Greek, and Turkish, and Spanish, and American; *ateliers* resounding with hammer and cog-wheel; and tents full of half-dressed savages chaffering uproariously; and *boulevards* thronged by the second-rate fashion of a French town planted, and growing fast, too, in the veritable desert. Beside it lie the shores of the Lake Timsah, "Crocodile Lake," which had a few pools when the canal was begun, but now it is filled with brackish water.

Only fresh-water shells are to be found in Lake Timsah, and the crocodile does not live in salt water. These facts seem to confirm the idea that a fresh-water canal existed here, and Glynn considers that the town of which there are ruins at the end of the Bitter Lakes, and which must have had a fresh-water canal (indeed, relics of it still remain), may have been destroyed by the same upheaving of the land which dried the lakes themselves.*

---

* A canal from the Nile to the Red Sea was begun 2400 years ago, and a branch of it went to Pelusium, in the Mediterranean. The "Bitter Lakes" were then navigable for small craft. About twelve centuries after that the

I rashly determined to spend a night on this lake, and launched the Rob Roy after sundown, with rod and line, net, deep-line, bait, flies, and trawling-hooks; after sailing everywhere until the wind died out, I took to fishing in four ways at once. The moon beamed brilliantly after midnight, and my little lamp, fastened on the canoe so as to be protected from the paddle by my knee, glittered on the water, and a hundred flies kept dancing round it always. I plied every means in my power to catch one fish, but did not get one single bite, and sad disasters happened to my gear.

The deep-line ran out overboard. The bait melted away without a nibble, my rod slipped into the water unperceived, and the "spinner" of my trawling-line got hooked in some rocks below. Wet and disappointed, I sought an island to sleep upon, for the shores of the lake were quite unsafe. In the preceding week two murders had been perpetrated; only one murder had come off in the present week, so it was still one below the average, where any man

---

canal joined the Nile near Cairo, and the navigation was kept open for 120 years. Napoleon I. resolved to revive the scheme long disused in practice. The Bitter Lakes were, doubtless, once a portion of the Red Sea. The marine shells found at the bottom of the lakes and those of the Red Sea are identical. These shells are to be seen on the sides of the lakes, and even on a raised beach, which is now above the level of the Red Sea. The ridge between the end of the Red Sea and the Bitter Lakes consists of tertiary strata, the fossils of which are identical with those of the London basin and of the hill of Montmartre, near Paris. "Egypt, England, and France are consequently of the same age."—"Glynn on the Isthmus of Suez," and discussion on the paper (Minutes of the Institute of Civil Engineers, vol. x. session 1850–51). In Smith's "Dictionary of the Bible" (article "Red Sea"), it seems to be considered that the Red Sea once extended to Lake Timsah, and receded thence, fulfilling prophecy (Isaiah xi. 15; xiv. 5; Zechariah x. 11). To myself it seems that the high land at El Gisr would be an effectual bar to an extension of the Red Sea beyond the Bitter Lakes. The project for a salt-water cut from the Mediterranean to the Red Sea has been a long time under consideration. In 1830, General Chesney reported upon the subject, and Mr. Stephenson and others in 1847. The concession to the present promoters was granted in 1854, and the work was to be finished in six years. Afterwards, it was arranged that the "Sweet Canal" was to belong to the Egyptian Government, but the French may use it for navigation until the end of 1869.

with five francs, or supposed to have them, is worth killing, and there is no policeman X, and no coroner summons his jury of quest.

The lake is girt by little hills of purest sand, a few shrubs perish by the margin, but farther back are rich deep jungles, full of water-fowl and small game—a perfect larder for the wild beasts of the bare desert around.

Under a sandy hill I grounded the Rob Roy, and rigged

NIGHT-VISITOR ON CROCODILE LAKE.

out her nightly cabin. Chill air and wet garments soon made me shiver under the cold moon, but I did not know then that this is about the worst fever-spot in Egypt. There was not fuel enough for a fire, but I lit up my Russian cooking-lamp, and this warmed the cabin wonderfully. Poor, however, were my pyrotechnics for this the 5th of November, yet it is well to remember Guy Fawkes. To my great surprise, although it was on an island, a visitor came, and he would not be denied an interview. He was only a jackal, and the conversation was entirely on his side, as he screamed his shrill cry, and would neither leave me in peace nor come near enough to be shot. The savory smell of hot supper, perhaps, found the poor beast desperately hungry. Next morning, on a return visit, I traced him by footsteps to his den, but he would not come out. Then to recover the lost fishing-rod I visited every cape, and bay, and beach, and reedy fen, and stony islet, where I had fished or walked upon during the night before. All these features appeared so different now in broad daylight, and at the very last place of all the rod was found, and with every hook still floating in the water.

At Ismailia, now again all safe, there met me the brave and faithful companion of my future journey, Michael Hany, well known to me as my dragoman in 1849, frequently trusted since by large parties sent to his charge; most welcome now as the man without whose aid I could scarcely have ventured to take the Rob Roy through the journey we are about to relate. My old friend was delighted with the new boat, and all her fittings had to be thoroughly explained to him. Perhaps this may be a good time to mention them briefly here.

The new canoe, named Rob Roy, like the other two, is, of course, fitted with every improvement suggested by former experience or kind hints from the two hundred members of our Canoe Club. She was specially built for this voyage (by Mr. Pembery, of London), and is probably the smallest vessel ever launched in which one can travel long and far, and sleep at the end in comfort. Moreover, she is strong and light, portable and safe, a good sailer, and graceful to behold.

The Rob Roy is 14 feet long, 26 inches wide, and one foot deep outside, built of oak below and covered with cedar.* A water-proof apron protects me from waves and rain. Her topmast is the second joint of my fishing-rod, and a third joint is ready in the stern. Her sails are dyed

* Minutiæ in her construction, and details interesting specially to paddlers, are given in the Appendix.

deep blue, an excellent plan, for it tempers the glare of the sun, and is more readily concealed from the Arab's eye. The blue-bladed paddle is the same that was wielded in Sweden over many a broad lake; and though an inch of its edge had been split off by an upset of the canoe from a runaway cart in a Norway forest, yet I loved my old paddle best of them all. To sleep in the canoe I always go ashore, and work her backward and forward on the beach until the keel is firmly bedded for a good night's rest. Next we form a little cabin less than 3 feet high, and more than 6 feet long, and then having inside the gauze mosquito-curtain, and over all a strong white water-proof sheet, 6 feet square, and drooping loose upon each side, we are made up snug, and can defy all kinds of weather. A "post-office bag," very light, but completely water-proof, has held our clothes during the day, and now it becomes a pillow. The bed is 3 feet long, and 14 inches wide, quite long enough for all one cares about, and no complaints were heard of its being too broad. It is only the shoulders and hips that really require a soft mattress if the head is pillowed too; as for the rest of one's body it doesn't matter at all. When travelling under hot sun, I place this bed behind me, with one end on deck, and the middle of it is tied round my breast, so as to bring the upper end just under the long back leaf of my sun-helmet, which is of pith and felt combined, a head-dress lately introduced by Tress, and entirely successful, for I wore it during about seven months, and neither rain, nor sun, nor duckings in salt waves, ever altered its lightness or good shape. The bed thus becomes an excellent protector against sun-stroke, and it was especially useful when my course was north, and my back was thus turned to the sun. Often I went ashore with the bed still dangling from my waist behind, while wondering natives gazed at the "Giaour" with his air-bag tail. The bed was useful too when I sat upon wet sand, or grass, or gravel, and it was always a good life-buoy in case of an upset.*

* This and all other fittings were made at Silvers, of Cornhill, where each of the four Rob Roy cruises had its outfit.

Every timber in the boat had, of course, been carefully placed, so as not to interfere with my comfort in sleeping, or to catch the shoulders, elbows, hips, or knees while turning in bed. In fact this canoe was built round me reclining, as my first one had been built round me sitting—in each case recognizing the one great principle, far too often forgotten, that a comfortable boat, like a shoe or a coat, must be *made* for the wearer, and not *worn down* to his shape.

CHAPTER II.

Rameses.—Sweet Canal.—Bitter Lakes.—Strange Leap.—Red Sea.—Pharaoh.—Camel Wading.—Wells of Moses.—Mirage.—Suez.—How to lose Money.—Shame!—Cairo Ragged Schools.—On the Nile.—Worship.—Paddle to the Pyramids.—Wild Boars.

HANY had brought a tent and a cook, and these a luggage-boat carried, while the canoe went westward by the Sweet Canal to spend the Sunday at Rameses.

The French seem to have settled it, to their own satisfaction at any rate, that this place is rightly named. It is now a dreary "wady" in the bleak desert, and a walk from it far away on the burning sand found for me only more loneliness. Yet hereabouts the Israelites must have lived in their Egyptian bondage. A railway passes near, and affronts our dreams of antiquity by its iron print of progress; and, worse still, the thin wires of the Egyptian telegraph, curving from their naked posts in the desert, seem to jar upon a half-sacred, half-poetic sympathy with the long-buried past. These little threads, never quite silent if there be but the faintest breeze to make them " hum " —a strange yet well-known music—are the nerves of the earth, running over land and under seas, and speeding the thoughts of the world through all its great round body.

I sat down in the desert under my white-topped umbrella. Only a little black spider seemed to be alive on the black gravel. The sand-hills in the distance quivered in the sunlight, or gently floated for a while upon a sea of liquid nothing in the bright mirage. Pictures came forward to the inner eye of fancy: crowds of Israelites, laden with jewels and kneading-troughs; countless cattle trudged along; a half-frightened, half-escaped multitude, beginning that wonderful walk of forty years. By the Sweet Canal the Rob Roy sailed again southward, and, hoisting her topsail to the pleasant breeze, she kept pace well with the luggage-boat, which was wafted along by her tall and graceful lateen.

Brilliant meteors shot across the sky at night, but softly the stars hung out their spangles, and the moon slowly rose. Then it was silent and cool and delicious for sleep: so far removed from the barking dogs of towns, and with only the wild jackal's scream, which is plaintive, clear, and not unmusical, but rather lulls to slumber. A rumbling in the distance came nearer as the express train rattled up, jingling, and swaying its red light like a great beast's angry eye. No wonder the Arabs ran up the bank to look at the hissing, puffing monster, and murmured a prayer to the Prophet as they came back amazed. Two active, merry Nubian lads were with our luggage-boat. They seemed never to weary or to quarrel as they towed her along with ripples simpering under the bows, and the red English ensign lazily fluttering against a sky of purest blue. One of the lads had all his wealth on his back—a shirt most uncommonly brief.

Sometimes, for a change, I lounged on the soft carpets in the stern, while the Nubians towed both our craft in the midday heat. Dinner was cooked on shore by Hany, and my table was set in the boat, while Sleman, the waiter, handed the dishes as he stood impassive in the cool water between us.

In this way we visited the Serapeion, and then Chalouf, where ten thousand men were hard at work, and a thousand donkeys and steam-engines and railways, all trying their best to hollow out the huge gap in the desert which by this time is filled with salt water, and floats the ships of the world from sea to sea.

Then came the vast hollow, called now the Bitter Lakes, where the sea has been rushing in for months to quench the thirst of many hundred years since water was here before.

As we passed this wide tract, the salt upon it glistened bright and dry. Men were loading huge white blocks of it into boats moored along the Sweet Canal, which here skirts the edge, and on a much higher level. There seems to be scarcely a doubt that all this hollow was part of the Red Sea when Moses led the people to it, and that over this very tract the Israelites passed.

But the canoe has no special work for it here, and all this can be seen from a camel or on foot. It was pleasant enough to sail over, but a very inactive voyage. So much is to be told of livelier work in the bounding waters of

DINNER IN THE SWEET CANAL.

Palestine that we must hurry through this slow canal, and even the Red Sea and the Nile, so as to reach the mountains and lakes and rapids, where discovery is open, and adventures are sure to be met.

We were now descending from the level of the Nile to that of the Red Sea, and so there was a lock to pass through. Many boats were waiting for the Turkish officials to open the gates, but these lazy fellows meant to keep the boats there all night. Our red ensign, however, soon stirred them up, and a few kind words persuaded the guards to let all the boats into the basin. At least a hundred passengers were on board one of these floating boxes, and all of them had to debark until the lock was passed. Then what a rush there was to get aboard again, pell-mell! and to secure the most comfortable places and softest boards to sleep upon in the cold.

Fish leaped and splashed in the still evening always. Once, in the midday, a man shouted to me to approach the bank, for he had a letter from Suez; so I moved the canoe to the shore, and, after reading the letter, I put it into my breast-pocket, when at the same moment a beautiful little fish leaped from the water into my pocket with the letter. The bystanders shouted eagerly at this as an undoubted sign of "good-luck;" and I had the fish broiled for dinner, occupying the centre of a large flat dish. The extreme length of the fish was under two inches, but the happy omen from it lasted among my men for months.

At Suez we camped, and next day (November 12) the Rob Roy was launched upon the Red Sea.* At the north end this arm of the sea runs up a crooked channel, where the variable tide of about six feet is magnified by the contracting bends, and very difficult currents whirled the canoe about uncertainly.

There is a ford across this twisted channel, nearly at the mouth of the Sweet Canal; and an island opposite Tell Kholzum, where the ford is, still bears the name of Jews' Island. The ford is not often passable, except at low water; and here it is that local tradition seems to place the passage of the Israelites. The water now filling up the Bitter Lakes indeed reminds us how they were once part of the Red Sea.† After considering all that I saw of the land and water, and what is believed to have been its

---

* The name "Red" applied to this sea may signify the sea of the "Red Man;" or it may refer to the red coral reefs, or to the very brilliant hues of the rocky shores which are noticed farther on.

† Robinson's "Biblical Researches" (1841), vol. i. p. 72.

ancient condition long ago, I think the weight of evidence is much in favor of the opinion that the Israelites crossed at or above Suez.*

The other place assigned by many for the miracle is much farther south, and where the water would be more than a hundred feet deep on the occasion of the passage, and at least ten miles across. Among other objections to this theory are the following:—1. The east wind would not have caused the water there to recede. 2. The water on each side of the dry passage would have been sixty or seventy feet high, which would rather have been styled a "mountain," whereas it is repeatedly called a *wall* on either side. This latter expression is quite intelligible when used for a heap of water even eight or ten feet high (and in the Bitter Lakes it would be thirty feet), and that depth, when the waves returned, would be quite enough to overwhelm the Egyptians. 3. One night would not suffice for the first and last of the long column of such a host to walk so many miles, nor would the women and children be able to do it. 4. It does not appear that Moses had special directions to go far south, and the natural desire of escape by the shortest way would lead him to the more northern part. 5. The relative positions of hills, valleys, and the sea itself, strongly favor the idea that the host passed over above Suez. 6. Pharaoh, coming from Zoan, would hasten his army to the upper end of the Red Sea (then farther north), and so bar the passage by dry land; and the subsequent "turnings" of the Israelites, as mentioned in the Bible account, would all be more intelligible.

The splendid range of Attaka rises grandly on the African side of the Red Sea, and the steep bare rocks glow ruby red in the setting sun. The ships of England, France, and Egypt rest on the smooth bosom of the bay, and the

* In Smith's "Dictionary of the Bible" (article "Red Sea"), the passage of the host seems to be placed about thirty miles north of Suez. The word "Pihahiroth" is said to mean a reedy place, and there is still much jungle-morass near Lake Timsah. The Septuagint has the word "south" wind where the A. V. reads "east" wind; but it is said to include a wind several points off the E. towards S. E.

Rob Roy dips her paddle-blades for the first time in bright waters of the south.

I paid a visit to the " Malabar," one of the magnificent troop-ships which, with the " Crocodile " and "Serapis," on the other side of the Isthmus, carry our regiments back and forward for the Indian reliefs. All the sailors were at once in love with the canoe. As for the captain and officers, they were profuse in their kindness. The visitors at the hotel, too, insisted on having a regular lecture and explanation of all her fittings, and a crowd of on-lookers hedged her round for the occasion. The gallery was filled by ladies and children from India with their native nurses. The Hindoo servants of the hotel stared with large black eyes from beneath their raven silky hair. Greek, Turkish, Italian, and French sailors, with Indians and negroes of every shade, up to the jet-black woolly pate of Central Africa, peered over the others' shoulders, and three Chinese sailors smiled at every thing.

Next day we started on a Red Sea voyage. A clumsy native boat took the luggage about ten miles down the eastern shore, to rig up the tents at Ain Moosa, where the " wells of Moses " spring up with refreshing sweetness from a desert of dry rock and illimitable sand.

In a fine fresh breeze—indeed, almost a gale—the Rob Roy scudded here over a very high swell, until she came to the luggage-boat, now aground in the fallen tide, and a camel was in the water unloading our gear.

More than a mile from the present shore, and on the *highest* point of the district round, but on what may have been the ancient coast-line once, fresh water, constant and copious, bubbles up, overflows into the sand, and sobbing, as it were, with a few fitful gushes now and then, loses its glittering stream in the ever-thirsty desert. About fifty feet farther down, water appears again in a pool about six feet wide, under one lonely, tall, and weather-beaten palm-tree. Not far off this, Arabs have dug about a dozen pits, in each case finding water, which is ladled up with a leathern bucket, and supplies the life-giving moisture to grow many trees and garden plots, while bleating sheep and cackling fowls soon gather about them too. The long-stepped, silent camel marches past in his caravan, stately and tall, and the Arab sings a plaintive song. The sea-bird shrieks as he wends his way aloft to the crags far over the waves, and our little boat is soon left alone by the unrippled beach, like a dead thing thrown there by the sea.

CAMEL IN THE RED SEA.

After two pleasant days here, the Rob Roy paddled back to Suez quietly in about three hours of a lovely morning. The clear water showed below bright sand and rocks of all painted hues, with patches of colored coral. Dipping my arm down, I grasped a beautiful shell as a trophy to bring home. The flying-fish rose here and there in a shoal at my paddle-blade, and danced along the tops of the little glittering waves, flashing light from their silver scales; and then, fresh and quivering with life, and after a glance at the sun-gleam of the morning, and most beautiful to see, they vanished.

Far off were the huge war-vessels, pictured above in the vapor and below in the sea, and twisted by mirage into weird and wonderful forms. Sometimes a great frigate would disappear from sight entirely; then a huge steamer would suddenly rise in the air, and mount up silently above a sailing-vessel's deck. All these views were increased in grotesqueness by the nearness of my eye to the water's surface. The whole scene had an air of enchantment which one can never forget, and there was a solemnity given to it all by the perfect noiselessness as the panorama changed. The Rob Roy hovered here a few minutes to look on this marvellous spectacle. Her bows were in Asia, her stern was in Africa; her crew had the mingled thoughts of years of travel—such thoughts as can not be seized for confinement in a cramping chain of words.

The hotel at Suez has a very motley mixture of nationalities rushing through it to all parts of the world. There is, of course, a regular tide of passengers, rising full for a a day in each week as the Indian mail comes in, either that from home or the other from the East; and next day all of these are on the wing again, either gliding over the sea to the Indies, or fast speeding home over the sand. Though most of these passengers are English people, yet the manners and appearance of the outward and of the homeward bound are very different.

The mail-train to-day has filled all the corridors of our hotel with passengers straight from England, the faces of many blooming with youth, and others freshened up for another spell of service by a year's leave at home. Their talk is of the latest London news and the Bay of Biscay, and their big strong boxes and new portmanteaus will all stream out again to-morrow into that barge by the quay for loading to Bengal.

Next day the living tide is rushing in from the distant East, from India, and Hong Kong, and Nagasaki, and the Australian mail. The clothes of these are well worn, almost threadbare, and their "puggeries" are ample and business-like round their hats; their faces are pale or careworn, or even haggard, and their fretful children battle on the stairs: pretty, and with brilliant eyes, but no bright English roses on their cheeks. What country but Britain could stand for ten years the exhaustive draught that India makes upon our health and energy? Many of the men who are thus turned into scarecrows by the heat and dust of that great empire will always deserve, and they do, indeed, obtain, full credit from all Englishmen at home for their brave and hardy work in the sun so long and so far away.

The *cafés* of Suez are a wretched jumble of East and West, combining the worst features of both. Better by far is that rude African dance of negroes and feathers and tom-toms in the open square, where the wildness of the savage has poetry and fitness in his outlandish yell. Let us leave Suez.

This is to be done by the railway to Cairo. Did ever any one see such a terminus as this? The door is locked, the guards inside are snoring, loud batteries on the wooden window wake up the clerk at last, and he makes no toilet for his morning work. Our boxes, and tents, and bundles, are tediously weighed on a rusty steelyard, which will tell any weight you please according to your purse. The Rob Roy itself is weighed, almost blushing at the indignity, and half an hour *after* the train is to start, we bustle all these things in. Of course there was no room in the carriage specially provided for the canoe. We had been foolish enough to take tickets instead of paying backshish to the guard.

My fellow-passengers laughed at this my greenness— "We *never* buy tickets," they said; "give five francs to the guard, he gives one to the engine-driver, and one to the station-master at the end, and you can then go anywhere you please."

This is what the viceroy gains by working a railway. while the fell plan of "backshish" reigns in his flat and sandy kingdom.* But though I had thus paid £6 for tran-

---

* I was assured, on good authority, that a million sterling is lost thus each year to the viceroy. Unless it had been declared by several passengers that to bribe was their custom, I should not say so thus distinctly.

sit, it was better than to sell one's honesty even dearly, and yet it was only at the last moment, and after regular battle for the point, that I could thrust the Rob Roy into a huge box, called a third-class carriage. There we tumbled over an entangled mob of miserable natives sprawling on the floor, for there were no seats, in a mess of pumpkins, and babies, and filth, and we tied the canoe against the windows —the open spaces, I mean—along the sides of the travelling shed.

At Zag-a-Zig there was a change to another train. Every body scampered off with his bundles, and a downright scramble began for places in the new carriages.

Entreaties here were vain, and so were threats. The whistle was shrieking, but it was just one of the times when to do the thing yourself is the only way to do it. Therefore I carried my boat in my arms, and shoved her right into a carriage already full, and tied her again to the side, and, what was most strange of all, not a single person protested, or said he would write to the "Times."

Cairo I had seen well years ago, and, at any rate, now is not the time to paint in words that gorgeous picture in the East.

Yet there were many changes here in twenty years: knocking down, building up, opening out, planting, fencing, painting, cleaning, almost civilizing, the old Egyptian capital.

Great gangs of workmen are all day toiling here at reconstruction. Puny children, herded in flocks by cruel task-masters who flog them with long sticks, are carrying on their heads straw baskets full of earth and stones. As they march they sing; but it is in a rhythm of slavery. The strongest repression of one's feelings is scarce enough to keep us from knocking that wretch over who has just belabored with his bludgeon a tender little girl; but this is Egypt, the product of idolatry, of philosophy without real religion and the Bible; and yet this is not half so bad as England would become if left to "philanthropy" without the love of God.

The evening brings a short relief even to the woe of these hapless little ones. Then they sit round in a circle with their baskets before them, while the roll-call is droned over by a task-master who can read. The little sketch here given records this curious scene.

And can *nothing* be done for these poor little babies, starved in mind and soul, slaved in muscle and life? Shall so many hundreds of happy English "Christians" hurry

SLAVE CHILDREN AT CAIRO.

past here every month to the work, the wealth, the honors of the East, without one effort to comfort or to teach the dark nation they pass by?

One brave British woman at least has nobly answered this, and has planted here the "Cairo Ragged School." Many as I have seen of schools, none struck me more than this, and a long and pleasant morning was well occupied in those cheerful classes, among those grateful little faces, however poor, and pinched, and wan—and with those bright teachers whose prayers and labor will have most certain fruit.*

But besides the young in Cairo, Miss Whately cares too for the ignorant old Arabs, even in the desert. Only one who knows their ways and their language—a woman—a lady, a cultivated mind, and a tender loving heart, could win room here amid the sand for the ever-advancing Gospel.

My tent at Boulak, the bustling port of Cairo, was placed close to the water, and the Rob Roy was launched into the Yellow Nile. Long lines of native boats were here with lofty yards pointing up into the blue sky. Splendid "dahabechahs" for the European traveller's use vied in their brightest paint and gaudy flags. I stopped at one of these, and a dragoman I had met years ago hailed the canoe, and handed a cup of hot coffee as I ranged alongside. On the other bank were steamers, moored head and stern, in a far-reaching line. Many of these were the viceroy's yachts, with trim sailors lounging on the bulwarks, and the reflected sunbeams sleepily waving on their upturned open ports of rich plate-glass.

Staid and passive as the Egyptians are, they stared astonished at the little "merkeb."† The word was passed along—some outlandish word of their own—and all eyes were set upon the Rob Roy, slowly moving towards them. Turning a point of land, I came upon soldiers at their

---

* The girls gave me a little sample-piece of very quaint and pretty needle-work (the same on both sides). People in London who wish to add tasteful colors to their drawing-room tables, and to cheer up the hearts of the teachers and children in Cairo, would do well to buy some of the neat and original patterns copied in this school. The little girls thus taught to embroider get better husbands by the accomplishments added to their charms, so the time spent on the work is not lost, but very well bestowed. The school was begun eight years ago. In September, 1869, there were 170 boys and 75 girls attending. The Prince and the Princess of Wales kindly visited the place. In 1849, I visited the Ragged School at Siout, far up the Nile, where little Coptic children were taught good doctrine and practice. This is the town where it is believed that our Saviour lived when He was a child.

† A boat is called "merkeb," and so is a camel—"the ship of the desert." The word is applied to any thing you mount upon for travel.

prayers. Of course I advanced softly, not to disturb them as they went through the regular kneeling, sitting, standing, kneeling again, and all the time muttering, with a look at least of intense and simple devotion. The Rob Roy came upon them suddenly, and they could not but see it in the field of vision, however straight they gazed away. Yet not one single glance was directed to the canoe. I doubt whether such a new sight could be thus received by people worshipping in any church in Europe.

It is a curious comparison that one makes in visiting the places of worship of different nations. Once I was in St. Peter's, when a new saint was being added to the calendar (next year it would be a new miracle, and the next a new doctrine, for the oldest thing in the Romish Church is to be always adding new bits of stucco and plaster to the stone). By good fortune I had a place very near to the Cardinals, who were all on their knees, Dr. Wiseman among them, and they passed from hand to hand a goodly snuff-box, while they were in this sacred act of devotion. The Pope alone of all seemed to be really devout.

To come to Egypt again and look at the Moslems there. I had an interview at the viceroy's palace with a pasha, one of his cabinet. In the waiting-room there was a Turk, a fine old gentleman, patiently sitting until his turn might come for business. But suddenly he rose and began his afternoon prayers upon the royal carpet, and he went on and on entirely undisturbed. I will give one more instance. At a far-off island in an Egyptian lake, a crowd of men were round the governor, who had brought them in a large boat to welcome the Rob Roy. There was scarcely standing-room for the excited visitors, yet on the deck and amid them all was one who had spread out his carpet and kneeled for his prayers, and he prayed on this boat in this bustle as if it were the quietest of private chapels in the world.

The Mohammedan has a very plain and majestic ritual. His mosque has no idols, or pictures, or ornaments, or pews, but on a carpet, or a mat, or on the floor, he kneels before

God. Indeed, he needs no church to pray in, no image to adore, no book to read, no priest to offer his petitions. The hour of worship comes, and wherever is the man there is his place of worship. On a ship's deck he spreads his carpet and kneels down. The stone-mason bows his forehead on his white marble block. The Arab kneels under his camel's shade while the sun is scorching the desert about him, and the shepherd bows adoring amid the green grass of the hills.*

To pray thus before men—a characteristic of outward religion—is all the more easy if it does not clearly signify that the worshipper is yielding what is asked by the demand, "My son, give me thine heart."

As the Rob Roy neared the water-palace of the Nile, so prettily posed upon an island, the watchful guards cried loudly to her to keep off. The life of the viceroy had been several times lately attempted, and the orders to his guard were now rigorous. But I wished to approach, though no boat is allowed to come here. To their shouts I shouted "Ingleez," and at length an officer was called who courteously told me in French that, being an Englishman, I might go where I pleased. A little time after this the palace was honored by the presence of the first gentleman of England, the Commodore of the Canoe Club.

Glorious old pyramids! it is you I see over the palm-trees, pointing your peaks to the sky.

"A paddle to the Pyramids!"

Can there be any two words so little and so great together? It seems, indeed, a desecration; so the Rob Roy floats back to her tent.

The jumble of barbarism and civilized life at Boulak was almost distracting. Camels grunting, and the rudest, nudest natives squatted on the ground, while yet a railway engine near us, built in Manchester, shrieks out with warn-

---

* Buckingham (p. 92) says that he saw, near Ras el Ain, two Arab women at prayer on the road, and that he "had never yet, either in Turkey, Egypt, or Arabia, seen a woman thus employed." I noticed a woman praying in public upon one occasion, but only one.

ing whistle, "Clear the line!" The Turks care very little about clearing any line if they are walking upon it, and every body here saunters between the rails at pleasure; men will even ride donkeys on the "four-foot way," and I have several times done it myself here, while the "down express" whisked by. As evening falls there are thick swarms of very large hornets hurrying to the water. It is wonderful how soon one gets used to these formidable-looking visitors, but when they are not teased they appear not to do any mischief. In the dark a shot was heard, and a bullet came through my tent. From my bed I asked what was the meaning of this note of emphasis, but the only answer was, "Somebody is firing at the wild boars." They would be as likely to find wild boars in Piccadilly as at Boulak.

CHAPTER III.

The Nile.—Inundation.—Raising Water.—Watering with the Foot.—Rob Roy the Robber.—Catching the Canoe.—Livingstone.—The Delta.—The Seven Streams.—Delight of the Natives.—Fog.—Pigeons.—Potters.—Pumpkin Raft.—Fiddle and Drum.

To descend the Nile, we now hired as a luggage-boat a very clumsy craft, with her top streaks plastered some inches thick of mud. The three men of the crew were not promising in appearance. They were hired by the day, and the wind was in our teeth, so the canoe could run round and round them under sail. But energetic argument accomplished a little with this stolid crew, and the stream of the Nile runs steadily here and fast.

A few facts may be jotted down that bear upon the country we are sailing in. The average amount of rain in Egypt is very small: forty days at Alexandria, seven at Cairo, and two or three at Assouan. The land, therefore, would never bear green things but for the Nile that brings water from far-off melted snow, and with this laves the rich soft loam which settles on the surface of the exhausted land, and makes it ever new again.* The Nile begins to rise in July, and is highest in the end of September, when, at Cairo, it is from 17 to 28 feet above its lower level. After this it gradually lessens again until June.†

The river at Cairo, when in flood, is about 70 feet higher than the sea, with a fall of about $5\frac{1}{2}$ inches per mile, and a velocity of 5 feet in a second. In "low Nile" the fall is only $3\frac{1}{2}$ inches per mile, and the velocity 19 inches a second. Thus the current is not sufficient to turn hydraulic

---

* The plain of Thebes has been raised about twenty feet by the deposit from the Nile inundations since the temples were erected there.

† Last summer (in 1869) it sank lower than for 150 years before. On October 10, an extraordinary inundation occurred ("Times," Oct. 27, 1869).

engines at the time they are most required. When at its lowest, the surface of the water is below the banks at the mouth about 4 feet, at Cairo about 16 feet, and Assouan (in Nubia) about 33 feet. The water in flood overflows Upper Egypt, but in the Delta it is restrained by high banks.

To use the inundations properly for agriculture, the water must be conducted to the plots of ground quietly, and so as not to tear them up by any violent current. Then it must rest, in order that the rich deposit may be precipitated, and when one level is watered thus the channels to another below can be opened. The water is led from the full Nile by numerous canals. Mehemet Ali paid great attention to this subject. He opened up again many of the ancient canals, and made cross-dikes in Upper Egypt, and strong banks along the two branches of Damietta and Rosetta, so as to control the irrigation of the Delta. Artificial irrigation has to be employed during the five or six months of the crops growing, and when the Nile has sunk far the labor of raising water is considerable.

A small proportion of this watering is done by the *shadoof*. This is a leathern basin, slung from a long pole, which is mounted on pivots, and balanced by a stone or counterpoise of clay at the other end. The basin end is depressed by the laborer until it dips into the water below, and, being freed, it is raised by the counterpoise until the leather basin comes level with the upper channel, into which it is then emptied, and the operation begins again. The men at this work are swarthy fellows, nearly nude, and singing a wild not unmelodious song. Sometimes two are alongside; sometimes one above the other, when the water is raised by stages. For filling with water any canal or pond quite near the river's level, the leathern basin is not slung to a pole, but by four cords held by the hands of men facing each other, who dip the bucket and swing it full to the level above. One or other of these men usually leans against a mud bank, but seldom both of them. I have seen some hundreds of these at work close together in a

D

gang of men and women, and they were always very good-humored whenever the canoe came near.

The irrigation of wider tracts of land, requiring a copious stream of water, is effected by hydraulic engines of more or less simplicity.

The "sakieh" was used, as now, in most ancient times, and consists of a wheel turning on a horizontal axis, and carrying an endless rope of hemp or withes, upon which are earthen pots so placed as to dip into the lower water, and to be carried up as the wheel revolves until they empty themselves successively into a shallow trough at the higher level. Sometimes, instead of jars on a rope, there are buckets, or compartments like boxes, in the hollow rim of a wheel, the lower part of which dips into the water and fills the buckets, and these empty their contents above through one side. Wheels of this sort and others are worked by oxen, horses, camels, buffaloes, mules, or asses, which move in a circle, turning round a horizontal frame, in the centre of which sits a boy or a woman to flog the animals. In the ruder forms of this machine, where wooden pegs answer for cog-wheels, much power is expended in friction. Much water also escapes by leakage, or bad adjustment of the upper flow, and a loud splashing noise generally tells how a large proportion of what is raised only falls back again through bad adjustments.

Wheels turned by men's hands and legs acting in unison are sometimes used in the East to wind up buckets from wells, but I never saw one employed for irrigation.

Robinson (vol. i. p. 542) thinks that this was the mode of watering alluded to in Deuteronomy xi. 10—"For the land whither thou goest in to possess it, is not as the land of Egypt, from whence ye came out, where thou sowedst thy seed, and wateredst it with thy foot, as a garden of herbs." But as we constantly see men watering land in Egypt at the present day by opening and closing the canalettes of mud in their fields with their feet, it is surely to be presumed that this more general characteristic is referred to rather than the use of a particular machine.*

A steam-engine, working the best hydraulic pumps, may now be seen in very many places, sometimes in those apparently most out of the way. These, however, were more employed when the cattle disease made animal power dear, and when the cotton culture became less lucrative, and steam-engines then were more at liberty, on account of the cessation of the American war. The steam-engine and the "sakiehs" often work night and day, and the sound of night labor in the East jars upon the wonted stillness and soft darkness. Music accompanies the watering, whatever be the mode employed. The sakieh, with its ungreased rickety axles, groans, rattles, and creaks with painful regularity. When the harmony stops, by the blind ass going to sleep, the laborer in charge of it is sure to be awakened, but he is generally too lazy to do more than to hurl a threat or a brickbat at the resting brute. The steam-engine pants with its hot strong breathings, and the men at the shadoof whine a vagrant music in no particular key.

About half of the area of the Delta is cultivated, and to water about one-fifth part of this it was estimated, in 1849, there were 50,000 sakiehs in operation (each employing three oxen), and managed by 25,000 men.

Of course the canoe was soon out of sight of the boat, and when, after sixteen miles, I came to the *Barrage*, at the fork of the Delta, I ran through speedily, at my very best pace, lest the crowd that came might send a shower of mud from the high walls above. There was noise in plenty, but I heard only one faint cry of "Monsieur!" from an irate official, and I was too much occupied to heed this while gazing upon the splendid bridge before me, which was built to head back the Nile water for thirty miles; be-

---

* Niebuhr, in 1776, mentions having seen only one machine turned by hands and feet at once ("Voyage in Arabia," p. 12). Thomson ("The Land and the Book," vol. ii. p. 279) does not agree with Robinson's view. The wheel turned by the current of the river Orontes is not, I think, to be seen on the Lower Nile.

cause even a few inches more or less of water flooding the land means hundreds of thousands of pounds gained or lost from the fertilized soil.

My luggage-boat came to the Barrage long after me, and she was detained two hours because the canoe had not been "inspected" by the *douane*. The dragoman and the crew were brought before the governor, and a very angry man he was. "I insist on your bringing the small *merkeb* back, that I may see it." "We can not, my lord, it is

THE BARRAGE OF THE NILE.

miles away." "Who is in it?" "An Englishman." "One?" "Yes, by the Prophet! one." "Impossible! He must be a robber escaping; bring fetters for these men." And chains were soon at hand. "Oh! my lord, we did not know the rule." "Catch the canoe, then, or go to prison." "Not a boat on the Nile can catch it, my lord." Two witnesses were then produced who swore they had seen the canoe, and that it was only the size of a large fish, but that it "flew like a bird." Finally, the Rob Roy was rated at half a ton's burden, and heavily taxed, and all this time she was far off, quietly in a shady nook, while I wandered over the lovely sand in the charming day, inspecting the plants, birds, fish, and deep rich loam, and waiting to see the English ensign of my luggage-boat flutter in the distant horizon.

Meanwhile I made a sketch of the Barrage. This great work was resolved upon in 1843, and begun in 1846. It acts as a long gate or weir across each of the two forks of the river, at the point of the Delta. The portion across the Damietta branch is about 600 yards long, and that over the Rosetta branch 500 yards. The weir consists of arches each of 16 feet span. Of these there are 72* upon the Damietta branch. On the branch to Rosetta there are 62. Mehemet Ali died† before any progress was made with this scheme, and his successor resolved to continue only the barrage proper without the canal, which formed its most important feature. At present it appears that the work has been entirely useless, and it is considered that, if any attempt were made to dam back the Nile by closing in the structure at high flood, the river would sweep away the whole mass together.

Until this point the Nile has run in one stream, and for a thousand miles of that without a tributary, pouring on towards the sea its gracious waters, whose birth is so far away, even (shall we not yet know it?) at "Lake Livingstone."‡ But the river now divides into two great branch-

* My dragoman counted 74, but this, no doubt, included the two arches ashore. The other dimensions given above are taken from "Annales des Ponts et Chaussées," 1851, p. 161.

† The traces of what this wonderful man, Mehemet Ali, began in building, in works of irrigation, in agricultural improvement, as well as in administration and foreign conquest, are already almost like old ruins of the Pharaohs. His amazing energies came not from the lotus-eaters of the Nile. He was "no true Ottoman Turk, but rather a Seljakian Koniarat of Cavalla" ("Saturday Review," June 26, 1869).

‡ At Suez I met the foreign correspondent of the "New York Herald," who was waiting there to receive Dr. Livingstone, then expected every day. This active little Yankee had accompanied the armies of India, Sadowa, and

es, and the triangular shape of the country embraced between these and the sea at the end is called the Delta, from its resemblance to the Greek letter Δ, answering to our D. I have voyaged along both branches of the river, but I do not feel able to say which of them has the largest volume of water. The left branch going towards Alexandria, has its mouth near Rosetta. The right branch, down which the Rob Roy is to sail, flows into the sea near Damietta. About the mouths of both these branches are large swamps and lakes. One of them—Lake Mœris—had long been dry, until the sea was admitted by the English army to protect Alexandria from Bonaparte and the French.

The other great lake is Menzaleh, near the eastern branch, and where our paddle is to ply in a day or two among the flamingoes and pelicans.

The boats on the Nile are truly picturesque. To catch the breeze over the lofty banks, the long lateen sail lifts its pointed head high up in the air. No rig is so graceful as this. One sees it on the Swiss and Italian lakes, the Rhine, and the Danube, and (in a modified form) all through the Levant; but by far the largest lateens are in the Delta of the Nile. Some of these have yards 150 feet in length. The sails are often striped with a gore of blue cloth, and delicate streamers are waving, or the sailor's charms like necklaces dangle from the farthest peak.

Boats with two and three masts are also common. Pressed by a strong north wind, they breast the powerful current with their white-bosomed sails, which lean over athwart each side, or as we call it, "goose-winged." This river was for ages the "seven-mouthed Nile." It was called by a Hebrew word, and is still called in Arabic "El Babr," with the same meaning, "the sea." These features do, indeed, remind us of the prophecy uttered by Isaiah when he says (ch. xi. ver. 16), "And the Lord shall utterly destroy the tongue of the Egyptian sea; and with his mighty

Abyssinia, and had now £1000 ready wherewith to telegraph to the American press every word he could get from the lips of the brave explorer. Such world-wide interest has this hero of Africa.

wind shall he shake his hand over the river, and shall smite it in the seven streams, and make men go over dry-shod."

The "tongue" is evidently what is now called the Delta, and the Egyptian "sea" is the Nile. The "seven streams" have now dwindled down to only two,* and by the bridge at the Barrage, for the first time, men can "go over dry-shod."

Nothing is more useless than a fanciful interpretation of prophecy, even of that which is fulfilled and past, but it is impossible not to follow the Scripture words into the next verse in this chapter, "And there shall be an highway for the remnant of his people, which shall be left, from Assyria; like as it was to Israel in the day that he came up out of the land of Egypt."

Whatever may be this "highway," we have at present a railway here from the Red Sea itself, and traversing probably the very ground on which the host of Israel marched. The railway is already finished to Mansoura, and a branch is next to extend to El Arish, the frontier post of Palestine.†

The Damietta branch of the Nile, which thus bears us along has all the grandeur of a noble river. It is wider than the Thames at Gravesend, and neither rocks nor rapids break the stately flow. The banks are high, and they are partly artificial. The foliage of green underwood often shades the water. Sometimes the shores are really beautiful with splendid trees and wide-spread park-like spaces, carpeted by richest grass. The current is quickened where the banks close in, and the Thames above Richmond Bridge was brought to my recollection by several turns in the Nile. In very few places is the scenery positively tame, and no two bends of the river are alike.

* In the days of the Romans the Nile was known by its eleven branches but of these, seven were principal ones. Herodotus states that of these seven, the Rosetta and the Damietta branches were both artificial. Thus at the present time the only mouths which are in proper action are the two artificial ones.

† Consider also verse 11 of this chapter, and in chapter xix. verses 23-25.

My reception by the natives was generally civil, often humorous, and sometimes exciting, when the boys who cheered the coming stranger flung sods and mud upon him for a parting salute as he retired from the bank. This conduct was harmless while I had the broad river Nile (or even its branch) to take speedy refuge in, but afterwards, in the narrow rivers, it was a serious concomitant of the voyage. Generally, as the blue sail was seen, a whole village rushed down to the bank, and half of them into the water; but with nods and smiles and "salaam" from her crew, the Rob Roy managed to get a good offing before the awe of wonder had subsided into the boyish desire to have a "shot" at the tiny craft.

We camped on a nameless island—no dogs howling all night, as in every town—no "ghuffeer" as a guard to snore under my tent-eaves, but the radiant moon shining in the eddies of old Nile as they rippled me to sleep. Next we stopped at Benha, the old Atribis, with huge mounds of potsherds, the remnant that never perishes from an ancient town. I dug long to get at a mummy here, having spied a bit of garment sticking out from the rubbish, but at last the whole piece came forth, much burned at one end, for the place was no doubt set on fire before it was deserted, and then buried forever.

The country on both sides of the river here is perfectly flat, teeming with verdure.* Five crops of clover had already been housed this year, and the sixth was to be the largest of all. Delicious Indian corn grew high, and my table was supplied with dainty fare. Working, eating, and sleeping well, I soon gained the exuberant spirits of buoyant health, and the whole journey of twelve days on the water was a continual delight and surprise, for indeed I had expected only a tame sort of trip, like a canal voyage in Holland, or a paddle in Lincolnshire.

---

* The English Consular Agent at Port Said, Dr. Yaab, has a very fine garden, with the rarest and most beautiful African plants growing, and a collection of others growing from seeds and cuttings in sand covered by small glasses. Moisture is supplied to these only once in several months.

By five in the morning our slumbers were done; at six three eggs appeared with tea and toast, while the tent was being struck, and then off went the Rob Roy into a dense but mild-tempered fog, which instantly concealed every thing around. Then I took out my Bible, or a traveller's "Book of Psalms," the kind parting present of the Earl of Shaftesbury, and while my canoe gently floated on the current, then was the time to read.

The sensation of being thus enveloped in what looked like dense white wool was most singular, and wholly undisturbed by any sense of danger. I *must* be going the right way. For the next hundred miles at least there was no new river to be entered. No boat could run me down, for there was no wind for it to sail with, and none of them dared to row in the mist. My luggage-boat, I knew, must be behind me, and at eleven o'clock I would somehow meet her again for luncheon. But by the time the Rob Roy had twirled round and round for half an hour, the cotton atmosphere was evidently thinner. Then rents appeared in it, and then patches of blue sky, and the faint green of trees, and the faint brown of mud villages, and the faint red flicker that I knew was the ensign on the tall yard of my consort. See, the veil rises now, and the silk flag flutters on my little mast; the whole bright scene comes out fresh and gorgeous, and a breeze has begun—yes, a south wind, favorable; so my blue sail runs up, and away goes the Rob Roy on another twelve hours of charming journey.

By the way we shall fish and shoot, and land to see the shore, and sing and talk with the natives, and sketch, and read, and soliloquize. There is one of the pigeon villages. It exists for pigeons. A hundred mud towers, about thirty feet high, are clustered together, and myriads of blue and white pigeons wheel in the air. Sometimes passing these in my little vessel, one could see what I had remarked before on the Nile, that when the banks are steep, and the pigeons can not well stand on them to drink, they settle on the water itself, and closing their wings and floating for a few seconds, they manage thus to slake their thirst.

Evening comes quick in winter, and near the tent there sleeps, on the ground, our "ghuffeer," or native guard, which personage you must take at every village, and pay this beadle of the Nile a franc or two for sleeping very loud to keep away the robbers. We were in a bad neighborhood last night, and even before this potent functionary had arrived, some thief had stolen a long piece of rope left out for two minutes. At another place our three boatmen absconded entirely, being displeased at some order I had given about their tattered but graceful sail. It is sometimes more pain than pleasure to know too much about what others are doing for you badly, and boat-sailing being a hobby of mine, I felt it hard to put up with the lubberly ways of an Egyptian crew. Here is the large town of Semenood, where I had hoped to have a boar-hunt, but my last experience of one in the Delta many years ago was not encouraging. The moment a boar ran out from the dense high covert of beans and prickles high above my head, all the beaters ran off, and as I fired into the brute's hindquarters my foot fell into a deep chasm in the mud, so I sprawled on my back with spear and sword and dagger all clinging entangled together.

In more pacific humor now, I spent an hour to see the potters at their work, near Semenood, the town being celebrated for this ancient art.* Among the tombs, in low clay huts, the nimble-fingered and prehensile-toed successors of old Egypt's potters were plying the busy wheels. The wheel that flies round by that man's naked foot is the same as when Amenophis died, and the vase that is now spinning swiftly is of the shape that Sesostris drank from —for "why should they change?" that is what the people always ask me. Yet they willingly go by railway even in the Delta.

In a pottery far up the Nile, I recollect, in my former visit, one of the men had his long chibouque suspended by

---

* Thomson ("The Land and the Book," vol. i. pp. 282, 283) gives a good picture of the potter of Egypt, and cites the texts Jeremiah xviii. 4, 6; Isaiah xxx, 14; and Paul's striking metaphor in Romans ix.

cords from the roof, so that with one end in his mouth he could smoke and yet have hands free to work. The idea of a shorter pipe seemed never to have occurred even to this man so conversant with the clay.*

Fishermen have odd ways of filling their baskets in the Delta. One of the most primitive is to see a man sitting on a sort of raft made of empty gourds, which are held together by a net below a small platform of river reeds.† How can he sit upon that for two minutes without an up-

GOURD RAFT ON THE NILE.

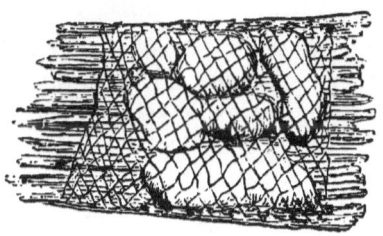

THE RAFT SEEN FROM BELOW.

---

* At a seaport also I remember a man up to his waist in water and calking a ship, while all the time, somehow or other, he managed to wield also a large "nargilleh" with two tubes, a yard long, stuck into a cocoa-nut, which every now and then was submerged by a wave.

† The sketch shows the man fishing thus, and the lower figure represents a view of the same raft turned up to exhibit the net-bag of gourds.

set? He asks me the same question about my canoe. Both of us conclude that practice will teach almost any thing. In the next river the raft was still more rude, merely a large bundle of reed shanks tied together.

Another mode of fishing practised in the East (but chiefly on the sea-coast) is to scatter on the water crumbs of bread soaked in poison. The fish eat these and die and float, and the man gathers them to sell.

All along the banks of the Nile is free luxuriant life, animal and vegetable, with a sense of profuseness and overflowing that is almost oppressive. And yet every person around us looks squalid and poor, although not one begged from me. The cry of "backshish" was heard only once, and then it may have come from a donkey boy who had floated hither from Cairo. Every body is getting water all day and most of the night. The Nile is every thing to the Egyptian. The women are filling huge earthen jars, while they stand gazing at me in the stream that laves their bare knees, and instantly they replace the long, black, dirty yashmaks, which hang by three brass rings on the middle of the nose, to screen their sallow features from masculine gaze. The men are lifting water either in a leathern bucket or by a pole and weight, or a long lever, and working the Persian wheel. Not far off you can hear the *puff, puff!* of a high-pressure engine, and this also is pumping water. Marvellous Nile, how far you spring from, how long you wander, how many millions all take water from you, and no wonder you were worshipped as a god! At eventide, the buffaloes wend their way to the river, and run the last few steps with neck outstretched, and eager thirsty eye, and wading forward they plump down in the mud, rollicking about in their bovine gladness, with only the nose above the surface, and a cloud of flies fighting to find room upon that. Warm red now creeps over the western sky, and our anchor hooks us to the shore. The Rob Roy meanders up some creek, while the tent is being smartly pitched by my admirable dragoman, and in half an hour my dinner is served up, having been partly cooked at the bows of the luggage-boat upon that clay slab you see there white with ashes. The repast is hot, and clean, and wholesome: excellent soup, one of the ducks I shot yesterday, peas, oranges, and coffee; can any travelling be more comfortable than this, in a canoe with a luggage-boat? And I mention the fare distinctly, for all the members of the Canoe Club soon get to know that, unless you are thoroughly well fed on a voyage, it is impossible to keep up both pace and spirits. The rising moon, now full, lights up the whole picture again, and makes it new with silver setting instead of gold. The oxen and asses for the night-work still keep grinding on the tedious round of the water-wheels, but the rather creaky tune is soon lost in the merry, plaintive song from every hamlet, with the shrill shrieking "trill, trill," of the women, and the deep-toned solemn sound of the Egyptian drum.* Some swains join in with reed pipes, and an old blind *maestro* will moan a sort of dirge while he plays, wonderfully well too, on a fiddle, called kamjeh, made out of half a cocoa-nut and only one solitary string.

Then begin the jackals, and, at their sharp whine of challenge, the dogs—arrant cowards both; you can make them scamper with a straw. Meantime, in my large and beautiful tent, I recline reading "Speke and Grant's Travels" in French, or Tristram's "Land of Israel," or add to my notes and sketches, or chat with Hany, or post up my log, and before ten o'clock I shall be in bed.

* I had learned to play this *darabookra* years ago, and brought a good one home. Music floats ever in the air of Egypt, as "backshish" in Turkey proper, and "dollar" in the land of the West. Crossing the Missouri River in Kansas, I thought there at least I was out of the range of Scotchmen and of dollars; but in the ferry-boat the only other passenger was a Macdonald, and from the opposite shore the first word—shouted at an auction—was "dollar!"

CHAPTER IV.

Nile and Severn.—Nile and Thames.—Bab el Hagar.—Misery.—Compass-card.—Mansourah.—King Cotton.—Shoeblacks.—The Zrier River.—A Water-puzzle.—A Run on the Bank.—Land of Goshen.—Wonderment.—Admirers.—Finding the Way.—The Makalolo.—The Governor.—Start on Lake Menzaleh.—Living Clouds.—Mataryeh.—Legs of Ingleez.—Egyptian Lock.

MANY of the reaches of the Nile were like what is seen from the window where these lines are written, as the heavy tide of the Severn runs sleepily past the red cliffs near Newnham. But substitutions must be made in the mind, if Gloucestershire is to look like the Delta. Those corn-fields are instead of maize; those bushy elms are put for palm-trees. The spires that point our English landscape must be thought of as minarets, gaudy and white, and this pleasant "Severn Bank Hotel" is a change from the doorless, wall-less, windowless "khan" of the East, with only a roof and pillars, and a general odor of donkeydom.

August here on the Severn will do very well for December on the Nile, and as the moon lights up at eve, the difference between the two pictures is only that between shadows. That lazy boat at anchor, fishing in mid-channel, would do for either continent, only in Egypt there would be gay turbans on board, and the soft, melodious drum, and gentle, careless song.

As night advances, the illusion is more complete that I am now in Egypt, and can fancy the bed is in the same old tent, for I hear quite close the roar of wild beasts; they are in the vans of Mander's "Unrivalled Menagerie," and their species and genera must be very terrible, for there is inscribed upon the caravan the following Latin—the whole stock, no doubt, of the composer:—"Sui generis," "Veni, vidi, vici," "Væ victis." Meanwhile the brass-band plays a chorus from Händel—an oratorio—at a show!

Even a better likeness of the Nile is seen upon the Thames, from the garden of the hotel at Purfleet, where the old Rob Roy on her first voyage passed her first night in comfort.

The dikes along the Thames are smaller than in Egypt, but equally strong. The Essex marshes stretch their flat landscape on either side, just like the Delta. When the setting sun casts a hazier light behind the shores, and fancy is more free, and colors are less true, then the tall tower of the new Asylum on the opposite hill might well be taken for a Moslem minaret, and the white-bait-fishers' boats for boats of Egypt. Greenhithe to our left from hence is shaded deep, but we can still discern the sharp masts of the "Chichester" Training-ship, the floating home for the homeless boy, and nearer, we hear a soft, sweet chant of the "Evening Hymn" from the open ports of the "Cornwall," where the poor lads who have slipped in first steps of life are put in the way upright, that they may cheer up and try again.*

We halted in a lovely bend of the Nile, while I walked about two miles through the cotton-fields to examine a wonderful ruin very seldom visited by travellers. Alas! to reach this relic of the past, we have to cross the rails of a new "iron road" of the present; so the romance is much spoiled of this "Bab el Hagar" (Stone Gate). No one can tell what the place was in ancient days; now it is a heap of stupendous cut stones, all granite and porphyry, all brought hundreds of miles, carved, polished, exquisitely fashioned, then all cast down, a huge pile of utter confusion—but how? Really no one has yet found out the mode by which the ancients could tear asunder the enormous blocks of these grand temples. A long green snake came out of the ruins to dispute the ground with us. Hyenas and foxes live in the tenantless palace, and the winding canal that watered its magnificent portal sleeps now forever, with a stagnant pool just here and there to trace it by.

* Details concerning the "Training-ships," and the "Reformatory-ships," are given in "The Voyage Alone in the Yawl Rob Roy."

At Ziftch the people were in holiday trim, on their Moslem sabbath, being Friday. The men had on their clean white turbans, and my crew asked to stop two hours for their mosque, which, of course, was allowed, because they seemed to care for their worship. Indeed it became a question whether it was not right for me to let the boat rest all their "Sunday," as it did during all of mine, but they have no such custom here.

Another scruple may now be noticed, as one of the very few things which even for a moment interfered with the continuous pleasure of this canoe journey.

When we had only one tent in Egypt, and when afterwards in Syria, with two tents for a larger party, we had still to accommodate some of them at night in that splendidly roofed spare-room—the open air—it was not easy to enjoy my comfortable bed, piled up with blankets, and shaded above from the dew, while some of my dependents were out the live-long night in a keen, cold, frosty winter blast, lying upon the bare ground.

'Tis true they were "used to it;" that I paid them highly for the additional hardship of a journey in winter; that for some at least, as, for instance, the "ghuffeer," or guards, it would be a breach of duty to come under cover, when theirs was the post of watchmen; and that none of them ever complained to me, and none would accept the rugs and carpets I freely offered for their comfort: still it was not quite a lullaby to hear men groaning with cold outside, huddled under the lee of my tent (at the best a rather bare shield against the bitter blast), and only separated by a thin bit of canvas from their fortunate employer, who was so intensely snug in his soft, warm bed.

Some of the men, too, had terrible coughs, for hours barking away by moonlight as if they must burst their very lungs before morning; and by our tent at Suez a poor woman, in a wooden hut beside me, coughed the whole night incessantly, as if each moment was to sob out her soul. It was a relief indeed to hear that in Egypt these colds in the chest seldom, if ever, prove mortal, but their trouble and their loud appeal to sympathy were scarcely less from this. Even the stout old muleteer would whine at the cold racking his hardy bones, and at dead of night I could hear the muffled prayer of "Yorub!" (God help me!), or a long-drawn moan—"Allā-ā-ā!"

Thick walls in England separate us from the dark, wet, freezing misery of the poor amongst us, and deaden to our ears their cries of hunger and of pain. Life would be impracticable if we could realize one tithe of the wretchedness around us; but his is a stony heart that does not think of this often, and get nerved by the sad thought to do his share in helping.

Our voyage so far had no need of a compass, for the river kept us in its own course; but among the sea-stores of the Rob Roy a mariner's compass was an article very specially prepared. In my voyage alone in a yawl, I had found some defects in the construction of the Liquid Compass, which had been kindly presented to me by the Royal National Life-boat Institution. Months of experience by day and night in the use of it at last resulted in several improvements as to the mode of lighting, and the diagram on the card, etc., which were adopted. The new card is applicable, of course, to a canoe compass. Messrs. Newton, the well-known opticians, presented to me one made in the new pattern, and by which for half a year my course was guided, and many curious observations were made, as will afterwards be noted in our log. The two forms of card are shown in the woodcuts on the next page, and the superior clearness of the new one will not need to be explained when it is compared with the other.*

Before a fresh breeze still favoring, and an onward current, too, our boat speeds fast and pleasantly to the large

---

* The Arabs, when looking at the compass, always speak first of the south point, "kibleh," as they call it. This is the same as among the Chinese, who "box" the compass by "South, North, West, East," and not, as with us, beginning at the north. I once heard a lecture upon "Great Britain," when the map used by the eccentric lecturer had its north point to the right hand, but the names all written so as to be read.

E

COMMON COMPASS-CARD.

ROB ROY COMPASS-CARD.

bustling town of Mansourah.* The sounds and sights, and even the very scents, around us now seem to tell at once that a revolution has been working here.

Mansourah is immersed in cotton, and "cotton is king!" The American war gave suddenly a start to the cotton-trade in Egypt. Even now, much of the cotton that reaches England comes from the land of the Pharaohs,† and cotton bursts forth on all sides. Children are plucking it in the fields, singing as they gather the fleecy pods into their little blue dresses tucked up for pockets. From country plantations a long string of camels stalks over the plain, all cotton-laden. Boats full of it are tracked along the sleepy lagoons of the Nile and the countless canals which intersect the ancient land of Goshen. At Mansourah the cotton-gins for cleaning the stuff and separating the seed are worked by steam; and the ceaseless sighs of the engine are not even stopped on Sunday, though the bell has been ringing long for the Greek Church prayers.

The tall, simple, smiling camel has found out this cotton-seed, too; and as he strides along, he turns his head, and (when his driver is turning *his* head) he bites a mouthful of cotton out of the sack he is carrying, and munches away with a look of guileless innocence.

Behind my tent is another railway, all made by Englishmen. See the "signal-man," with a bright turban and no shoes; he is spinning with the distaff, and the "points-man" lies prone on the ground and fast asleep. In front are the steamers, with the crescent flag shining red again below in the deep-flowing stilly Nile. Thus the spirits of fire and water, raised by James Watt, are, in the locomotive, the marine engine, and the land-engine, haunting us everywhere.

The English vice-consul at Mansourah was kind and

---

* The name means "a delightful place," and several towns in Syria are so called.

† The export of cotton from Egypt from Oct. 1, 1868, to August 13, 1869, was 217,596 bales ("Times," Aug. 26, 1869). From America, in 1868, '9, it was 1,000,000 bales; the total American crop, 2,750,000 bales.

hospitable, and he already knew the Rob Roy well by name. He told me the following strange story, quite typical of Turkish ways. An accident happened a few days ago in a factory, when one of the cotton-gins tore and mangled a little lad's arm. The necessity for amputation caused great excitement; but a terrible delay intervened. First, the boy's consent had to be given; then, being a minor, it was found his father must assent; next, his mother, too, had to be persuaded; and when all had agreed, the wise officer of justice had to re-examine each and to take their evidence in writing; after which, and other formalities occupying three mortal hours, the operation was begun which should have been finished long before. As a set-off to these evidences of barbarity, we noticed, at any rate, one plain sign of civilization at Mansourah: there are shoeblacks in the streets. Cairo, Beyrout, and Alexandria have also their blacking brigades, though they are not so organized as we have them in London, but each boy works on his own account as a "freebooter."*

After a blood-red sunset, empurpled far overhead by heavens of deeper blue, we had a sudden and fierce gust of wind from the west, which whistled through the lofty masts and marred the sleeping landscape of the evening with a rushing storm of sand. My tent quivered again, and all inside was dust and darkness, as the poor fainting candle soon gave in. Loud cries now for the mallet to hammer down our iron tent-pegs; so I must close my ink-bottle for the night, and give an extra brush to my hair in the morning.

I left the Nile at this town, and chartered a luggage-boat on the Zrier River (small river). Our ryis, or captain, is a veteran seventy years of age, but he objects to being called "old." His two sons are the crew, both able

---

* The "Ragged-School Shoeblack Societies" of London earned during the twelve months ending June, 1869, nearly £9000. The oldest of the Societies, begun in 1851, and of which 100 boys occupy chiefly the City and the Strand, earned during the same time, as part of the above amount, the sum of £2400, and this year will earn £3000.

lads, and the moment the bargain was struck (now made "by the piece," and not "by the day") the ancient mariner begged us to hoist our ensign upon his boat at once, for that, he said, and only that, would keep him from being at the mercy of the soldiers, who could claim his boat at any moment and at any price they pleased. Next morning we launched our little navy, with a fine breeze behind us, and tropical verdure thick on the banks of the Zrier. The oak, sycamore, and weeping willow overhang us now; gorgeous butterflies flit from the tall reeds, or rest as if poised on the sunbeams; the black and white kingfisher hovers in mid-stream, and the large Indian kingfisher, arrayed in red and blue, twitters as he launches on the breeze. Eagles, hawks, and bustards, wild ducks, and the graceful ibis now and then, and the crook-necked flamingo, and the pretty little hoopoo, with its crest and bill in a line till it settles on the sand, and spreads its chignon to be admired by its partner, for they are always conjugal in pairs.

We have, of course, a sort of "family worship" with my dragoman and his servant (both professing Christians—one, I hope, more than that); but, before this, it is a strange sight to see the crew of our boat every day at their prayers. They first wash their faces, adjust their garments, and then on the cloak of the ryis each man will kneel, bow, stand, bow, and rapidly repeat his words of Moslem worship, turning still to Mecca as our boat is wheeled round in the current. Then they give willing silence while a chapter of the Bible is read for ourselves. Some only of these men can read Arabic; to them, and to such others as it seemed advisable, I gave Arabic tracts, or French, or English, and they were always gratefully accepted. It seems strange and unfriendly to live with men for days, and not to say or give one word to them about the great eternity that they and we shall meet in again most surely.

The Zrier River we are now upon is not visibly joined to the Nile, though once it was. This little river is one of many hundred streams that seem to rise out of the surplus water which percolates the soft loam of the Delta, coming underground from the Nile itself, by working through its narrow banks of clay. An elaborate map is before me of the canals and rivers in the Delta. Years must be spent in learning the outlines of an aquatic network like this, and the clearest head would be very long puzzled in arranging their outlets and overflows, so as not to require some of them to run up hill.*

The fish are so numerous that no bait need be used: the hook is sure to catch a fish, even if the fish does not catch the hook. When caught, the fish are tasteless—as they are, in my opinion, all over the Mediterranean—and not worth cooking. This curious, economical mode of fishing is practised all over Egypt, but was particularly well suited to a narrow river like the Zrier. A man flings a brickbat with a string to it across the little channel—fifty yards. By this another man draws over a long string carrying large hooks upon it (but no bait), attached by a span of cord at every three inches. A float of cork is at each three feet, and some brickbat sinks every six yards. These were all neatly tied on by the fisherman with one hand and his teeth. A dozen lines are thus stretched across the stream, and fixed by pegs to the bank. The two men then take the ends of the string they first laid down, and so drag the hooks slowly under water against the current. Each of the strings is worked in succession, and thus in half an hour the two fishers catch, at any rate, a few of the more sleepy of the fish. Besides this plan, the Delta fishers also use a triangle of bare hooks dangling from a short rod, and the more ordinary drag-net and the seine.

The trees became rather troublesome, now that they branched so far across the little river, and there was scarcely room for the sail to pass between their green boughs,

* The map is a photograph of one made by Mr. Lutfy, C. E., and it was found to be very correct. By a decree ("Times," Aug. 20, 1869). "Omar Pasha Lutfy" has been appointed the Director of the Egyptian Canal Works. From part of this map has been prepared our map at p. 93, engrafting on it from the official map of the Suez Canal, and from a tracing of the last new lines of railway.

which almost met in a leafy arch from bank to bank. Still the current ran fast, and the wind freshened up until we had to take in a reef; while our ensign, floating off to leeward in the breeze, often lapped the foliage on the tree-tops with its long red tongue. Tall reeds on either side choked up the channel, and as the wind down in the hollow between such high banks could not reach the little sail of the canoe, I reluctantly tied her painter to the luggage-boat that she might be towed, while I climbed the bank for a scamper over the country alone. It was exceedingly amusing to see the astonishment of the natives when they suddenly perceived a human form entirely clad in gray, and trotting steadily along. But they were never uncivil to me, and they always returned the salutations of the runner. By cutting across the windings of the channel it was easy for me to keep up with the boat, which was now tearing along at great speed through the water. The view from the high bank was very interesting, for before me was the "Field of Zoan," where once was the pride of Egypt, and where mighty miracles were wrought through Moses.

GOSEIN, IN THE "FIELD OF ZOAN," SEEN FROM A BANK ON THE ZRIER RIVER.

The horizon on every hand was one straight line, with only a few very distant mounds, or "tells," to show where cities had stood of yore.*

All the vast plain was deep brown in color, not the sombre hue of wild, bleak savagery, but that of a rich and mellow land. Between the trees and just beside our sail-top, as it hurried past, there was a little row of dots on the distant limit, a village still called Gosein.† This was the only relic I could find to tell of the famous land of Goshen, and the sketch here given was taken on the spot.

Berimbal was the name of a village where we camped, with fine trees all round it, and a peaceful look of plenty and intelligence on many faces. The river here was not twenty yards broad, and a good deal resembled the wooded stream under Magdalen Bridge at Oxford.

After another day's delightful sailing, on December 1, we arrived at the lively town of Menzaleh, with its mosques and minarets, and its bazars, its street-merchants squatted beside their pile of gourds, and dates, and pepper, and round flat bread, eggs, sweetmeats, oil, embroidered shoes, copper pots, mule-saddles, and a host of other things one does not want, although loud voices roar the names.

The Zrier River has a barrier here, which no persuasion could induce our boat-captain to pass; therefore, yielding to the custom of the place, it was necessary for us to hire another boat to enter upon Lake Menzaleh; and we were sorry to part with the nimble sons and the juvenile father, and they were sorry too.

We camped in the highway, just outside one of the town gates, and in full view of the broad lake of Menzaleh. A dense crowd soon assembled, but they behaved most courteously, ranging in a wide circle with the first few rows squatted down in the usual Eastern fashion. The tent was a delight to them, but a tent they had seen before. As for

---

* Several large villages were visible to the north, and beyond these were the minarets of Damietta.

† This is marked on the map. There is also another of the same name, which I did not see.

the canoe, it was so entirely new to every man that the oldest shook their heads when asked by the juniors in a timid way, "What in the world is *that?*" In the various cruises of the Rob Roy the wonder or inquisitiveness shown by the natives of different countries has always been a study to her captain. Where boats are unknown—as upon the Upper Danube and Moselle, the canoe was greeted with an unmeaning stare, which often became a gaze of fright, especially if she was seen first in motion on the water, or dragged over the grass. In parts of Palestine, where not only no boat had ever been seen but no picture of such a thing which might give an idea of a boat to the Mohammedan mind, the feeling of the spectator on a sight of the canoe generally began with fear, and sometimes ended in a brave attack, as will be told before the end of the Rob Roy's log.

Again, where boats are known, as in Norway, Sweden, the Elbe, and Schleswig-Holstein, as well as here in Egypt, the natives were all admirers, rather than amazed. They smiled with a yearning to examine the canoe more nearly, and their animated discussions about the matter showed how much they appreciated her delicate construction, and beautiful finish, and diminutive size, compared in each feature with all the best models of naval architecture which the oldest sailor of them had ever seen before.*

But now came the difficult part of the work—to find any man among these wonderers who could point out our way over the lake to the ruins of San, the modern name of Zoan, whither the Rob Roy was bound.†

* In Canadian waters the Indians examined only the crew of the canoe I paddled alone. They saw plenty of the bark canoes and of "dug-outs," and the craft therefore was no novelty.

† From Lynch's "Visit to the Suez Canal" (1868), p. 58, we learn that Menzaleh Lake was formerly called Zoan, or Zan, or Tanis, or Tan; and in Scripture the fertile district round was called the "field of Zoan." Strabo mentions fields and villages on its site, and the word used by him ($\tau o \mu o \varsigma$), "pasture lands," corresponds with the word employed by Arab geographers, who also call the lake Tanis, from a word meaning clay or mud. The Hebrew "Tan" means "clay," and the Greek $\pi \eta \lambda o \varsigma$, found still in the modern name Pelusium. An Arab tradition from the tenth century states that this

I selected three of the likeliest fishermen for consultation, and (Hany interpreting) the plan of travel we had formed was explained for their opinion. We were standing in full view of the lake, and with an excellent map, and these three men to help us in counsel, yet, after a good hour's earnest talk, of which, however, almost half was wasted in an animated debate between the guides, who at last came to blows, we found it utterly impossible to make out how the canoe was to paddle to San.

"Toweel" was the place most difficult to fix in their different versions of directions. At one time we were to go outside of "Toweel," at another it was evident that "Toweel" was to be left outside of our route. "Nobody lived at Toweel," and yet there were "always men" at this very place. The canoe could not sail nor paddle to "Toweel," nor could "the howaga* walk to it."

Even by a careful sketch of the coast I made for them, no man could tell us the proper course for San. But I have found that explaining things by drawings is seldom of any advantage, except when only common objects are outlined. People who have never before seen a map or a plan have no idea of it as a miniature of the land and water.† Dr. Livingstone told me that the intelligent Makololo chief, "Setcheli," was perfectly incapable at first of discerning any figure even in a plain picture. The doctor tried him at last with the simplest sketch of a few men in a group, but the puzzled clever African, though truly anxious to make the best of what was put before him, only turned it round and round in his hands, and upside down,

district was once covered with villages: that many hundred years ago the sea overwhelmed all except Tooneh and others on high ground, and that the surviving inhabitants carried their dead to Zoan. Funereal hieroglyphic inscriptions found at Memphis mention "the land of Tannen."

* In Egypt the Arabic *g* is pronounced hard, whereas in Syria the word would be with the soft *j*, as "howaja."

† Once upon a steamboat I observed a Turkish lady studying an atlas. The map represented Turkey, not only as the centre of the earth, but as occupying nearly all the circumference; while England and America were two red dots on the farthest verge. I was generally spoken of as a native of Belad Ingleez—"the town of England."

and still stared intensely at the paper utterly bewildered. At last a gleam of light seemed to flash upon his mind, and he pointed to a man's arm he could just descry in the drawing; then gradually, but very slowly indeed, he seemed to catch another limb, and then a head, until the whole of the pictured group became intelligible. After his eye had been thus tutored to look for form represented in miniature, he could always make out the meaning of pictures; and the process his mind went through is, doubtless, like that which a little child must graduate in before he can point to a cow in his nursery picture-book, and tell us that he knows it by saying "Moo!"

I retired from the bustle to consider the conflicting evidence as to the best route, and the verdict was "to start next day, and find the way myself."

Four fowls must be roasted at once, and bread and eggs made ready for four days' food. To lighten the canoe, I left every possible item behind, even the boat's topsail; and thus, prepared for all chances, there was encouragement in the reflection that surely this insoluble Menzaleh could not be worse to get over than the Mälar Lake in Sweden, where the Rob Roy had found her way to the end, though eleven hundred islands had to be threaded to get there.

It was a wide and novel view to sit and meditate before that open lake and the strange fishermen around us. The sun just setting showered upon the water a flood of fiery red. On the large marshes near was a company of fowlers at their work, while more than thirty beaters spread out in a great semicircle and plashed along wading. The ducks and water-fowl rose in advance by thousands, and whole clouds of winged game flew straight into the range of men posted with guns in little bowers far out in the water. Many reflections crowded into my mind as to the strange things I should meet there on the morrow; the men, the birds, the water, even the land, so entirely different from what could be seen anywhere else. Thunder in the night rumbled from far, and a few drops of rain came sprinkling in the dark. My mackintosh sheet was soon rigged out to cover us from a storm, but it did not come to-night, and only pleasant sleep.

Before our start on this doubtful journey to San, a crowd came to see us, and in the middle of them, arrayed in full state, was the governor himself. In almost every town where we stopped in Egypt, the chief ruler was courteous enough to honor us with a visit, but this governor at Menzaleh was particularly complaisant. He was venerable and dignified. He was dressed in most brilliant colors. His suite encircled him with pomp, and the boy-slave, his pipe-bearer, carried for him a magnificent chibouque, all gold and gems, which reached from the old man's mouth even to the ground.

His interest about the canoe was excessive. All its contents had to be explained—the cabin, sails, lamp, curtains, compass, paddle, and cuisine. He felt the long lithe sides of the Rob Roy with his hands from end to end, because he was nearly blind. How vague must have been, after all, his notions about the whole affair! Explanations from this worthy fellow soon cleared up the meaning of that mysterious word "toweel," which we now found to signify any piece of land not solid enough to walk upon, and not covered enough to sail over. In fact, there were fifty "toweels" around us, and the particular "toweel" that was marked on the map near Matarych, and described as a village in the guide-book, had no special existence whatever—nay, the natives protested against any such town in the world.

Plans fully made in a campaign should be carried out at all hazards—if only you have made them after weighing all the evidence. But in canoeing one learns, among other lessons, that an important fact, though new, must be duly considered in our plans, even though its intrusion discomposes all. Thus it was now plain that the route I had settled to start upon, all alone, would entail a full half-mile of sheer haulage of the Rob Roy over deep mud and very shallow water; and yet there was a far better way to San,

START ON LAKE MENZALEH IN EGYPT.

for the lake was wide, and 3000 fishing-boats upon it all had ample room.

At once my plans were changed, then, and a luggage-boat was hired to take us for five days at the price of eight napoleons, of which sum the large proportion of five napoleons went to the Government for their share as a tax. By this boat we were to enter the lake at another side from the west, and to double the Cape of Mataryeh instead of crossing a marsh, and so to push on to San, which place I was more than ever resolved to visit by water, now that the difficulty of getting there in this way was fully proved.

Camels came to carry our luggage and tent, as our camp was now going to sea. The tall palm-trees bent gracefully over the gazing crowd, and shaded us to the last. Two stalwart fishermen shouldered the canoe, amid loud plaudits, and Hany singing led the way. My parting address to the Mayor of Menzaleh was earnest and eloquent, if not intelligible, and in a few minutes more we had borne the canoe through the cotton-fields and launched her on a beauteous river hemmed in deeply by the weeping willows and other pendent trees.

Four miles of a winding course upon this brought me gradually down to the west limb of the lake, where a very fresh breeze was blowing, and quite a new scene awaited my arrival. We had been told of the enormous flocks of wild fowl to be seen on this lake, and especially in winter. I had seen thousands, nay, myriads of these, and wondered at the multitude in the air. But I never expected to see birds so numerous and so close together that their compact mass formed living islands upon the water, and when the wind now took me swiftly to these, and the island rose up with a loud and thrilling din to become a feathered cloud in the air, the impression was one of vastness and innumerable teeming life, which it is entirely impossible to convey in words. The larger geese and pelicans and swans floated like ships at anchor. The long-legged flamingoes and other waders traced out the shape of the shallows by their

to be shyly ignored between men meeting for once in the wide, wide world.

Three sailors and a boy were our crew of the luggage-boat this time, but there was another little fellow, almost a baby. I did not know at first he was with us, for they had locked him up for safety in the forecastle, an apartment about the size of a portmanteau, and when he whined inside, and I ordered him to be let out, they brought the key of the Egyptian lock, just like a tooth-brush, with wires for its hairs, each wire corresponding to a ward in the lock. The plan is simple and sure, and it certainly contains the idea too of the well-known "Bramah lock," which is used all over the world.*

The wind being contrary, the paddle had now to drive the Rob Roy for about four hours, ascending the river Mushra, but I ran her up the winding creeks, and soon began to replenish our larder by shooting my first wild duck from a canoe. People had foreboded an upset as the sure result of a gun's recoil. However, it was only the duck that was knocked over.

---

* The Egyptian lock and its key are both of wood, and when a man has locked his door, he throws the key over his shoulder, where it can hang all day suspended by a string round his neck. This custom, no doubt, explains that verse of prophecy, "And the key of the house of David will I lay upon his shoulder; so he shall open, and none shall shut; and he shall shut, and none shall open" (Isaiah xxii. 22); which passage again leads us to the further and clearer mention of the solemn truth in the Book of the Revelation, "These things saith he that is holy, he that is true, he that hath the key of David, he that openeth, and no man shutteth; and shutteth, and no man openeth" (ch. iii. 7).

CHAPTER V.

River Mushra.—"Field of Zoan."—Strange Creatures.—A Lost Needle.—
"Fire in Zoan."—Qualms.—Flamingoes.—Rigs.—A Yarn.—Lubbers.—
By Moonlight.—Port Said.—Parting Shot.—Squall.

AFTER a long and winding voyage on the Mushra, which leaves the Delta with a score of others, and, passing by Zag-a-Zig, conveys Nile water, partly from filtration, partly direct from the Nile, finally into Lake Menzaleh, and once, probably, in much greater volume, into the sea, we came near the vast tells, or mounds, of ancient Zoan, and I started on foot to explore them all alone. It is far the best way to be alone in examining a huge relic like this, where desolation reigns, where all may be seen without a guide, and where the sentiment of silence adds to the loneliness of the scene.

For a mile I crossed a marsh, not without frequent difficulties, and then climbed up to the highest mound, perhaps 200 feet above the water. All was seen from that point, and indeed it is a noble view. The horizon is nearly a straight line on every side. Looking west, the tract before us is a black rich loam, without fences or towns, and with only a dozen trees in sight. This is "The Field of Zoan."*

Behind is a gleam of silver light on the far-away shore of Lake Menzaleh. Across the level foreground winds most gracefully the Mushra, and down there below the Rob Roy floats on the ripples of a gentle breeze. But be-

---

* "Now Hebron was built seven years before Zoan" (Numbers xiii. 22). In Psalm lxxviii. 12, we read, "Marvellous things did He in the sight of their fathers, in the land of Egypt, in the field of Zoan;" where Stanley considers that "field" may be the translation of the Hebrew signifying "to level." Cruden gives "motion" as the meaning of "Zoan." The name is referred to again in Isaiah xxx. 4.

tween that winding river and the mound we look from, there is lying bare and gaunt, in stark silent devastation, one of the grandest and oldest ruins in the world. It is deep in the middle of an inclosing amphitheatre of mounds, all of them absolutely bare, and all dark-red from the potsherds, that defy the winds of time and the dew and the sun alike to stir them, or to melt away their sharp-edged fragments.

THE "FIELD OF ZOAN."

M. Mariette, of Cairo, lately had these ruins uncovered (by forced labor, I was told, of 500 men at a time). They are wide-spread, varied and gigantic. Here you see about a dozen obelisks, all fallen, all broken; twenty or thirty great statues, all monoliths, of porphyry, and granite, red and gray; a huge sarcophagus (as it seemed to me) was of softer stone, and enormous pillars, lintel, and wall-stones are piled in heaps one over the other, most of them still buried in the earth. The polished statues are of various sizes, and of beautiful workmanship. Some sit with half the body over the ground, others have only a leg in the air. One leans its great bulk sideways, covered up to the ear; another lies with chair and legs appearing, but the head is buried deep in the mud.*

The buildings seemed to have formed a temple, with three outlying edifices. Some of the obelisks must have fallen long before the dust and refuse of ages had filled the courtly halls, then tenantless. Others fell on this new stratum, and these now lie, say, ten feet higher than the floor, while a few of the taller columns lasted perhaps for another thousand years, and then they toppled over on the lonely plain with a crash unheard by a regardless world. The sand soon buried them there, and even the memory of Zoan faded away.

The words in Isaiah† may well be read here with so plain a comment round us:

"Surely the princes of Zoan are fools, the counsel of

---

* In the exfoliating granite of these old walls I found some very curious insects. They were crowded in groups of many hundreds close together, and they seemed to lie dormant until disturbed. Each was like a small grain of corn, but flatter, and more of the shape of a lady-bird. The color was a uniform pale yellow, and they had many legs. I could not discover the slightest trace of moss, or any vegetable matter, in or near these groups, though I carefully examined the stone with a lens. Some of them I brought away, and sent in a letter to that amusing and excellent weekly paper, "Land and Water," being quite sure that a description of them there would educe full explanation of their proper names and habits, if they did not eat their way through the envelope on their passage home—like some bats sent from Australia to my friend Mr. Gould (the king of ornithologists), and which, though asleep when they were posted, awoke, and ate up the other letters in the mail-bag and bit the postman's fingers at the end. However, the following appeared in "Land and Water," September 18, 1869:—"With the kind assistance of Mr. F. Smith, of the British Museum, I have compared their damaged remains with the specimens of this class of insects in the national collection, and find that there is only one individual there which at all resembles the Rob Roy specimens. This is an unnamed coccinella from China. It has the same buff-yellow elytra with very faintly discernible spots of a slightly deeper shade on them, and, so far as we could ascertain, the same number of black spots (nine) on the thorax, placed in the same form and position. Mr. Smith hopes to be able to make a perfect insect for the collection from the *disjecta membra* of more than one individual."—HENRY LEE.

† Isaiah xix. 11-13.

the wise counsellors of Pharaoh is become brutish: how say ye unto Pharaoh, I am the son of the wise, the son of ancient kings?

"Where are they? where are thy wise men? and let them tell thee now, and let them know what the Lord of Hosts hath purposed upon Egypt.

"The princes of Zoan are become fools, the princes of Noph are deceived; they have also seduced Egypt, even they that are the stay of the tribes thereof."

Think of the labor of transporting hither these stones, each many hundreds of tons in weight, from the Upper Nile, whence several of them *must* have come, and yet we Englishmen have left the splendid obelisk, "Cleopatra's Needle," close by the sea at Alexandria for fifty years, though it belongs to England, and it would grace our finest site in London. In 1849 this neglected gift was only half buried, but in 1869 it was so completely hidden that not even the owner of the workshop where it lies could point out to me the exact spot of its sandy grave!

The mounds that now hedge in the ruins of Zoan—so that from no point in the plain can you see even one stone of the grand silent pile—were probably the houses of a great town built of mud, and an extensive pottery. All over and under and among the stones are large masses of vitrified bricks, evidently the produce of the kilns and reminding us of what was predicted in Ezekiel (ch. xxx. 14), "I will set fire in Zoan."

Many as are the celebrated ruins I have seen, I do not recollect any that impressed me so deeply with the sense of fallen and deserted magnificence.*

---

* In the 13th verse of the 30th chapter of Ezekiel it is said, "And there shall be no more a prince of the land of Egypt." The country has been for ages subject to foreign rule. Lately the present viceroy seemed to have acquired almost the place of an independent sovereign, but the Sultan has just reminded his highness (in no measured terms) how entirely dependent upon the Porte is this governor, who would set up as "a prince of Egypt." In Isaiah (ch. xix. 4-10) is the following further prophecy: "And the Egyptians will I give over into the hand of a cruel lord; and a fierce king shall rule over them, saith the Lord, the Lord of Hosts. And the waters shall fail

Our wandering up and down the Mushra was like a quiet walk along a country lane to see a deserted town, only the way was by water. In the lake again once more, the journey was livelier as the Rob Roy dashes out upon a wave-flowing sea. Islands innumerable block up the horizon. Sea-birds by thousands sail upon the wind. Flamingoes hover in flocks, and spread a pale pink cloud of beauteous plumage painted by the sun. Pelicans in groups of ten at a time gently rise and fall on the ground-swell, or lumber through the air with heavy wing, and pouch well filled with fish.

The life of a water-bird seems the most full of enjoyment, for it has three elements to sport in, and on the earth and the wind and the wave it is equally at home. But what is to be said about the fourth element, fire? There is good reason to cut short even so happy an existence if the dead bird is really useful for the mind or the body of man, to be stuffed for a museum, or for a side-dish, or to grace the head of a girl. Still I own to some tender qualms when the pretty gay feathers are fluttering at the other end of my gun-barrel, unconsciously waiting their doom; and it may even be a consolation to the sportsman that a "miss" of his trigger will disappoint only one of the parties concerned, while it sets the other free. 'Tis better to grumble at one's bad luck or bad shooting than to be haunted by the ghosts of orphan ducklings, or the cackling of a web-footed widow.

To the bird-fancier, or the scientific ornithologist, one

---

from the sea, and the river shall be wasted and dried up. And they shall turn the rivers far away; and the brooks of defense shall be emptied and dried up; the reeds and flags shall wither. The paper reeds by the brooks, by the mouth of the brooks, and every thing sown by the brooks, shall wither, be driven away, and be no more. The fishers also shall mourn, and all they that cast angle into the brooks shall lament, and they that spread nets upon the waters shall languish. Moreover they that work in fine flax, and they that weave networks, shall be confounded. And they shall be broken in the purposes thereof, all that make sluices and ponds for fish." How much of this is already fulfilled can only be seen by going to the brooks, and ponds, and fishers for one's self. The word "aroth" is said, in Smith's Dictionary, to be wrongly translated "paper reeds" in this passage.

might well suppose that a month on Lake Menzaleh would be the very least he could give. As for myself, I did not go for the water-fowl, but for the water, and yet every day there was some new feature of winged life to be noticed on the lake.

One of the most amusing sights was the odd clumsy manner in which the flamingoes (*nehaf* in Arabic) rise from the water to the air when they are hard pressed by such an intruder as a canoe.

The bird, with the utmost reluctance, having at last resolved to fly away, up he springs, with his long legs dangling upon the wave-tops, and walking on the water might and main, while his wings are struggling above, and his

FLAMINGOES TAKING WING.

neck is crooked out in front. It is only after a long doubtful scramble between earth, water, and air, that the scrimp little body, with its pretty pink wings, can finally manage to carry off the whole concern, in a hurry packed together, the long snake-like neck and the lower encumbrances called legs. The various phases of this process of locomotion are shown in the sketch above.

It will be seen by Map I., at p. 93, that Lake Menzaleh has a very irregular outline, especially on the southern side. Its length from north-west to south-east is about forty miles, and when the water is full, the breadth from Port Said is fifteen miles. A distinct chain of islands runs along the middle, and many others of various sizes dot the surface, or disappear just beneath the water when that is full.

The depth of the lake is nowhere great, and for many square miles we found it not more than four feet, even in the channels. On first thoughts one is apt to suppose that a shipwreck in water only a yard deep would not be a very serious disaster, even if the solid land were several miles away on every side; but, on reflection, it is soon found that this shallow pond-like area is more dangerous for the lone sailor who may be overturned, or water-logged, or benighted, than a deeper lake would be. For while it would be very difficult or impossible, without complete exhaustion, to reach the shore by wading several miles over such shallows, it would also be a severe tax upon both pluck and patience to find for the first time a channel deep enough for a boat, where so many parts of the lake are mere pools joined by surface-water only a few inches in depth. For when you get into one of these, desiring to cross it in some determinate direction, the channel leading to another of the pools in the chain may be in the most unlikely side of the pool you have entered, and thus for hours the boat would be caught in a *cul-de-sac*.*

The various rigs of vessels on the lake are not numerous, but we may be allowed to spin a little yarn about them. Small boats, especially at Port Said, carry the orthodox lug-sail, some of them also a jib. Fish tank-boats, very low in the water, and (without any conceivable reason I can see) depressed on deck at the bow and stern, have the lateen sail on their masts, but are much propelled by poling. All the larger vessels also have long poles to punt with, and of course they row with "sweeps." The large lateen sail of the Nile is much used on the lake, but without the good reason which justifies its use in the river: that its uplifted peak may catch the breeze over the top of the high

---

* On one occasion, long ago, voyaging alone, my boat found its way into a pool of this kind; but it was more than six hours before she could get out again, and all that time there was nothing to do but to read the only book I happened to have on board, "A Table of Logarithms."

banks. For lake-sailing, and wherever any attempt to beat to windward in regular boards has to be made in rough water, and in narrow bounds, the lateen is used by the Menzaleh boats most absurdly. Often they tack ship without shifting the sail to leeward of the mast, and they are content to lose all weather progress whatever while sailing on the "short leg," besides cutting the sail itself to pieces by grinding it on the shrouds.

The sail is not like a "dipping lug," for the yard is permanently slung at the mast-head, and when the vessel comes about, the sail has to pass above all, so that the after leech goes over the mast and yard and is brought round to the other side. Then the yard itself swings over the mast-head, and finally the sheet can be hauled aft.

This dangerous and lubberly process is so much more easily done by "wearing ship" that in most cases you find the pilot put his helm up. Sometimes, when the loss of weather-way would be too bad to justify this, the vessel is actually stopped, and held by a pole (or even anchored!) while the sail is got over. In such cases, and often when "going large," and wearing, the sail is triced up for a minute or so, while a boy is sent out on the yard to hold it up and to gather it with his arms, in order to prevent the canvas from catching too easily in the upper gear. The braces, too (or vangs, as they would become in an ordinary cutter-sail, with gaff and boom rig), bind the sail in an extremely dangerous manner, and, if taken aback in a squall, the boat is most apt to subside for a ducking, like a man in a straitjacket sent adrift on the waves. The crew, however, care very little indeed about the prospect of a capsize, being fatalists in the most illogical fashion. Once, when my "dahabeeh" was sailing on the Nile in a fresh gale, the hardihood of the men was beyond all bounds, and the boat reeled about several times, within an ace of upsetting. To the sailors personally it was no matter if she did go over; not one of them had any luggage to care for but his pipe; so after they had disobeyed my directions once too often, and the vessel heeled down under a long mountain squall,

I quietly went forward and cut the sheet in two with a knife at the time in my hand, being then at breakfast.

Had this been done with any semblance of anger, it is not easy to say what the consequences might have been, for it was of course the highest possible affront to the seamanship of the crew, but being perpetrated with serene calmness, and even a smile, they only wondered and muttered, and put it down in their memories as another of the extraordinary things that those "Ingleez" will dare to do. But many occasions occurred when the extreme ignorance of sailing on the part of a crew, willing enough, but utterly lubbers, grieved me, in the hopeless knowledge that it was no use to protest, far less to instruct, and the only thing was to sit still with an air resigned, but a deep wounding of one's sense of the "ship-shape," and an excruciating pain concealed.

There was thus always plenty to occupy the mind of any one who cares for boat-sailing, besides many other interesting and ever-varied sights. Camping for the night on a lonely islet in this lake is truly a new lodging. It was quiet enough until the jackal's scream woke up some distant echoes on the main-land, but yet the shrill music near us being a solo made the other silence more impressive. Not far off were the fishers' stations, little bowers of rushes, each at the end of two lines of wattles fixed obliquely zigzag in the shallow lake. The fish swim along these hedge-rows seeking an outlet, and they find themselves at last in the net at the end. This net is held by the strange baboon-like native, whose fire for the evening is now alight, and the smoke feebly curls in the dark glooming of eve. He will stop there for days and nights together, and boats will take away his basketful of fish, which at Mataryeh will be salted and thence sent all over Egypt. The wonder felt by these men may be imagined—sitting in silence in their funny little nests—when I visited them suddenly in the canoe. The moon rose in state to brighten long rows of white sea-birds dotting the dark water, and the horizon was only broken by the distant mast-tops at Mataryeh. Then gliding back in the moonlight, the Rob

Roy brought me to camp again, and her covering was thrown over her now resting in bed and well "tucked in" by Hany. The absence of all sounds but the faint ripples on the shore is intensely refreshing. Our party are all at rest now, but yet we can hear at times the latest flocks of geese speeding homeward to roost in the fens, and the beat of their instant tireless wings sounds sharply musical, but unseen, as if you were to whisper loudly and very fast the words "Tiff—tiff

NIGHT ON LAKE MENZALEH.

—tiff—tiff," lowering the voice as the sound dies away in the night, and the moon shines calmly still.

By sunrise our tent is melting into a bundle, while a lovely morn is welcomed and a friendly breeze. With compass and map I cheerily sail out alone, and after a long cruise with my gun, and a rest on the islands, peeping into the wild ducks' homes, we board the luggage-boat as usual, when sharp hunger, after five hours' work, quickens the nautical sense, for it is wonderful how soon you can

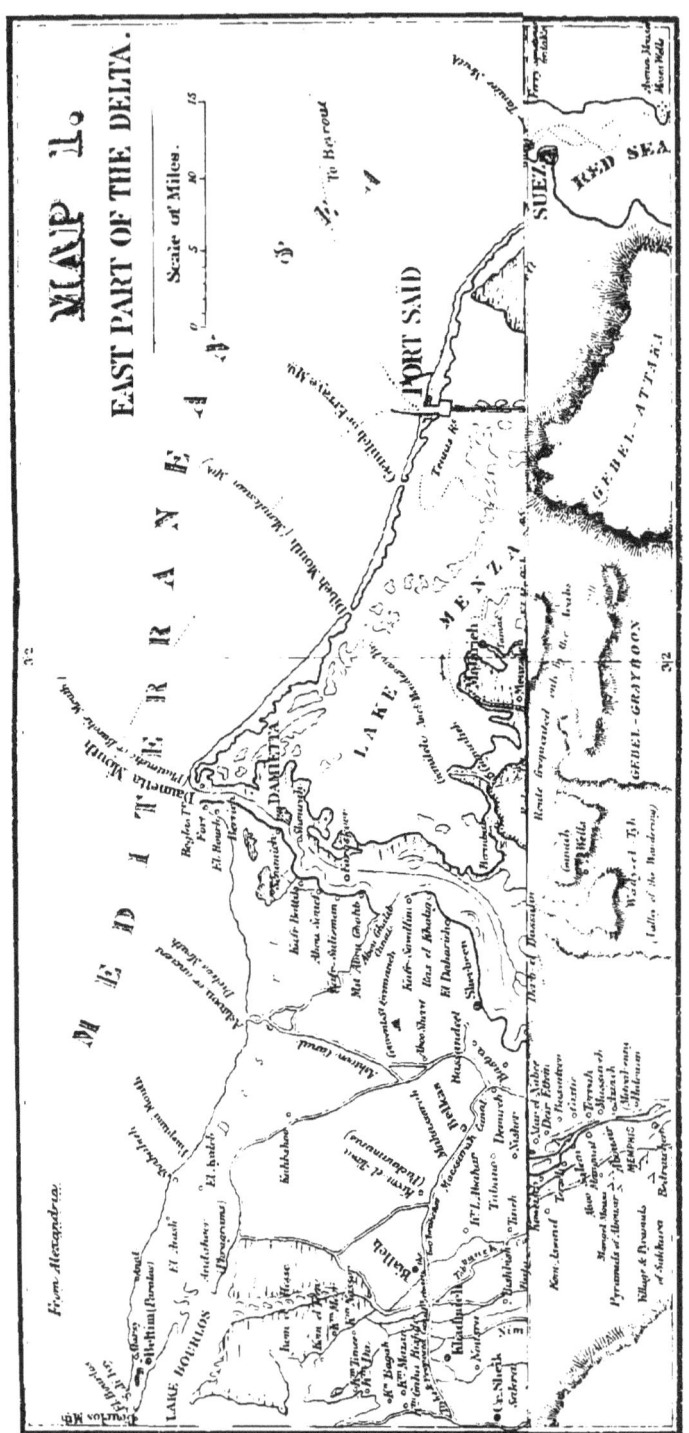

"find the way to food" if you have but a good appetite, and know where it will be appeased. Thus we sailed on till, in the far horizon, blurred and quivering with mirage, the ships at Port Said could be seen. The Arabs called this "Bult," a way of saying "Port" when their language has no *p*. Safely landed at our old quarters there, we looked back on the past six weeks of travel with unmingled pleasure, and forward to the Syrian tour with hope.

Next day I took a long walk by the sea-shore, which here is of unsullied sand. The temperature was perfect— cool enough to walk anywhere, warm enough to sit any time. The tide came quietly in upon the glittering beach, and rushed among the colored shells. Wave after wave gracefully bent its thin crest, and, toppling over, flung athwart the sloping shore a long, wide, tongue-like sheet of glistening water, which lapped around it with a gentle sweep, and then left the cool wet sand to shine in the sun, verged by a rim of pure white foam, melting away. 'Tis in such days one can walk fast and far, singing unheard. It was my last walk in Africa, and a good twelve miles, rather too long for a morning stroll.

The heavy luggage and the second tent which we had not taken through Egypt were all waiting for us at Port Said. The officers of the canal very kindly permitted our party to camp in their well-kempt ground, an excellent place for a Sunday rest. Hany was delighted to be no longer shorn of half his dignity by ruling over only a half-equipment, so he rose to the occasion, and spread abroad our English flag in this French town of wood.

Next day all was bustle in preparation for the farewell dinner in my tents, to which were invited four of the French Company, who had been most kind to the Rob Roy, and while plate and glasses, and viands and decorations, and hangings and flowers, were being prepared, the canoe took a farewell paddle down the canal, for a parting shot at my old friends the pelicans. A fine rolling swell in the bay poured its blue waters tumbling through the long-armed piers projecting seaward.

The pelicans were swimming, and had been daring us to come out for hours, but they could be seen only at rare intervals when the canoe and floating birds happened both to be high on the waves. It seemed as if it would be impossible to use a rifle in such a swell, but it was impossible to resist the desire to try it. No one can tell what excitement will not urge him to dare if once the idea seizes the mind that a shot can be had at a fine large bird like a pelican.

To shoot was not easy, for when I brought the Rob Roy as near as possible to the birds, and then lowered the paddle and drew out the double-barrel, the very next wave was sure to turn round the head of the boat, and the next turned her more; and so while the little canoe was brought "side on" to the long rollers, my body had to be screwed round at a most crooked angle to get the barrel in line with the birds, which now were behind my right shoulder. Nothing but daily use of the boat would enable one to balance himself while aiming thus, and without the paddle, and without regarding in the eye the waves as they came, for the boat must now be poised by only the sense of *feeling*. At length came the supreme moment when the gun and the bird were each on a wave, and I fired, and I missed, and that was an end of it.

On the pier which we approached, so as to reload in more quiet water, there were some pilots waiting for a large vessel seen in the offing. They shouted to me that a big squall was coming, and truly it was looming in the sky, and a rainbow framed the picture. As we got out on the pier, the waves dashed full upon it. Down came a furious gust of wind and drenching rain while we cowered under the huge blocks of the jetty, and the men told me all the secrets of their craft, and entirely confirmed the impression I had received after carefully going round the whole area of water here inclosed, as a place of safety for the future navies of nations that are to hie them in a body to Port Said.

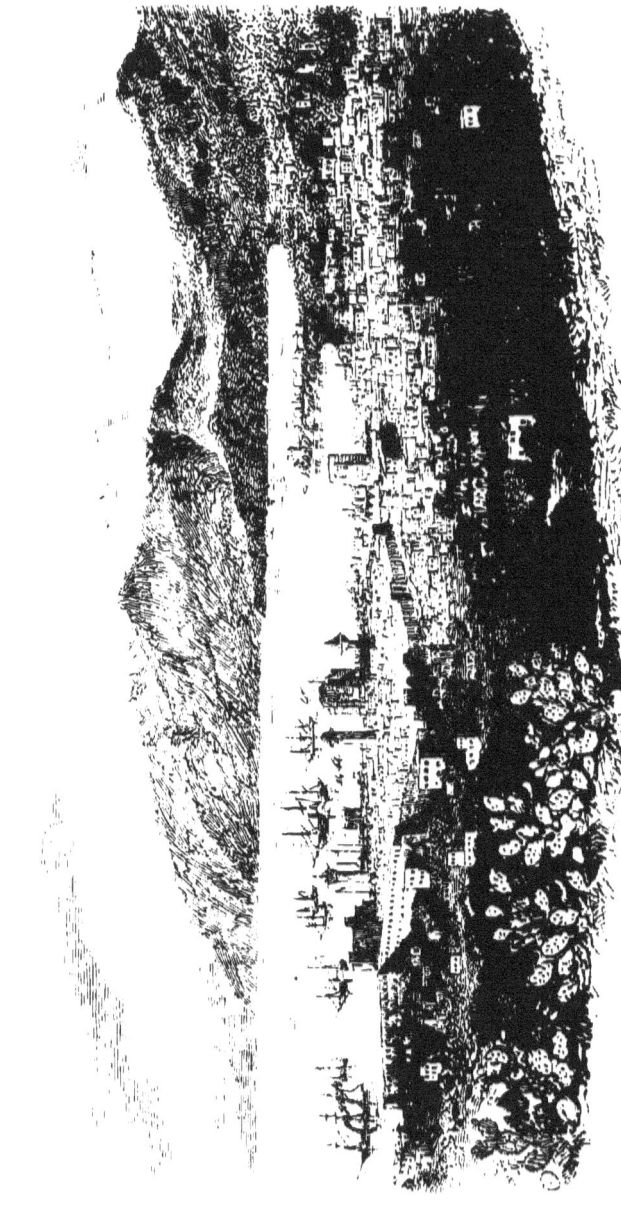

BEYROUT.

CHAPTER VI.

Beyrout.—Massacre.—Good News.—Schools.—Bustle.—Blind.—American Mission.—Moslems.—Prince of Wales.—Agrippa.—Our Flag.—French Lake.—"Gratias."

SPLENDID old Lebanon, snow-capped, young Beyrout smiling in rain-tears, and all the boys running down to the beach to see the canoe—that was our way of landing in Syria. Yet it was only with reluctance that I could bring her to the shore and leave the fresh-flowing waves of that pretty bay. Egypt, indeed, is grand with the sublimity of vast flatness. But now we have the mountains for a happy change, and, after all, the plain can not please like the hills. Quaint oldness is the feature of Egypt, lovely beauty is the charm of Beyrout.

A rapid glance at this thriving town soon shows one that it is now the focus of civilization for Syria, perhaps of the evangelization also of this district of Asia. My faint recollection of it many years ago was still enough to let me judge how wonderful is its recent advance. The town is increased in size. Its roads and streets are far better kept than most of those in Alexandria or Cairo; its houses are altogether superior externally to those of Egypt; its people well clad and wholesome-looking—women comely and tidy, children mirthsome and intelligent, a "school-going" race, whose mothers, too, can look men in the face as equals. Most of these improvements here have been effected during the last eight years, since the terrible massacre of the Christians by—but we shall not name the assassins.

While family ties were cut asunder then with a bloody violence, the bonds of priestcraft were broken by the same rude shock, and people were set free from worn-out crazy systems, to unite again under new associations of religion or nationality. Hence Beyrout has become a camp-ground for both truth and error. Popery is intrenched here. The Greek Church has enormous buildings and collegiate ap-

STREET IN BEYROUT.

paratus (if we extend the title "college lads" to the merest schoolboys). Prussian deaconesses congregate and toil with zeal and success. The American Christians are banded in close array—they who almost first won the ground here for the Bible. The practical action of British Protestants may be seen and closely studied in Mrs. Thompson's schools, and even the dull cry of the Moslem prophet is quickened by these intruders, so as to have, at any rate, a Mohammedan college too.

It is scarcely fair to any of these institutions to visit one or two of them and to describe only these, when so many are clustered in the beautiful slope of the town, looking out upon "that goodly Lebanon," now decked to its waist in purest snow, and skirted below by the azure sea. But my time here was limited to the few days required for preparing men, horses, mules, tents, luggage, supplies, and porters for my own journey, and, this being unique in its kind here or anywhere else with a canoe as the centre of the cavalcade, I felt it would be out of place to inspect Beyrout, however interesting, if the time thus consumed would be taken from that absolutely needful for success in the main purpose of my voyage on the "waters of Israel."

Let us, however, go into that airy, cheerful, and substantial building, where the chief schools are carried on by Mrs. Thompson. Her husband, well known years ago to travellers who went to Damascus, bravely did his duty in the Crimea, and fell a victim to disease. As a widow, she felt sympathy for the widowed wives and bereaved mothers and sisters in these mountains, when "all their men" had been butchered for their Christian name. She assembled these poor hapless ones, and told them of the aid sent out by England. Lord Dufferin had come to dispense this British present, and he did it well. The widows were grateful for the help, but far more than gratitude moved them when they were told of the *sympathy* of our queen, and of English ladies, and that these had even wept for the poor Syrian mourners. Sympathy is more, or seems more, than money-gifts when the heart is sore. She spoke to them of Christ, and the story of his love was news to many. They would not leave the room where such good news had been heard. Their new friend was forced thus by heart-pressure to begin a noble work.

Her schools are chiefly for girls, as most needed for the country and most fitting for a woman to manage. What a pleasant school-room this! Nothing can be more cheerful or inviting. Children of all ages, nations, and ranks are here, busy and happy together. Those of them who are the best learners now will be teachers soon under this excellent training. See that first class of girls, with their bright-hued dresses, the natural and therefore graceful colors of their land, toned down a little by the neat, plain pinafores, sent as presents from England. How many lovely faces there are among those maids from the mountain! Druse girls, with gay kerchiefs and black hair; Arabs and Mohammedans, some who will not show their faces, and others who smile at every look from a visitor. One coming in state with nine servants; another sent to school in a carriage; the next one a mere pauper from the street; and beside them both an Abyssinian with her frizzled locks. Two or three English are here, too, but all seem equally happy and equally loved.

No wonder this little family should gladly meet in such a place, and with such kind ladies to direct them, and such excellent, active, and intelligent teachers to instruct them. They read in Arabic, French, and English; they trace the maps or sew embroidery; they write and cipher. A few recite some simple drama, wherein one is the "spider," one the "fly," and one the wise fairy who tells the moral to us all at the end. Then how well they sing! and what sermons their very manners *must* preach at their several homes, even if they never speak a word of what they have learned! But there are several branch-schools besides at mountain outposts in connection with the head-quarters of Mrs. Thompson's work in Beyrout, and we shall visit some of these as we go farther on.

Coming so recently from Egypt, with its vast plains, to Syria, with its lofty mountains, it was natural to compare the countries and the people of the two; also to regard together the ragged school at Cairo with this training-school at Beyrout, and to consider the separate fields occupied by Miss Whately and Mrs. Thompson, working in the same vineyard. Both are, of their kinds, most interesting, useful, and worthy of all support. In Cairo the degradation of the ignorant is deeper, the bonds of women are more cruelly slavish, the position of the Christian teacher is more isolated, the lack of sympathy and companionship is more depressing. Nothing, in fact, but positive heroism could attack such a difficult post as that, or win it, or hold it when a footing was secured. In Beyrout there is an atmosphere more free, and the brighter faces of the pupils are more gladdening to the teacher's eye; but yet in each place,

FOUNTAIN AT BEYROUT.

Cairo and Syria, there is a most signal evidence of the constraining power of Christian love for souls; one more proof of the influence of woman in the world when patient, persevering work is to be done, and one more sign that, of all women, British ladies are the best for noble deeds.* Every moment of my time here was soon engaged by kind friends on one side or another. An address to this school, an examination at that, a peep into a third, a lecture on canoes to the English residents, and a service on Sunday for the

* Information may be obtained by those who would help those Beyrout schools from Mrs. Smith, Morden College, Blackheath, Kent.

school children, etc., these filled up pretty well the time between packing and buying, walking and visiting, settling those nameless nothings without which, well arranged, a special journey of this kind is certain to break down.

Besides these efforts on behalf of the ignorant, and the orphans, and the sick, a very interesting but very difficult work has also been commenced for the blind, and one for the maimed. Mr. Mott's little class of blind men reading is a sight, indeed, for us who have eyes. Only in February last that poor sightless native who sits on the form there was also in the mental and moral darkness of ignorance. How glorious now the change, as his delicate fingers run over the raised types of his Bible! and he reads aloud and blesses God in his heart for the precious news, and for those who gave him the new avenue for truth to his soul. "Jesus Christ will be the first person I shall ever see," he says, "for my eyes will be opened in heaven." Then even this man becomes a missionary. Down in that room below the printing-press of the American Mission, and in the dark, for *he* needs no sunlight in his work, you find him actually printing the Bible himself in raised type, letter by letter, for his sightless brethren. This is one of the most impressive wonders I ever looked upon. As we leave the place, some of the maimed, and lame, and halt, scramble along the road to their special class for a lesson, so that all kinds of suffering are here provided for; and this mission of Christians is following closely in the actual personal work which He, the great missioner himself, described as His mission to mankind. The woodcut on the opposite page is from a photograph of this blind man reading God's Word to the maimed.

The American mission and schools and college in Beyrout are in amicable Christian fellowship with their British brethren; and this is most happy, for their premises are near one another, and their work is to the same end, though by different means and in distinct departments. While the "British Syrian Schools" are educating children and training teachers, the American College is intended to instruct

BLIND READING TO THE LAME.

youths willing and able to give some years to deeper study, and to aim high at learning, so as to enter important professions, and to become ordained ministers or doctors of medicine.

The college* is a large, plain, and practical-looking edi-

* The following information is derived from Dr. Post, of the medical department in the Beyrout College:—"The College (in January, 1869) numbers sixty-seven students, of whom forty-six are in the literary and twenty-one in the medical department. The latter all pay their fees in full; and as these, for the new class, are quite heavy for this country (10 gold medjidies =about £9), we consider this a great success in the direction of self-support. The students in the literary department are in part supported by scholarships; but a considerable number defray all their expenses. They are from six different religious sects, including Druses. The students of the literary department study the Arabic language and literature, English, French, the natural and physical sciences, and will ultimately advance to the higher departments of intellectual and moral philosophy, and the analogy of natural and revealed religion. The mathematics are also thoroughly taught. An air of studiousness and decorum, unusual in Arabic schools, pervades the building. The religious influences brought to bear on the students are of the strongest kind. The medical students for the most part room out (i. e., in English, 'lodge out') of the college building, and can not, therefore, be brought so much under college discipline. The students have gone through a thorough course of anatomy, chemistry, and physiology, and are now receiving instruction in materia medica and practical clinical medicine and surgery. Not a few of them attend the services of the college and mission chapels."

fice, with halls and dormitories, and a medical school and dissecting-room, and with a pretty new chapel, nearly finished then, but doubtless now all ready. This is a prominent addition to the beautiful buildings of other kinds ranged all around upon the same hill. When I walked into this church alone, an old gentleman addressed me. He is the architect of the building, a native Syrian, the brother of one well known in England. He was the first Protestant convert in Syria, but soon after the change he had a difference with the missionaries, which resulted in a separation. Then his former friends came round him again, insisting that he should return once more to his old discarded creed; but he answered, "No; I have a quarrel now with some other Christians, but not with Christ. I love Him more than ever, and I will never separate from Him." Restored friendship enabled this steadfast man again to work in harmony with his foreign brethren, and now he is building their church; and when its marble floor has been laid, and its clock has been set a-going, and its bell a-ringing, he will have just reason to be proud of the part he has been privileged to take in the American Mission.

Dr. Bliss is at the head of it, and Dr. Van Dyck, eminent as an Arabic scholar, and another able professor of medicine, and all the appliances for education—broad, sound, if not refined—which our Western cousins know so well how to keep in action on strictly economical terms. The Bible is, of course, their solid foundation. Their curriculum requires four years' study before any youth is deflected into one or other particular line by choice and fitness, and at his entrance he must be sixteen years of age, and pass a creditable examination. I could not judge of the aptness of the scholars, because, very properly, their studies are not allowed to be interrupted by the examination often given in other places when visitors call to see a school.

In one of Mrs. Thompson's schools I found the man who calls the Moslems to prayers from the top of their mosque

—one of the Muezzim whose faint shrill voices sound in the hot sun of noon; but now he is reading and praying over the Bible. In another school, that at Zahleh, one of the pupils is the best painter of church interiors in Syria. Many a "Virgin" and "Saint" has he limned upon their idolatrous walls; but now he knows the pure faith, and at a great sacrifice he has given up his former profitable business, because it was inconsistent with his obedience to God's word.

After a service at one of these schools, all the girls pressed forward to shake hands with the "Howaja Ingleez," and one of the little creatures confided to me a very loving message I was to carry to her former teacher, now in Damascus. They were, indeed, a happy and affectionate party, more like a family than a school, and amongst them were the little Druse girl, and the Abyssinian child, the intended bride of Theodore's son, who found so far away from home a nestling place upon Mrs. Thompson's knee. One of the pupils then recited, with a clear and distinct voice, in English, that striking piece of poetry, "The Starless Crown," which she afterwards wrote out for me as a *souvenir* of this visit.

It was truly kind of the Prince of Wales, who had visited these schools himself, that he did not forget to commend them to the Sultan when that phlegmatic monarch came to England. Let all nations see for themselves, and let them hear besides from the mouths of our princes, that education without religion is like an atmosphere without its oxygen. We can breathe it so, but it is not the "breath of life." The prosperity and progress of Beyrout, and the remarkable stir to be seen there in the matter of education, and the great quickness and aptitude of the Syrians to learn, are all exceptional features in the East, and are the more striking because of so much sluggish dullness at this end of the Mediterranean Sea. It is well to remark that Beyrout is beyond the strict limit of the Holy Land, and it seems also to be outside the borders of the curse which rests upon the land of Israel—only for a time, we know, but still heavily now, and for good cause too. But fast comes the day when the blessing will embrace them again, and "all Israel shall be saved."

Not many notices of this town of Beyrout can be found in ancient authors, but Josephus tells us something of what Agrippa did for the place.*

While the English, after the massacre in 1860, did the real work of helping the poor, and the widow, and the fatherless, the French blew their bugles and marched their Zouaves throughout the land. A splendid road was made by the French from Beyrout to Damascus. This is a hundred miles long, and the Suez canal is just the same length over Egypt. Thus Paris has two arms stretched over the East: one on the land, the other on the water; and both seem to clutch, if they do not embrace, the country of Osmanli.

The road is more French than any thing in France—a strict monopoly to begin with, and it does not by any means "pay," except in political influence.

The very same carts, with big wheels, gawky shafts, thin bodies, canvas tops, and cerulean-bloused Frenchmen inside and out, are rumbling along here, precisely as they rumble in Algeria to the Atlas, or, in France, to the mountains of Grenoble.

The sea, too, is scored deep with French ruling. Splen-

* "Now, as Agrippa was a great builder in many places, he paid a peculiar regard to the people of Berytus, for he erected a theatre for them, superior to many other of that sort, both in sumptuousness and elegance, as also an amphitheatre, built at vast expenses; and besides these, he built them baths and porticoes, and spared for no costs in any of his edifices, to render them both handsome and large; he also spent a great deal upon their dedication, and exhibited shows upon them, and brought there musicians of all sorts, and such as made the most delightful music of the greatest variety. He also showed his magnificence upon the theatre, in his great number of gladiators; and there it was that he exhibited the several antagonists, in order to please the spectators: no fewer indeed than seven hundred men to fight with seven hundred other men; and allotted all the malefactors he had for this exercise; that both the malefactors might receive their punishment, and that this operation of war might be a recreation in peace. And thus were these criminals all destroyed at once."—"Antiq. of the Jews," book xix. ch. vii. sec. v.

did steamers run up and down the coast incessantly, and so long as the enormous subsidy is paid them by Government, they will never cease to run.

Russia, jealous, sends her steamers too along the same route, which brings pilgrims to Jerusalem by thousands from Odessa, and garrison the holy places by battalions of stout women, who start from the steppes of Moscow, where I have seen them on their way, each in a universal garment, with its hood about her sturdy cheeks, and a staff in her hand. Half a year is their holiday for the crusade, and they fight their way to Rachel's tomb, and then, satisfied, stump back again.

Austria buys steamers too in Scotland, and sends them along this coast. England, alone, is entirely absent on this line of travellers, for she will not pay for an "idea," nor for that will her merchants equip a passenger-line of Syrian steamboats.

But a good quiet trade in merchandise is done by Britain here, and if you go farther round the African headlands, and look at the flags in Lagos, and along the bights, on to the Cape of Good Hope, it is the brave old ensign of our island that is waving there, as it always will do when freights are found, and dividends are to be earned by sheer work. Still this absence of England from the Palestine coast is not pleasant to notice for an English traveller. 'Tis true the mercantile attractions for shipping are but meagre now, at any rate for passenger-boats. From Alexandria right up to Skanderoon there is really not one good port all along this iron-bound shore.

Port Said is of the future. Joppa is utterly bad. Acre has skeleton hulls bleaching on the shore to warn you off. Haifa is a mere tossing roadstead. Beyrout has no dock, but squalls and swell in plenty, and if the Turk would invite good commerce to his country, he really must provide or *allow* that a port should be made to receive it.

Besides this want of harbors in Syria, the distance between the present ports is wasteful of steam and of seamen's wages. Joppa must be entered by daylight, so the steamer runs six hours in the dark to Port Said, and then waits a long time there, so as to arrive next morning at Joppa. Again she leaves Joppa so as to enter Beyrout in the morning. In fact, the whole eastern side of the Mediterranean is inconvenient as yet for legitimate commercial venture, and it is precisely in the condition when France finds scope for Imperial advancement at any cost, however great, to her tax-payers.

All this clever policy has one purpose; Algeria, Egypt, Syria, and so on round the coast, are to be attached to Paris, until the Mediterranean becomes a "French lake." France is *the* nation here in Syria, and napoleons are the common coin. French is the best-known foreign tongue here, and the very shops in the streets have French signboards besides their own. England, which is, after all, dearer to the hearts of these people than any other "Feringhee," appears to be, it must be confessed, most lamentably absent from the sight and the hearing of the common people, except by these schools we have mentioned, by the large number of English travellers in Palestine (about fifty times the number of the French), and by the impression, still very vigorous and fresh, of what Albion achieved in her Abyssinian raid.*

* In one good policy, however, all the steamers I used in the East did well—they carried the Rob Roy *gratis*. England had set them the example when the "Peninsular and Oriental Company" kindly took her from Southampton to Alexandria, and brought her back again, quite free. The French steamers did the same, the Austrian too, and the Russian likewise. For this I thank them all, not as for a money boon (a few pounds is little in a six months' journey here), but because it showed kind feeling to the voyager, and an approval of his purpose.

CHAPTER VII.

Over Lebanon.—Canoe on Wheels.—The Rob Roy in Snow.—Odd Quarters.—"The Young Lady."—Generous.—Zahleh School.—River Litany.—Hanged.—An Eagle.—The Fiji.—Source of Abana.—In-doors.—Cats.

Our ride over Mount Lebanon need not be described, but it is impossible not to mark the rapid change in a few days from Egypt and the yellow Nile to the rugged cliffs of the mountain, the whirling mist, the dashing torrents, and, at last, the snow. It was unusually early for the winter garb to clothe even this the "White Mountain," as its name signifies. Yet for miles we plunged on in snow a foot deep, driven about by a keen, cutting wind, and hundreds of men were required to clear this away that the French diligence might ply its daily course in time. On arrival in a dark night at a little village, I found my saddle-bags had dropped off on the road. At once two hardy mountaineers volunteered to go back and seek for the valuable lost property, and off they trudged with lanterns, and splashed through the mud and slush and sleet, and they happily found the bags a long way off where I had suspected they must have come loose.

The road is excellent; it is all marked in kilometres (French again), very well kept, and rolled down and fenced and drained. But the toll of three francs for each mule is enough to deter hundreds of these from using the road; so they plod on their way along the old worn-out, steep, muddy, slippery, winding bridle-path, which runs often for miles alongside the carriage-way, and thus you see strings of heavy-laden asses, camels, and mules, toiling among boulders and sharp rocks, with their drivers ankle-deep in mud, while the even flat surface of the new road is used by a scant few; and no cart or carriage goes upon it except as part of the "Company's" monopoly. It is a miserable sight, and this gift of France to Syria is like a crust to a toothless beggar.

Our first intention as to the mode of transporting the canoe through Syria was to have her carried by two men, with two others in reserve at intervals, for the weight of the Rob Roy, when lightened as much as possible, could be reduced to about sixty pounds, which would not be an oppressive burden for a couple of stout Syrians.

But after careful consideration of this plan, I came to the conclusion that something better must be devised, and the events of the very first day on Mount Lebanon clearly showed us how difficult it would be to carry a boat by hand, especially on slippery ground, and that it would have been more than could fairly be expected from mortal men to plash through the half-thawed snow, while a canoe was upon their shoulders or in their arms, constraining their motions, and making the troubles of their way ten times more irksome. Therefore, for this part of the journey, at any rate, we were glad to be able to hoist the Rob Roy into its covered cart again, and happily she got over the high pass just in time to avoid the worst part of the second storm, which came in sudden fury soon when the road had been opened for us after the first fall of snow for the year. The diligence had been stopped here for many hours, buried in a drift up to its axles, but the French showed great energy in clearing the road again, and our cart went over easily, bearing its precious cargo.*

Is it maudlin that one can not help personifying a boat like this, the companion of so many happy hours, the sole sharer of great joys and anxious times? When we see even

---

* Some thousands of persons have seen the Rob Roy since she returned to England, and was shown for three months at the Palestine Exhibition in the Dudley Gallery. Many of these visitors, well aware of the numerous scars and scratches which a six months' journey would inflict upon so light a craft, are astonished to observe that the canoe has weathered it all, and is almost unscathed, for she is far less knocked about than the former Rob Roy was in her trip to the Baltic. There is not one crack in her planks or her thin cedar deck, after all sorts of hardships from weather, and carriage, and hauling on land, and never spared for a moment in waves, or rapids, or morass.

deal tables merrily turning round, and can fancy a smile on the face of a clock, are we quite sure that there is no feeling in the "heart of oak," no sentiment under bent birch ribs; that a canoe, in fact, has no character? Let the landsman say so, yet will not I. Like others of her sex, she has her fickle tempers. One day pleasant, and the next out of humor; led like a lamb through this rapid, but cross and pouting under sail on that rough lake. And, like her sex,

CROSSING MOUNT LEBANON.

she may be resisted, coerced, nay, convinced, but, in the end, she will always somehow have her own way. Yet however faintly other people may feel with me in this matter, it will be allowed that any one who keeps a boat for a journey, and expects her to go long and far, and to be always stanch and trim, must at least be careful of her safety in dark nights, in doubtful places, or when left alone. Few boats can have had greater variety in their night quarters than this canoe. In hotels she was often locked up in a bedroom, and once she floated on a marble basin under the moon. In private houses a place was kept for her near the fire, and away from the children. By lakes, canals, and rivers, the Rob Roy was sometimes my house, and so it covered me; or, when the tent was used, she was covered up herself from the dew by a carpet, and snugly placed under the tent-lines safe from the mules. The straw hut of the Arab gave her shelter once, and, at another time, a buffalo's byre. Her polished deck was shielded from sun by hiding her below the long grass of Gennesareth, and for two nights she rested on the shelly beach of the Red Sea. She was lodged in a custom-house, or on a steamer's deck, or down in the hold, or she floated on the Nile under the protection of her rough sister of the sail, whose sides were of Delta clay, or at times she was taken on board, so as to be quite out of danger. Great deference was paid to the canoe by all the men of our retinue. She had not one tumble or accident, and no wonder that Hany always called her "the young lady." Perhaps through this pleasant fiction the voyage was safer, certainly it was more fortunate, and it was impossible for a cruise to be more successful in all the course prescribed. At present, however, the Rob Roy was safe on the rice-bags in a Frenchman's wagon, while we rode on to meet her at the Abana River.

Our traveller's morning lesson was now on horseback, as it had been on the Nile in a boat, and it was soon found to be quite easy to read aloud while riding over the grassy plain. From this we hurried off to Zahleh (pronounced with a strong aspirate on the letter *h*, almost as if it were the Scotch *ch*). This is the largest village in Mount Lebanon. It was all burned down in the "massacre time," an epoch of suffering which seems to date so many changes here.

Frenchmen soon rebuilt the houses, all with flat roofs, while at Beyrout the sloping tile is beginning gradually to appear in large new buildings, where they wish the house to be dry, and to last a long time.

A gush of waters sounds loud at the bottom of a deep

and winding valley, with poplars at the bottom, and vine-terraces to the top. The houses are all neat-looking, and most of them white in color; and, as there are no chimneys and no streets, the appearance of the whole is very peculiar, even to the eye well used to Eastern buildings. What strikes one about it is that the irregularity is so very regular. The houses nearly all face to the same point, but they are not in rows. We stumbled up one side and down the other until our horses reached the new school-house of one of Mrs. Thompson's branches, chiefly aided by kind friends in Glasgow. The old school-house being too small and too far off, a new one, in every way suitable, was most generously offered free during the remainder of the lease, if taken after that for five years. This munificent aid from a native is of itself a real proof of the value set by them on the operations of a school.

The new building is wide in its front, and stands high in the town. The excellent Scotch lady in charge was delighted to receive her visitor, and soon men and women came in from other houses, all evincing by look and manner, and earnest salute, how glad they were to see an Englishman; for the place is not often thus visited, being a few miles out of travellers' paths, and only otherwise interesting because of its picturesque situation. Nearly all the inhabitants of this village are Christians in name, most of them bigoted Papists, with lazy priests for guides, and the church and the convent bells ring on the hill; but no mosque is there that I could see. A deeper Christianity seems lately to have spread in Zahleh, and many are eager to read the Word of Life. Perhaps it was by some of these that, within the last two months, more than three hundred Arabic Testaments had been *purchased* at one shop alone in Beyrout, as I heard from the person who sold them. Surely this one fact gives hopes that the people are seeking the Bible, while from other evidence we know that the missionaries are seeking the people.

Comfortable airy rooms, and a cheerful court-yard, open to the fresh-blowing mountain air; these are the features of Zahleh school. All the children are away. The house just occupied is to be whitewashed to-day, so the scholars have a holiday, though the *women* who are to whiten the walls have not arrived, and it is noon.

But a pith helmet, with the Canoe Club cipher upon its black ribbon, and a water-proof coat, and a dragoman with a double-barrelled gun, these are novelties that do not scramble through the lanes of Zahleh unnoticed by the

ZAHLEH SCHOOL—OPENING DAY.

boys of the town. They followed us, so that when called to come in, there was soon a large and motley array, first of little girls (for whom the school is meant), who sat quiet and well behaved in a room open to the air, and then of boys from the American school, just opened, under the Sultan's sanction, given to the English female department (by a clever extension of the boon, whether legal or not); and then of men of various ages, fringing the background with their graceful head-gear and their many-colored robes. An address to the children was very well interpreted, each sentence at a time, by a girl, and another interpreted a prayer, to which all listened.

It was a pleasing, strange, and solemn sight. The congregation half in-doors and half in the open air; half children, half old men: the words half spoken in English, half in Arabic; and to think (and to say) that never again in this world, but surely again in the next, we should all meet each other once more. The men were anxious for a longer interview, and some of them sat down on chairs (a very unusual thing here), while they were spoken to apart. Then being invited to ask any questions, one of them wished to have our "jury system" explained, which was, of course, soon done, and my dragoman gave, in round guttural Arabic, *his* version of the Templar's picture of our English law. All kissed my hand, and we were soon in our saddles again. As a memento of Zahleh, I made the opposite sketch of the new school on its opening day, from the roof of another house, though there is little chance of forgetting a visit like this that we had enjoyed.

Soon we cross the Litany, the largest river flowing

BRIDGE OVER THE LITANY.

through Palestine into the Mediterranean. It was not easy to resist the desire to paddle at once upon this fine strong stream, but strangely enough, there are scarcely any historical associations, and no sacred ones, about this river at all. We shall see some of its grandest beauties farther on; meanwhile it flows steadily here, yet enlivening the landscape at once. Land without water never can be perfect in scenery. The veriest pond on a plain is like a dimple on a smooth cheek. The lightsome glitter of a lake or a river bend is like a sweet smile on the face of a beauty.*

With the first glimmer of day, it was most pleasant to walk over the rich plain of Cœle-Syria breathing the fresh air of the morning. My horse's bridle was slack upon my arm, and our tread was light on the footpath winding through the loam made fat by many battles.

The pretty crested larks,

"That *tira lira* chant,"

rose into the merry blue sky twittering their song to the sunrise.

Thus in advance and alone until Hany overtook me, I gradually ascended the pass through Antilebanon, and in charming enjoyment of unfettered thought, and lovely scene, and healthy exercise.

* "Ain," the Arabic word for "eye," and also for a fountain bursting out from the earth, is very expressive, as representing a glittering "eye" on the face of nature. The word has the same meaning in "Hebrew and Syriac, and is in that form in Amharic, Arkiko, Hurar, Gindzhar, and Gafat" (Paper by H. Clarke, "Athenæum," No. 2178, 1869, p. 116).

If the "face of nature," is to have fountains for eyes, and hills for cheeks, and forests for hair, our fancy may as well make it sentient at once, by putting telegraph wires for the nerves, by which quick pleasure or neuralgic pain thrills through the great dull body.

The electric wire is spread over Egypt. There are two lines of telegraph from the south to Damascus. The posts cresting the rocky mountains, over some desolate pass, remind one of those in Switzerland. Turkish reforms are by jerks and starts, but it is a steady maxim never to repair. More than once we came upon broken wires in coils on the plains. Nothing is more dangerous to ride over than an iron trap like this, for an Arab horse becomes furious if his legs get entangled. The Arabs themselves are compelled to respect the telegraph. One of them who defiantly struck the wire with his spear was ferreted out, and hanged upon the very post he injured.

In a former travel of this road some twenty years before, I was so weak from severe illness, that I had to fasten a chair on the saddle-bow, and to lean forward upon it for support. Getting worse, and yet determined not to delay, I had a long pole lashed on the back of a mule, and sprawled upon that, face downward, and forced to dismount each half-hour to get a short rest on the ground. But all was different now, and the intense enjoyment of the present journey was quite in keeping with the vigorous health vouchsafed.

Not far from the ruins of old Chalcis is the beautiful temple at Mejdel, from which our view is magnificent over the wide-spread plain of Bukaa. For many centuries this had sounded with the shouts of warriors battling for the mastery of Palestine, in the struggles related by Josephus. But now it is all sad and silent here, and the only noise at Chalcis was the chirping of a little bird under a thistle in the sun. From these graceful ruins a large grisly beast came out to stare, but I could not get near enough to see whether he was a hyena or only a jackal, and at five hundred yards a shot from my gun merely splintered the rock. Unfortunately the rifle itself had no claim to my confidence, for it shot always to the right, as is often the case when a gun-barrel for shot and another for ball are welded together as a double-barrel.*

A cold biting breeze from the snows of great Hermon gave zest to the ride, and brought us to Dimes, where I went off for game with the rifle, but marched in vain over the mountains, until, after two hours, I met on the highest peak a splendid eagle, feasting on some quarry, with his broad wings outstretched, as he stamped with his talons and chuckled, tearing with ravenous beak the bloody living flesh.

Our meeting was so sudden, and after so long with nothing to do, that I lost my presence of mind, and, instead of stalking up to easy distance, which my gray coat and gray

---

* The bores are seldom parallel, and the thickness of metal being unequal for the two, there is a deflection caused by their expansion when heated.

helmet would have facilitated, especially when the hungry bird was carving his dinner, I at once unslung my rifle, dropped on one knee in "Hythe position," and aiming at three hundred yards, flashed quick the sudden trigger, but only hit the hare, which was being devoured piecemeal, and was yet quite warm, nor had its glazing eye yet ceased to quiver, while the eagle mounted in reluctant circles only half fed.

EAGLE'S NEST.

It may well be evident from these records of failure with the gun that, if my paddle had not been better than my powder, the Rob Roy's cruise would have been rather a bore; but it is one thing to hit a target on a rifle-range, with the distance known and the shooter cool, and a very different thing to fire at rough game on the open. Next day at El Hameh, the Arab host of the house we put up at received very gladly a little paper which I was very sorry to find was not in Arabic, but in Turkish—the same in letters, but not in words. However, this man could also read a printed sheet in French, and he went on translating it to a congregation in the next room, while at every sentence every body said " Um !" as a token of assent.

A stormy sky and cold rain next morning were all in keeping with a wild ride over the bleakest of hills, and through deep dales gushing with waterfalls to Ain Fiji,* a source of the Abana, not the highest, but far the largest of its springs. In a dark dell here, all shadowed by rugged cliffs,† is a sudden change of scene, where water perennial quickens life in the soil, and while the snow is thick above, and reaches down in long streamers as far as it dares to enter the warm vale, the blooming little garden by the fountain below is redolent with walnut-trees, apricots, olives, and long trailing vine branches, tangling the tall poplars. Here stand the ruins of two bluff old temples, and the massive stones of an arch, from out of which bursts a pure and copious river, rushing at once into light with a roar as if free, and staggering over rocks and boulders for about seventy yards, till it tumbles into the ravine and meets the other branch, and so forms the Barada, the ancient Abana, the river by which the Rob Roy will enter

---

* My dragoman, who seemed to have a minute and delicate apprehension of Arabic, his native tongue, said that this word Fiji means, "premature, unripe, or sudden." Mr. Palmer, the traveller in Sinai, whose acquaintance with the language may be acknowledged as almost unrivalled, appeared to think that "Fiji," if it be the word with a short first syllable, "Fidji," denotes a source from which the water ascends and then spreads, and that in an Arabic poem it is contrasted with another word, indicating a source where the water descends or trickles down. This meaning of the term Fiji compounds with the actual character of the source so named. Can the word "Feejee," as a name of islands in the Pacific, be related to this Arabic term? Reland makes the " Figa " the Belus.

† The dip of the strata here is 49°, according to the observation of Captain Wilson, R. E., who, with Lieutenant Anderson, R. E., on behalf of the Palestine Exploration Fund, surveyed part of Syria and Palestine in 1865-'6. The unpublished MS. notes of their journey have been kindly lent to me for perusal, and when the information obtained from this valuable and accurate source is embodied in these pages, the reference to it is made simply under the name " Wilson."

FIJI SOURCE OF THE ABANA.

Damascus. We took shelter from rain in a Moslem house, and the inmates were amazed to see my "canoe cuisine," by which in ten minutes I prepared four cups of good English tea. They had, never heard of "tchai" (tea) before, and a wax-match to each of the pretty daughters pleased also their grave papa, who said it was the third day of the Ramadan, when none of them eat, drink, or smoke, from 4 A.M. to 5 P.M., but then the whole night is passed in these three engagements. Such is Mohammedan fasting.* He and his family and visitors were respectfully quiet while the Bible was read at our morning prayers.

While the rain patters at Dimes, we can glance round our lodgings and take notes. My room, then—vacated of course by the family—is about twenty feet by fourteen

* Abd-el-Kader, the brave veteran Arab of Algeria, resides near Damascus, but his observance of the fast is so strict a seclusion that I found it impossible to get an interview with him.

wide. I know the breadth exactly, for the Rob Roy reclines by my side, and just fits into the apartment. The walls are mud, but well plastered, and neatly whitewashed. Hollow arched spaces are left in them here and there as cupboards and shelves, just as one sees in the stone dwellings of old Bashan. There is a window, with shutters, but no glass. The floor is raised eighteen inches above the doorway entrance, and is spread with mats, but there are no tables or chairs. Our table and camp-stools from the tent supply the want. The ceiling is of two logs unhewn; across them are barked trees, about two feet apart, and again across these are bundles of sticks, over which is a flat mud roof. After rain you will see a little boy with a stone roller smoothing the roof to fill up the sun-cracks. In one corner of the room is a great copper salver, three feet wide, and a candlestick three feet high. A mirror is near; it is evidently made in Damascus, with the golden crescent on its frame. This is the first mirror I have looked into for many a day, and surely the glass must be of a rich brown tint—or is it my countenance that colors the portrait? The door is closed by a wooden bolt, with a key such as I have described before, and the lock can only be opened from the *inside;* but near it there is a hole in the door through which the hand can be put from the outside, for a friend to open with the key and so let himself in. Does not this remind one of the beautiful expression in Canticles, which seems to tell that Christ is an intimate of the believer, and can admit Himself into the heart-home of his friend. Outside the room are my little band of followers; we are in all, as yet, only seven men, six mules, and two horses. A dog with me as a pet would have been great fun, and good to keep off the cats of the house, which pester me sadly. I don't like them, but I don't like to hurt them, though they spring on the table and nibble my bread. Throwing nutshells at them answered at first, but then boots had to be thrown, and at last I found that cold water was what they most fear, so they all scamper off when I take up a tumbler, and they escape in a bound through the hole in the door. At night I stuffed my large sponge into this hole, and that puzzled the cats, but at 2 A.M. they had pulled this out, so I had to rise in the cold and fasten the entrance by a riding-boot, which they tugged at for an hour in vain. .

CHAPTER VIII.

The Abana.—Sources.—Abana and Pharpar.—Their Names.—Canalettes.—Start on Abana.—Change to the Taura.—How to do it.—Pleasant Toil.—Procession.

WE are now about to descend the first of five or six rivers explored in this journey, and which run through channels where important parts are entirely inaccessible except in a boat, and as no voyager has been mentioned in history to have floated on them thus, it may well be supposed that their full beauties and all their dangers have never been seen before. The Abana passes straight through Damascus, the oldest inhabited city in the world,[*] and so we may linger on its wavelets with the deep interest aroused by the far-gone past, while telling how the stream flows as newly seen.

When we are asked where is the source of a river, it is necessary to agree about the meaning of the term "source."

"The "historic source" of a river, or that which is written about soonest, is by no means sure to have been the most distant or the most copious one, or the most constant origin of its waters, though it may be the most accessible, or the most striking in appearance and interesting from local associations. Thus it will be seen hereafter that the "historic source" of the Jordan at Laish is not that which we should now style "the source of Jordan," if describing or exploring the river for the first time thoroughly.

Then there is the "geographical source," that which ought to be reached by following up the largest perennial

[*] Josephus says that Damascus was founded by Uz, the son of Shem ("Antiq. of the Jews," ch. vii. sec. iv.). The Arabic name of Damascus is Sham.

stream where the river is formed by tributaries. But here again there is the doubt whether we ought not to follow up the *longest* tributary rather than the largest, so as to reach what may be termed the "theoretical source" of the river. The Mississippi flows into the Missouri, but as the former was probably seen first, it gives its name to the united stream, though every one who has been upon them both knows well that the Missouri is the longest and is also the largest of the two at their junction. This difficulty as to whether we should cite for the source of a river the water which has run the longest, or the largest, or the loudest, occurs constantly in our paddling tours. It was a puzzle on the Danube to say whether that, the largest river of Europe, rises at Donaueschingen (whence the water comes to it most) or at St. Georg (whence the water comes to it farthest); and with respect to the most interesting rivers of Syria, the Abana and the Jordan, the question is even more difficult, for to displace the "historic source" of either is to tamper with the tradition of some thousand years.

The splendid gushing forth of the Fiji under the cliff at the end of the Antilebanon is at once the most striking and most copious source of the Abana,* and we have pictured it already at p. 122, though it was very difficult to make a satisfactory sketch of the scene; but the limb joined there has come from the west through a marvellous glen, so steep that I could only see it in safety by lying down on the cliff to look over; and opposite were the ruins of Abila, the city of Abel, under high snow-peaks.†

* The three other more distant sources are marked in Vandevelde as follows:—(1.) Near Ami El Hawar, north of Zebedany, under Jebel Ruzma, not far from a tributary of the Litany, which river falls into the Mediterranean; (2.) west of Zebedany, running through the Wady el Kurn, but this seemed to me quite dry; (3.) west of Rukleh, under Hermon, near Kefr Kook; but this, though the ground was very wet and marshy, appeared to have no flow. The springs of Abana here are near a source of Jordan, and the river Orontes rises not very far away. Thus four rivers rise and flow north, south, east, and west. Porter states that the Abana rises in a little lake, 300 yards long, in the plain of Zebedany, 1100 yards above the sea-level, and falls 400 yards before reaching Damascus, *i. e.*, 50 feet in the mile.

† Another Abila, now "Abeel," is marked on Map V.

It may, however, be stated broadly, that the Abana rises from the Antilebanon range, while the Pharpar rises from Hermon. These rivers are entirely distinct in their rise and in their flow,* their characters and their use, as well as in their terminations, and yet the "Abana and Pharpar" are represented in many maps as united, for their identity is disputed, and their very names are interchanged even by Jews at Damascus.†

The Arabic word "Barada" means small hail or hard snow, and is very appropriate when the hail and sleet are felt so near the river. After a careful reading of what is written by the best authorities upon this subject, it seems plain that the Barada is the old Abana‡ (the middle *a* of both words

---

Whiston states that the city Ablemain (or Abellane in Josephus's copy) is the same as Abilo, and considers that Christ referred to the shedding of the blood of Abel the righteous within the compass of the land of Israel, in His prophecy, Matt. xxiii. 35, 36; Luke xi. 51 ("Antiq. of the Jews," book viii. ch. xii. sec. iv. In ch. xiii. sec. vii. Josephus speaks of the prophet "Elisha of the city of Abela."

* Except by the artificial conjunction of their waters led off by a canal from each, meeting at half a mile from Muaddamych; I heard that the united water is delicious (see Map V.).

† It appears clearly from the following passages in p. 54 of Rabbi Schwartz that he makes the Pharpar to be the north river, and the Abana the south one. "Not far from the village Dar Kanon (Hazar Enan), there is a village called Fidjeh (the Figa of Parah; viii. 10), north of which is the source of the stream of the same name, which flows south-easterly to Damascus, and unites with the Amanah near the lake Murdj. Now this stream is the Pharpar, as it is still called by our fellow-Israelites in the vicinity, according to a tradition which they have. In case, therefore, that a divorce takes place in Damascus, they write in the letter of divorce, ' at Damascus, situated on the two rivers Amana and Pharpar.'"

"About 1½ English miles north of the village Beth al Djana is found a large spring, called Al Barady, that is to say, "the cold." Its waters are clear and excellent for drinking, and it flows north-east to Damascus. This river, formerly called Chrysorrhoas (Gold River), and known in the Talmud Baba Bathra, 74b, as the Karmion, is the identical Amanah of the Bible, as it is actually called by all the Jews of Damascus." Neubauer says the Karmion is the Kishon ("La Géographie du Talmud," 1868, p. 32).

Pococke seems to suggest that the Fiji, or, as the Arabs called it, Fara, may be the Pharpar, and the Barada the "Abna" ("Pinkerton's Voyages," vol. x. p. 503).

‡ Meaning "made of stone" (Cruden), perhaps from its rocky bed.

is pronounced short), and the Awaj is the Pharpar, which latter name in Chaldee means "crooked," as Awaj does in Arabic. Benjamin of Tudela, who lived A.D. 1160, calls[*] the Abana the Amana. This may be a mode of pronouncing the word Abana (readily passing into "Amana," as will be found from trial). Porter cites it as probably giving the name to the mountain whence it flowed, and as part of his strong argument for the identification of the Abana and the Pharpar with the Barada and Awaj. It is in Solomon's Song (chap. iv. ver. 8) that we find this beautiful name of a mountain: "Come with me from Lebanon, my spouse, with me from Lebanon: look from the top of Amana, from the top of Shenir and Hermon, from the lions' den, from the mountains of the leopards."

Josephus[†] speaks of the "mountains Taurus and Amanus;" and again, "Syria and Amanus and the mountains of Libanus." Pliny mentions the "hill Avanus" (lib. v. ch. xxii.).

Having traced the Abana on foot from very near its farthest source to the Fiji, and thence on horseback clearly to the bridge at Doomar, I consider that its course so far is well given in Vandevelde's map. But here we notice at once that, just as the Nile, as it runs on, lessens in volume partly by evaporation and absorption, partly by the artificial conduits which bear away large portions to water the country around, so the Abana is early seized upon for distribution, and grows thinner as it runs. The highest conduit from it above Doomar, called the Yezid, runs among the hills northward, and was said to go as far as "Tadmor in the wilderness;" but it ends in the plain. This flows in a winding channel, seven feet wide and three feet deep, which I followed on foot for miles. A second, about twelve feet wide, the Toura,[‡] branches out below Doomar;

[*] Purchas's "Pilgrims," ii. 1448.
[†] "Antiq. of the Jews," book i. ch. vi. secs. i. and vi.
[‡] Query from the Taurus of Josephus? In an Arabic version (of the eleventh century) the Pharpar is called Tourah in 2 Kings v. 12, and the Abana is called Barda. Vandevelde marks the Berdy River flowing into the Awaj (see Map III.). The Awaj was no doubt crossed by Jacob (Gen.

and there are said to be other canalettes on the south side of the river made for the same purpose, to irrigate the plain. The best detailed account I have met with of these waterways is by Pococke (in "Pinkerton's Voyages," vol. x. p. 503, written so long ago as A.D. 1745). According to these the Yezid and Toura do not enter the town of Damascus. The Acrabane, or Serpentine River, passes close by the north wall of the town (and by this I entered the place), while the other four streams pass through the town, and one more waters a village in the plain. Some of these rivers are under-ground, and may often be seen and heard through holes in the surface. Numerous other tunnels are formed by connecting wells opened at successive levels. Some of these are marked on Vandevelde's map by a line on the plain where they are spent in irrigation. Most of the streams indicated on maps as if they were tributaries do in fact run *out* of the main river. Two days were employed on foot or in the saddle in examining these complicated waterways. The time was not spent fruitlessly, for it showed me why Naaman[*] might well speak of the Abana as superior to Jordan, seeing that the former river waters a whole city and about a hundred villages and thousands of acres of richest land ; whereas the Jordan, below the Sea of Galilee, waters only a strip of jungle. Certainly, as a work of hydraulic engineering, the system and construction of the canals by which the Abana and Pharpar are used for irrigation may be still considered as the most complete and extensive in the world. A previous examination of my course on the Abana was also necessary before launching

xxxi.). As to the Yezid reaching Tadmor, it may be remarked that Josephus says ("Antiq. of the Jews." b. viii. ch. vi. sec. i.): "Now the reason why the city lay so remote from the parts of Syria that are inhabited is this; that below there is no water to be had, and that it is in that place only that there are springs or pits of water."

[*] In the account of Elisha given by Josephus, he has omitted all mention of the miracle wrought upon Naaman. Whiston considers that a part of the original is wanting here. Lepers are alluded to in another place, and amongst them "great captains of armies" ("Antiq. of the Jews," book iii. ch. xi. sec. iv. ; and book ix. ch. iv.).

I

the Rob Roy upon a stream too strong to remount, and too much hemmed in by forest and crags to let any man come near for help, however much the need might be.

The village of Doomar was all astir when the canoe came down to the bridge for a start. Although I had resolved to begin there, and all the spectators were expecting, amid silence almost enforced upon them by the loud rushing of waters, I altered my plan at the last moment, for there was one particular rapid with a fallen tree across which on closer inspection seemed absolutely too dangerous, at least for the first essay upon rapids in a new boat, and with so many rivers to come, and unknown and unavoidable dangers to be met in them. The people were much disappointed by this prudent refusal. Some of them had ridden out from Damascus to see the wonder (having heard of the expected event by telegraph); but it is one of the small, useful bits of wisdom one learns in canoeing, not to mind in the least what the natives say or think upon matters about which they are profoundly ignorant.

The river we are now launched upon is like a Scotch salmon-stream, with high snow-clad mountains on one side and bluff rocks on the other, leaving now and then a green flat sward between crags and boulders and gravel-banks well clothed with trees, among which the French road winds. This is the only piece of real carriage-way in all Syria, and its presence in this valley at once Europeanizes the scene; but the Abana soon runs out of sight of all such detestable civilization, and pours its old stream, as it did in Abraham's time, gushing under the thickets and round the lonesome rocks with a merry onward gait, too fast to let you stop to look how fast it runs or how wide. Part of the river—the Taura arm, branching to the north—passes, like a broad mill-race, under the road; and for variety the Rob Roy followed along this on a higher level, while the main water soon gets much lower, running at a more headlong pace; but the Taura goes at last through a dark tunnel in the cliff, and it would have been madness to follow it there, so I dragged the canoe down again to the old river,

GORGE OF THE ABANA.

and plunged once more out of sight into places perhaps never seen before, though very beautiful. The pace quickens as we approach the cut of the great gorge, and there is a goodly sound of waters echoed from lofty rocks. After months upon the quiet level of the Suez Canal, and the oily-running Nile, and the waves of the Red Sea, and the broad sheet of Lake Menzaleh, it was true luxury to be whirled in the swift eddies of Abana, and to speed at a river's galop among rocks and forests, where the midriff is tickled in the paddler's breast by the sensation often felt on a high rope-swing, and the mind expands into an exulting glee, always begotten by rapids encountered alone.* Many birds and animals were roused from their uninvaded haunts, and splashed into the stream or scurried away, rustling among the dusky brakes. The canoeist soon finds that it is impossible to note these pretty companions when he is in this sort of river; for the stream carries you suddenly to where a dozen prostrate trees are tangled in the water, while their straggling roots hold fast to the bank. A heavy, treacherous rock overhangs on the left, and the right shore is steep with soft mud. The whole picture of this is presented in an instant as you round a point, and the decision how to deal with it must be instantly made, or the current itself will decide.

"Strong to the left hand, seize that bough with the right. Swing round a quarter-circle, then duck the head for ten seconds under that thorn, and shoot across below the second tree, drift under the third, and five strokes will free us, surely." After settling all this as the course to be pursued, at the first paddle-stroke out splashes a shrieking bird, rattling the close thicket of canes as he plunges into the water.

Now if you look at him, even for an instant, in such a place, the whole programme above is in confusion—the

---

* It was soon found that this new canoe, with its long floor adapted for sleeping in and sailing, was thereby rendered much less "handy" in rapids than my Norway Rob Roy. Every canoe is a compromise between the qualities of steering, stowage, sailing, strength, and speed.

bough knocks your hat off, the rock catches your paddle, and the third tree gets hooked in your painter. This comes of mingling ornithology with canoe-craft, and yet it is in just such a place that strange birds are most likely to be flushed.

My dragoman on his horse, and a muleteer on mine, rode along through orchards or water-meadows, and closing to the rapid river wherever they might get a glimpse to see me pass in safety, ever shouting among the crags that echoed his voice, "Rob Roy!" the usual hail we had for each other. Meantime I was swiftly borne away into a thicket of trees, with magnificent towering crags and snow behind them. The Abana here was about sixty feet broad, but every mile we go down it has less of water, for the canalettes lead off the precious liquid right and left, to far-away meads and long dry plains. The stream is swift, and tumbles along in a rugged bed, with a very lively noise. I had to jump out into the water at least twenty times, and used a strong pole as a prop in fording the powerful current. At one or two places I had to haul the boat round on land, where the trees met over the water and their branches were interlaced, or their trunks had fallen in root foremost. Next came a weir for a mill, a waterfall and torrents of foam with dense woods all round, through which no one could see me as I waded, and shoved, and dragged away, but always, somehow, getting onward, and most thoroughly enjoying the varied exercise on so bright a sunny day. The amount of labor involved in a voyage of this kind will be understood by the fact that with every effort to get on, the canoe was five hours in reaching a point which is only one hour distant by the road at a walk. After I had battled with all the difficulties which could be crammed into this time, panting with a tried but wholesome excitement, the sun suddenly appeared, that had been hidden by rocks or trees; the gorge had loosed its hold of us, and the canoe soon floated along the now placid river, while Damascus, old Damascus! gleamed out brilliant before me in the evening light, with its groves of green, and white shining walls, and airy minarets, a glorious scene. The far-famed approach to this city from the west, which unfolds upon the traveller all its gentle beauty from a lofty hill, I had well remembered nineteen years ago; who could forget it? That is one of the sights of the world, but the sudden emerging now from rapids, and rocks, and dense jungle, into the broad day, with such a picture before me, was more striking by far than the other view, especially to one who was the first to see it.

And now the river itself seemed tired of the struggle, and it gurgled, almost sleeping, between the green meadow banks. There a most pleasant repast was spread on the soft grass, and the little knot of wondering Turks which soon collected, was good proof that even Moslems, with all their apathy, could not help looking at a boat on the river. Then the Rob Roy glided into the town itself, under the bridges, round the dripping aqueducts, past the barracks, close up to the Pasha's palace; and two men carried her wearied hull safe to the hotel with colors flying, Hany singing, mud splashing, Moslems wondering, and the hotel folks bowing.

CHAPTER IX.

Damascus Dock.—Pretty Girls.—Eastern Desert.—Reconnoitre –The Rob Roy on Horseback.—Latoof.—On Abana.—Celebrated Canoeists.—Brave Guards.—Tent-life.—Harran.—Mirage.—"Abraham's Well."—Plunging.—Ateibeh Morass.—"Ko-ax Ko-ax."

DEMETRI'S HOTEL is like other houses of Damascus, with the rooms round a large court-yard, looking inward upon a broad marble basin, where fountains copious and cool sprinkle soft music, with gentle splashings never ceasing; and little rivulets pour in as they gleam under the colored sunbeams that dart through vine-branches, and orange-trees; and gaudy-hued dresses are flitting about—for it is the people's clothes you see in the East, the faces of the fair are all closely bandaged up.

There, on the cool water, I placed the canoe, with her blue sails set, and her golden flag reposing. Soon began the long line of visitors; each one, as he left, sent in a dozen friends to see. Even the Pasha of Damascus came, and the English Consul; and the Arabic newspaper gravely chronicled the arrival of the canoe, in the same page with the movements of the Greek iron-clads, stirring up their fires then for a European war.

On Sunday (December 21) the Consul had an English service, and among the five present was Mrs. Thompson, of Beyrout, who—indefatigable woman—had come here to open her new school-house. This is large and roomy, and very suitable for its purpose. After you have struggled up and down dingy lanes, ankle-deep in mud, you enter a substantial pile of buildings, and under the gilded carving of these roofs, the girls of Damascus stand silent and smiling, to wait for their kind Christian "mother," with Bibles in their hands. Not long ago a Giaour dared scarcely to ride through the streets of the town, and in my former visit there our very mules were taken by force, because we were "Nussarenes." Now there are schools and "Bible-women," supported by the ladies of Turkish harems here, who saw their own children able to read, while the mothers were ignorant and cried to their husbands, "Why are *we* to be less blessed than our children?" Among the forty-four young people who had assembled in the school, there were Jewesses, Greeks, Moslems, and Christians. I never saw so many pretty faces among a like number of girls. As for their dresses, they were so varied, so graceful, so suitable to womankind, that one could not but lament that our climate (for of course the fault is not *ours*) has so grievously contorted our feminine toilet. Mrs. Thompson was received with a gush of welcome and sweet greeting. She went round the circle of girls, and kissed each of them in turn, not with a mere "general salute," but a tender look from heart to heart, a special clasp for every one, that made each child feel her embrace was meant in good earnest. This was indeed a pretty sight for a rough-bearded traveller to see.

I do not enlarge upon the importance of sustaining this school. One thought of Saul and Paul stamps Damascus on a Christian's heart, and fixes it as a post of duty for the brave and the generous, who have gone out there to labor for Christ's sake. Nor is it only Paul of the past, but shall we not see him ourselves in a future we know not how near, and speak to him then of Damascus? Let us cherish a vivid sense of heaven in its reality as a life.

The girls sang gentle hymns, and then the whole of them listened to an English address, which was very well interpreted, as also a prayer. At Damascus I met Mrs. Digby, the English wife of a great Arab chief, and, when in English society, her quiet manner as a lady makes one forget that her husband has some thousand spearmen at his beck, and that to get to Palmyra with their aid, the curious traveller must pay a heavy black-mail of yellow gold.

On a hill above Damascus is the celebrated "wely," or little domed chapel, where first, as you journey eastward, the splendid panorama bursts upon the view. Looking from this over the vast plain, long ago I had observed in the distance, tremulous with *mirage*, two huge black vapor pillars, which drifted slowly across the limitless flat. These were sand-clouds, whirled aloft by the breeze, and I was told that they were coursing over a silent and desolate region, almost unknown, through which the river Abana ran, and though it had run there for ages, the life-blood of thousands, and was praised in every language, and sung of in melodious verse, and fabled in prose, it melted away in the desert somehow, nobody knew how.

The Rob Roy had come to this region, and to probe the inviting mystery of the ancient river's end. But all inquiries as to how she could follow the Abana to the east were baffled more every day by the stolid ignorance or stupid exaggeration with which natives complicate any stranger's effort to do what ought to have been done long ago by themselves. The united testimony asserted that the canoe might be taken by land if I could mount her upon a horse, but to float her by water all the way was impossible; and this was precisely what we meant to do. They all agreed, too, in describing the bleak morass at the end as "impenetrable," full of whirlpools, which sucked people down; of hyenas, panthers, and wild boars, which ate people up; and of fevers, agues, snakes, jungle, sun-strokes, and many other horrible things.

As usual, we found that there was just one peg of truth in each of these warnings whereon to hang a huge fiction, and that nothing in the tale had the merit of pure invention. To reconnoitre the land and water of at least the first day's route, Hany and I rode along the banks near Abana. The river's speed was moderate now, for it was running through a plain, but the intricacies of its navigation were most perplexing, because the water branched out right and left into numerous channels, of which one only could be the right one, and nobody could tell us that one. It is only by a ride of this sort that one can appreciate the richness and beauty of the Damascus plain, or can understand the marvellous ingenuity and perseverance with which the Abana has been led through the desert to water it. In Egypt, indeed, the sluices and canalettes are intricate enough, but nothing to what is done here. Banks, dams, lashers, and weirs, seem to force the water into every nook of the country; to force it underground, and, as it were, even up hill, until every available drop has been wrung out for use. Below the shady groves, athwart bright level meads, oozing over, murmuring beneath, and softly hurrying by, there is water everywhere, and nearly all this from that one river which has fed millions of people for ages of time, and if this river stopped, Damascus would perish. The problem of carrying the canoe on a quadruped was new and difficult, but it must be solved, as complete preparation for months of journey, where much was over mountain and plain. *Ali*, my chief muleteer (an excellent fellow to the limits of his calling), was therefore consulted, and he looked grave for two days, after which he proposed that the Rob Roy should be slung crossways over a mule, so of course his further suggestions were useless.

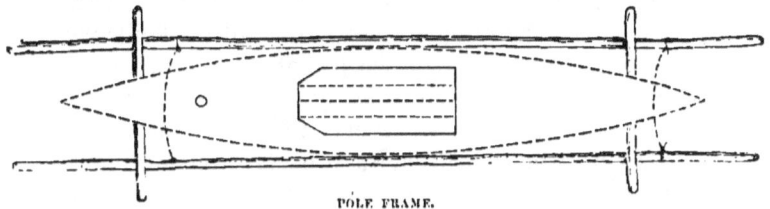

POLE FRAME.

After thought and experiment, I went out and bought two strong poles, each sixteen feet long, and about three inches thick at the larger end. These were placed on the ground two feet apart, and across them, at three feet from each end, we lashed two stout staves, about four feet long, which resulted in a frame like that shown in the sketch. Then a "leading horse"[*] was selected, a strong, docile,

[*] Most good caravans have a "leading horse" in the van. He costs double the price of the others, but he is well worth the expense: he finds the way for all, keeps up the pace, and is very soon recognized as a guide by the other

sure-footed creature. On his back a large bag of straw was well girthed, and flattened down above. The frame of poles was firmly tied on this, and a crowd looked on as we wrapped the canoe in carpets and placed her on the frame, and the moment it was there I saw the plan would succeed. For three months this simple method enabled us to take the Rob Roy over sand and snow, over rock and jungle, across mud and marsh—anywhere, indeed, where a horse could go; and therefore, perhaps, it deserves to be described. The frame was elevated in front, so as to allow the horse's head some room under the boat's keel. Two girth-straps kept the canoe firmly in position above, and carpets were cushioned under its bilge.

It will be seen from the sketch of this boat-frame that, in the event of a collision with a rock or a tree, or if the horse had a stumble and fall on the ground, the shock would be received upon one or other of the four projecting points, instead of striking the canoe itself. To lead the horse by a long rope (though for many a day he was ever shortening it), we told off *Adoor*, a gentle, half-witted, raw-looking youth, who was brought with us because with a charming voice he sang so sweetly that all his faults were drowned in his music. In sharp contrast to him was *Latoof*, a powerful fellow, purposely chosen at Beyrout to hold fast to the canoe in every difficulty, grasping the frame as he trudged through the pools, or clambered the rocks, or swayed the high top-heavy burden right and left, when fierce gusts of wind threatened to overturn us all. To guide these three came Hany next behind on his plucky little Arab, with a hundred and one things in his saddle-bags (and always the things one wanted most), his cocoa-nut nargilleh dangling at his side, and his double-barrel rifle slung upon his back. Without him personally, and his care over all, there is no doubt in my mind that our long new way of travel in the East could not have been finished, as it was, without one check, or disaster, or

mules, horses, and donkies. Indeed, they are restless without him, and wander about in straggling disorder.

break-down, without one day lost, or the slightest injury to any of us, men, horses, mules, donkeys, and boat.

Another secret of success was the elaborate preparation of minutiæ, and the stern resolve that every thing to be used should be of the best, as the clearest economy in the long run, when any failure might cost a day's delay, and the cost of a day was never less than three pounds.*

Those delights or dangers of the river which the canoe-man might meet with anywhere, we need not describe in this story, having plenty to tell that is peculiar to the place and the people. However, as this stream of Abana has not been boated upon before, it may be well to inform the next canoeist that, below the first mill beyond Damascus, we found it full of interest and variety.† The water was now red in color and two feet deeper than before, being swollen high by mountain storms, and the channel led us away and away among orchards and groves and thick osier-beds and smiling water-meadows. Tortoises sleeping on the bank toppled into the stream as we passed, and land-crabs lazily crawled out of sight. There were many wild ducks in the river brakes, most of them too fat or lazy to rise, and I had to get out only seven or eight times to haul the canoe past obstructions, until on a sudden the ruddy current bore the Rob Roy right into an impassable jungle of osiers ten feet high. This sort of obstacle, or a marsh full of deep holes, are the only real troubles to the canoeist, if we except (as very unusual) a river covered with small hewn logs, such as I met in Norway on the River Vrangs; but even then I had only to drag the boat for a mile through a lonely wood. Rapids however long, waterfalls however high, can be passed on the land by persevering

---

* The same dragoman, providing also the best materials in 1849, charged £2 per diem for myself and a companion. The increased expense now of about 100 per cent. is accounted for by the Crimean war, the Abyssinian expedition, and the cattle murrain, which raised the price of animals and labor.

† The general route of our journey may be traced on Map VIII., while Map II. (p. 142) and Maps III. and IV. (p. 171) give portions on a larger scale.

patience. The sea between Ireland and Scotland was traversed by one of our Canoe Club in his canoe; another member sailed his Rob Roy from England to France, and a third paddled from France to England, all in one summer.* Still, though a canoe can start from any part of Britain, and struggle all the way to Hong Kong, there will always be much difficulty in passing it through a forest of small trees, which may be too dense to allow the canoeist to shove his craft by the water, or to drag it along the bank. An invariable policy in such cases always brings relief: "Persist in the assurance that you *must* get through; pull up to the side; ponder on the best place, and shout aloud." Who would have thought that in such a strange jungle on the Abana there would be any one within reach of a call? Yet a man was there, cutting the osiers, and soon his head was stretched forward. Then he ran off at once as fast as his legs could carry him. Smiles and soft speeches speedily brought him back, and we soon shouldered the Rob Roy together, and so passed the obstruction. I slept that night at Jisrin (Map III., p. 171.)

The Abana now ran eastward, steady and deep, in a tortuous way between high grass banks, with a lively day for enjoyment. No trees now, and no thickets, but wide and fruitful plains, and oxen that stopped ploughing while the peasants ran from their teams to see the "shaktoor." For miles they ran with me thus, a good-humored, smiling band, men, women, and children, shouting with joy, while statelier Turks on horses and mules kept pace alongside with more dignity, when any path on the bank could be found. Thus we came to El Keisa, and pitched our tents in the cemetery, while at least a hundred people sat round the camp in a picturesque circle, staring hard till sundown. It was important to make friends with these people, who were being rather drilled than delighted by the officious orderings of two Turkish soldiers I had taken with me as guards, splendidly mounted, miserably clothed, wretchedly

---

* The names of these three members of the Canoe Club may well be recorded—Mr. R. Tennent, Mr. Bowker, and the late Hon. J. Gordon.

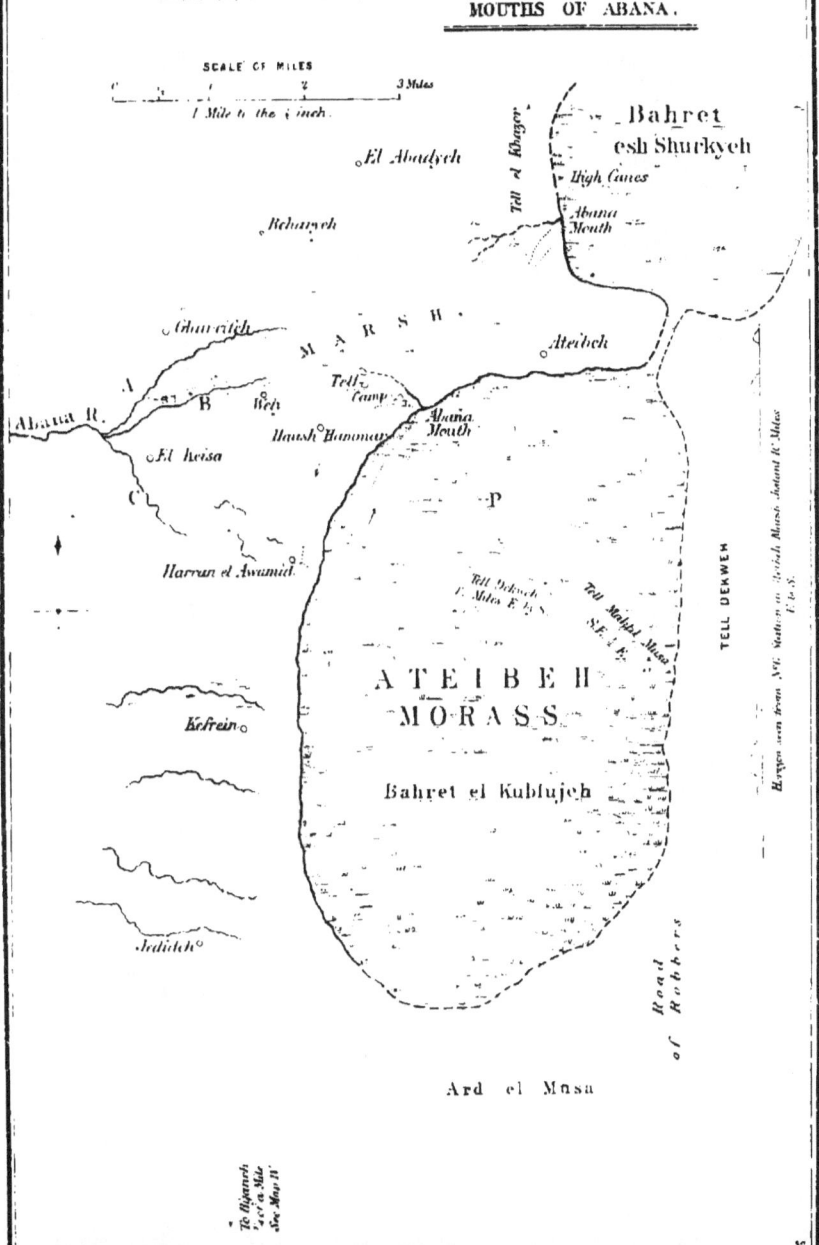

armed, and thoroughly prepared for their only duty in danger—to run away. The peasants' red coats reached to their ankles. Every man had a staff five feet long. Some of the women had yashmaks, and a few of the men wore a black cotton kerchief (the *mandeel*) tied over the face, to moderate the reflection from the ground, and concealing the nose, but used in a manner I had never seen before.*

These quaint people were easily amused by a few pleasantries, and they laughed very heartily. Patting the children's heads pleased the little ones, and their mothers too. One copper-colored youngster, wallowing in the mud, asked me for a farthing (the only beggar), but when I gave it to him, he asked that it might be "put by." Poor fellow! he had no pocket for his purse, being as perfectly naked as on the day he was born.

A long string of my new friends followed in procession to the village, which was of mud, but far better built than in Egypt. A shepherd was dozing by his flock, with a sword girt round his waist. A few Arab tents were near, and keen eyes in them eyed me askance. I slept now in my tent, feeling far more lonely under canvas than when lodging in my canoe. It was a small square tent, sent from England as a present to Hany—double, of course—and made by Edgington, so it ought to be good, but we shall have it tried by jury farther on. The other round Syrian tent was henceforth used by the servants.

Sweet sleep follows such a day, but the winter's dawn next morning can not soon struggle through English canvas. Yet one awakes by habit or instinct, or by a previous resolve; and, without lighting a match to see my watch, it was easy to tell the time by the sounds outside. First, there is the feeblest bustle heard in the dark, and a tinkling sound as the charcoal briskly kindles in the cook's fire. The cock-crows (so many and loud in Palestine) are absent here. Soon the men around are whispering more loudly,

---

* This, however, reminds one of the Towaregs one sees in Algeria, a tribe to the extreme south of the French settlements in the hot Sahara, where all the men wear black crape masks entirely covering their faces.

and then a horse neighs. The sharp "whish" of swift pinions is from a wild bird overhead hieing off thus earliest to the lake; then the soft regular beat of the cook's bellows gets louder, it is a turkey's wing waved with a sound like "fam, fam, fam!" At last a donkey brays. Up now! An end to sleep forever, and let the joyous splashing of my bath bespeak me eager for the happy hours of another bright day. Hany hears the sound, and soon after a "Good-morning!" times the hot wholesome breakfast to a minute.

Among the chief features of the Abana River is the fine Tell of Salahiyeh, a green mound that looks like Primrose Hill, in Regent's Park. The excavations made here for the Palestine Exploration Fund, in 1866, by Mr. Rogers, are described in Part II. of the "Quarterly Statement." Some of the articles dug up were shown in the Society's Exhibition last autumn.

The tell had an imposing grandeur, and, at the same time, an air of lively interest, as the huge green mound seemed to turn slowly round, while my canoe bore me floating by in the bend of the river; but nearly all the researches in these artificial hills, so common in Palestine, have been barren of valuable results.*

* The following is the conclusion of the account Mr. Rogers gives of the excavations at Salahiyeh:—"Close to this cutting, and to the east of it, I made another, in which was found much broken pottery, black inside and red on the surface. A few stones, similar to those already mentioned, with bricks, mortar, and strong cement, were found. It was opened to the depth of 32 feet.

". . . At the south of the mound, the regular layers of brick are very distinct and perfect; these bricks are about 18 inches square and 4 inches thick; some pale yellow, others pale red, joined by strong mortar; . . . some stones of a heart-shape were found, as if belonging to a pavement.

"The people in the neighborhood came to me, and said that, if I wanted to make any discoveries, I must first propitiate the sheikh, whose tomb is on the top of the tell, by sacrificing a sheep in his honor. I immediately gave them half a sovereign, with which to purchase the victim, and my workmen partook of the feast.

". . . It seems to me that the tell is a solid mass of brick-work built over, perhaps, one chamber or more in the centre, similar to the Pyramids of Egypt; for wherever I dig I find layers of brick and mortar. If the tell

After El Keisa, the Abana has some very intricate navigation. Against my opinion—for experience points the way even in new places and by indications that can not be explained—I was directed down the wrong branch of three into which the river had forked. At last my faithful compass told the tale so clearly that it was plain we were going astray; so I took the Rob Roy across the fields to the right way, and we halted at a point about sixteen miles straight from Damascus, the village of Harran el Awamid, that is, "Harran of the pillars."

These are three handsome basalt columns in the middle of this village. Sculptured fragments also are amongst the mud hovels. The pillars, standing forty feet high, served as a landmark to my journey for a whole fortnight, and I took a careful sketch of them,* and some bearings by compass, while the most exemplary silence prevailed among the wondering villagers.

Then, by a "silver argument," the sheikh was persuaded to let me mount the minaret of the mosque, and for the first time to get a good general survey of the country about us, the snow hills behind, the river winding below, the far-off desert, the nearer plain with its hundred villages, and the weird morass I had come to pierce.

Not a drop of water could be seen in this "Lake of Ateibeh," painted so prettily blue on the travelling maps. Mr. Rogers told me he never could see water in the marsh. On the other hand, Porter saw, in November, 1852, "a large expanse of clear water in the midst of the marsh," a little south of the Abana mouth, where there was not a

---

were the mere store of a brick factory, there would be no mortar between the layers. The work, affording no promise of further discovery, was then abandoned."

Captain Wilson gives the position of this tell as in 33° 30′ 28″ N., and 36° 28′ 02″ E. The mound is 60 feet high, the largest side nearly east and west, and the Barada washes its southern slope.

* It was unfortunately lost overboard, but a beautiful photograph of the pillars is in the series published by the Palestine Exploration Fund. The side pillars are not equidistant from the corner one. Wilson gives their height of shaft 29 feet, base 2 feet 3 inches, circumference 11 feet 7 inches.

pond visible to me.* In his visit to Hijaneh also, where I traversed a full lake with five feet of water in it, he found a basin "perfectly dry."

With such variations of the surface we are about to map, we must expect the contours of these marshes to be very different as sketched by different travellers, or at different times. The maps of them in Porter's "Five Years in Damascus" are different from those in his excellent guide-book ("Syria and Palestine," Murray). The Maps II. and IV. of the district are made from my own compass-bearings, of which a list is given at p. 173, while the other parts are taken from Vandevelde's map, which I found to be more correct than any other.

As for the branch of Abana passing by Harran, it was only a few disjointed pools. We were now on almost unknown territory, and it was something to know that; but I instantly resolved to carry the canoe north to the next arm of the Abana, for it was plainly impossible to get her into the morass from Harran.

By the mosque here they showed me a very ancient well, about six feet deep, with stones exceedingly worn.† This is called Abraham's Well, and Dr. Beke and others consider the village to be the Harran where Abraham dwelt "between the two rivers" (Abana and Pharpar).

* Partly this may be accounted for by different times of the year, and by wet or dry seasons, though his visit was in a season "unusually dry;" partly because the *appearance* of water is deceptive in hot regions of mirage, as one soon discovers by journeys on rivers and lakes, and Porter himself describes a phenomenon of this kind in this very plain (vol. ii. p. 11). Thomson ("The Land and the Book," vol. ii. p. 288) says that the mirage, or scrab, "thirst of the gazelle," is meant by the word translated "parched ground" in Isaiah xxxv. 7: "And the parched ground shall become a pool;" and certainly this rendering gives much force to the passage. The mirage on the river St. Lawrence is perhaps the most wonderful one can see.

† Stones are sooner worn at wells than elsewhere, and as an indication of antiquity this is deceptive. The edge-stones of the tanks in the Haram at Jerusalem are seamed several inches deep by the bucket-ropes; but Lieut. Warren, R. E., the clever explorer of the Holy City, told me that a year or two of use is enough to make a deep cut in the stone when a wet rope (always carrying grit with it) is constantly worked.

Josephus ("Antiq. of the Jews," bk. i. ch. vii. sec. ii.) states that Berosus writes: "Now the name of Abram is even still famous in the country of Damascus, and there is showed a village named from him — 'the habitation of Abram.'"*

We bade good-bye to the amiable village "sheikh," a man with long, shaggy, red hair, very intelligent, and very sorry we were not to stop a night in his mayoralty.

Our route lay across the verge of the morass (see Map II., p. 142), but we went too far eastward, and the work was now very troublesome and dangerous. We soon found that the experienced "marsh-walker," who acted as guide, had never led more than cattle over these wilds, and the amphibious oxen here can plunge through pools that are impossible for laden mules and restive horses. It was a wide sea of shallow water, concealed by grass in tufts, like an Irish bog, and with soft deceptive mud, deep holes, and trickling streamlets.

Hundreds of cattle stood up to their stomachs in the water, as our mules plunged deep above their girths, and the men sank down repeatedly. The guide now fairly lost his head, and I had to push on in front to lead, with a feeling of some responsibility in having brought to such a place our long cavalcade, numbering eleven men and twelve animals.

At length mule after mule slipped in till only his shoulders were visible, and one of the little donkeys disappeared under water completely, head and ears and every thing, but a clever muleteer caught him by the tail, and we pulled him out. Then he began to bray—a piteous performer, all wet and muddy. I noticed that particular donkey's music for months afterwards was always at least double his natural allowance, but, in consideration of his gallant behavior on this occasion, he had special license to bray on continually to the end. The men lamented

---

* Dr. Beke wrote again upon the subject of Abraham's sojourn here, in the "Athenæum" (April, 1869), having previously suggested that the well mentioned above might be Rachel's Well.

their moist bread (the load of the ass submerged),* but I cheered them up with a promise of Christmas fare, and then I dismounted, and punted and paddled the Rob Roy, for she might have been injured by a fall if carried any longer on horseback.

By the route-line on the map it will be seen that we were travelling nearly north along that edge of the marsh until at last we struck upon that branch of the Abana which passes near Haush Hamar; we camped by its

MORASS OF ATEIBEH, EAST OF DAMASCUS.

mouth, on fine solid ground, to spend our Christmas Day, and the red ensign of England was soon hoisted on a high pole, to wave over as wild a spot as ever was seen. The river narrowed here to four or five yards across, with a deep and quiet stream.† No jackals sang out now their usual

---

* In such a wild district, of course, we had to bring all our provisions from Damascus. In the above sketch is shown the Rob Roy on horseback.

† The course of the branches is explained in a note farther on. Porter

lullaby we had nightly listened to before, but it is said that where larger beasts are near, the jackal does not cry, and I have generally found this to be true. The frogs owed no such tribute of silence, and their chant was from a thousand-throated chorus, each one croaking as loud as the quack of a duck.*

states the breadth as 30 feet, but though it widens to this at a long pool by the ford, the average above and below that place is only one-half of this width.

* The croak of a frog has been one of the best means of informing the modern world of the mode in which the ancient Greeks pronounced their beautiful language, for in an old Greek author, the frogs are made to sing what would now be written in English " Brech-ech-ech-ex ko-ax ko-ax." Now the frogs of the nineteenth century have probably been faithful to the pronunciation of their race in former times, and as we listen in the still night to their curious music, it is exactly as if one set of them—perhaps the tenors—the gentlemen of their choir, kept saying, "Brekekekex!" while the softer wooing of the ladies is uttered always as "Koax koax ko-ax." The din made by millions of these songsters, in a marsh many miles extended, is astounding. Those in the distance are heard like the sound of a railway train when it passes over a metal bridge. The nearer croakers, being more articulate, are more disturbing. Sometimes they all stop, as if by command, and, after a few moments of silence, the catch-note of some flippant flirt just whispers once, and instantly the whole Babel resumes its universal roar.

CHAPTER X.

Ateibeh Morass.—Drowned in the Lake.—Menagerie.—Embarking.—Dangerous Day.—A lonely Wold.—End of the Abana.—Retreating.—Christmas on the Abana.—Thoughts.—Northern Lake.—Mouths of the Abana.—Tell Dekweh.—Tell Hijaneh.—Hijaneh Lake.—Paddling to Bashan.—The Giant Cities.—Nimrim.—The Island.—In a Boar-track.—Channel.

HERE then we face this dread lake of Ateibeh, which I have carried the Rob Roy over the snow to explore. Behind us is a vast plain, bounded by the rocky hills and snow-capped mountains, and great Hermon in his cold white robe presiding over all. Small mud villages are scattered upon the grassy level. The inhabitants are very interesting to look at, tall, very handsome, men, women, and children, strong, good-tempered, healthy, and intelligent, also well dressed. They wear long robes of most brilliant colors, bright red predominant. Even if a man is in tatters, his rags are crimson. The better sort have embroidered coats and earrings (not in the lobe of the ear, but in the small projecting flesh), and their faces are tattooed. Their boots are of red leather, with long turned-up toes, and the women seldom conceal their faces. Scores of these have often run a mile alongside the canoe, but I never had an unkind word or act from one of them. Their villages are nearly surrounded by water, and not very dirty—one gets used to all things being reasonably dirty here. Compared with Egypt, this verge of house-habitation in the East (bordering the real Arab tent-folk) is a paradise.

Great excitement was caused by the Rob Roy coming to such a place, because the only boat which had attempted this lake had a miserable end three years ago. I made particular inquiries as to this accident, and went to the spot where she launched, and saw one of the men who helped to find her sad wreck. From these inquiries it appeared that two Moslems and a Christian from Ateibeh (a village near the lake) brought a boat from Damascus. They were all "fowlers," and wished to shoot more ducks for the market. The boat was shorter than the Rob Roy, but broader, evidently a poor tub, and the three men having been absent in her for five days, an offer of 500 piastres* was made to any one who would find them. The villagers selected a man who was a good swimmer, and they made a raft of reeds and sticks, upon which he set off naked, and after fifteen days he found the boat upset and the bodies of the three drowned men—none of them could swim—and each of them, in true Arab style, had strapped to his body his gun, ammunition, and food. So I was put quite at ease about this foolish adventure.

Before us the Abana ran straight into the marsh for a quarter of a mile; so it was evident we were at the right place for our essay at quagmire navigation, and the next thing was to determine the best mode and time and direction for penetrating to the centre of the morass. Not an atom of information could be got on this subject from the books or the maps, of which I had three, and the best that the inhabitants could tell us was not reassuring; for, according to these, besides the panthers, hyenas, and other beasts, there are, worst of them all, wild boars. In ordinary times a wild boar avoids a man, but if I came upon him in my canoe in a marsh among tall reeds, he would most likely "charge" the new-comer, and one blow of his tusk, I knew, would finish the Rob Roy. In such a case she would not float, for when mud gets inside it, even a life-boat will sink. Then I could not swim ashore for the reeds, and I could not wade or drag the boat through the deep pools if it were broken and jagged, nor could any help whatever be given from shore, because the water jungle completely hides you.

Still the thing must be done somehow, and plans for new projects of this kind can not be hit off in a moment. Long

---

* A piastre is about twopence of our value. Not many years ago its value was sixpence.

consideration, and a resolve to leave nothing hap-hazard, are the true secrets of insuring success, and here comes in one of the great advantages of travelling alone—you have time and silence to consider maturely. You do not mar your plans by feeble compromises. You see, hear, and think a great deal more than if a " pleasant companion " is beside you all day, whose small talk (and your own) must be run dry in a month, and neither of you is *free*. In these solitary expeditions I have never a sensation of loneliness. Hard work, healthy exercise, plain food and plenty of it, early hours, reading at night, and working, moving, noting, drawing, observing, and considering all day, one's plans are quietly perfected, and there is no more of tedium or solitary dullness than is felt when you read or fish alone, or paint or write in a town—the place one can feel most lonely in, after all.

Our object was now to trace the Abana River until it flowed no farther, and to see whether its end is in a mere morass or in a lake—that is, a sheet of water reasonably open all the year round. For this purpose it was plain that our course ought to be always in the strongest flow and towards the lowest depression, which, after careful scrutiny, appeared to lie to the south-east.

At break of day the compass-bearings of the chief objects around us were accurately taken, and their alignments with the snow-hills far in our rear. This was done to enable me to get out of the marsh by the way through which I came in at the end of the river, for at no other place could I hope to bring the Rob Roy close to the margin.

The canoe-compass has been already explained.* In taking bearings by it when afloat, I found it best to hold the compass to the eye with both hands, and to keep the lid slanted back so as to allow a long black line on its inside to be directed by the eye to the object, when the pressure of the right forefinger acting upon a stud will fix the needle for reading off, and this being done four or five times, and a mean taken of the angles noticed, it is easy to obtain bearings within a quarter of a point.

* See *ante*, p. 66.

Having thus made every possible preparation, I ran the Rob Roy to the river's mouth, with the sun just rising over the illimitable desert on the other side of the lake, and gilding bold Hermon with a bright morning ray. I had food for two days, a double-barrelled gun, one barrel loaded with ball, a long pole for working in the reeds, and a number of strips of calico two feet long, which I tied one by one at various points to the loftiest canes, that I might have perhaps some chance of finding my way back to the river's mouth. This last object was important, because, if in the return I arrived at any other place, it would still be a quarter of a mile from the verge, without water enough to float in, or land enough to stand upon.

Hany, my invaluable dragoman, was to hail me every ten minutes until he could not hear my voice. In the first ten minutes I was invisible, and he saw me no more all day. The river ran to a clump of bushes, widened to twenty feet and four feet deep, and then branched out into five or six small streams among the reeds. The current became stronger, and it was impossible to forget that this would be all "up hill" in coming back. I had soon lost sight of the tents, but part of the red flag was always visible when I stood up. Taking my bearing from this, I wound a long strip of calico round the tops of three highest plants tied together, and carefully entered the particulars in my "log-book;" doing this all very deliberately, for certainty in such matters is better than speed, and any confusion or excitement might ruin the whole proceeding. From this, called "Station No. 1," I worked on until it was nearly invisible, and then placed "Station 2," and so on. The plan answered admirably.* Soon I put my paddle away below deck, and worked with a long pole. As the water shallowed, I had to "punt" the canoe, standing up in her, and with my shoes off for better foothold, and to lessen the danger of making a hole in her skin, which would probably have let in the mud so fatal to the boat,

---

* As this method may be a hint to others paddling where they can not see twenty yards in front, the exact notes are given at p. 173.

or by its rough edges outside would prevent her progress on her return. I had shot a few ducks, for there were hundreds quite close, but it was impossible to retrieve them when they fell even a few yards off; and, moreover, it was soon found that all one's attention in such a place is required for navigation. Sporting with either the rod or the gun is, in my opinion, incompatible with proper progress in discovery when only one man has to do all.

At length I reached a point where all stream ceased, as was shown when the mud stirred by my pole did not advance beyond my boat at rest—in fact, the Rob Roy was now in the middle water of the marsh, and to be quite sure of this, I got out and waded, dragging the boat to the point P in Map II., at p. 142; but the deep holes concealed by clumps of grass were very troublesome, though of course a good wetting had to be counted on at starting, and the water was warm, while the mud below was cold.

Some of these holes indeed seemed bottomless, and now I understood what had been so often stated to me before setting out: "There are whirlpools (as they styled them) which drag men down—every year men are lost even on the edges, and no help can reach them." These are the Arabs who shoot ducks which fall a few yards off in the marsh, and the men, eager to retrieve them, soon get overhead. It was one more proof added to hundreds in my voyages that natives speaking of what they don't understand always give the worst view of danger, but that there is generally something meant by them which it is well to understand for one's self.

Having fully satisfied myself that I was now going up hill to the other side of the lake, and it being noon with a hot sun, after four hours of tremendous labor, and craving for food, I sat down and enjoyed an excellent luncheon. How silent, how solitary, how desolate the scene in this wilderness of marsh. No ducks rose now, for I was quiet. I saw three very tiny fish, but could not catch them. One mosquito came to me, but he did not bite. Perhaps he had never been taught that man is the sweetest morsel for his ravenous tooth. A beautiful fly buzzed about me, like a bluebottle of the most brilliant green.

The faint buzzing of that fly made the silence of all else far deeper, for the ear was aroused by the sound, and yet found only that sound for its listening. It was a position, this, entirely unique, sitting most comfortably in a boat, aground, hidden, absolutely still; time passing, but nothing doing. If you are floating on a lake, there is at least a scene around, or catspaws on the water, or cries from the shore, for variety. If you are alone in the sea, be it ever so glassy, there is sure to be a ground-swell gently curving the clouds pictured on the waves. If you rest thus on a river, the boat will turn round, and so a panorama seems to pass before the eye; and lastly, if you are alone on the water in the dark, you can at any rate strike a light for company's sake.* In every one of these cases some new object is likely to appear, or, if not, it may be hoped for, while, if sickness or death come suddenly then, there is the grim consolation that somebody would find the boat and the body. But now in this marsh I was out of the network of things: no change took place in the view about me, no event happened, I was farther away from the world than on the highest mountain's peak, or in the deepest mine— and the world was getting on very well without me. Let us go back to it, thoroughly convinced that the Abana dies in the marsh of Ateibeh, yielding its vapory spirit to the hot sun, as Jordan faints away in the Dead Sea, and so, rising into the clouds again, both of them perhaps wafted aloft to the snow-peaks where they were born, pour down their old waters in a current ever new, in that circuit of death and life which God has ordained for all.

The end of the Abana, then, may be less sublime than that of the Jordan, but it is not less grim and mysterious.

---

* In sailing alone from Havre to Portsmouth in my yawl, there was a sense of isolation when each port was fifty miles away, and no other vessel was in sight, but then there was always *action*, a movement of the waves and of the boat; and isolation to be felt in all its force must have absolute rest and silence.

A trackless marsh has horrors worse than the Dead Sea. You can float in water, but in mud you can neither swim nor stand, and the great slime volcano in Sicily seemed to me more terrible than even Etna itself.

To turn the boat required a sweep of half a mile, and then I could see snowy Hermon in front, and a flutter of my English ensign at the tents where poor Hany, like a distracted mother, was waiting long hours in despair, for these Easterns jump from exulting joy to deepest distress at a bound.

Beginning with "No. 6" guide of cotton, I traced back to No. 5, having recorded each one clearly in my note-book. One of the most important things, I repeat, in such expeditions is to do every thing very slowly, and to keep every idea clear and separate.

Much sooner than in the outward voyage I reached the river again. An Arab fowler was there, wistfully gazing at a large bird which was out of his reach. I shot it, and the bird flew towards him wounded. He put a bullet through its head as it lay on the rushes with dishevelled outstretched wings, and then he brought it to me, but of course I gave it to him, which made us great friends. The bird had a beak like the "great bittern's," and a large crest on its head.

The men at our camp were rejoiced to hear my hail again, "Rob Roy!" long before they saw the canoe. Orientals speedily identify themselves with their master's cause, and these fellows had believed all the nonsense told them about this lake. Besides, their promised Christmas feast depended a good deal on my being among them. For this I bade them collect materials to make a huge bonfire, and these were piled up high. Hany brought in a splendid stuffed roast turkey for me, and then a capital plum-pudding swimming in the flames of brandy. Fancy such an orthodox dinner in the desert of Atcibeh!

The moon shone clear, and our fire had become embers when the Howaja joined the party round it and asked silence for his address. He told them that we had now reached the farthest point of our journey. After this we were going south, and west, and homeward. Then he turned to the journey of life, and the home for us pilgrims—then to the Christmas Day just finished as a great mark in time's road to eternity—and then he gave them a condensed history of the world from the creation—the law—the prophets, and the Saviour—the apostles—the martyrs and ourselves.

CHRISTMAS NIGHT ON A MOUTH OF THE ABANA.

Hany interpreted each sentence, and every sentence was heard with intense interest. It was indeed an open-air sermon, and what with the time, the place, the audience, and the occasion, we might well feel solemnly the heavy responsibility we incur in speaking to others who will listen on subjects like these. Long after the hour for sleep these men were talking of it all. Perhaps no one of them had ever heard so much truth before, or will ever hear it again.

Those who are not convinced of the truth of the Gospel must at any rate admit that Christianity exists. How it came here, how it thrives, and how it works more than all other energies, are questions that no man has solved without assuming far more unlikely things than the existence of a Christ such as the Scriptures describe.

The phenomenon appeared, they must allow, some eighteen centuries ago, and among a few fishermen upon Bethsaida beach. These simple folk carved out the only Godlike image ever seen. These crafty conspirators arrayed it with a glory that eclipsed first of all themselves hopelessly and forever. They devised the most novel and successful scheme of moral conduct, and kept on preaching doctrines that convicted every day their own falsehood and deception. They invented the very best plan for benefiting other people, but they utterly failed to get any thing out of it for themselves except weeping and loss. These simpletons, that could not see through the flimsy veil of fable, saw deeper into human hearts than any other men, and gave voice to yearnings that were felt everywhere, but were never understood before. These dupes exposed all other deceptions that had deceived the wisest of philosophers. These dullards conceived a system that outreached the loftiest fancies of the cleverest thinkers.

We who are of course so much wiser, and cooler, and better altogether—we are the only fair and shrewd judges to try this case. A whirlwind of clashing thoughts is sweeping in thunder through the darkness above us, and an earthquake rends the rocks, but we are placid, and can sit unmoved, while we rake among the chaos and sift out grains of truth. We have not taken sides—we are only standing aloof from every thing. It does not tell upon our verdict at all that, if these prisoners at the bar are in the right, then we are utterly in the wrong, and must lay our mouths in the dust and confess that we are miserable sinners, and give up our dearest idol—self, and change our whole course of life, and labor and suffer and die for the truths we are now judging.

'Tis true that we have ourselves no rival system that will bear five minutes' comparison with theirs—that our advance towards any better truth from the beginning of mankind, say fifty thousand years ago, is rather minute; but the day after to-morrow we shall have explained all mysteries by our sunlike inner light, without that dim candle of revelation—our existence in flesh and spirit, right and wrong, happy and wretched, poverty, sickness, death, and the illimitable past and future of it all. Oh, it is a delightful thing to live in an age so modest, impartial, and serene, and to trace back my pedigree with honest pride to the ancestral oyster in a metamorphic rock, to feel a patronizing regret that no light from heaven could ever penetrate his thick shell, but that all truth is revealed to my soul by me, and that *my* law of life is what I think right, and (for I am charitable as well as infallible) your law of life is what *you* think right, and that nobody can say any body is more right than any body else, and yet we are all right together —and that's the way to make things pleasant all round.

Next day I rode to the village of Ateibeh to examine the northern lake. Pools of water made this town nearly an island, but its five hundred inhabitants seemed healthy and comfortable, and the sheikh was most hospitable in his palace of clay, with pictures on its outer walls, which sloped like those in Egypt.

A dense white fog shaded the morning sun, and bedewed the grove of trees. Through this we galloped over a fine plain to the mouth of the Abana's northern stream, which ran into the lake, only five feet wide in one part, and five feet deep, with a current of a mile an hour, until it suddenly branched into five, exactly like the palm of a hand, and so oozed forth into deep water, closed not far off by tall dense canes—a scene quite different from that in the southern lake we had left.

This was the place where the three men had perished in the only boat known to have traversed these lakes before. I waited till the fog cleared away, in order to get compass-bearings, and then commenced a long, tedious, and dangerous search for the course of this northerly branch of the Abana.

The route-line on Map II., at p. 142, indicates the general direction, which was sometimes over low mud-plains and hollows, at others across numerous canals and streamlets, or deep, treacherous morass, or golden-colored herbage.

The general conclusions arrived at during this ride were as follows:—Above El Keisa the Abana had separated into three streams. The most southerly (marked C on Map II., and seemingly rather modern and artificial) is spent in irrigation, but in floods it may run by Harran. The middle one (marked B) we had followed in the Rob Roy, and, soon after the place where we left it, the stream is lost in an upland marsh, until about a quarter of a mile from its mouth. There the water appears again as a river, and, passing near the hamlet of Haush Hamar, runs into the lake through the mouth we had camped by for Christmas Day. The northern branch (marked A) also merges into an intricate spongy bog, until the waters unite in the stream which enters the northern lake. Between these last two branches is the land separating the two lakes. Porter states that this neck of land, about a mile in breadth, divides them permanently, except where the deep channel through it allows the water to run. Vandevelde marks the land here only as a peninsula, and he indicates the channel called El Hawar through this narrow tongue. Porter says that the water flows from south to north through this, but the sheikh at Hijaneh stated that the water runs either way. All the people at Ateibeh assured me that Tell el Khanzir[*] is not at the place so named in Vandevelde and in Petermann (and which is called Tell Namy), but is north and west of Ateibeh. Porter (who visited the actual spot) places Tell Maktil Musa near the channel above mentioned, while Vandevelde calls another tell by that name. The misty cloud which hung about us for

[*] Wilson, however, mentions the tell by this name as being near the canal, though he did not reach it, owing to a robbery at his camp.

several hours prevented me from taking reliable bearings of the villages in this district, but, on the whole, they corresponded with the position marked in Vandevelde.

According to Porter, the northern lake is about eight miles long, by four and a half wide, and receives part of the Yezid water, and in winter a stream called the Mahrabrit at the north. It also receives water from some springs. The most copious of these, Ain Halush, waters five villages. The southern morass is about six miles long, and four broad. The plants I saw upon it were seldom higher than five feet.

On the east of these lakes, and, according to my compass-bearing, about sixteen miles from Ateibeh, and eighteen from Hijaneh, is a high mound, call Tell Dekweh, one of a line of tells close together for fifteen miles. These form the most remarkable, and, indeed, singular feature in the eastern horizon. The land between them and the lakes must be high, Porter says thirty feet, and the outline sketch of them given on Map II., which was taken from my post P in the marsh, shows that they are nearly hidden by the shore when looked at from the water.

Three strange ruined buildings lie between these hills and the lake, but no man lives in that solitude, and all around and beyond is a desert of silence.

It was difficult to resist the powerful attraction of a visit to such places on the eastern shore, but the Rob Roy had no business there, and plenty of work was awaiting her which could only be done in a canoe. So she was mounted again on her pony, and we filed along the edge of the morass by Kefrein ("two villages") and Jedideh, easily finding a far better route than our herdsman guide had led before; for there are very few places where a traveller is not his own best guide when journeying in a mode unknown to the natives.*

* The plain of the Abana is considerably lower than that of the Pharpar, and Wilson describes a canal leading from the Pharpar to the Damascus plain. In one place it is crossed by a Roman bridge, so it must have existed in Roman times. This may be the canal alluded to before, p. 127.

L

In the lovely evening our tents were pitched at the foot of the large and very remarkable mound of Hijaneh, which, looming out from the horizon, deep blue-black and vivid, against the evening sky, had long been our landmark from afar.* To run up this for a new view of old things, and a sight of what was hidden behind, was of course one's immediate delight. Such pleasures never pall on the voyager.

This huge tell is about one hundred feet high, and one thousand yards long, by four hundred in breadth. It seems

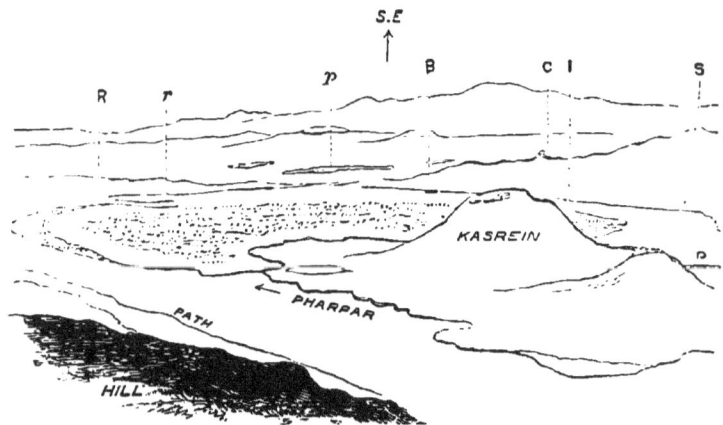

HIJANEH LAKE FROM THE TOP OF THE TELL.

R, The first river.   r, Second river.   p, Pools in Bashan.   B, Butreya ruins.
C, Cairn.   S, Summit of Fashal.   I, Position of the island.
P, South limb of the Pharpar.   The dotted part in the lake is densely covered by canes.

unlikely that it can be wholly natural, yet it is far too large to be formed by man. On one end is a fort. Ruins are in the middle, and enormous stones are piled in circles all about, while a small modern cairn crowns the southern end, as a look-out for the soldiers here to spy the robber Arabs.

Towards the north I could not see a speck of clear water in Ateibeh marsh, but to the south-east there stretched the

* It is strange that this very striking object is not noticed in Murray's Guidebook. It is marked on Map IV.

new lake of Hijaneh, its ample basin full, and ready for tomorrow in the canoe, where myriads of water-fowl were darkening the air, or busily crowding amongst the tall yellow canes.

Here was our first view also of the river Pharpar, which divides into two as it nears the lake,* and from this point the accompanying sketch was made, looking south-east towards the giant cities of Bashan.

This was one of those many charming spots to camp in which make the traveller revel in joy. The air balmy and serene, the prospect grand, the floor of one's little mansion dry and salubrious, the village not too close to mar by its odors and noises, the sky melting from the azure of day into the dark repose of night, where only the stars seemed alive, until the last plaintive wail of the last jackal for the night was blended in the first bark of the most wakeful dog next day. What must it be for a sentimental man to live in scenes like this?

Goats in a flock wending to the river showed us the ford where bushes and wattles laid on the water formed a rude bridge. Then we mounted the little hill, and next Tell Kasrein, to reconnoitre the lake. On both of these are ruins of black basalt, squared as in the giant cities of Bashan. At the eastern top of Kasrein there is one enormous stone, twelve feet wide, and a yard in thickness, covering a subterraneous store or chamber. This stone I observed had been blasted by gunpowder, and, descending below it, I came upon the skeleton of a man, from which I brought back a tooth, to remind me to ask about it. Then they told us that, many years ago, some " Frangi " (that is, somebody not dressed or speaking like Turks) had excavated here for " treasure," but that they suddenly left the spot when an " accident " had occurred; and, doubtless, the skeleton was that of the one who was killed.

Next day the Rob Roy dashed into the reeds of Hijaneh.

* Inspection of these confirmed the evidence of the natives that the branch running south of Tell Kasrein is the larger of the two. Vandevelde marks only one, and that on the wrong side of the tell.

These were from ten to fifteen feet high, counting the root. The longest I obtained was twenty feet, allowing for five feet of immersion, as the water was usually of that depth. These canes were a barrier not easily forced. However, it was quite a different matter here from the slow dull "punting" across a shallow marsh in Atcibeh. My pole easily caught the long stiff reeds, as a purchase to act upon, and, by standing up in the canoe with a compass to direct, and the clumps of canes to haul upon with my hands, I soon crossed right through them, and came into open water, and so landed at the foot of the long hill of the Fashal, which bounds the lake on the south; and thus in the Rob Roy I entered the land of Bashan. Here I left the canoe and ran up the mountain to a cairn near the end, whence a new and splendid prospect opened out grandly from a point not visited before by any traveller, so far as can be found. Our mode of progress was at any rate unique, thus landing on the Hauran* in a canoe, and entering alone upon a district where a guard is always required for protection. My first care was to see that no lurking Arab should intercept my return to the water. For miles around the place was utterly desolate. In case of an armed party appearing, I must be ready to retreat to my boat, and, by gaining the reeds, be out of reach of their guns. Meantime, with cocked pistol in one hand, and a stout staff in the other, I was fully prepared for any single Arab, or even for a couple of them, who might try to make a capture in hopes of the usual ransom. Ruins with huge black basalt rocks crowned the hill-crest, to which I had run up rather than climbed, and the sight all around me was magnificent. The day was bright, the air was clear, no sound whatever came to the listening ear, however still, no moving thing could be seen on that dread wilderness. In the far-off picture, which was all black basalt, I could see the mounds and ruins of at least ten towns, apparently tenantless of man, desolate for ages, but sternly defying time and weather still, and

* Hauran, from the Hebrew word meaning a hole. The people there lived in caves, the "Troglodytes."

telling loudly to the world in their very silence the truth of prophecy, and the sureness of the curse of God. To the north was the wide marsh of Ateibeh, and the unmeasured plain beyond. The Jebel Tinyeh chain stood out from the plain of Damascus, and a long line of snow-peaks gleamed in the blue sky. Hermon, that ever-present mountain, here again asserted his majesty, and pierced the only cloud. From below this, like a long winding thread of silver, the Pharpar flowed, and, sweeping to the south, just under the sun, were the rugged hills where Og had ruled and revelled ages ago. In the middle of this ancient panorama was my pretty little floating home resting by the water-side. All the Bedouins of the desert could not catch us when afloat, nor could they reach me with their rifles, for, in two minutes, I should be hidden by the reeds. At such a moment the Rob Roy seemed more than ever *dear* to me, if such an expression is ever permissible respecting an inanimate object, and as I wended my way down the hill again through huge ruins and rank vegetation, there was a feeling of exhaustion and repletion of excitement, and the conviction in the mind, "I have had strange thoughts here." A chain of far distant pools shone with light to the south. Among those nearer was Bala Lake, but, unfortunately, I did not sketch it. In the fac-simile sketch at p. 162, the farthest water must be Bala, and the long streams of Nimrim,*

* "The waters also of Nimrim shall be desolate" (Jeremiah xlviii. 34). The name occurs again in a passage of such exquisite beauty, and with other names so liquid and grand, that it is inserted here. This is in Isaiah xv. 2-7.

"He is gone up to Bajith, and to Dibon, the high places, to weep: Moab shall howl over Nebo, and over Medeba: on all their heads shall be baldness, and every beard cut off.

"In their streets they shall gird themselves with sackcloth: on the tops of their houses, and in their streets, every one shall howl, weeping abundantly.

"And Heshbon shall cry, and Elealeh; their voice shall be heard even unto Jahaz: therefore the armed soldiers of Moab shall cry out; his life shall be grievous unto him.

"My heart shall cry out for Moab; his fugitives shall flee unto Zoar, a heifer of three years old: for by the mounting up of Luhith with weeping shall they go it up; for in the way of Horonaim they shall raise up a cry of destruction.

while the oak-forests darkened the way to the ancient Bozrah.

In all this panorama of sable rock and hills one man only could be seen, and he was miles away, though he seemed near enough to hail as he marshalled his little flock of desert sheep and a camel, all unconscious that a Giaour was staring at him from the hot sharp peaks of the mountain.

A hasty examination of the ruins marked Betraya in Vandevelde's map found nothing of interest there. But I noticed at once with great delight that there was, indeed, an island on the lake, and buildings upon it. This can be only just discerned from one part of Hijaneh fort, for it is otherwise hid by Kasrein; and I can not explain why I did not remark it from the top of Kasrein Tell. Carefully taking its bearings, I descended from my eyrie, and the Rob Roy was soon again in the thick of the reeds.

By careful steering I reached the spot desired, and was soon made aware of my nearness to it by the tracks of wild boars cut through the reeds as the water shoaled to less than two feet. With necessary caution I went all round the island first, ever ready in an instant to dart out into deeper water, if by misfortune I should come on some sleepy "tusker" who might charge the Rob Roy, smash her to pieces, and leave me helpless on the concealed island. The ground was a few acres in extent, and torn to pieces with innumerable boar-ruts, while for two hundred yards the massive walls of four strong buildings rose to the height of three or four courses of masonry. I determined not to land in so dangerous a place, but with the full conviction all the time that I *must* land nevertheless. Very quietly then I punted in along a boar track and stepped ashore, and with pistol and club stole noiselessly into the silent inclosure. I was the only animal then on the isl-

---

"For the waters of Nimrim shall be desolate: for the hay is withered away, the grass faileth, there is no green thing.

"Therefore the abundance they have gotten, and that which they have laid up, shall they carry away to the brook of the willows."

and, or the others were very well hid. Indeed I have seen only two wild boars at all in the East, and these certainly were not pleasant-looking, with their enormous heads, yellow tusks, and stiff red bristles erect on their back, fully three inches long. I entered chamber after chamber, always pistol in hand, but all was silent. My boat was so buried in the reeds where I had left her that I could not find her again, and for a little time there was a qualm in her

BY A BOAR-TRACK ON LAKE HIJANEH.

captain's bosom, but soon we were afloat again. From observations here and in hunting the wild boar in Egypt years ago, I came to the conclusion that in two feet of water the boar is compelled to swim, and he is then more concerned to retreat than to attack. As I slowly paddled round the shores of this lonely isle, I saw deep at the bottom many huge stones and ruined walls and piers as of a bridge, squared and cut for unknown purposes by unknown men at a time unknown. At the north angle of it there is a channel of open water straight to the shore, in a direction north-west; this is two hundred yards long, twenty yards wide, and with water seven feet deep, so that it was evidently a fortress in old times cleverly placed, though one may well pity the garrison of such a keep. The channel led to a little tell, no doubt an outwork once, and busy with life of a people long since passed into another world.

I know not whether this place had been visited before, but it would be quite easy to reach the island by the merest raft. As for getting through the reeds, that could only be done by a canoe. A row-boat needs room on each side for her oars, and it would be next to impossible to wade, with mud below and four feet of water above, and the reeds between. I brought away one of the twenty-foot reeds trodden down by the wild boars in this island as a trophy for my traveller's museum in the Temple, but to my great regret it was afterwards thrown aside by a muleteer heedlessly. There was great rejoicing in the village at the return of the shaktoor (boat), and until a late hour at night the people haunted my tents, and the sheikh, a fine handsome fellow, had coffee with me to learn the news, which afterwards and for many a day he would retail to his subjects with all the additions which a romantic Arab can so pleasantly hang upon a simple tale.

CHAPTER XI.

Hijaneh Lake. — Jungle. — Plain of Pharpar. — Maps. — Bearings. — Off to Bashan. — Brak. — Stone every thing. — Cut-throat. — Stone Gate and Shutter. — Mr. Bright. — King Og. — Paddle on the Pharpar. — Sources. — Adalyeh. — The winding Pharpar. — Damascus. — Spur of Hermon. — Ice.

OUR next day's start in the Rob Roy was made farther north to survey the rest of the lake, and to determine its nature, depth, and size. Open spaces were frequent, and the countless wild-fowl made the scene lively and exciting. When undisturbed, the noise of these birds feeding all unseen was extraordinary. It sounded like a strong river gushing, and yet it was only the chittering of their bills. The dotted route-line on the map shows the course of the canoe, with arrow-points to indicate its direction. At the round promontory on the north-east I noticed a wolf stealthily drinking, and I landed for battle, creeping low with my pistol and bludgeon, but he decamped with a snarl of defiance. Next the canoe entered a canal, to which a deep channel conducts through the bay. The water was fifteen feet wide and four feet deep, and the current about a mile an hour, between banks gradually higher as we floated along, merrily singing, in the bright sunny day. But after a mile or so of this, as the current increased rapidly, we had to think of the journey against it for return, and so I landed in the wilderness to rest and take bearings.

The next promontory was low, and led out to an insular track of shallow in the lake; so I hauled the canoe over this and entered a second canal. This seemed to be much older than the other, and it had no current, but ended in a deep dry brake with banks nearly twenty feet high. We were told that these two canals were made to drain off the surplus of Hijaneh Lake, that it might not flood the arable land.

The canal first entered was made about thirty years ago, and it leads by the Asyah Haswch to the pool called Bala in Vandevelde's map. When the canoe could go no farther in the second channel, I left her for a walk.

The jungle became rapidly thicker, and exactly the sort of place where wild beasts lie at noon. Numerous marks of their feet were there, and the turf was torn up freshly by the tusks of boars. Having thus gone as far as prudent towards the "Road of Robbers," I sat down on the level plain to rest and enjoy myself and to take compass-bearings. Some at least of these angles were less accurately observed than they ought to be, especially when the fear of robbers and beasts hurried the work of the surveyor, who, besides observing the compass, had to look on each side of him for danger, just as a monkey does when every thing about him is suspected. Perhaps at first sight it may be considered of little consequence to ascertain the nature and shapes of these places, but a different estimate of their interest and importance is formed when we consider their relation to the ancient city of Damascus, the evidence around them of nations once existing, but now extinct, to whom Hijaneh must have been a well-known feature, and besides all this, the halo of undying celebrity attached to the Abana and Pharpar by Naaman's comparison of them with that other more blessed stream we are soon to sail upon.

Let us rest a bit in our tent this fine evening to collect our memoranda from the note-book hurriedly pencilled. Yet it is not easy to withdraw the eye from the beautiful picture before us, framed by the curtains of our canvas boudoir.

Hermon insists on being sovereign of the scene, and there you see him high over all in the sketch opposite. The plain, long-stretching from the carpet at our feet, is that which is watered by the Pharpar, and to the left is the root of the Fashal Tell, while the mound of Abu Zid and other less prominent hills are grouped in front at the foot of imperial Hermon. The villagers have come to gossip and drink our coffee, so the short reverie is closed.

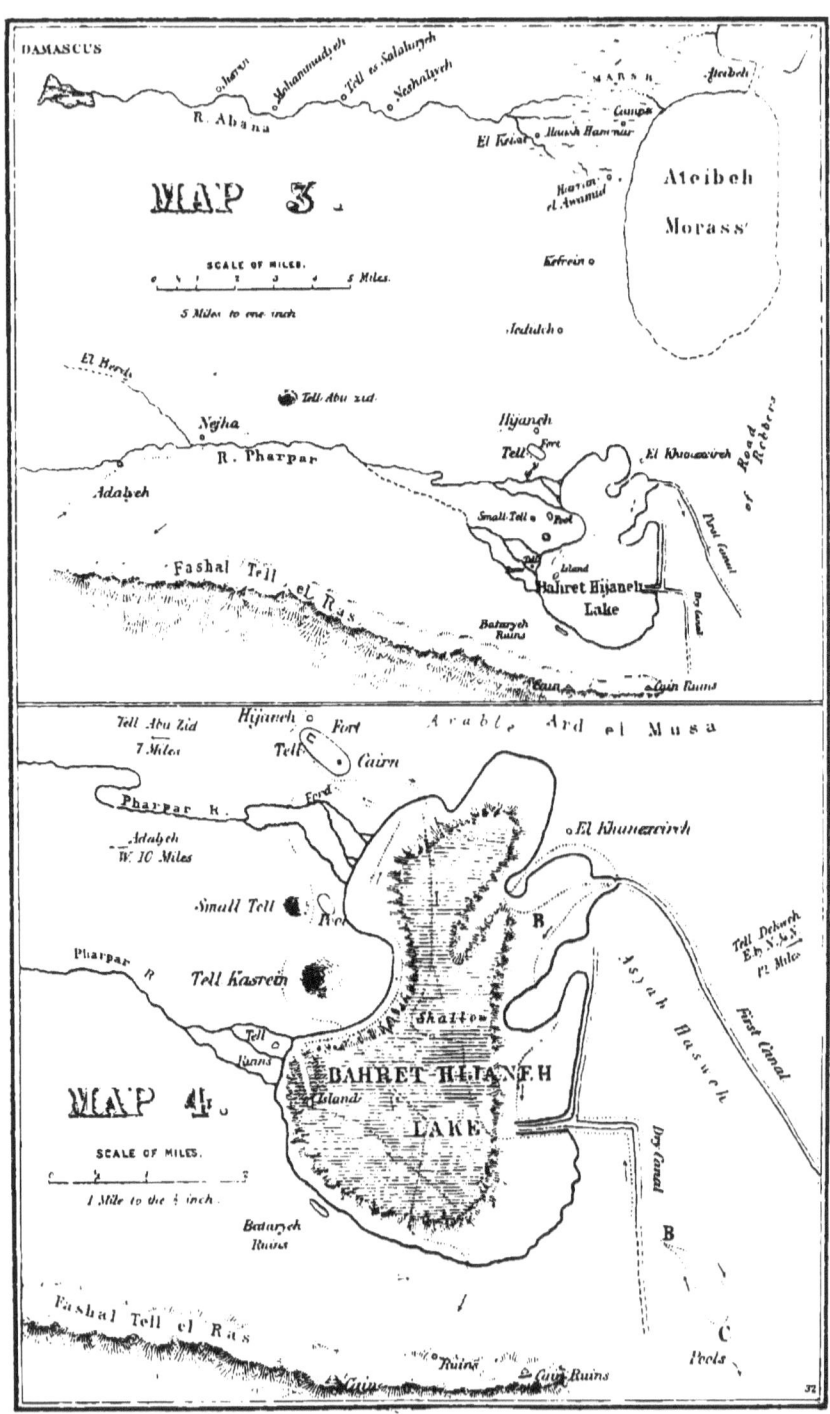

HARPER & BROTHERS, NEW YORK

After examining all the best maps hitherto drawn of this lake of Hijaneh, it is evident enough that none of them have been made by personal survey from each side.* Por-

HERMON AND PLAIN OF THE PHARPAR.

ter declines to imagine where he has not inspected, and rightly merges the lake in the desert without any southern outline, though Hijaneh has a very distinct shore-line all

* Unless the contour varies much in different seasons. But this is not likely here.

round it. Vandevelde's map is distinct, but rather inaccurate. Petermann's is worse, for the whole is imagined, and not even imagined well, though distinctly. Ritter's, however, is the worst of all, for it "lumps" the three lakes in one, and marks all sorts of bays and capes as if they had been accurately surveyed. This pretentious accuracy is equally fallacious in his delineation of the Abana and Pharpar, the Jordan, the Lake of Hooleh, and the Sea of Galilee.

Keeping to facts ascertained by those who have actually seen the places, we may consider it to be proved that there are four lakes; that a channel unites the two northern ones; that the margins of these are vague, and that the Abana runs into them without ever escaping again except in vapor. Also that the two southern lakes, Hijaneh and Bala, are united by a channel, and that the Pharpar falls into Hijaneh only to be evaporated again like the Abana. Lastly, the water in the two sets of lakes does not increase and diminish together, but one may be dry while the other is deep, and *vice versâ*. Probably the Abana and Pharpar, therefore, do not flood or dry up together. One may be more influenced by the melting snow, and the other by rain. The investigation of this interesting point is still open to some careful observer.

The principal bearings obtained by our little compass may now be given from the Rob Roy's log. From these were constructed the maps of the lakes. A few of the bearings are evident mistakes, or at least can not be dovetailed with the rest, but it is better to record them all, with the excuse for a little confusion which any one who follows the Rob Roy will need for himself when he uses together both a canoe and a compass.*

* Those who are interested sufficiently to investigate these bearings in detail, will remark that the maps of the two lakes are connected in *position* only by one observation from Hijaneh Fort, and in *distance* by the interval between Jedideh and Hijaneh taken as a base. The length of this base I could not measure, but estimating it from the time taken to ride over it, Vandevelde's map, and Murray's account, I reckon the distance as nearly two miles and a half. The time occupied in riding from Hansh Hamar

COMPASS-BEARINGS NEAR ATEIBEH MARSH.

From
Harran Mosque ....Tell Dekweh, E. by S.
Haush Hamar Mouth....................Harran Pillars, S.W.
North Mouth of Abana.................Tell el Namy, E.S.E ½ E.
                                     Ateibeh, S. ½ W.
                                     (?) Tell el Khanzir, N.*

LOG OF THE COURSE IN ATEIBEH MORASS.

Time.   Stations   Bearings of Last.
         No.
Started 8 38
   At   9 36......1......N.N.W.
                  2......N.N.W. (tent-flag midway between 1 and 2).
        10 30......3......N.N.W.   Pillars at Harran, W.S.W.
                  4......N.W. by N. (turn to left).
        12 10......5......N.W. ½ N.
        1 05......6......Bearings from this:
                         Harran Pillars, W.S.W. ½ W.
                         Hijaneh Tell. S.S.W.
                         Tent-flag. N.W. by N.
                         Ateibeh, N.N.E.
                         Dekweh Mount. E. by S.
                         Tell Maktil Musa. S.E. ½ E.
                         Tell el Namy, N.N.E.
        The position of Station 6 is marked P in Map II.

COMPASS-BEARINGS IN AND NEAR THE LAKE OF HIJANEH.

From
Hijaneh (N.E. corner of the fort) ....Jedideh. N.
                                     Kefrein, N. ½ E.
                                     Harran, N. ¾ E.
                                     Ateibeh. N.N.E. ¼ E.
                                     Tell Meskin and ⎫
                                     Deir Hagar......⎬ N.N.W.†
Hijaneh (south cairn)..................Pharpar Ford, S.S.W.
                                     End of fort. N.W. ½ N.
                                     End of reeds, E.S.E. ¼ E.
                                     End of next promontory. S.E. ½ S.
                                     Small tell near Kasrein, S. ½ W.

mouth to Hijaneh was four hours and a half, but the ground being very heavy at first, and our horses tired by a long morning's work, our pace was not more than two miles an hour, which would agree very well with the distance given by compass-bearings. 8½ miles. These maps had been printed before it was thought desirable to allow for variation of the compass, which in the other maps is 5° west.

* This was pointed to by the native guide, but it was not seen in the fog.
† This seems too far N. to be correct.

COMPASS-BEARINGS IN AND NEAR THE LAKE OF HIJANEH.

From	
Entrance of first canal (first river in plan at p. 162)	Hijaneh, east end, W.N.W. ½ W.
	Kasrein Tell, W.S.W.
	Bataryeh (?) ruins, S.W.
	End tell on Fashal, S.
	Tell Abu Zid, W. ½ N.
	Jedideh, N.W. ½ N.
Entrance of second canal (second river, p. 162)	Ruins, W.S.W.
	Kasrein, N.W. by W.
	Fashal Cairn, S.W. by S.
	Tell Dekweh, E. by N. ¼ N.
	Hijaneh, N.N.W. ½ W.
Post B, on south bend of dry canal	Hijaneh, N.W. by N.
	Fashal, S.W.
Second start-point on Lake Hijaneh	Ruins, S.W. by S.
	Fashal point, S.*
	Hijaneh fort, N. by W.
N.E. corner of the island in Hijaneh	West corner of Hijaneh fort, N.
	Kasrein to E. covers the rest.
	Direction of the channel to shore, N.W.

I thirsted to see near what I wistfully gazed at in the Hauran from afar, the "Giant Cities" so graphically described by Porter, and I determined to visit at least one of these. For this we went up the Pharpar to Nejha, a little village full of Arab tents, but built itself on so steep a rock that we could scarcely find room for our camp alongside. Next day, leaving our tents, and all our valuables, and with only a mule for light luggage, and with the village sheikh as guide, and one of our soldiers as guard, we rode into the "Land of Argob," as the Bible calls it, the "stone country." Here are the Druses in force, and the Turks have the mere name of possession without rule over the Arab hordes, but an Englishman is safer here than other travellers. They like us, they welcome us, and now and then they plunder us.

This part of our journey need not be minutely de-

* This seems too far W. to be correct, or the point was not that at the end.

scribed, for it has been done well by other travellers. The village sheikh who came with us was mounted on a very small saddle made of bones. His wife was weaving cane mats with black strings, each of them tied to a stone. Bleak was the way amid wave-like hills of unnumbered stones. Camels fed in them nevertheless, and long-haired goats, and the black Arab tents were in many valleys, with the blue smoke listlessly curling towards the sky, but not very particular as to its direction here or there. Rivers marked in the map we found utterly dry. Yet we went down for miles until a blacker black in the distance showed we had come to the nearest "giant city."

This Bashan town of Brak looked like a mass of crags without order until we came close. It was far more curious to behold than I had even anticipated. You come upon a mile of rock and stone in piles, the ruins of the commoner houses along a ridge, and at one end of this you perceive with amazement that fifty or sixty of the ancient houses are still standing almost uninjured. They are built of massive basalt blocks, a stone which resists time and weather, and yet is so rough that it will scarcely slip to tumble down even when ruin has begun. No one can tell when these cities were built.* Porter says it may have been in the days of Ham. We lunch meantime on the roof of one, and then for four hours wander over and under and through the others, at every step more puzzled about them and more pleased.

Stone is every thing here. The town has some hundred stone cisterns, but no well, and the rain-water is stored in these; hence its name Brak (cistern). The walls of the houses are four or five feet thick, sometimes six feet, of roughly hewn basalt. Several houses have the stone well cut, almost polished. Many are of two stories high, and a few three stories. The joists and rafters of the great rooms

---

* Mr. Freshfield, who recently visited the Hauran, thinks that the buildings are modern. They seem to be of two kinds, where very ancient remains are interspersed with structures of Roman character and of a different form, and certainly not "giant" in the height of their gates, or roofs, or ceilings.

are all of stone. Some of these are twelve or fourteen feet long. The doors are large slabs of stone, the stables have stone mangers, and the spouts on the roofs are stone. I could not find any chimneys except holes in the roof, but there were stone cooking-places, and stone troughs in the kitchens. There is no wood here at all, and every single thing is stone. In several houses fine semicircular arches support the roofs of large halls, and until quite lately all these buildings were entirely untenanted. The Arabs like their tents better than any houses, and they even live in tents pitched in the court-yards of the empty streets, and they would not let other people take lodgings here. The sight of this town is a new sensation, a bewilderment; and upon looking at house upon house, built, finished, lived in, deserted, and yet unsought by any of the homeless, houseless folks of this world, there is an inward protest against the conclusion, mingled with a romantic interest in the whole affair. Yet, I regret to say, much of this will be lost to future travellers. They will see the houses indeed, but not so silent and tenantless. People are beginning to inhabit them again. Within the last three years a hundred persons have taken up their abode in this one town of Brak, which Porter speaks of as without an inhabitant at the time he wrote. A man came here from Aleppo to avoid the cruel conscription for military service, which is one of the self-inflicted wrongs of the miserable Turk. He collected others round him who liked this convenient " tenant right," with no landlord to give notice, and no rates to pay. So these people settled in Brak, and now the chief defies the Government to wrest from him his freehold! "By all means," I said, "let us call on him." He was not at home, but his son, a fine youth of twenty, received me well, and I invited myself as a lodger for the night.

Turning to the Turkish soldier who was with me, he said with most courteous ferocity, "I should like to cut your throat, sir;" we told him not to joke with the military, but he said it again, said it to his face, and was in earnest too. However, because of the "Howaja Ingleez," he would let the poor Turk alone. I had a bedroom given to me in this ancient house, the largest and best in the town. Perhaps Og, the king of Bashan, may have slept in the same room; and let me now describe it, after we have swept out all the grain which fills the floor in a heap.

We have entered the yard of the dwelling through a gateway where two massive stone doors still turn on their pivots, and folding together are fastened by a rope through

STONE DOOR OF A HOUSE IN BASHAN.

holes in their inner edges. These slabs are about seven feet in height and six inches thick, and the pivots about four inches long and three in diameter. I can close them with one finger. A stone door of this kind has been sent to the British Museum. Inside the court we find a stable with compartments, all of stone, and up stairs my room is now ready, the steps to it being in the wall outside. The floor is perfectly smooth; the walls, of cut stone, well joined. The window, on a level with the floor, and opposite to the

M

STONE SHUTTER OF MY BEDROOM.

door, is actually furnished with a *stone window-shutter*, four feet by three in width. Somebody may have looked through this window when England was a desert, and long before the Britons were painted blue and hunted the elk in Wessex. A Greek inscription is on a wall of the courtyard relating to some monument, and dated five centuries before Christ. At night I took my candle and went up stairs to bed (holes in some stairs for banisters are noticed), and then read the "Times," telling that the new Ministry had been formed with the Right Honorable John Bright in the Cabinet. My bedroom window stone shutter opened outward. The stone doors opened inward, and when there are two leaves, they overlap. In several of the houses there were small stone rollers to smooth the clay on the roof outside exactly like those now seen elsewhere and described before. One of these rollers was in use at this sheikh's house, and he assured me that he had found it there. Our bedroom is fourteen feet long, and nine feet wide, and eleven feet high. Stone slabs neatly jointed project inward from the end walls, and on them are laid six stone rafters, each ten feet long, and about fifteen inches wide. The stones to support the joists were sometimes let into the wall at a slope, and in other cases with a flat part let in and an angle turned up. Rough stones are laid across these above, and then rubble and earth to form the roof. One side wall has three recesses, about three feet from the floor, each of them about a yard deep and high and wide. These form cupboards, and in most houses in Syria, whether of stone or mud, the very same plan is adopted at the present day. In the stable below the mangers are recesses of this kind, and the oxen eat their fodder from this sort of recessed shelf, the lower ones being open to allow the sheep and goats to pass. It occurred to my mind at once that, as Bethlehem has many houses built against rocks, the manger of the room in which our Lord was laid may have been precisely of this kind, and if so, it would be the very safest and most convenient place in the apartment for the infant Saviour to be placed. At one of the watering-places in the ruins there was assembled a picturesque group of men and women, cattle, sheep, and goats, camels, horses, and asses, all awaiting their turn as a man let down a bucket by a rope thirty feet long, and then poured the water into pots and pans and troughs for the beasts, just as it was done, no doubt, in the days of Og, that lofty warrior-king.

Wild beasts infest these ruins, and they ran about all night wailing with greedy hunger as they scented the bleating kids. The dogs of the house were equally active, and rushed through my room and clambered on the roof, baying at the moon and barking furiously as the wilder quadrupeds shrieked again for prey. The sheikh, a man with long red hair, was most complacent in the morning. He reviled and defied the Turks and their government, and then extolled the English and our gracious Queen. He said the river Khuncifis never ran water, except in heavy rain-storms. This stream is marked in the maps as if it were a regular river. I passed four times over its bed, which had not the semblance of water then, but was tilled and verdant with crops. The river Leiva (or Looa) must be a good deal imaginary. The ground near Brak seemed to be below the level of Lake Hijaneh. The Matkh Brak (marked as a lake in the maps) was dry and covered with crops. The pools I saw from the Fashal and the Bala Lake were not visible from the highest point at Brak, though I spent about six hours there in carefully inspecting all that could be dived into or clambered over.

Returning by another route, we visited Merjany, a smaller town, and with houses just like the others, except that they were utterly vacant and still. As I came near them, riding a mile in advance, a wild-cat skulked in one of the kitchens, the only sign of life. The pavement of the inclosures here was absolutely as perfect as it ever could have been in old times, but no flock ever bleats now in these ancient folds. Brak was grander than this, and, at first, more striking; but the mud now plastered on the walls of the houses full of living men has covered up much of the sentiment there, and which still reigns in Merjany supreme and overwhelming amidst absolute silence, and black gaunt loneliness.

It was a pleasant ride back from the Hauran and the stony land of Argob, and soon our horses' hoofs again sank softly in the rich loam by the Pharpar, and I chose for my encampment a charming bend on the river. The water ran smoothly round a low grassy bank, which was warmed by a genial sun, and dotted with early flowers. How peaceful it was for a moment! But soon our long string of mules came near. Boxes and bundles were loosed from their backs, and quickly sprinkled the sward. Men shouted, and horses neighed. As if by magic, two snowy homes fluttered into being, and the wild plain resounded with hammer-knocks on tent-pins. Perfect method and order always ruled our camp. Lax discipline gains no respect from the Moslem; so, when our red ensign was flung out to the breeze, I left the men to their duties and paddled up the river. The boys of Adalych were frantic with a new delight. The women forgot even to cover their faces. The men ran pell-mell to see the "shaktoor," doubtless the very first boat they had ever seen in their lives, even in a picture. Above the village is a curious aqueduct, and beyond it a sort of dam with a waterfall. Here, as we mount the stream, are the first trees on the Pharpar, and from this spot I could just discern the fort of Hijaneh, near which the river enters the lake. After healthy exercise like this—riding half the day and canoeing the rest—it is pleasant, indeed, to haul up the Rob Roy on the velvet turf, and to enter one's canvas citadel, sure to find every single article, great and small, precisely in the same relative position they occupied yesterday, and every day before.

The thick Turkey carpet, the tressel-bed, the wooden box I had got made at Damascus twenty years before, the portmanteau I had brought from America, the camp-stools, with the large tin basin on one, the cleanest of table-cloths spread daintily, and the brightest of plate; all these, and every little knick-knack, are the same every day, and not an instant is wasted about the furniture of our room, but all attention may be riveted at once upon the splendid prospect outside, seen as we recline in peace and gaze through our tent-door framing this lovely picture. The Pharpar rises in Mount Hermon in two streams. According to Porter, the north and principal branch has its spring in fountains near Arny, and the second rises from Beit Jenin, at the foot of Hermon. These unite after eight miles at Sasa, and form the Awaj,* which then runs about six miles south-east, and then eastward to Kesweh, five miles more, whence it soon falls over the weir near Adalyeh, and meanders quietly to its noiseless end in the lake.

Reveries are sweetest when you are half tired; but the most poetic traveller *must* eat, if it be only as a duty. The jingling of plates and glasses foretells that faithful Hany has elaborated his *ménu*, and Sleman approaches with a low reverence to say it is "hadir" (ready). The tinkling

* Jebel Jar seems to form a portion of the dividing ridge, as the waters flow to Pharpar on one side, and to the Yarmuk on the other. It is near Jebba, in lat. 33° 09′ 36″ N., and long. 35° 52′ 34″ E.—Wilson.

of mule-bells shows the beasts have come from their watering, the quiet outside shows that the men are at rest, the soothing gurgle of the nargilleh proclaims that Latoof is in the height of enjoyment. Our long chibouque, less vocal, is equally serene. Not one disturbing thought or care jars on the mind, not even about the waiter and the "bill." This is luxury, a terrible luxury too, for if not earned by labor and energy, it can not be enjoyed by him who counts the hours that fly.

At least a hundred visitors formed a respectful circle round our camp, all sitting on the grass, until the sun sunk into Hermon's snowy lap. Then one by one they left, the last one being a depositary for all time to come of all that the rest of them had heard or imagined about the wonderful "Frangi" and his marvellous "shaktoor."

Next day she was launched again, and sped down the river swiftly on a rapid stream. The whole course of the Pharpar from this to the lake is dull and monotonous to a degree, without any interest whatever, except as a new lesson in canoeing.

The excessive winding of Pharpar can only be completely realized by following its channel in a canoe. Of course, any other kind of boat would very soon be unbearable in such a river as this, unless the voyager could turn his face permanently backward. Though the stream ran from four to five miles an hour, and my speed over the land must have nearly doubled this in actual progress, yet the Rob Roy was two hours in accomplishing a distance between two points which the mules, at an easy walk (under three miles an hour), finished in thirty minutes. Thus we may estimate that the channel bends so much as to make the river's length about seven or eight times as much as the real interval measured upon a straight line.

To exhibit this more clearly, I have given here in the plan a copy of my map of half a mile of the Pharpar. In nearly all rivers we have a bend to right and left of a general course. In some there is a "wind within a bend," but in the instance referred to on the Pharpar it will be seen that in several parts there is "a turn within a wind within a bend."*

Some of these gyrations were performed in so small a

HALF A MILE OF THE PHARPAR.

compass that Hany used to stand still on the bank and converse with me while the Rob Roy carried its crew away from him, and then back again several times, but yet seldom out of sight during the excursion.

It would have been waste of time to spend it on much of this work; so at the bridge where the "Hadj road" takes the Mecca pilgrims over the river on their long tiresome route to the air-hung coffin of the Prophet, the canoe was brought ashore.

Here we part from the bare and bending Pharpar, so slow, so silent, so solitary; winding to the lake to die, and yet in dying to rise again—a subtle vapor drawn up to heaven by the sun. There in the sky it meets the rapid Abana, which has rushed over rocks and through the ancient city, and then oozed to the marsh, and has melted into a cloud. We leave these streams, that we may see their rivals in Palestine, and so answer the question of the Syrian prince, "Are not Abana and Pharpar, rivers of Damascus, better than all the waters of Israel?"†

On New-year's Day the Rob Roy returned to Damascus. It is easy to lose count of the days of the week while we are travelling among people whose mode of reckoning them is not ours. And one collateral benefit to the traveller from the Sunday rest (besides its refreshment to soul, and

---

* At Nejha, the river Berdy runs into the Pharpar, according to Vandevelde's map. In Porter's, no confluent is marked here. The stream at Nejha appeared to me only a tiny canal, banked up behind the village, and being but two feet wide in many places, it was not large enough to embark upon. Unfortunately I forgot to notice accurately the junction of these rivers, but my impression is that the water of the canalette was wholly absorbed in irrigation. † 2 Kings v. 12.

mind, and body) is the preciseness with which it checks the computation of time's unnoticed flow.*

At Damascus again the Pasha came to see the canoe with his suite. He spoke French, so we could converse, and he asked very pertinent questions. He is an earnest Freemason, and a clever agreeable man. His dress, semi-European, was a bad compromise between the two kinds of costume—theirs so loose and flowing, so bright and graceful, so useless for action, so dreary in rain; and ours, as a contrast, fitting our forms, dull in its color, but perfection for manly exertion, and exposure to sun and storm. Damascus has never yet, I think, been well described, and the reason may be that the traveller who has enough acuteness to paint a good word-picture of the town has sense enough to see that it is a sentimental humbug. In vain he tries to feel an admiration which he can not support by the appearance of the place. It may be the oldest, but, in wet weather, it surely is the filthiest of towns. It may be rich, but the mud walls are what you see, and not the wealth. Damascus is a disappointment; its situation is its chief beauty, and, once inside it, you can not realize that outside these dirty lanes, tumble-down walls, gloomy shops, and crooked bazars, are the lovely groves, the gushing fountains, the teeming gardens, and the glorious hills. For the fourth time, then, I leave Damascus, and without any deep regret.

After a night at our old quarters in Dimes, we wended round the spur of Hermon to Deir el Ashayeir, with its splendid temple.†

* Some years ago, I entered Cairo on Christmas Day—the bursting of a waterskin for the camels having deranged our set days for travel—and we overtook a party of Englishmen, whom we had journeyed with some months before. "We shall have our turkey together to-night," I said; and they inquired with surprise, "What turkey?" "Why, of course, at our Christmas dinner," I replied; and they answered, "Christmas? we have eaten our Christmas pudding ten days ago!" They had tried to gain time by losing Sundays.

† A curious incident is mentioned in the remarks on this place and its people in Murray's Handbook:

"This is a small village, inhabited by a few families of Druses and Chris-

The mountain pass between this and Rukleh presented a totally new set of difficulties to the traveller carrying a boat. In the marsh and quagmire of Ateibeh it was the horse one had to fear most for. In case of his sinking, his legs might be easily broken; but the canoe in falling there would at least descend upon reeds and rushes and water, and from a diminished height.

But now we had a narrow, steep, and very crooked path, at sharp angles, down, down amid slippery rocks, projecting trees, loose stones, and deceitful mud, where the two men could seldom hold the canoe steady as the cold winter blast from the snow alongside us swayed the lofty top-heavy burden this way and that with unwonted violence. In some places the ice under our feet gave way suddenly with a crash. In others the gnarled trees blocked up all passage, or the sharp jutting rocks made it impossible to get the boat through between them. This was the sort of work that really tries a dragoman by difficulties entirely new in his experience; for who ever before carried a long delicate boat on horseback over these rocks in winter?

Hany behaved splendidly in this business. A dozen times we had to carry the canoe by hand, or to slide it down cliffs, guiding it by the painter, until the horses, left to themselves, could find their way down to meet us below.

Muscular strength and sheer pluck and endurance were needed for this, combined with gentleness, caution, and judgment, and backed by indomitable perseverance. One slip of their feet on such rocks would have smashed our best oak plank in a moment; one sign of ill-temper would

tians; the former, like their neighbors of Halwy and Yuntah, have a bad character, and deserve it. They are the hereditary pests of the Damascus and Beyrout road; never missing an opportunity of shooting a postman, or plundering a caravan. Franks, however, have little to fear from them; indeed they look upon the English as their friends and protectors. On one occasion, some years ago, a Yunta chief committed a most cold-blooded murder by night, in a house in Sûk Wady Barada; but having learned the next day that the English Consul of Damascus had been sleeping in an adjoining room, he sent him a polite apology for having unconsciously disturbed his repose, and assured him that had he known the Consul was there, he would have postponed his work to a more suitable time."

have dissolved the allegiance of our muleteers, who must have been sorely tried at times to put an end to the cause of all this trouble and toil—that incomprehensibly useless Rob Roy, carried so far and so tenderly for a purpose they could not possibly appreciate, and requiring that the boat should be handled so softly while their own limbs were bruised, their shoes and garments torn, and their steps directed with peremptory exactness into mud, or shingle, or ice-cold water, all for its sake. Yet the men had learned to love the boat (who would not, if he had any heart?), and when they did not like the canoe, they feared it. They saw it do things impossible to be done in any other way. They were promised good payment for success; they deserved this, and they received it.

CHAPTER XII.

Rukleh.—Bust of Baal.—Mount Hermon.—Kefr Kuk.—Rasheya.—Search for Jordan.—Earliest Spring.—Jordan's Eye.—Sad Loss.—Leeches.—The Hasbany.—Wady et Teim.—Hasbany Source.—First Bridge.—Start on Jordan.—Colored Cascade.—Pitch-pits.—Jordan Vale.—The Litany.—Storm.—Dripping Bedroom.

RUKLEH is a curious place, and not like any other. Our tents were pitched there in a deep valley, hemmed in by piles of the sharpest gray rocks tumbled one upon another in extraordinary confusion. Climbing these, you soon perceive that once, in time gone by, every nook of the jagged heights had been occupied. Endless winding avenues; gardens hanging upon steeps; huge walls girding amphitheatres where the slightest level space admitted of any such expense; and ruins and temples and altars harbored in rock clefts, all lone and speechless now, but once, no doubt, sounding out a busy life; and tombs and sculptured caverns, the longer-lasting records of ages of death—all these are crowded, almost huddled, together in Rukleh. To sit on a high peak and look upon it all is very quaint. Some hours passed here richly rewarded the steep clambering, and from a rugged edge, out of sight of the camp, there were splendid glimpses of the dark Damascus plain: while sheer down below there gaped two huge chasms just like the crater of Etna. At the foot of the larger temple here is a large medallion in stone, about four feet long, representing a human face which stares out straight upon Hermon, while its curly locks hang on both sides. Most likely this countenance is intended for the face of Baal himself.

Wistful glances could not be restrained from eying Hermon here; it would be so splendid a summit to gaze from on all the land of Israel. The ascent is easy at a proper season; but now, with fresh snow every day in the cold of January, I came reluctantly to the conclusion that the main object of the tour must be kept to, and the water of lakes and rivers was our proper field.

Yet it was impossible not to urge the plea that the very source of the river we were now to examine was up in that white shining snow which clad the high summit above us, burying the temple there in its soft bosom, and streaming down as the long folds of a robe to cover the valleys beneath. Nay, that snow itself had, no doubt, come up from the Jordan and the Pharpar, and was only resting now for another devious journey when once more melted from its cold sleep by the summer's sun.

Porter's description of the ascent of Hermon and the view from the top must have incited many travellers to enjoy the climb and the prospect. Respecting the general features of this mountain, related as they are so closely to the "waterways" we are to traverse in the canoe, I venture to extract his account.

"The name *Hermon* was doubtless suggested by the form of this mountain, 'a lofty conical peak,' conspicuous from every direction; just as *Lebanon* was suggested by the 'white' color of its limestone strata. Other names were likewise given to Hermon, also descriptive of some striking feature. The Sidonians called it *Sirion*, and the Amorites *Shenir*, both signifying 'breastplate,' and suggested by its rounded glittering top, when the sun's rays were reflected by the snow that covers it (Deut. iii. 9; Cant. iv. 8; Ezek. xxvii. 5). It was also named Sion, the 'elevated,' towering over all its compeers (Deut. iv. 48; Psalm cxxxiii. 3). So now it is called *Jebel esh-Sheikh*, 'the chief mountain,' a name it well deserves, and Jebel esh-Thelj, 'snowy mountain.' When all the country is parched and blasted with the summer sun, white lines of snow streak the head of Hermon. This mountain was the landmark of the Israelites. It was associated with their ideas of the northern border almost as intimately as the sea was with the west. They conquered all the land east of the Jordan, 'from the river Arnon unto Mount Hermon' (Deut. iii. 8; iv. 41; Joshua ix. 12). Baal-Gad, the ancient border city before

Dan became historic, is described as 'under Mount Hermon' (Joshua xiii. 5; xi. 17), and the north-western boundary of Bashan was Hermon (1 Chron. v. 23). In one passage it would almost seem to be used as a synonym for 'north,' as the word *Jam* ('sea') was for 'west,' and the word *Kibleh* (the shrine at Mekkah) is now for 'south'— "The *north* and the south, Thou hast created them; Tabor and *Hermon* shall rejoice in Thy name' (Psalm lxxxix. 12). The reason of this is obvious. From whatever part of Palestine the Israelite turned his eyes northward, Hermon was there terminating the view. From the plain of the coast, from the mountains of Samaria, from the Jordan valley, from the heights of Moab and Gilead, and the plateau of Bashan, that pale-blue snow-capped cone forms the one feature on the northern horizon. The 'dew of Hermon' is once referred to in a passage which has long been considered a geographical puzzle—'As the dew of Hermon, *the dew* that descended on the mountains of Zion' (Psalm cxxxiii. 3). *Zion* is probably used for *Sion*, one of the old names of Hermon (Deut. iv. 48)."*

* The snow on the summit of this mountain condenses the vapors that float during summer in the higher regions of the atmosphere, causing light clouds to hover around it, and abundant dew to descend upon it, while the whole country elsewhere is parched, and the whole heaven elsewhere cloudless.

Hermon is the second mountain in Syria, ranking next to the highest peak of the Lebanon, behind the cedars, and probably not more than 300 or 400 feet lower than it. The elevation of Hermon may be estimated at about 10,000 feet. The whole body of the mountains is limestone, similar to that which composes the main ridge of Lebanon. The central peak rises up an obtuse truncated cone, from 2000 to 3000 feet above the ridges that radiate from it, thus giving it a more commanding aspect than any other mountain in Syria. This cone is entirely naked, destitute alike of trees and vegetation. Here and there gray, thorny, cushion-shaped shrubs dot the ground, but they can scarcely be said to give variety to the scene, they are as dry-looking as the stones amid which they spring up. The snow never disappears from its summit. In spring and early summer it is entirely covered, looking from some points of view like a great white dome. As summer advances, the snow gradually melts on the tops of the ridges, but remains in long streaks in the ravines that radiate from the centre, looking in the distance like the white locks that scantily cover the head of old age. Late in autumn only a few white lines are left, round which the clouds cling until early in November, when the winter raiment is renewed.

The little lake of Kefr Kuk soon attracted attention in our journey from Rukleh to Rasheya, for the surrounding hills were complicated in their watersheds, and it was necessary to be on the *qui vive* for the very first streams that enter the Jordan.

The lake was full,* and waterfowl played upon it in merry whirling groups; but who could be astonished by these crowds of wild birds after seeing the myriads circling on the bare lake of Menzaleh, or rustling in the reeds of Hijaneh?

It was a charming day's journey over this district to Rasheya, with weather perfect overhead, and clear, crisp, silvery hoar-frost, melting into shining drops as the sun rose warm.

All this was singularly fortunate for allowing the canoe horse to pass.

Yet we had to carry the Rob Roy by hand over many obstructions, and amid much difficulty and delay. On all these occasions the operation of dismounting her had to be carefully performed. First, Adoor held the horse's head; Hany and Latoof loosened the girths which strapped the canoe to the frame; then they bore her each with one arm, the post of danger and responsibility in every instance being that in the rear, where it is harder to see one's footsteps and to advance or retard the pace, or to raise or depress, or move the boat sideways through or over rocks, stumps, or other obstacles.

The horses followed, or found their own way. It was play to them; and to the mules the worst places seemed alike with the best, always managed with patient intelligence—indeed, they were often quite hilarious under their heavy loads, and many a caper they cut with redundant energy. Each of the animals had plainly a distinct char-

---

* A hundred yards from the shore the water was three feet deep, with soft sandy clay below, and rapidly shelving. Hany assured me that in summer this basin is often quite dry. Its waters may percolate to Jordan, but I can not see how they could run there over-ground, so as to constitute the lake a perennial source.

acter and mode of thought, but each had a high opinion of his own importance, and would fling out his hoof at a neighbor with playful jealousy of precedence, or a sort of rough humor if his rival was a friend. The donkeys alone had always true dignity in their gait, never stopping, never prancing, ever sure to find out their way somehow or other, and often enduring many a needless thwack with stoical indifference.

To get past Rasheya there is a cut in the rock, for many hundred yards only about six or eight feet wide, and the same in depth, with the roughest footing for horses, and so narrow and slippery that we had to carry the canoe all the distance, about half a mile, and thence reached the pretty hamlet of Bekafyeh, where a lovely meadow gave ample room for the camp; and all the villagers sat looking on in mute array until the latest moment that the cold night wind could be braved.

In these altitudes day and night were as summer and winter in the change. Sometimes I was cold even in bed with five blankets over me and my thick cloak, besides my day-clothes all kept on, though beneath the sheets. It was not very easy to write up a journal with fingers tingling, but perfect health makes even a frost-nip enjoyable.

Early next day I went off alone to scour the country, in eager hope of finding the first springings of the sacred river. Even Vandevelde's map was at fault here, and no wonder my way was soon lost entirely for the rest of the day. But little mattered that, or any trifling hardship: with such an object for pursuit, one could readily pass the night under the coldest, loneliest rock.

From the hill north of Bekafyeh, and between that and El Akalab, I found streams from a tiny spring forty feet below the sheep-path, but on following it, these only sank back into mother earth exhausted.

From the same point could be seen two pools on the west side of the valley, and bearing W.N.W., but they appeared to be shut in completely.

Searching again very carefully—for now was the right

time to find the Jordan's source, when no rain had fallen for weeks, and the cold hindered snow from melting—I noticed a spring in a field, south-west from which a streamlet wandered past a house. This gradually increased in definite direction and size, and at last ran down the bare sides of the Wady et Teim, where was the dry but ample bed of the Jordan channel. This is here full of huge white stones and mountain-gravel, with steep sides, and the water-worn

AIN ROB ROY.

tract of a powerful stream, which no doubt runs deep with violence and great volume in stormy times, though the river it forms then is only of surface water.

My little streamlet tumbled into this dry bed—the earliest water I had seen actually on its way to the Dead Sea. Dismounting, as the only way to investigate, I forgot all about my horse in the excitement of the inquiry. The rivulet fell in a pretty cascade over a horizontal ledge of strongly stratified rock, about thirty feet wide and five feet thick, with a deep grotto-like cavern hollowed out beneath and forming a beautiful background to the water, which, after its fall, is gathered together again as a clear brook, and runs down among stones into the desert rocky sun-dried channel we have before described.

About thirty feet to the north-west of this point is the ruin of a little building, with only one pillar erect, and two prostrate in the grass. Evidently this had been built here to look upon the bright cascade, for no other view is open.

Has this ever before been recognized as the youngest babblings of Jordan?* May it not now be regarded as the water farthest from the mouth?

The opposite bank is steep and rugged, and, as I climb-ed the crags, one stone at the top looked rather *unnatural*, and this on inspection proved to be the jamb of a sculp-tured gate still erect, and about eight feet high. Beside it lay (north and south) a well-cut slab, the lintel of the door, which must therefore have looked straight upon Hermon splendidly rising in front, as the other Baal temples do, from their posts round the mother-mountain of the idol's cult.†

Along both sides of the glen are many hewn stones, so scattered and mingled with the natural rocks that only a close inspection can detect the difference. A wall lies near to the river's brink on the eastern side, a sort of quay of huge stone blocks, but the water of our fountain, once it has run into the channel, seems too soon satisfied by as-serting its claim to be Jordan's earliest rivulet, for it dies away in the sand and gravel. Only a few pools appear be-low this, though I followed the very precipitous banks closely, and had to cross the dry bed of boulders many times to get along by any means.

Of course there was no road here, and, walking myself,

---

* The stream that runs into the Hasbany Pool was remarked, in 1834, as having "its origin to the W. or N.W. of Rasheya." The pillars were sketched separately, and are more distant in reality from the bed of the rivulet.

† Bekafych is not visible from this stone, but, judging by the smoke of the village, it bears E.S.E.

I drove my horse from point to point, where he could be tethered to graze, while his rider clambered up and down in the exciting search.

Three gazelles pranced out of the wild rocks gracefully, and I chased them on horseback through many a turn, always keeping above them, but in vain, for they were never within pistol-shot.

The position of the hills and villages on distant peaks puzzled me now exceedingly. Vandevelde's map is certainly incorrect in this district, at any rate, in its names for places.

Wishing to take bearings again, I discovered that my compass was missing. Only one who has become fond of such a silent but self-moving thing like this, his "intelligent" companion in months of happy solitude, can tell how sad was such a loss.

How could this have happened? Surely in chasing the gazelles. Shall I give it up as hopeless to find the compass again? But how can I survey the waters of Merom and the Sea of Galilee without a compass? A minute's weighing of doubts, and I resolved to go back and trace, if possible, all my devious zigzag from where I had last used the compass upon the ruined temple slab. My poor horse, already wearied, seemed to wonder at this backward move. How much I wished to explain to the faithful spirited beast that dire necessity imposed this threefold traverse of one way!

It was only when by long labor we arrived in sight of the prostrate stone that I could see, and with delight, the little brown box still lying on its surface, open to the sun and telling its own tale silently, with the needle ever true, and no one there to regard it. Thus three hours were added to my wanderings, and at length I descended to a mill very deep down, where a confluent from the east brings in an ample stream by Es Sefiny—undoubtedly, then, the first continuous water of Jordan.

Three men were in this deep glen, and I begged for bread, being very hungry. They laughed outright to see me roll up their wafer-like scones and bolt them in a moment. But they refused all payment, for they were Druses,* and I was an Englishman. One said he had been at Beyrout, and liked the "Ingleez," for they were "tyeb keteer" (exceedingly good fellows). When he had guided me over the hills, and would take no pay, I got off my horse and shook both his hands, and we parted. The country was now rough and stony, with deep deceitful valleys, which seemed at first quite possible to cross, but on trial were reluctantly acknowledged to be impassable when one had got halfway down them into the shade; and after much of this work, and plunging about in a deep morass, I forced my way to the western road, and there found Hany overpowered with anxiety and long waiting, but with the canoe reclining quite at ease by a pretty stream, fit place for a wanderer's dinner. It was under a steep rock, and in some of the clefts of this we found several small leeches. How they came there was a mystery; how they lived there without a shred of moss in the stony holes, not two inches deep, was still more wonderful, but there they were and lively too.†

It was night when we crossed the first bridge which spans the Jordan, a short distance below the highest recorded source, not far from the village of Hasbeya, which is perched on a knoll encircled by hills, and gives its name to the river itself, here called Hasbany, as if it were still too small to be called Jordan, being only a babe among streams, and not yet christened by its own great name.

The travellers who have camped here all speak with favor of the lovely spot: the spring flowers and crocus spangling the green grass, the deep shade of olives, the graceful oleanders by the banks of the young and beautiful river, cradled here in hills, and watched over by great Hermon, stately and shining, the prince of them all.

---

* The name of this strange sect is derived from Derazy, their founder, in the eleventh century, and their original centre was at Hasbeya, in this neighborhood.

† This is called Ain Alil, the "high fountain."

It was a happy walk, on January the 7th, to wander up the glen and rest by its deep crystal pools, listening with rapture to the eloquent voice of solitude. But these waters, we were assured by all who know them (and Vandevelde had the same information),* are only winter rivulets.

The sketch given below represents the outlines of the country through which they flow, and whence we had come in search of the earlier stream, as seen from the cairn on the hill above the bridge. The Hasbany is winding in the glens below, but it is hidden there until it sweeps round the foot of the hill on which we stand, on the top of a cairn marked C in the sketch, and which is about east from the bridge.

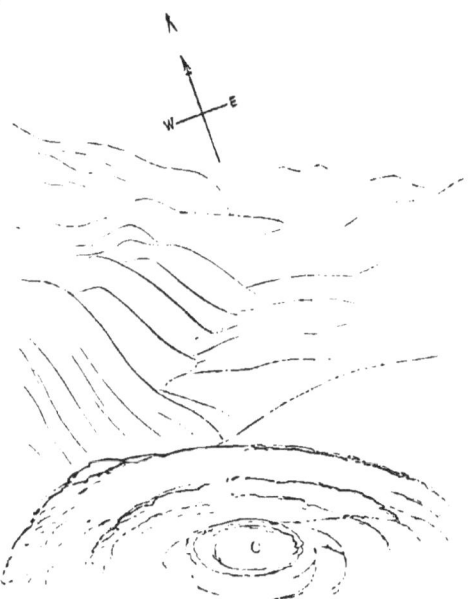

WADY ET TEIM, NORTH OF HASBEYA.

Young Jordan is like the prettiest tiny stream in Scotland, with white hollowed rocks and weird caverns, but

* Vandevelde's "Syria and Palestine," vol. i. p. 128. The high fountains of Jordan are described by Wortabet in "Journal of Geog. Soc." vol. xxxii. p. 101.

the gravel is prettier here than any in my own land; pebbles of yellow and bright blue banked in by fruitful loam of a deep rich red, and all so silent and unaffected. So it winds until steeper rocks gird the water, narrowing where wild beasts' paws have marked the sand. Returning from a long ramble, we came to where a bold cliff dips into a pool of deepest green. Here I launched the Rob Roy, certainly the first boat that ever floated on the pool. The few natives round us stopped in wonder, sitting—that is their posture for lost astonishment. They assured us this pool of Fuarr is a thousand feet deep.* It is entirely unapproachable for sounding from the cliff overhead, so imagination has full sway to fancy it fathomless. The cold matter-of-fact sounding-line let down stopped short at eleven feet. I was astonished at the illusion, for the water

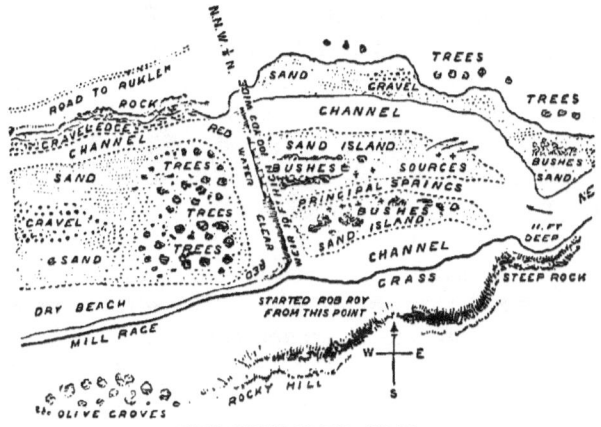

FIRST SOURCE OF THE JORDAN.

here looked any depth you please. Of course the people did not believe my word for this, but nevertheless it is a sturdy unromantic fact that less than two fathoms measures this abyss.

The plan here given was carefully sketched from the

* Newbold says it "appeared to be of immense depth." In the above plan the pool is marked at the right.

hill above, and corrected from various other points, as representing the true beginnings of Jordan.

Just opposite the cliff, and a few yards away, is a three-cornered island of sand and small gravel, with many low bushes on it, and luxuriant spotted clover, and under and from out these there bubbles, gurgles, and ascends the first undoubted subterranean source of Jordan.*

There are about twenty of these very curious fountains on this islet, and the water runs from them in all directions. That which pours out towards the north runs a few feet *up the stream*, being at first a foot higher in level. The island and the rocks near it are formed into a weir, for the terribly practical purpose of supplying a mill. Perish all the mills and millstones that spoil the birthplace of such a stream! But the weir, happily, is moss-grown, and delicate cascades tumble through its broken edges, unite below in a narrow pool about 150 yards long, under the fall of ten feet high, and then escape at one end, just as in the great falls of the Zambesi, if these could be scanned on a Lilliputian scale.

Camp struck and all things packed, we floated the canoe again just below the falls, to begin our descent of the river. In front was the bridge, with two pointed arches about eighteen feet span,† and sixteen feet high, with a narrow roadway of twelve feet broad, and only three or four small coping-stones left upon the edge. The stream was swift and shallow here, but it occupied only one arch of the bridge.

It was thus on the loveliest of sunny days that we shoved off from shore to begin the Jordan, and the iron keel of the Rob Roy sounded sharp on the pebbly beach as she gladly rushed into the water, with a cordial but faint and doubting cheer from the thin attendance on the

---

* This, the Hasbany, was first noticed as a source of the Jordan by Fürer von Hämendorf, in A.D. 1566 (p. 206, Nürnberg, 1646, see Newbold's paper, 1856, p. 15). Next Seetzen did the same, then Burkhardt and Buckingham.

† These were studiously measured with an umbrella 33 inches long. Newbold gives the length of the bridge as 135 feet.

SOURCE OF THE JORDAN, NEAR HASBEYA.

bank, every one of them certain that now, at any rate, she must capsize.

The sketch of the bridge, and the weir and the island of springs above it, I made before starting.*

I saw that the numerous rapids now to be encountered would endanger my paddle, so a long pole was taken aboard, and, as I might have to get out often, it was more convenient to adopt the plan of sitting first used at the Rheinfelden rapids on the cruise through Switzerland, and which was always found very good for such places. For this you sit, not in the "well" of the canoe, but on the deck astern, with your bare legs in the water, or tucked up in front, when you have learned to be very steady. This action, of course, raises the bow of the canoe entirely out of the water, and by depressing the pole to the rocky bottom below you can *drag* it hard over stones and gravel, so as to retard the speed in a powerful current, and, indeed, to stop altogether if this be necessary, and if you do not mind the cold waves invading your seat from behind.

As the stream bears the boat among rocks, you meet them with one foot or the other in the water, balancing carefully the while, and see that you do not meet the rocks with *both* feet at once, or the canoe will instantly pass away from under you altogether. If you are whirled on to a shallow, the bow runs in so far that you can stand on the ground and allow the boat to pass on (keeping hold of the painter) until, in wading alongside her, the water gets too deep, when you spring on the stern again, and so are charmingly ferried over.

* A part of this sketch appeared (a good deal grandified) in the front page of an April number of the "Illustrated London News." The village visible north of the source is that called Mimes. The town of Hasbeya is not seen from the river, as it is perched on a hill, quite encircled by higher mountains. Rabbi Schwartz says of this (p. 65): "The Jewish inhabitants of the town of Chaspeya carry their dead across the stream to Abel al Krum, because they have a tradition that the river Chaspeya formed the boundary line of Palestine, and they wish to inter the dead on the Holy Land. But this boundary line was only so after the return from Babylon, as I have shown at the proper place above." A tributary falls in from the east near the ford.

After a little practice I found it not very difficult to get out from the " well " to the deck of the canoe without stopping the boat, even in rough water, and this saves a great deal of time. Indeed, the variety of positions and pranks that the canoeist can practise with advantage and pleasure in paddling, punting, poling, sailing, towing, and dragging his faithful floating house over land and water, soon makes him weary of the everlasting monotonous swing of a row-boat, where he goes into dangers and beauties back foremost, gains no rest from a favoring breeze, and smashes his oars, or his boat's hull, or his own face, whenever there is a narrow among rocks, or an eddy among trees.

The river bends below the bridge with all the waywardness of a trout-stream in the Highlands. Thick trees hang over its clear surging waters, and reeds fill the bays twenty feet high, while rocks, and a thousand hanging straggling creepers on them, tangle together over silent pools. Who had seen these before the Rob Roy? It can scarcely be supposed that any other boat had been here, and so no man had yet looked on these earliest beauties of the hallowed stream.

I had often to get out of the canoe, and to drag her over or round obstructions, and sometimes we went down a mill-race for variety, until at last the white tents of my camp shone homelike through the thick trees. The sketch at p. 204 represents this part of the river.

Torrents of rain poured upon us all the night. The last rain we had met was on December 17, so that the Jordan had been seen at a time of drought (for winter). This was exceedingly fortunate, both for an auspicious beginning of the voyage and for a special examination of the effect of rain upon the river.

Next day, therefore, I rode back to the waterfall, and the flood pouring over it was now bright red and resounding. But it was not all thus colored. In the middle, and where the stream from the subterraneous springs came over the fall, only the brightest, clearest, limpid water came. It was a piebald cascade, red, white, and red again, curious, though not more beautiful than if no such phenomenon appeared. The full stream now occupied both arches of the bridge, and ran wildly, careering over islets that were warm and dry the day before. The rain continued, and next day I came back to look at the waterfall; but there was the same crystal gushing between muddy torrents. Once more, and to certify the fact, I returned early next morning, and still it was the same—the unsullied waters from the deep-fed fountain—protesting in unchanging purity against the fitful upstart surface-puddles of a passing storm. These rain-flows had no right to mingle with the true source born high in the snow of Hermon, and running below through dark channels in clean rocks, far out of reach of rain.

The current had doubled in force and volume, and its ruddy waves welled high over the banks, and covered the trees a yard deep, roaring the while with anger, and by no means inviting to paddle upon. So I climbed one hill after another round the camp, and from each had a new and splendid prospect.

It was a pleasant walk to Hasbeya, where eight hundred Christians were so barbarously massacred in 1860; but now they have Missionary Bible Schools there—the true retribution of Christianity.

There are some curious bitumen-pits near the Jordan. The people live beside them in very simple huts, and they go down fifty feet into the earth to fill baskets with the black shining treasure, which "grows," they say, however much they dig.

A climb up the hightest hill on the west had shown me clearly all the Hasbany vale. Looking north, one sees on the left a hill range north and south bounding Wady et Teim, and from it smaller white knolls are trending always eastward. A parallel group of conical hills is to the right of this, and again another larger one to the east. Through this last the Hasbany cuts its way steadily, meandering southward, while eastward again are wedge-like ridges and the long roots of Hermon, but its head is in the clouds,

VALLEY OF JORDAN.

sullen and dark. To say the very least of this scene, it was at any rate *curious*. What it would seem if bereft of its holy associations and the remembrance of a hundred armies that came this way from Babylon or Parthia to the battleground of Judea, I really can not tell, having failed (and willingly) in every attempt to look at the vale of Jordan as a mere river's banks.

Then I rode alone over the hills to the river Litany, where it bursts through cliffs one thousand feet high, and is crossed by the bridge of Burghuz. This is said to be the old river Leontes,* which rises not far from the Abana, and runs south as if trying to find an exit that way. But the hills rise into mountains on either side more impenetrable, until at last, as if with a desperate effort, the torrent cuts straight through the west range in a gorge of magnificent grandeur, and so it rushes out to the sea.

I wandered long without road here, over many a rugged and bleak mountain, and returning by the village of Kaukaba, which clings to its perch aloft on the scarped hill, I found our tents newly pitched on a fine grassy mound; in fact, the roof of an old deserted khan.† Nothing could

---

* But Stanley remarks that Ritter shows this to be a mistake, and that the Litany had no ancient name, except the "Tyrian river" ("S. and P." p. 414 *d*). Now it is called the Khasmyeh, the "divider," perhaps because, after a long course south, it cuts its channel westward.

† Marked K on p. 204, where B shows a bridge. When a map is so very good as Vandevelde's, it may be presumptuous to add to its information, or even to correct. Still I venture to make three remarks: (1.) There is a good road to Khan from the Hasbany source on the west side, and without

look prettier than this for a place of camping, but it was a great mistake to pitch the tents there. For at night there arose a furious storm of wind, almost a hurricane. Each moment I feared the worst—that the tent would fall—and then what to do? Of course to get out from the ruins, if not already wounded by the tent-pole; but what next? The other tent and my men were a long distance off, and between us were several holes in the arched roof upon which our camp stood. To fall down any of these would be instant death, and in the dark it was impossible to see them, because no lantern could live in the gale, nor, in the din, and darkness, and confusion, could we recollect exactly where these holes were.

To care for the Rob Roy was, of course, my first thought —the men being in a safe place, and the horses and mules ensconced in strong quarters below. I lashed the canoe to the earth, mooring her like an iron-clad in a cyclone, yet the wind still lifted the light little craft, and a sad remembrance came into my mind of a gale in the Baltic, where my canoe was so blown about *on land* that in my efforts to hold her down I was upset several times myself, and was bruised and spattered all over with mire.

The first strange thing one notices in a storm under canvas on shore, is that, however violent the wind, it is the tent only that shakes under the pressure. The strongest stone house vibrates even in the lower stories in a gale, but unless your bed in a tent actually touches the canvas walls, the sleeper is perfectly unmoved, while the roof and walls of his tabernacle rattle and quiver as if they never could hold out for a moment. And is it not a good thing in the storms of life to have the living soul, the real self, firmly set on the rock steadfast and unshaken, though blasts do harry and shatter the frailer tabernacle wherein we lodge?

passing the bridge (not marked). (2.) There is a road from Khan to Burghuz, by the hill defile, without going to Kankaba (not marked). (3.) "Zuk" is marked here as the name of a village, for "Suk," which indicates the "fair" held at this place.

As this was the first good honest storm of rain and wind which this new square tent from England had endured, I was careful to see how it stood the trial. For resistance to the gale it was perfect. The excellent ropes, the long iron tent pegs, the sturdy pole, and the doubled laced sides, so well pegged down all round, these sufficiently kept the wind from getting under the canvas, and unless you can do this in a tent, the whole structure gives way in an instant.

On a former tour a storm overtook us at Gaza, and both our tents were overturned, when at once the wildest confusion ensued. Water ran deep on the floor of softest mud. Wet canvas caged us in. Camels and horses entangled in the ropes, and screaming, fell in a jumble together in the dark howling night, and all the men roared and bellowed at each other to calm the excitement, as in duty bound, according to their light.*

As to wind, then, our English-built tent was secure, but not as to water. The seams of the roof, instead of being along the edges, where the inclination is strongest, and therefore the rain runs fastest away, were joined in the middle or flattest part of each slope of the roof. In an hour or two, therefore, water worked through this, and soon it came through the inner tent too, until at length the rain fell sprinkling cold on my face in bed, and then methinks the laziest sleeper *must* get up.

But for just such times as these I had brought a piece of sheet water-proof, seven feet long and five feet broad, the cover of my cabin in the canoe, and this secured aloft over the bed received the invading stream, and conducted it in a continuous patter all to one corner, where it could run off harmlessly, and with a sweet harmonious lullaby that gendered sleep even in a dripping bedroom.†

---

* In the great storm of 1839, in Britain, a small bell-tent, pitched on a gentleman's lawn, near Belfast, was swept off by the wind, and was carried a distance of nearly *fifty miles*.

† The ornamental dentellated "flaps" round a tent's roof make a ceaseless disturbing chatter in high wind. This I could not put up with, though not

Sunday came next, with morning bright and warm. The grass was soon covered by our wet dismantled garments spread out to dry, and a half-sleepy life began after the sleepless night. The only pleasure was that listless one of quiet, and a feeling as if one was having one's hair cut by a dumb hair-cutter—the rarest case in London. Still the neutral stagnant hours of such a time are not altogether without benefit. Dreamy tiredness has its slow-paced thoughts, and they may not be brilliant or deep, but they are very pleasant. These are breaks in the lines of life's story, but they may give emphasis to the quicker action which comes after. The compulsory rest of illness is a different pause, though it also has its benefits, some of them inestimable; but what I speak of now as pleasant and profitable is that half-slumber of mind in a healthy but unslept body, relaxed, not lazy, when peace and fine weather are outside, no pain within, no particular anxiety, no feeling that "it is all our own fault," and no doubt is felt that the very best thing to be done (unless we mean to lose time) is to rest entirely all to-day. Our more orthodox slumbers at night were rudely broken by loud shouts and bustle. Every body seemed to run everywhere and to knock down every body, and all this was only because a wild beast (species and genus probably imaginary) had alarmed the horses. Hany immediately fired four volleys into the universal darkness, "to compose" us all.

very nervous, but "silence for sleep" is a good maxim, so I had these useless appendages sewed firmly down. The tent-maker who would make a good tent ought to live in a tent in a storm to acquire experience.

CHAPTER XIII.

Across Jordan.—Bloody Fray.—British Officers.—Our Ignorance.—Jordan's Streams.—Tell El Kady.—Dan.—Laish.—The Golden Image.—Sounding the Source.—Justice and Mercy.—Name of Jordan.—El Ghujar.—Hazor.

THE first valley of the Hasbany ends a little below Khan. Wady Sheba, a tributary, enters it on the east, crossed by a two-arched bridge. Then the two ranges of hills close in upon the river, which tumbles and foams and hisses between them, a headlong torrent, quite impossible to put a boat upon for several miles. Therefore we carried the Rob Roy across it here, and round or over the mountains towards the next source of Jordan.*

A FISH FROM THE HASBANY.

We are now on *terra firma*, and so my tale must be brief, for it is meant to be only a *log* of the waterways, and my pen should be quiet when my paddle is ashore.

The bridle-path on the east side of Jordan was very troublesome for the mules. Once, and for the first time, the Rob Roy's horse fell on his knee over a broken stone. I heard the shout behind me, and looked round stoically prepared for a catastrophe, but nothing happened.

A very old bridge led us over a noisy torrent, hastening its tribute to the Hooleh plain. The canoe was floated

---

* A Greek priest, fishing in the river near the bridge, brought me his whole bag as a present. It consisted of two small fish, very like trout. A sketch (natural size) of the smaller one is given here.

over, but at the same time there came a string of asses, each bearing a huge load of fragile earthen jars made at Hasbeya el Fokas, and now carried for sale into Bashan. These were cleverly packed with one great pot in the centre, and the others grouped round it in light matting. The sure-footed asses trod their ways thus laden, when one single fall or one brush against the jutting rocks on either side would have instantly smashed the whole cargo.

The men joined us for company's sake, and our midday meal was spread beside the beautiful stream. Later in the afternoon, when suddenly rounding a rock, we came upon a fray. One of the pottery merchants had driven his ass near a field to avoid the mire and marsh alongside, and the owner of the unmarked domain instantly rushed at him and broke his ox-goad upon the offender's head, which instantly streamed with blood, while the unappeased assailant whipped out a long curved dagger, and was just aiming a blow when we appeared. Our muleteers closed upon the man in a moment, seized the sharp dagger and pitched it into the marsh, and then brought up the prisoner for judgment. The sentence was that he must run the gauntlet of our avenging muleteers, but at a suitable wink from me he was let off a moment too soon for their preparations, and I never saw a man run away faster than he did. The district did not seem to be a peaceful one for residence. A short time before three dead men had been found under a tree close by. Not far from this Hany had taken a party of travellers, three English officers. At night the Arabs came and stole all the horses. Next day they had the impudence to send for a sum of money, and then again for, at any rate, half the sum. Hany waited until next morning early, and found the Arabs all asleep in a mill, and the stolen horses inside. The officers, each with a double-barrelled gun, were quietly posted so as to command the sleeping robbers, who were then awakened, and in sudden bewilderment of fear they allowed the horses to be quietly recovered by their owners. Vigorous means were taken to force the Turkish government to bring these

O

men to justice, and at length one and all of them were hunted up and punished.*

All endeavors could not repress the increasing excitement which this part of the journey stirred in my mind. Now the Rob Roy is to enter on territory absolutely unknown and yet world-wide in its interest, where new discoveries are possible and likely, but only to the traveller journeying thus. Some parts of the Danube, it is true, are entirely inaccessible by land, and so these were first seen when the Rob Roy wandered there four years ago. Large portions of the rivers which she descended in Norway were also first unveiled to her. But what part of the Norse Vrangs or the Hohenzollern Donau can compare in interest with the bends of holy Jordan? Yet in the brief run of this venerated river, so looked upon by mountains, so watched by ancient tribes, and so often pencilled by travellers, there are actually portions which no map delineates rightly, because no observer has been privileged to see them. For ten miles the course of Jordan is almost unknown, or its description at any rate is not published, and three miles of this interval have most probably never been seen before.

* In a former journey in Asia Minor, I recollect two British officers of the Guards were attacked by sixteen robbers, who stripped them of almost every bit of dress, and even of their rings. Long, tedious "representations" ended in nothing.

In 1849, while among the Greek islands, becalmed in a little schooner, I heard the sharp rattle of musketry, and the big boom of cannon behind a hill. To get at the cause of this we entreated the captain to lend us the boat. Pirates were at their work, and had murdered the crew of a brig. This we told at Smyrna, and instantly an English war-steamer, then in port, started in pursuit of the sailors' common enemy, the robbers of the sea. We were informed afterwards that the pirates were captured, and seven of them were hanged.

These instances are cited to show how much may be done for the repression of crime (which is the sad but dutiful prerogative of true humanity) by the power and influence of the wiser and more powerful nations, acting even in the Moslem's land of hot-blooded murderers. But since the "massacre year" (1860), and the energetic action of England and France, the peace of the high-roads and the security of the towns of Syria may be said to have become "tolerable," considering the people who rule, and the people who are ruled, there.

Of Palestine itself we are shamefully ignorant, though the whole area of the country is not larger than Lancashire and Yorkshire together. Jerusalem, in a sense the metropolis of the world, has still many nooks not even visited by men who can use their eyes and pens, and yet all that is left of that city would easily be contained in Hyde Park. In full keeping with this unaccountable ignorance of the Holy Land and the Holy City would be our acquiescent permission for the Holy River to run on with any portion of it still untraced. Jordan is the sacred stream not only of the Jew who has "Moses and the prophets," of the Christian who treasures the memories of his Master's life upon earth, of the cast-out Ishmaelite who has dipped his wandering bloody foot in this river since the days of Hagar, but of the Moslem faithful also, wide scattered over the world, who deeply venerate the Jordan. No other river's name is known so long ago and so far away as this, which calls up a host of past memories from the Mohammedan on the plains of India, from the latest Christian settler in the Rocky Mountains of America, and from the Jew in every part of the globe. It is not only of the past that the name of Jordan tells, for in the more thoughtful hours of not a few they hear it whispering to them before strange shadowy truths of that future happier land that lies over the cold stream of death.

Therefore, as our view of the wide plains under Hermon opened southward, it was with an intense impatient longing to reach such scenes of interest. Step by step brought our caravan nearer to the waters of Merom, and our gaze was soon riveted upon the heavy silent morass that had so long guarded the unseen course of Jordan.

Meanwhile our horses plunged about in very wet ground on the plateau above Hooleh, where there are several ruins worth visiting, until, deserting the usual track as almost impassable (in winter), we reached the well-known Tell el Kady by a way of our own. Here is the ancient historic source of Jordan, and though the real source is, as we have seen, a long way farther north yet this latter has only been acknowledged about three hundred years, while the springs we have come to visit now were known and reverenced ten times as long ago. As the Jordan itself attracts us most, because of the part it has played in history, rather than the course it now runs as a river, so its ancient reputed source will always command more attention than the actual origin of its highest waters; and we may enter somewhat minutely into particulars here because the springs of this stream so renowned are precisely what the Rob Roy came from afar to see.

Tell el Kady is situated on the east side of the Hasbany, which runs crooked here and out of sight in a ravine torn roughly rather than cut by its furious waters. About us is a ragged bleak jungle of stream-worn plateau shelving southward gradually, then at a quicker slope, some five hundred feet, down to "Ard el Hooleh," a district low and level, about twelve miles long, and five or six in width. This is bounded by the hills of Naphthali on the right, and those of Bashan opposite, until these two chains approach in the distant horizon, and clasp the little lake of Merom glittering in the sun. So sweeps the gaze of the eye until, satisfied, it rests once more on the giant mountain, ever present in the scene, but now, for the first time, behind us—

> "That lifts its awful form,
> Swells from the vale, and midway leaves the storm;
> Though round its breast the rolling clouds be spread,
> Eternal sunshine settles on its head."

The tell itself is a mound of great size, and its shape, as will be seen by the plan on page 215, is rectangular, with rounded corners. Its length is about 300 yards, and the breadth 250 yards.* The space within is hollow, and nearly flat, while the sides or walls are like those of a railway viaduct, with an average height of thirty feet, but much higher at the south-west end, and steep.

* Captain Wilson's estimate. It appeared somewhat larger to me. Other travellers have strangely cut it down to half the size, even Vandevelde, Porter, and Newbold.

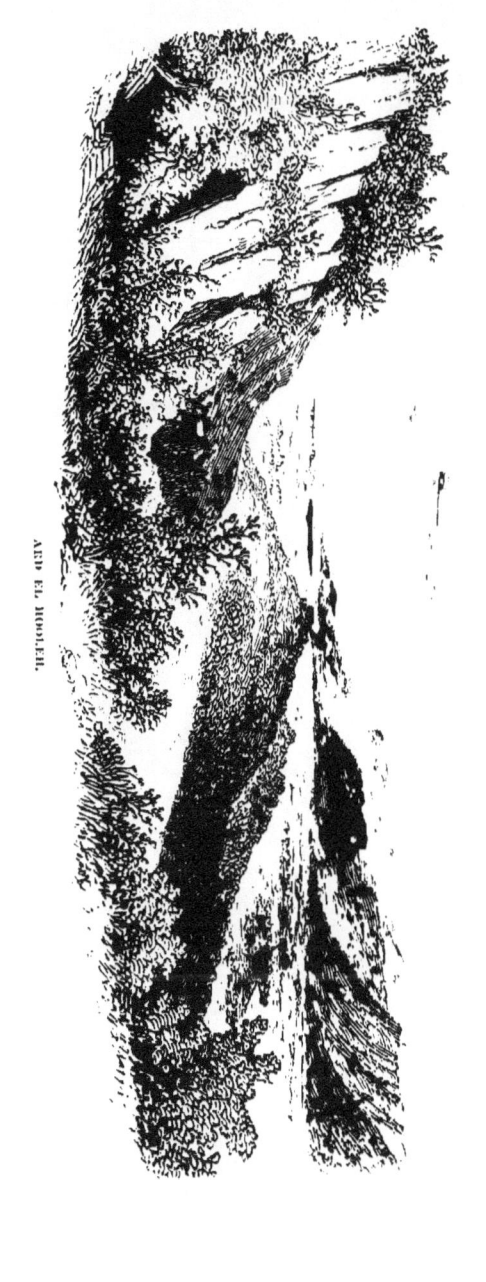

AIN EL MODLEH.

Ruins are at various parts visible all around and within and upon the mound itself, which seems to me to be wholly artificial; but it is said to be partly formed by a volcanic crater.

At the south-west corner of the tell is the reputed spot where the idol was set up by King Jeroboam.*

The word "Dan" in Hebrew means "judge," and "Kady" in Arabic has the same meaning; and there seems to be no doubt whatever that the town of Dan once stood where now is Tell el Kady. But Dan itself

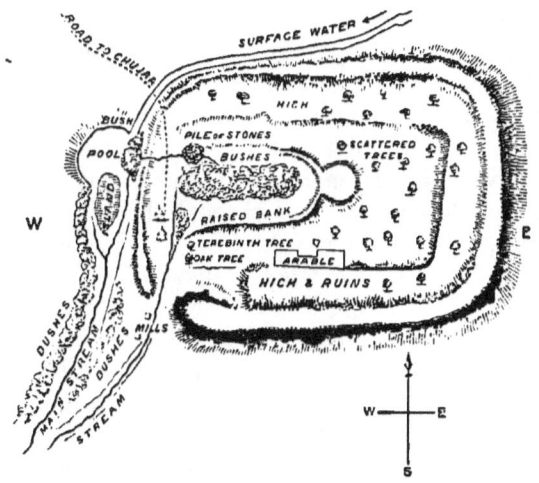

SOURCE OF THE JORDAN AT DAN.

had formerly an older name, as we read in the book of Joshua (xix. 47), when he speaks of the various tribes receiving their inheritance by lot: and the coast of the children of Dan went out too little for them: therefore the children of Dan went up to fight against Leshem, and took it, and smote it with the edge of the sword, and pos-

* This is related in 1 Kings xii. 28–30: "Whereupon the king took counsel, and made two calves of gold, and said unto them, It is too much for you to go up to Jerusalem: behold thy gods, O Israel, which brought thee up out of the land of Egypt. And he set the one in Beth-el, and the other put he in Dan. And this thing became a sin: for the people went to worship before the one, even unto Dan."

sessed it, and dwelt therein, and called Leshem, Dan, after the name of Dan their father." A more particular account of this incursion is given in the Book of Judges,* where we are told that the Danites, feeling their border too narrow, sent five men out to spy the land, and they came to Mount Ephraim. Here dwelt Micah, a man who had stolen some money set apart by his mother to make an idol with. He had found a young Levite, whom he appointed as his priest, with a salary of ten shekels a year and his board.

The five spies met the young priest, and talked with him. Then they "came to Laish, and saw the people that were therein, how they dwelt careless, after the manner of the Zidonians, quiet and secure; and there was no magistrate in the land, that might put them to shame in any thing; and they were far from the Zidonians, and had no business with any man. And they came unto their brethren to Zorah and Eshtaol: and their brethren said unto them, What say ye? And they said, Arise, that we may go up against them: for we have seen the land, and behold, it is very good: and are ye still? Be not slothful to go, and to enter to possess the land. When ye go, ye shall come unto a people secure, and to a large land: for God hath given it into your hands; a place where there is no want of any thing that is in the earth." The Danites then set off and passed Micah's house, and after some parleying, they enticed the Levite to come with them as priest to their band, which numbered six hundred chosen men.

"And they took the things which Micah had made, and the priest which he had, and came unto Laish, unto a people that were at quiet and secure: and they smote them with the edge of the sword, and burnt the city with fire. And there was no deliverer, because it was far from Zidon, and they had no business with any man; and it was in the valley that lieth by Beth-rehob. And they built a city, and dwelt therein. And they called the name

* Chapters xvii. and xviii.

of the city Dan, after the name of Dan their father, who was born unto Israel: howbeit the name of the city was Laish at the first. And the children of Dan set up the graven image: and Jonathan, the son of Gershom, the son of Manasseh, he and his sons were priests to the tribe of Dan until the day of the captivity of the land. And they set them up Micah's graven image, which he made, all the time that the house of God was in Shiloh."

But Tell el Kady, besides its claim to attention as being Dan, and farther back old Laish, is the spot where the Jordan issues from the deeps of the earth in a noble spring, said to be the largest single source in the world.

In the four-sided inclosure already described is a most tangled thicket, quite impenetrable to man, and perhaps almost to beasts. Round it is a low quadrangular raised dais, and the remains of what once was evidently a splendid amphitheatre, often, perhaps, thronged with spectators of the idol's rites.

Scattered trees, still in some sort of order, dot the wide space beyond, but the thorns of the brake itself, a dark and thick screen even in mid-winter, must be ten times more dense in spring, or in the luxuriance of summer growth. These cover a hidden pool, which defies all efforts to enter its retreat, but, under a pit half filled by heaps of old gray stones,* you can just hear the smothered murmuring of pent-up secret waters, and on the west side of the embankment, beneath a mass of fig-trees, reeds, and strongest creepers, the water issues free into the day, and filling up to the brim the circular basin a hundred feet wide. Here the new-born Jordan turns and bubbles, and seems to breathe for a while in the light, and then it dashes off at once a river, with a noisy burst, but soon hiding its foam and waves in another thicket, and there its loud rushing is

* These should be taken out by the Palestine Exploration Fund. Something worth finding is likely to be there. Josephus, when describing how stones were heaped upon a dead body after a battle, plainly indicates that the body was in a hollow, and so the heap would only fill up this to the level of the ground about it, which would therefore be unnoticed in a few hundred years.

shrouded in darkness as it hurries away to the mysterious plain.

In much less time than is required to read these lines, the Rob Roy was dismounted and was floating on this pool, while the muleteers stood round to see, but now quite prepared for any wonder. After their recent experience of the boat on the Abana, the Pharpar, the lakes of Damascus, and the swift Hasbany, they thought that the canoe could do any thing she tried.

As before, so now, they told me this pool also was bottomless, and, to be prepared for the strange current gurgling from below and circling about in all ways right and left with uncertain eddies, I sat upon the deck with my legs in the water and a sturdy pole in my hands.

Behold the abyss of the Dan source of Jordan, it is only five feet deep! After a full examination of it all, the canoe was carried to our tents, which were pitched inside the inclosure, and almost hidden by the rich foliage of the inner stream. This last* has been led to the south-west corner of the mound, and then through that (broken down for the purpose) it rushes out to turn a mill, which nestles among the brambles, and seems half ashamed to drive its trade just under the old altar of the golden calf. A splendid terebinth and a not less splendid oak droops over this little stream, and the soft breeze of a dank evening waves the countless old rags hung upon the branches in honor of some long-dead worthy of the Mohammedan sect.

A crowd of men came next day as a deputation on the matter of the ass-driver's broken head. These pleaded for our pardon. His bloody cheeks and gashed forehead urged grim justice. After long parleying to establish the enormity of their offense, I gave an Englishman's merciful sentence, and restored the dagger we had captured in the fight. Then all of them went off well pleased and—quite

---

* That all the water in both the confluent streams comes evidently from the same source within the inclosure is, I think, quite clear on examination. What is hid from the eye is plain enough to the ear, in the pile of stones.

ready to do the same deed again! Not long ago it was a matter of risk to camp long in such a place as this, even with guards. But here we settled to stay and without any escort, and I roamed the savage country round without any attendant whatever. No bravery is needed for this, but only quiet attention to a few simple rules.*

We are now at the second source of Jordan, and the stream that gushes forth here from Tell el Kady is named the Leddan. Of the three several fountains which form that wonderful river, the Hasbany may be considered as the Arab source, the spring at Dan as the Canaanitish source, and the fountain at Banias as the Roman source.

Josephus speaks of Dan as at "the fountains of the less-

---

* One of these rules was not to heed *one* man at all, but if two were in sight, and they seemed to be in concert, then to go straight up to one of them, when the other was sure to come too. I had my pistol then, not a revolver, but a far more useful weapon, with only one barrel, and a bayonet which jumps out when you touch a spring. This I have carried on such occasions for twenty years, and find that, when people come near in out-of-the-way places, and some of them are *curious*, an admirable effect is produced by asking them to "look" while the bayonet leaps out. Arabs (of this prowling sort) all know the revolver well, and there is no excuse for exhibiting it to them; besides they would ask to handle it too. But the other pistol is a novelty, and one can offer to show it as such. The moment the bayonet darts out, there is sure to be surprise, or even a start; and while its unexpected power can be exhibited (and with the bayonet thus fixed, you are a match for any man quite close), the show has the *air* of a gratuitous favor, not a warlike challenge, though virtually it is a vivid symptom that one party at least is ready for action.

With more than two men, a single traveller does wisely to rely on moral means alone. If actually attacked by three armed Arabs, his chance would be small indeed, and suppose that he was justified in killing two, and able and willing to do it, the vengeance of their more distant comrades would be certain. With the whole tribe it might become a religious duty to wipe out blood by blood.

Besides this, it is to be remembered that, while one man or two might attack to rob and plunder, the united advance of more than this would usually be made with the intent, not to murder or to rob, but to capture and get a ransom. The first kind of attack is mere footpad's war; it is right to resist, even according to the laws of the wildest horde; but for the second—the endeavor to catch a European, who has not taken the proper course of procuring a guard or escort—there is more than a shadow of reason in favor of the aggressors, and one can not forget that other tribes than these have drawn their broadswords for blackmail.

er Jordan,"* and an imaginary derivation was early given†
and even long maintained for the very name of "Jordan,"
as compounded of "Ghor" and "Dan." But the name of
Jordan occurs in the time of Abraham, five centuries before
the title Dan was given to the town of Laish. The Jordan
is never called in Scripture "the river" or "brook," or by
any other name than its own; and it may be considered
as proved by Robinson and Stanley that the word "Jordan" is only the word Iarden of the Hebrew, which signifies "the Descender"—rightly due both to the fast flow
and the enormous fall of the river, which also "descends"
into the earth lower than any other in the world.‡ The
Jordan is also said to be the most winding of rivers, but
the Pharpar certainly winds more.

After examining the runlet of surface-water which bears
a muddy tribute into the clear pool of the source at Dan,
and being satisfied that this is only the drainage of the
morass behind, and is dried up entirely in summer, I rode
to the old Hasbany again, which had cut its channel so
deep as to have eluded our sight towards the end of the
day's journey. This ride was very difficult, when so much
rain had lately drenched the teeming plain. For an hour
Latoof and myself were struggling through water-courses
and thick bushes. In two of the four larger streams the
current almost carried us away. Arrived at the river, we

* "Antiq. of the Jews," book v. ch. iii. sec. i.; and book viii. ch. viii. sec. iv.
† Even in Jerome's time (Robinson, vol. iii. p. 352); and in the Talmud.
‡ Stanley says that only the Sacramento has so great a fall as Jordan has from the Lake of Galilee to the Dead Sea ("Sinai and Palestine," p. 284). The physical features of the river in general will be alluded to in a summary farther on.

Captain Newbold differs in some particulars from those in my notes. He says the mound at Dan is about 300 paces in circumference, that the volume of water is at least as much as from the Banias fountain. He cites an Arab authority for the usual erroneous supposition that the united stream enters the lake "nearer its eastern than its western angle." He says Abulfeda called the Jordan "El Urdun." ("Journal of Asiatic Society," vol. xvi. pp. 12, 13). He considers it highly probable that Banias was Baal Gad (p. 27). He never mentions the papyrus, though a list is given of the plants about Jordan. His paper is, however, the most full description of Jordan's sources hitherto published.

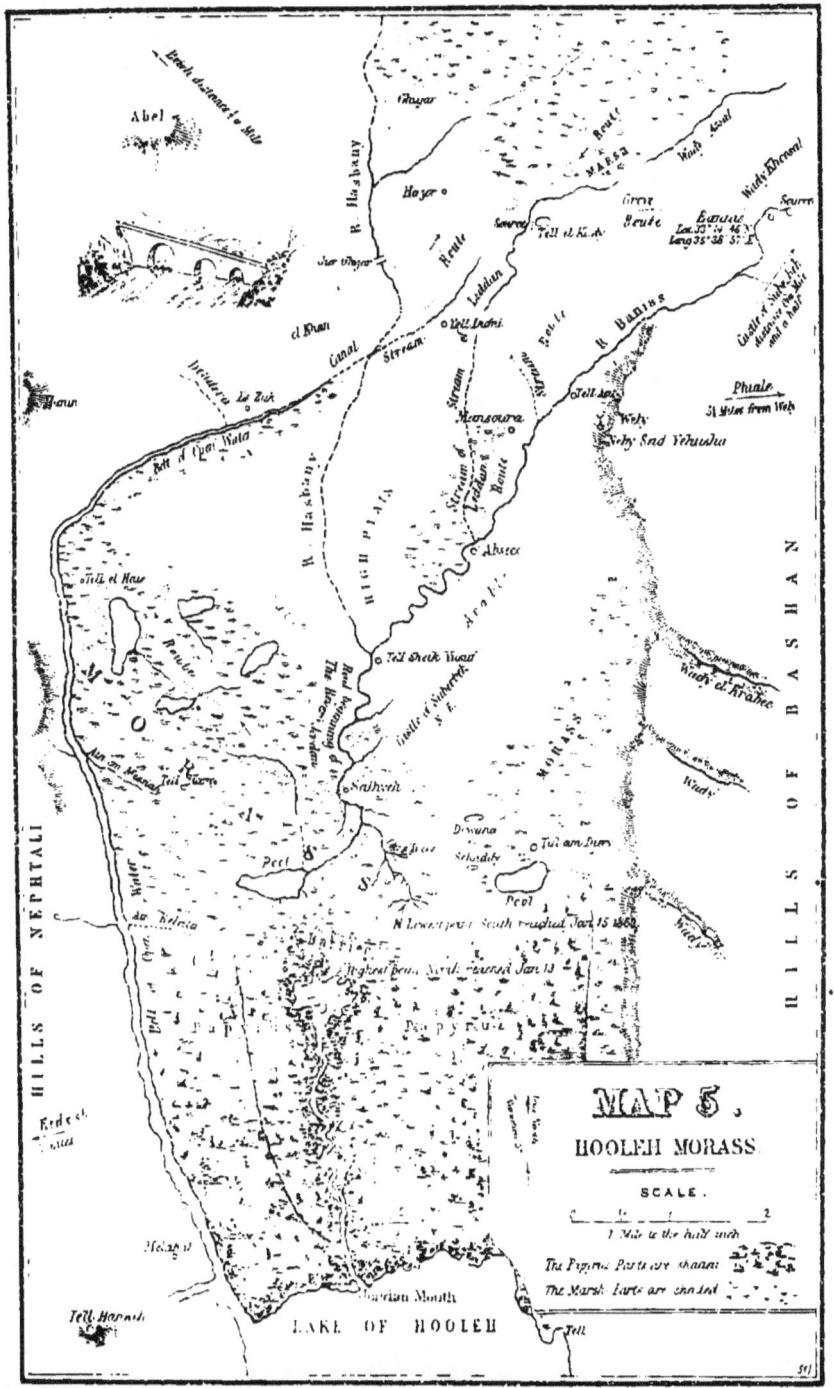

followed it for a mile down to the bridge of El Ghujar,* which with three crooked old arches, all of unequal spans, crosses the Hasbany as it roars in a wild glen. The bridge itself is, of course, more easy to reach, even on a dark winter's eve, as being in some sort upon a thoroughfare; but we then turned, where no path leads, along the Hasbany to its latest traverse of the high plateau before the torrent rolls over headlong into the Hoolch marsh. Latoof was thoroughly well versed in the intricate waterways of this wold; and unless he had been so, it would certainly have been dangerous to make such a circuit, with night approaching, and when every streamlet was swollen into a red and angry torrent, and several times so deep as to cause us to hark back and try to ford elsewhere.

But for this toil there came reward in finding, for at least a mile, huge blocks of stones laid out in circles and squares, far too many and too big, and in a place too wet, to be old Arab camps, but plainly, in my opinion, the relics of a very ancient city. These stones extend quite up to the river's bank, which here is very steep, and their weather-worn aspect, their enormous size and vast numbers, their strange aggregations, wherein form and method were clearly visible, though amid such confusion and wreck, impressed me very strongly with the conviction that this might be the site of ancient Hazor. Other travellers have been here, and usually not in winter. In dryer seasons they could, therefore, move more easily amid these stone blocks by riding on harder ground; but their bare desolation in January was better than the high rank undergrowth of summer for exploring, and it also enforced our attention by laying bare great numbers of these stones at once, and giving to the whole scene a wide significance. Care-

---

* Finn says ("Byeways in Palestine," p. 370) that his guide called the river itself El Ghujar. Porter does not seem to mention this bridge as El Ghujar. Wilson saw the water running through only the western arch, but it filled all three channels during my visit. The bridge is 65 paces long, and four paces broad; two of the arches are slightly pointed, the third being round. A rough sketch of the bridge I have inserted in Map V. The Luisany enters near this as a tributary.

ful examination of some of the stones showed that a proportion, at least, of them had been hewn. I looked for inscriptions in vain, but the writing of old time was there without letters; and I would earnestly suggest that this district should be far more diligently scrutinized than it appears to have been from what is told about it in travellers' books.

Subsequent examination of the texts in Scripture and the Maccabees and the notices by ancient and modern authorities upon the site of Hazor have convinced me that De Saulcy is right in his supposition that Hazor was here. In his "Journey round the Dead Sea and in the Bible Lands" (1854), he describes a visit to this place, and how he found the ruins of a vast building like to the Temple in Gerizim in plan. His investigation seems to have extended chiefly along the southern ledge, but much farther north I found the ruins quite as thickly strewn. Three venomous snakes from under the stones attacked De Saulcy's party. This, and the utter devastation of the scene, may well remind us of the prophecy of Jeremiah (ch. xlix.) —" And Hazor shall be a dwelling for dragons, and a desolation forever: there shall no man abide there, nor any son of man dwell in it."

CHAPTER XIV.

Banias.—Cæsarea Philippi.—Cavern.—Josephus.—Three Streams of Jordan.—Phiale.—Our Saviour's Visit.—The Great Question.—Peter.—Crusaders' Keep.—View from Subeibeh.—Anxious.—Mansoura.—Parliament. — Catechism. — Costumes. — Nose-rings. — Water-ways. — Bright Eyes.—Enter Arabs.

THE Rob Roy had now floated on two of the great sources of Jordan; but another and the most interesting had yet to be seen.* This is at Banias, about an hour's pleasant ride from Tell el Kady eastward though a well-wooded district and over springy turf. Here we are just within the bounds of the land of Israel, reaching " from Dan to Beersheba;" and here at once we come upon a hallowed spot, for Jesus himself had tarried in the place, had wrought there miracles of mercy, had spoken deep loving words of wisdom, and had manifested forth his heavenly glory after a manner never seen elsewhere.

For at this little village of Banias was once the town of Cæsarea Philippi. Like some other old places, it had several different names. According to Robinson and Rabbi Schwartz, the place was that called in the Bible Baal Gad.† Then the Greeks named it Paneas, and the Romans

* A fourth, but minor, tributary to the Jordan, not mentioned by the ancients, is found in the springs of Esh Shir, $2\frac{1}{2}$ miles east by north of Phiale Lake. They form a rivulet a yard broad, and a foot deep, which runs by the north side of the lake, between it and Majdel, increased by several springs in its course down the deep defile of Wady esh Shir, and passing close to the south of Banias, by Wady el Kid, joins the Banias River in the basin of Hooleh. Captain Newbold "saw it in the month of May, when no rain had fallen for many days: it was then six yards wide, and two feet deep, clear and rapid." The Arabs assured him it never dries up ("Journal of the Asiatic Society," 1856, vol. xvi. pp. 15, 16).

† Schwartz says (p. 61): "It was there that the image of the cock-idol was worshipped by the Cutheans, in the town of Tarnegola, consecrated to the god Nergal (2 Kings xvii. 30). . . . The more recent name of the time of the Crusaders of 'Belias' for 'Banias' is founded upon the original appellation of the same Baal-gad (Joshua xi. 17)."

Cæsarea, while the Arabs, who have no letter *p*, now call it Banias (as "pasha" becomes "basha"). A long time might well be spent in examining the curious relics here, and to describe them fully would occupy some pages; but this has been well done by Porter with his usual clear succinctness, and our business now is only with what concerns this source of Jordan.

In riding up a gentle rise from the morass, we soon meet the new river tumbling its young waters among beautiful old ruins, bridges, walls, and fallen pillars, the broken relics of grandeur and elegance, mingled with trees and undergrowth of most exuberant forms. The hum of runlets underground and the louder dashing of cascades above give animation to what else would be desolate. The head of all is in front of a steep-faced cliff about eighty feet high, of white and pink stone, much scathed by weather and cut about by man. Niches aloft, but empty, tell plainly of great statues and idols. Numerous inscriptions upon the cliff speak even now of Pan, though with a mutilated story.* Above them is a *wely*, dedicated to *El Khudr*, the Moslem St. George; and thus we have grouped round this grotto the emblems that show it was sacred to the Baalite, the Jew, the Greek, the Roman, the

---

Again (p. 80): "It was there that the idol Baal-gad, already existing in the time of Joshua, was worshipped as late as the days of Isaiah (ch. v. 11), 'who set a table for the *Gad*' (English version, 'for that troop,' which, however, hardly means any thing; whereas it is highly significant when taken as the name of a heathen divinity)."

Stanley places Baal Gad at Baalbek. Thomson seems to think that Rehob was at Banias ("The Land and the Book," vol. i. p. 391). Schwartz tells us (p. 202) that "About three mill north of Banias, there is a mount, on which there is an old building having several cupolas. There is a tradition that the 'covenant between the pieces' with Abraham (Gen. xv. 9) was made on this spot; the Arabs call it Meshhad al Tir, *i. e.* the covenant or testimony of the bird (turtle-dove?), in reference to the 'bird' referred to, ibid. v. 10."

It had one more name given to it according to Josephus ("Antiq. of the Jews," book xx. ch. ix. sec. iv.): ". . . King Agrippa built Cæsarea Philippi larger than it was before, and in honor of Nero named it Neronias."

* Some of these are copied in Finn's "Byeways in Palestine" (Appendix). The stream of Banias is crossed by a bridge of one arch, very slightly pointed.

CAVE AT BANIAS.

Christian, and the Moslem, each in turn. A lofty and wide cavern opens deep in the rock, and just in front of this, outside, and *not* from within, but apparently from at least the level of the cavern's present floor, a copious flood of sparkling water wells up and forward through rough shingle, and in a few yards it hides its noisy dashings in a dense jungle.*

Josephus† thus writes of this rock and cavern: "So Cæsar bestowed his country, which was no small one, upon Herod; it lay between Trachon and Galilee, and contained Ulatha‡ and Paneas, and the country round about. . . . . So when he had conducted Cæsar to the sea, and was returned home, he built him a most beautiful temple, of the whitest stone, in Zenodorus's country, near the place called Panium. This is a very fine cave in a mountain, under which there is a great cavity in the earth, and the cavern is abrupt and prodigiously deep, and full of a still water; over it hangs a vast mountain, and under the caverns arise the springs of the river Jordan. Herod adorned this place, which was already a very remarkable one, still further by the erection of this temple, which was dedicated to Cæsar."

In another passage Josephus§ varies his account of the

---

* Wilson mentions the stream that flows above ground to swell that from the cave as formed from springs in a shallow valley, near Jebata Khusseh, while on the other side of a ridge there the springs flow to the Yarmuk. Newbold estimates the width of the front of shingle as 150 yards, but it appeared to me much less. The position of the fountain, as given by Captain Wilson, is lat. 33° 14′ 45″ N., and long. 35° 38′ 57″ E. He says that in the cavern there is a large accumulation of rubbish, and some little moisture, and that the spring appears to have issued directly from it at one time, and there was probably a large pool, over which may have been erected a temple, similar to that at Ain Fijeh, though on a more extensive scale. The fountain issues from the limestone, just at its juncture with the trap formation. In front of the wely the limestone has a dip of 15°, and strike of 250°.

The stream bridged in W. Zaareh, joining the fountain stream, had (in January) about one-fourth of the volume of the latter stream; the W. Khoshabé has about one-twentieth of that volume, and joins it a little higher up.

† "Jewish War," book xv. chap. x. sec. iii.

‡ This evidently means the Ard elHooleh.

§ "Jewish War," book i. ch. xxi. sec. iii. Schwartz tell us (p. 203, note): "In 'Bereshoth Rabba, ch. xxiii., it is said 'Three springs of Palestine and

BANIAS SOURCE OF THE JORDAN.

cavern and source, but by combining the two versions, it appears to me that the springs did always in old times, as now, issue from the front outside the cave, and not from within. The cavern was quite dry when I visited it.

The plan of this place given above is merely a rough map of the land and water in front of the cave.* This is the "greater source" of Jordan, that longest recognized as a beginning of the river; and it is not easy either to tell how much water comes from any one of the three sources separately or to compare their relative quantities, when you are looking at one only, and the other two, being distant, can only be reviewed by memory.

On the whole, and after a careful examination of them all, and a further inspection (to be described later) of the Banias and the Hasbany at their point of junction, I come to the conclusion that the Hasbany source is less than that at Banias, though the former river is the larger where the two unite, and that the source at Dan is larger than that at

---

its vicinity remained not closed up after the flood (Gen. viii. 2), the springs at Tiberias, Abilene, and the one of the Jordan issuing from the cave at Paneas.'" The Talmud says the same (Neubauer, 34, 37.) Pliny speaks only of the fountain here as the source of Jordan ("Nat. Hist." xv.).

* A photograph of part of the springs is published by the Palestine Exploration Fund, and several views about Banias.

LAKE PHALE.

Banias, though the Dan waters disperse afterwards and fail to reach the others in any one particular channel.

Josephus mentions* that Philip the Tetrarch discovered a still higher source of Jordan than Pan's Cave, in the little cup-like lake of Phiale, four hours distant from Banias. To test the matter, he put chaff into this pool, and it came out at the rock of Banias after passing underground. This is frequently referred to in travellers' books. From Irby and Mangle's account (p. 288), it seems to have been considered by them, and Robinson agrees (vol. iii. p. 350), as well as Stanley ('S. and P.' 394), that this discovery of Philip was barren. It is given as a reason for this that the water could not pass underground from Phiale to Banias because it would have to go beneath a certain streamlet described as lower than the level of Phiale. Wilson says the lake (Phiale) lies at the bottom of a cup-shaped basin, and has no outlet, though there is no stream running directly into it; it appears to receive a great portion of the surface drainage of the plain or sloping ground on the north-east.

Captain Newbold,† who also examined the Birket er Ram (Phiale) with care, says that the lake is three thousand paces in circumference, the taste of the water " a little brackish and flat," the temperature 75° Fahr. (air 78° in shade). The temperature of the Banias spring at the same time was 58°. The lake abounds with leeches and frogs. Then he says: " I repeated the experiment of Philip the Tetrarch, but the straw thrown in remained motionless on the surface. The loss by evaporation would be amply sufficient to account for the lake's never overflowing." A water-mark showed the lake had been six inches higher in winter.

Though Captain Wilson sought for subterranean passages leading from the fountains of Banias, none could be

* "Jewish War." book iii. ch. x. sec. vii.
† "Journal of the Asiatic Society," vol. xvi. (1856) p. 8. The small lake south of Banias, and shown in my picture (*post*, p. 237), is also called Birket er Ram.

found. The impure water of Phiale is very different from the sweet water of the fountain. The deep ravine of Wady em Keib lies between Phiale and the fountain. The cleft of W. Khoshabé cuts off communication between the fountain and the pool near Sheba, which some supposed was a source of the river; the rapid dip of the strata westerly would not allow the water to run to the fountain. The sheikh at Banias said straw had been put in at Sheba and appeared at the Banias fountain. This was most likely a fabrication, built upon accounts of the other experiment already noticed. The amount of water from the fountain was doubled after rain. It may, therefore, be considered as quite settled that the fountain of Banias is the first real source of Jordan in that direction.

A little stone shanty beside the great rock* served me as a shelter from a shower of rain, as I came here all alone, and my horse was put into Pan's Cavern, while I heaped wood on the still warm embers of the deserted fire, and made myself at home.

The house of this trustful shepherd had no door. He had left every thing quite open inside, so I was very soon comfortable, and greeted the venerable proprietor when he returned, telling him the one cardinal fact that I was an Englishman.

Cæsarea Philippi would have been interesting enough to see with what has been told already as its features—the grand mountain views around it; the worships of Pagan, Turk, and Jew, each with their symbols; the Crusaders' ruined keep, and the fights of the Cross; and, oldest of all, yet ever fresh, the source of the Jordan.

But a higher holiness was printed on this rock when the foot of Christ came here, seeking for "the lost sheep of the house of Israel,"† even on the outskirts of the land where they wandered.

---

* Thomson, in "The Land and the Book," gives woodcuts representing this rock and the Phiale pool.

† The wely marked in Map V. as Neby Seid Yuda—the "tomb of the Lord Judah"—may be (Thomson thinks—vol. i. p. 390) what is alluded to

He had healed the blind man of Bethsaida.* If this was the eastern town of that name, our Lord next went by the waters of Merom until He "came into the coasts of

NEBY SEID YUDA.

Cæsarea Philippi."† Then was that searching question put, and that solemn pledge was given, which is recorded in these verses:

"He asked his disciples, saying, Whom do men say that I the Son of Man am?

"And they said, Some say that thou art John the Bap-

in Joshua xix. 34, when he describes the borders of Naphthali as reaching "to Judah upon Jordan toward the sunrising."

* Mark viii. 22. So "He is gone to Kisrin" (*i. e.* Cæsarea; to express the farthest limit).—Neubauer, 238.

† Matt. xvi. 13. The word "coasts" is expressive as describing "the towns" (Mark viii. 27) on the edge of the wide watery plain.

tist: some, Elias;* and others, Jeremias, or one of the prophets.

"He saith unto them, But whom say ye that I am?

"And Simon Peter answered and said, Thou art the Christ, the Son of the living God.

"And Jesus answered and said unto him, Blessed art thou, Simon Bar-jona: for flesh and blood hath not revealed it unto thee, but my Father which is in heaven.

"And I say also unto thee, That thou art Peter, and upon this rock I will build my church; and the gates of hell shall not prevail against it.

"And I will give unto thee the keys of the kingdom of heaven: and whatsoever thou shalt bind on earth shall be bound in heaven: and whatsoever thou shalt loose on earth shall be loosed in heaven.

"Then charged he his disciples that they should tell no man that he was Jesus the Christ.

"And† he began to teach them, that the Son of man must suffer many things, and be rejected of the elders, and of the chief priests, and scribes, and be killed, and after three days rise again.

"But when he had turned about and looked on his disciples, he rebuked Peter, saying, Get thee behind me, Satan: for thou savorest not the things that be of God, but the things that be of men."

Too often the latter part of this conversation is omitted when the first is given. At the same place and time, when Peter was called a "stone," he was called "Satan." We are content to be built in with Peter just so long as Peter is a "living stone" on Christ, the "Rock of Ages."‡

Where this scene took place can not be ascertained now. Mark says it was "by the way" (ver. 27), but a fond fancy would fix it dramatically under the rock at Banias.

---

* The people were likely to say this, if it was here that Elijah appeared with Moses. † Mark viii. 31, 33.

‡ Let those who assemble under the dome of St. Peter's, encircled by the promise given to the apostle, written there on a blue band above them, think well whether the "lively stones" of Christ's Church are new doctrines invented by man, or new men converted to Christ.

God seems to have withheld from us precise knowledge as to the places of His most glorious deeds, that the lessons taught by them might be free from mere local interest, being for all people everywhere, and for all time—aye, for eternity itself and every universe.*

Then "after six days" our Saviour took his three apostles "into a high mountain" to be transfigured, and to speak with the prophet and the great lawgiver. He had called himself the "Son of Man" to the apostles; now he was proclaimed as "My beloved Son" by the very voice of Jehovah. All this took place near Banias, and much better is it that no one can say exactly where. The words and deeds are glorious and thrilling, but they are meant for the whole earth, and not for a single spot to make its own. From this farthest point of his walk of mercy through Israel, the Saviour turned back again to scenes of agony and death. He had fortified his faithful ones by his kinglike promise; he had been fortified himself by his Father's voice out of the "bright cloud;" and now and for the last time "He set his face to go unto Jerusalem."

From Banias I rode to the splendid ruin of the castle of Subeibeh. This still stands proudly on a height guarded by sheer cliff all round, except at the entrance gate; and to reach this—the only way in—the pilgrim must pass a long narrow path, wholly opened to the view of a defending garrison, and completely at their mercy if he comes as an enemy. Murray's Handbook almost entreats the traveller not to miss this place. His words are not too urgent, for it is, on the whole, the most magnificent relic of such a fortress to be seen. Heidelberg is not so large, nor has it any thing like the view we have before us here. Towers and bastions are round about, and huge walls and courtyards fill the ample space within.† A thousand men here,

---

* Perhaps the spot most nearly known and quite undoubted is that where the Great Preacher "sat thus on the well," and preached a full sermon to the most empty of congregations, even to one fallen woman.

† Thomson describes the vast number of scorpions found here in summer. The inhabitants, to avoid these, build little booths on long poles to dwell in.

more or less, would not crowd the "visitors' rooms," or weigh upon the grand old masonry. Built by the Herods first, perhaps, or by Phœnician masons, it was an outwork afterwards of the Holy Wars, when nations were fired with frenzy for the Land of the Cross. Now we can scarcely beg a few guineas from the world to uncover the buried ruins of Palestine.

My rifle beside me, but no one in sight or hearing, I had a fit of melancholy meditation here, deploring our degenerate days that leave such a noble stronghold in the hands of the feeble Turk—his, too, for the last seven hundred years. But it was not to be moody I climbed up to Subeibeh, nor, indeed, was it to see this old castle with its cold gray stones. I came to scan from hence how the Rob Roy could paddle through the marsh of Hoolch; to get, if possible, some little inkling of where the Jordan spreads its lost waters, and how they are gathered again into one before the last long leap of "the Descender."

From this lonely perch, about 1500 feet above the plain, the panorama is superb. The hills of Bashan are cleft in front, and they frame the wide-spread picture. To the left, and farthest off, are the gleaming waters of Merom. In front is the Galilean chain, and on the right is Hermon—

"Like Teneriffe or Atlas unremoved."

Down in the level hollow stretches the wide morass, of dark and even color, gloomy, but with pools and lakes and strips of disjointed water shining in the sun like the last snow-wreaths of spring on a half-melted lawn. The most careful scrutiny could not detect any method or sequence in these water-patches.* Viewed as a mere landscape, one might fancy, indeed, some possible channel between them; but a more practical connection must be discerned before the canoeist can trust his boat on such a patchwork of water, without at least some possible route determined. Oft-

---

* They are inserted in the drawing here as accurately as I could make them out. Thomson gives a sketch, but from a lower point of view. See *ante*, p. 213.

POOLEH MORASS, FROM THE CASTLE OF SEDFJEIL.

en in Sweden I had to climb high hills to spy out the way through the archipelagos on the great lakes, several of them eighty miles long. But the grand difference there was that the canoe might be stranded a dozen times or lost altogether, and yet there would be no danger to its crew from man or beast; and it certainly is one effect of experience in such voyages alone that, while a certain class of dangers gets more despised, and boldness increases as to one class of difficulties, another kind of possibilities becomes more realized as truly formidable, which, at first starting on such cruises, would never be thought of at all. However, after all the moralizing about the morass had been done, it came to this in the end: that there was very good reason for not trying to pass through Hooleh marsh, and that there was much better reason for a determined effort to do it now. Next day, therefore, with Hany, I made a *reconnaissance* from our head-quarters by the mound at Dan, that we might find the best way, or any way, by which to carry the Rob Roy into the soft green plain. He was quite as anxious as myself to do this well, and up to a certain point of perseverance a good Eastern dragoman is as resolute as any Englishman. Where the Orientals break down (as seems to me) is when the difficulty is an unknown one, and has to be overcome in a way entirely new. It is just then that is wanted the Saxon's positive resolve, "It *shall* be done." And this was needed now. To take a horse down these rough rocks was easy. To steer a mule, even a laden one, among the bogs and gushing streamlets, and through hedges and reeds and thickets, could be done by bearing bumps and bruises and duckings in the mud. But we had to find a way for a tender cargo to be carried here—the ever-precious Rob Roy; and this, so strong in waves and rapids, might be smashed by a single fall of the horse, and then the journey could not be begun again without long delay, or, at best, would be continued with the enfeebling sensation of paddling over a new and rapid river in a crippled boat. Nevertheless, we found a way here even in this winter season, and with all the ground flooded by recent rain; and we settled upon a house, the last on the plain, where the Rob Roy might lodge the first night, and there we bespoke for her the best bedroom in a buffaloes' byre, the landlord, no doubt, being puzzled out of his wits when he was gravely told that next day would come a "shaktoor." And come it did, on January 4th, all safe, to Mansoura, after far less struggling than was expected, and no hurt.

This place is at a clump of trees seen from Tell el Kady. Two stone houses are by a little mound, and, so far as I could make out, this is the ground of the Difne Arabs, evidently connected by name with the ancient Daphne, the longer way of saying Dan. What in such sparsely peopled places may be called a crowd was waiting to receive us, and indeed they were a rough-looking set, but civil enough, and strongly reverencing my double-barrel while they worshipped the canoe.

So great was the pressure about me that it was very difficult to take compass-bearings here, but it was far more difficult to obtain from the numerous Arabs peering at us any one name of the villages in front—the clumps, I mean, of straw-mat huts, and Arab tents, and every cross-breed compromise between the animal and vegetable orders of architecture.

First, it was scarcely possible to point out any of the knobs on the horizon, so that any two men beside me should agree upon what they were asked to look at. Then their arguments about the matter had to be filtered through faithful Hany's rendering of the case. Next the names had to be marked in pencil on my plan, and lastly the whole list was found to be wrong.

This was the usual routine, and it happened so many times, and after long periods of rest had been given to cool down the conflicting geographers, and to allow some *consensus* of their versions to be precipitated for use, that I was driven to the reluctant conclusion, first, that the places had no names, and, second, that none of the men knew the places. As this never happened thus before to me, and as it must have been caused by one or other of these reasons, I feel pretty sure that the maps of Hooleh will never agree if we take the names from what the people tell us, and that the time is come for some inventive tourist to christen all the localities himself.

After a stormy session of this parliament in the grove of Daphne,* I peremptorily silenced all the self-elected speakers, except a fine clear-eyed fellow, who seemed to be the least garrulous and the most knowing man among them; and having overruled in my favor all points of order, I noted down this man's version of the Hooleh Domesday-book as a comment in explanation of a careful sketch made previously from a point five hundred feet above the plain. From this the few names are given in Map V., and, perhaps, they are as likely to be right as any other list.

The following catechism will show what had to be digested into knowledge fit to record in a map, and in the colloquy Q. is the English inquirer, and A. is the answering Arab.

Q. You see that little group of huts near the big tree?

A. Yes, where the water flows quiet; that is Absees.

Q. And the next huts to the left?

A. Tell el Schady. By the Prophet! it's a fishing-station. Great for fishing is the Ingleez; but this is in the reeds ("rab").

(Voice in the crowd): "'Dowana' is the name."

Q. What name did you say last?

(Voice): "Zahmouda" — (which voice, after much wrangle, turns out to be not the same that spoke first).

Q. Which is Zahmouda?

(Three people point in three directions, and instantly begin a subsidiary debate.)

---

* Another Daphne, near Antioch, is mentioned by Josephus, and in 2 Maccabees iv. 3. The Dufneh Arabs are to the west of Mansoura, and the village is marked on Map V. Schwartz (p. 47) places "Dafne" at Berim, or Riblah. I observe that almost every writer of travels here has a Daphne of his own.

Q. Look along my ramrod. Now, what's the name of the hamlet it points to?

A. Dowana.

Q. Why, it's what you said was Absees?

A. El Aksees the Howaja sees to the right of Zahmouda.

Q. But where *is* Zahmouda?

(First voice, and a general chorus—the second voice being stifled by cuffs): "Next to Tell el Schady."

Then, with rough eagerness, the strongest of the Dowana faction pushes his long forefinger forward, pointing straight enough—but whither? and with a volley of words ends " Ah—ah—a—a—a————a—a."

This strange expression had long before puzzled me when first heard from a shepherd in Bashan. I thought the man was a stammerer, then that he was laughing at me, then that he was crazy himself. But the simple meaning of this long string of "ah's" shortened and quickened, and lowered in tone to the end, is merely that the place pointed to is a "very great way off." Nor is the plan a bad one for giving by words a long perspective distance to the place we are pointing out.

The festival ending Ramadan happened to fall at this time, so that all the people were idle, joyous, and boisterous in their fashion, and they had donned their gaudiest finery. A procession of children came over the marsh with guns and flags, green boughs, long sticks, and music of tom-toms and singing. When they saw the Rob Roy on horseback, the ranks burst into disorder, and rushed to our group with wild shouts. They believed (said they) that the canoe had come to honor their holiday show. Each one in turn came up to see my pith helmet, and the older men to gaze on my compass. Their dress was the most various possible, long and short, colored and plain, scanty and ample, of camel's hair of Damascus, silk of Lebanon, and Manchester cotton. All the women had their faces stained with blue patterns. Most of the men were tattooed, and some not merely punctured, but gashed hideously in diagrams on their cheeks. A good deal of jewelry was displayed. Many of the men wore earrings. Nose-rings were the fashion among the young. Heavy dirty coins (kesh) chained together hung from their hair and rattled on their cheeks. One had this chain of money linked at one end to the ear, and at another to the nose.

THREE HOOLEH HEADS.

The moment I tried to sketch any of these, the happy subject of the pencil became at once grave, important, and stiff, putting on his "best looks," and (as generally in such cases) looking the most unlike himself. These portraits were bespoken and eagerly received as presents, and so I secured only three for my album, which are given above. One of these dandies thus sketched had a head-dress with fur woven into his hair, and two long side-locks pendent, and another was the likeness of a mischievous little scamp, very unlikely to be regular at his ragged-school, with three tails on his head, and, plainly, by his manners, a sprig of nobility, or, it may be, a prince from a mud palace near, and, at any rate, privileged in general as a "flibbertigibbet." The third portrait represents the young fashionable with the chain from nose to chin. I thought that the wearer was a girl, and even then this ornament would be wonderful enough, though what finery can be too extravagant for feminine coquetry? But my sketch-book shows that the wearer of the *parure* was a man; nor is this warrior of Hooleh the only man who, with a string of coins, can be "led by the nose."

The name of this village, Mansoura, means "delight," and there are many other places called by this name, besides the large town in the Delta already described in our log.

Fine oak-trees shade the green tell here; south of it is the cow-house, where we docked the Rob Roy for a night, and a corn-mill turned by a noisy sluice of water. It will be seen by Map V. that the river on the east is the Banias,* which has wandered down here from the cave of Pan, while behind and around the tell are several streams complicated in their relations, but on a higher level than the Banias, and apparently not always here uniting with that river; at all events, not when we saw them. These upper streamlets are parts of the Leddan, which has broken its channel into many pools and brooks, soon after leaving the source at Dan, and is then dispersed by canalettes over fields, and absorbed by marsh-land, from which the waters again debouch, unite, and branch out once more at half a mile from Tell el Kady. One arm of this, I was told, reaches to the Hasbany River, but, if so, it is a mere brook. It may be safely said that the Leddan spreads generally into Hooleh plain, but to follow up this network of water-

---

* I can not understand what Dr. Thomson says ("The Land and the Book," vol. i. p. 388), that, starting from Mansoura, and "crossing the Baniasy at Sheikh Hazeib, we came to the main branch of the Leddan, and in ten minutes more to another branch with the name of Buraij. Half a mile from this all the streams unite with the Hasbany, a little north of Sheikh Yusuf, a large tell on the very edge of the marsh."

ways on foot was not easy, for I found them often too broad to leap on foot, and their banks were too treacherous to ride over. The exact geography could be better deciphered in summer, but fever, ague, and plenty of other ills would be, of course, rampant then upon the marsh.

The crowd under the oaks had increased in number as I returned from the rough survey of their amphibious territory. In a large semicircle they stood at the open door of the house until the buffaloes were expelled, protesting in loud bellows and angrily rushing through the mud.

Our host was a dull, sad, and silent man. He had come to the place a year before. Four of his children had been slaughtered in the massacre—for he was a Christian—and the only one left was a little girl of ten years old. She was most beautiful in face and figure, and with a happy, angelic look, very winning to regard. Her gentle kindness to her father, her graceful alacrity in the household bustle of preparing for a howaja, her dignified restraint of the rude urchins about us delighted me exceedingly. With tears the fond father held out her little right hand to show me how it was gashed and worthless for needlework, and shook his head, sorrowfully weeping, and sympathy watered in my eyes.

He seemed too down-hearted and woe-begone to feel the panting thirst of hot revenge for this Moslem's outrage, and in lack of other consolation he lighted his chibouque. I gave the pretty child a "British Workman" with its cheerful pictures, and an English knife and other presents. Then, to get peace, we closed the few boards called a door, and which admitted plenty of light, though there was no window. For company's sake the man stopped the hours of evening by me. My converse with him was by few signs and fewer words, though they were all I knew of Arabic; but even these cheered him, for my hand pointed him upward, and he knew the meaning when that signal came from a "Nussarene." A heap of corn was in the room, and a steelyard to weigh it, and some ox-yokes. Not a single article of furniture was there but the one straw mat on which I stretched out to sleep, with my boat-bag for a pillow.

Loud kickings at the door soon knocked in its feeble fastening, and a dozen Arabs entered. They had come to buy gunpowder from the Christian miller. After much bargaining he pulled out the old canvas sack I had been leaning upon for hours, and wherein was the gunpowder perfectly loose, and we had been smoking too, and now a man came in with a nargilleh (water-pipe). The powder was weighed in handfuls. Each of the Arabs flashed a pinch of it in his rusty gun, and then blew down its mouth. Some put their powder in bits of paper in their belts, others carried it quite free in a goat-skin bag, others in their pockets, with a dozen more things. Each man wrangled all the time of weighing his portion, and he always got a spoonful more thrown in extra to quiet his murmurings. They all departed at last, and we were at peace. But they all returned with loud imperious mien to say "their change was wrong." My wearied host only sighed and gave half-farthings round, and I did not wish to see any one of the miller's customers again, but to-morrow will tell about that. The cats scampered over me all night; no doubt they smelt the large pudding in my bag. In dreamy struggles to explain how the eyes of cats will glance bright like diamonds through black darkness, sleep seized and overcame.

CHAPTER XV.

River Banias. — Strange Rock. — Afloat alone. — Riding. — "Waltzing." — Meeting of the Waters. — Pursued. — At bay. — Fired at. — Caught. — Captive's Appeal. — Carried to Captivity. — Before the Court. — Sentence. — Taunts. — Revenge. — Escape.

"DEFT little lassie, good-morning! Your bright eyes, how they sparkle! your neat and modest dress, how tidy! One only spared of his children, and a darling to your father—fair Christian maid, good-bye!" Now mount the Rob Roy, and be careful, Latoof and Adoor.

We were taking the canoe as far as possible on horseback straight over the plain to save the time of floating her on the crooked river, and so gain a fine long daylight for the voyage itself. The Banias takes long bends here, keeping well eastward to our left, and at intervals I rode to its banks to inspect them. Near Mansoura it passes a most curious obstacle, an oblong level rock, probably—certainly, so far as I saw—the last rock in the plain. This projects from the west bank, due eastward. It is rectangular in shape, about six feet thick, and three feet out of the water. Against this barrier the river runs full tilt, and foams back, turning on itself as if in anger. The swift current sways to the left, and rushes quite round the end of the rock in a narrow passage which must have rock on its other side too, else it would soon sweep out a broad bay in the bank. I never saw a rock so placed in a river, and therefore I made the following sketch of it.

The banks of the Banias are otherwise uninteresting here, and about six feet high along the plain. Shrubs line them at intervals, but they are mostly bare and gravelly. Buffaloes and horses browse on the luscious green grass. All the horses appear to be of one color, for they are thickly coated with mud. Clover, I am sure, would readily grow on their backs. As for the buffaloes—the "bulls of Bashan" —their favorite pastime is to stand, with outstretched gaping head, just up to their stomachs in slush. A herdsman was out thus early to drive this mixed flock somewhere. He rode a splendid Arab without saddle or bridle, and perfectly naked himself. With a long stick he dealt heavy blows on the horses before him, and heavier upon the buffaloes. All these plunged and scampered, and squealed, bellowed, and kicked, with their tails in the air, a loud wild orgie of savage animal life.

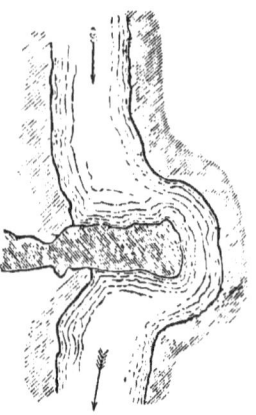

STRANGE ROCK IN THE JORDAN.

The few hamlets in the marsh are curiously various in their architecture. After the stone house and flat roof we had left, there is the mud wall with a round hump-backed top of reed matting. Others have side mats for walls, and the roof shaped like a pulpit cushion, of which the tassels at the corner are heavy stones tied by straw ropes to keep the light covers on; black Arab tents succeed, and with woven reeds at the sides, and then the long tent pure and simple: all the varieties, in fact, of tent and thatch, and mud and mat, combined. The sketch at p. 264 will show these "Beit Shahr," the reed demesnes of Hoolch.

We joined the Banias River where it runs between the houses of Aksees, or Absees, or Absceyieh, as it was called by each of my instructors yesterday. The stream was about one hundred feet wide for a little, but narrowing and expanding at every turn. The water was turbid and in flood, whirling with eddies, the banks of reddish clay, and thick reeds nestled in the bights. Nobody was aroused in the village when we noiselessly launched the Rob Roy to float on the third stream of Jordan, as it had already floated on the other two.

Slowly we numbered each article that had to be stowed

away, so as to see that nothing was taken that could possibly be left behind (for lightness), and nothing left that ought to be taken for safety. Hany was now to return towards Dan, whence the mules and baggage had already gone away, and he was to press on to Mellaha, near the end of Hooleh Lake, where he was to wait for me, and by relays to watch night and day until I might arrive, "any time during the next forty-eight hours."

It was bright sunshine above us and the river-stream looked hearty and strong below, but there was more than usual pressure between our hands as the Rob Roy glided off with my dragoman's earnest "God bless you!"

Once more alone, the interest and excitement were strung up to the highest pitch. It was not like the Atcibeh morass, where my tent was on shore, and I had only to get back to it. Here, on the Jordan, the stream was far too powerful to think of returning against it; and where, indeed, could I come back to?

The interest arose from the hope of discovering the real course of the Jordan.

Suppose we had ten miles of the Thames still uncertain in our maps, would it not be a reproach to English boatmen? But Jordan was an old river before the Thames was heard of, and the Thames will be forgotten when Jordan will be remembered forever. What an honor, then, for the Rob Roy to trace even one new bend of this ancient river!

As the Hooleh Arabs seemed to be an ill-looking set, and had but a poor certificate of character from the tales of travellers, I tried to slip by them unperceived under the high banks, and this was the first place in my voyages where the natives were to be eluded.

On the Abana the difficult parts for the canoe were in deep rocky defiles, where no man, friend or foe, could come along the banks; but here, on Jordan, the banks were level and open to the prowling robbers. Moreover, I was to meet them, if at all, without the constraining pomp and presence of a retinue, and once captured, I would be lawful prize for a ransom.

No one caught sight of the canoe as she stole past the mat houses of Abscos under a few palm-trees. Then the river wound very crookedly, but with steep banks and jungle concealing me. The bends were so angular and the current so swift that in the turns it was utterly impossible not to run into the thick overhanging canes. Then it was I invented a new way of getting round sharp serpentine corners, and which I beg to commend very warmly to canoeists.

The diagram will show this manœuvre. We are supposed to be speeding fast round a bend shaped like the letter S, and this is the way to manage it:

Run the bows of the canoe gently into the left bank at the first angle, and let the stern be swung by the current until you can back into the right bank of the next angle, and run the stern in there. Let the current again swing the bow until you can paddle ahead in freedom, and so escape from the double bend.

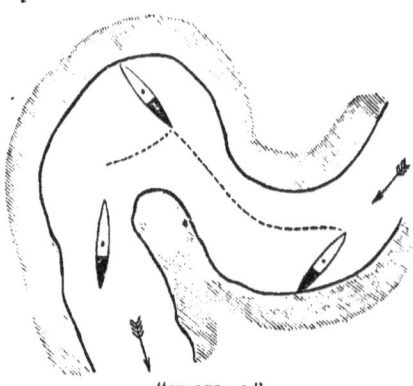

"WALTZING."

It will be found that the eddies are all in favor of this plan, and the jungle in the bends is an aid rather than hindrance; but the operation requires quiet attention and good balancing, especially when steering back foremost; and a good look-out must be kept, lest in the narrow parts of the stream both bow and stern might be caught at once, when an upset would be a moral certainty.

This new *pas* in the canoe I called "waltzing," the Rob Roy being my fair partner; and as we were whirling about in this dance without music, I saw a head gazing over the reeds in amazement. His eyes opened large, up went his hands, and he disappeared with a yell. Soon I heard others shouting, and soon—too soon—they all ran near to see. In a moment I noticed how very different they were in manner from any other spectators that so often had run alongside me in Europe and America. They were dancing in frantic excitement and shouting ferociously. The bounding current bore me along too fast for their running, but while I had to go round the long bends, they crossed by shorter routes, and saluted my approach with a volley of clods. All these fell harmless, and at the next bend the Hasbany River ran into the Banias; so the men were left at the point of junction, high on the steep bank, screaming until I disappeared.

The Hasbany joins the Banias in a proper orthodox way, each river yielding its tribute quietly to the united whole, and now for the first time is formed the veritable Jordan. Vandevelde marks this spot near Tell Sheikh Yusuf, "the Mount of the lord Joseph;"* and he is quite right, for there was the green hill close by the shore, the junction of the geographical and the historic streams of Jordan, the wedding of the line of largest waters with the line of largest fame.† Here I intended to land and take bearings, but the banks were perfectly steep. However, in the middle there was a beautiful island of small round black gravel, and I ran the boat on that and got out to

---

* On the eastern hills is shown the place where Joseph was sold to the Midianites.

† Robinson rode (with Thomson) from Tell el Kady to Sheikh Yusuf in an hour and forty minutes ("The Land and the Book," vol. i. p. 388). Josephus says: "Now Jordan's visible stream arises from this cavern (Panium), and divides the marshes and fens of the Lake Semechonitis: when it hath run another hundred and seventy furlongs" ("Jewish War," book iii. ch. x. sec. vii.). The distance he mentions would be about fourteen English miles. But the position of Tell Sheikh Yusuf is settled by the observations of Captain Wilson, R.E., and Lieutenant Anderson, R.E., whose survey reached to this spot, and from these the tell is marked in our map, as well as Mansoura, Banias, and Jisr Ghujar, fixed in relation to Tell Haroweh (on the south-west of Map V.), where was an astronomical station. Thus far the features of the district of Hooleh are now published for the first time from proper data, and it will be seen that all previous maps are wrong. The details of Map V., and the whole of Map VI., are from my own observation.

rest, to collect my thoughts as to the new complexion things had taken, to prepare my pistol, and settle whether it was better to lie concealed for an hour, or to push on swiftly and try to outrun the wave of excitement which had evidently arisen, and would quickly propagate itself among the Arabs in the fields. Each of the rivers here seems to be about seventy feet wide, and seven or eight feet deep. The waters of both were pale brown in color, and their united stream was about a hundred feet broad.

Launching again on the river, the current bore us on delightfully. The banks were from twelve to twenty feet high and quite vertical, with grass upon the top. Two buffaloes looked at me over this, and soon their driver too. I gave him a most polite "salaam!" but he stared as if he saw a ghost—and a most terrible ghost, too—then he ran away hallooing.

With all my might I pressed on now, but soon heard the men behind me. In a straight reach, and with a good current like this, they could not keep up with the canoe.* But here these pursuers cut across the bends on shore, and so they overtook me in ten minutes. Then a dozen of them were running high above, and they speedily increased to fifty—men, women, and children.

It was of no use now to paddle fast, but better to reserve my strength and keep cool for what might come. Suddenly every one of them disappeared, but I knew I must meet them all round the next corner. There they were, screaming, with that wild hoarseness only the Arab can attain, "Al burra! al burra!" (To land! to land!) That was the chorus, and a royal salute of missiles splashed in the water. I bowed to them quietly, and answered "Ingleez;" but they ran still with me in a tumultuous rabble, and seeing some of them give their scanty garments to the others, I knew what would follow; about half a dozen jumped into the water

They swam splendidly, and always with right and left

* In the last "long race" of our Canoe Club, the winner's canoe accomplished 12 miles in 85 minutes.

hand alternately in front; but of course I distanced the swimmers, who murmured deep, while the others shouted and laughed. Then the naked ones got out and ran along the bank again, and all disappeared as before for another attack.

It was a crisis now; but as there was no shirking it, the Rob Roy whirled round the next point beautifully; and here the river was wide, and the rascals were waiting in the water, all in a line across, about a score of them wading to their middle.

For a moment I paused as to what was best to do, and every one was silent and stood still. Then I quietly floated near one of the swimmers, splashed him in the face with my paddle, and instantly escaped through the interval with a few vigorous strokes, while a shout of general applause came from the bank; and they all ran on except one, who took a magnificent "header" into the river, and came up exactly by the stern of the Rob Roy, with his arm over her deck. But my paddle was under his arm in an instant, and I gently levered him off, saying, in my softest accents, "Katerhayrac!" (thanks!), as if he had been rendering a service. The shout renewed, and the best of them all retired discomfited.

At this time we must have been quite near the village of Salhyeh (a name I can never forget), and the number of people on the banks was now at the least a hundred. Many of them had ox-goads, some had spears, the rest had the long clubs with huge round knobs at the end peculiar to that northern district. Another shower of missiles came, yet, strange to say, not one hit the boat. There rose the cry, "Baroda! baroda!" (the gun! the gun!).

I let my boat float quietly that the excitement might cool down, and, looking at the mob quite close, I saw several point their long guns at me; one kneeled to do so, yet none of them at first seemed really in earnest to shoot.

But soon on a little point in front I noticed a man posted methodically for a purpose. He trimmed his priming, he cocked his hammer, and, as I came straight up to him, every other person stopped to look, and not a voice was heard.

I could not escape this man, and he knew that well. Up went his gun to his shoulder: he was cool, and so was I. The muzzle was not twenty feet from my face. Three thoughts coursed through my brain: "Will hit me in the mouth; bad to lie wounded here." "Aimed from his left shoulder; how convenient to shoot on both sides!" "No use 'bobbing' here—first time under fire—Arabs respect courage." The clear round black of the muzzle end followed me covering as I passed. I stared right at the man's eyes, and gave one powerful stroke; at the same moment he fired—fiz, bang! and a splash of the bullet in the water behind me. Loud shouts came out of the smoke. I stopped, and said, "Not fair to use a gun!" In an instant the water was full of naked swimmers straining towards me. It was shallow here, and in vain I tried hard to avoid them. Suddenly my canoe was wrenched down behind. It was the same black giant I had elbowed off before; but now he came furiously, brandishing the white shank-bone of a buffalo. I warded off that with my paddle, but another had got hold of the boat's bow. I was captured now, and must resort to tactics. The crowd yelled louder in triumph, but I motioned my captors to take the boat to the opposite shore. The man cried "Bakshish!"—a word I had somehow heard before! I said, "Yes; but to the sheikh." The villain answered, "*I* am the sheikh;" but I knew he was not. His face was black, his cheeks were deeply gashed and tattooed; he had one big earring. His topknot stood erect, and the water glistened on his huge naked carcass as he roughly grasped my delicate little paddle. My pistol lay between my knees full-cocked, and my hand stole down to it. Better thoughts came instantly. "Why should I shoot this poor savage? it will not free me. Even if it does, it would be liberty bought by blood." Still I parleyed with the man till he softened down. I pointed to his bone weapon, and said it was not fair to use it. He pointed to my paddle, and said that was not fair. Poor fellow! I felt for him; his vanity had been wounded by discomfiture before. Soon we became good friends, chiefly by my quiet smiles and patting his wet shaven pate.

I kept him yet on the far side of the river, that the others might sober a little, for the Arabs quiet into calm as suddenly as they flash into rage. All the village was out now on the banks, and many swam over to the Rob Roy.

CAPTURE.

I formally appointed my captor as my protector, and he became proud instead of angry. Little as I knew of the language, I could make him understand my meaning, and he *did* understand—nay, there is scarcely any idea of *facts* that you can not make intelligible without words if you are at once calm and in earnest.* Then we crossed—he swimming and holding on with excruciating twists to the

* It is quite another matter to understand *them*. They speak as if you knew their language— you gesticulate as if they don't know yours.

poor prisoned Rob Roy. How frantic the people were! Some of them in the crowd tumbled over into the water. They did not mind that a bit. I commanded silence, and all obeyed. Then was pronounced this most eloquent oration. I said, "I am English." They replied, "Sowa, sowa" (friends), and then rubbed their two forefingers together, the usual sign of amity. I said it was not fair to use the "baroda" (gun). Holding up one finger, I said, "Ingleez wahed" (one Englishman), then holding up both hands, I said, "Araby kooloo" (all the rest Arabs). At this the crowd applauded, laughing, and so did I. A little girl now took up a huge lump of red earth, and from the bank, about eight feet above me, she hurled it down with violence upon the canoe. This was a crisis, and the time to be perfectly calm. If the quick spirit had seized them then, the boat would have been smashed to pieces in three seconds. Turning, therefore, slowly round I pointed to the horrid mess the mud had made on the clean white waterproof of the canoe, and looked up in the faces of them all with a pleasant but beseeching air. It was a turning-point this. They looked at one another for a moment silently, and then, as by a general impulse, they rushed at the hapless girl, and as the whole mob of them disappeared over the bank, I heard her screams and the thumps of discipline that caused them. In the confusion caused by this absence I had almost escaped once more, when they angrily captured me again. But they could not persuade me to get out of the boat, and for this reason: my pistol was still open and at full cock lying on the floor-boards of the canoe. If I got out, they would see it, and surely would scramble for the prize. Every time I put my hand inside to stow the pistol away out of sight, they tried to wrench my paddle from the other hand. One hand was, therefore, needed for the paddle, but the other could not be spared from its duty of patting their wet greasy heads, which affectionate caress seemed to be an unwonted but most successful mode of propitiation.

The water mob of swimmers closed nearer and waxed

larger as more crossed the river. Their curiosity was boundless, and every hand tried to undo my apron or to get somehow under the deck. Their patience was on the ebb, and while I considered what to do next, I felt the Rob Roy heaving this way and that, and then gradually, and despite all my smiling but earnest remonstrance, the canoe began to rise out of the water with all her crew inside. Loud shouts welcomed her ascent up the bank as a dozen dark-skinned bearers lifted the canoe and her captain, sitting inside, with all due dignity graciously smiling, and so they carried her fairly up the steep bank and over the smooth sward some hundred yards towards the tent of their Arab sheikh.

See this strange progress depicted in the frontispiece of our volume, and it may safely be said that no prisoner before was ever thus taken into custody.

'But it was an anxious journey this from river to tent. The men were rough and boisterous. The boat heeled and plunged as if in a terrible sea. I clasped the two nearest bearers round their necks to steady these surgings. Then they let the boat down while I clung to their clammy cheeks and swarthy shoulders, and I had soon to loose hold of these and descend to the ground with the Rob Roy, for I would never desert her. Up aloft again! and laughing and shouting we waddled along, while the crowd was denser than ever, until the sheikh came slowly to meet us with a few of his ancient councillors.

I insisted that the canoe should be placed in his tent. After much resistance he suddenly allowed it, and then I got out. But what to do next? The first thing to recollect in this sort of adventure is that *time* is of no consequence to such people, but that stage effect and dignity are very important to your case. Therefore I made long preliminaries, and had every person ordered out of the tent. The crowd obeyed, after some had been beaten with sticks to convince them. The sheikh seemed puzzled at the whole affair. I looked at him carefully, and saw he was a second-rate man without much decision in his mien,

R

and one who would, on the whole, like events to happen under other orders than his own.

Having now a fair stage scene around the central figures, I came forward slowly, hat in hand, and bowed to the sheikh very low, and shook hands with him heartily, and told him I was a wandering Briton on my way to the lake, and I would rest at his tent until the sun was cooler.

The crowd was attentive and silent. Men in the rear beat off the boys, and the women went behind the tent and peered through the matting, so that a whole regiment of feminine noses was ranged over the little Rob Roy, now reclining safe on a carpet. The sheikh retired to consult with his cabinet. I asked for two men to keep order, and he gave them, and desperately tyrannical they were upon the mob. After an hour, about mid-day, the chief and his ministry came back, and ordered "silence," and said, "You can not go to the lake." I said, "I *must*." He answered it was "impossible." I said I must go to see that. He gave me the very smallest wink that could be given by a man's eye, and I answered by one a little smaller. Then I knew he could be convinced—*i. e.*, bribed, and so finally, at any rate, I would have my own way.

The tent was cleared again. About twenty women came forward in a group, and the sheikh's wife, quite refined in manner and very intelligent. I behaved to her as if she were an English lady. She was lost in amazement when I exhibited my little bed, my lamp, compass, and cuisine. She looked with kind and feminine interest upon me when I said I was losing all the fine sunshine of the day, a prisoner alone among strangers. She fetched her husband by himself, and, under cover of showing him the inside of the canoe, I managed to let him see a gold napoleon in my open hand, and with a nudge to his elbow for emphasis to the sight. He whispered, "Shwei, shwei" (softly, quietly). I knew I had bought him then. The "council of ancients" came with their final decision, "You can not go to-day, but must have a horse to-morrow. There are reeds (rab) quite impassable." I explained how the canoe went through reeds in the lake of Hijaneh. "Yes," they answered, "but there is water in Hijaneh, now here the reeds are so," and they placed a sort of hedge of sticks at the bow of my canoe to explain.

I then began to amuse them by making sketches of men and horses, next I gave a lesson in geography by placing nut-shells at various points to represent "Sham" (Damascus), Musr (Cairo), El Khuds (Jerusalem), and Bahr (the lake of Hooleh), and at last placed one little shell at the extreme end of the tent to represent England so far away. They exclaimed loudly in astonishment at my long journey to see them. At intervals several of these men kept boring me for "bakshish." One was an old deaf cunning fellow, who whispered the word in my ear. Another, a sharp lad, who said he had seen the "Ingleez" at Beyrout, spoke incessantly to me by signs only, and he did it admirably. I was much interested in the clever variations of his noiseless pictures, always culminating in the same subject, "bakshish." A third applicant used no such delicate coyness in the matter, but merely roared out the hateful word before all, and louder every time.

No one had as yet offered me any food. This gross neglect (never without meaning among the Arabs) I determined now to expose, and so to test their real intentions. My cuisine was soon rigged up for cooking, and I asked for cold water. In two minutes afterwards the brave little lamp was steaming away at high pressure with its merry hissing sound. Every one came to see this. I cut thin slices of the preserved beef soup, and, while they were boiling, I opened my salt-cellar. This is a snuff-box, and from it I offered a pinch to the sheikh. He had never before seen salt so white, and therefore, thinking it was sugar, he willingly took some from my hand and put it to his tongue. Instantly I ate up the rest of the salt, and with a loud, laughing shout, I administered to the astonished outwitted sheikh a manifest thump on the back. "What is it?" all asked from him. "Is it sukker?" He answered demurely, "La! meleh!" (No, it's salt!) Even his home secretary laughed at his chief. We had now eaten salt together, and in his own tent, and so he was bound by the strongest tie, and he knew it.

The soup was now ready and boiling hot. They all examined my little metal spoon, and my carving-knife went round (it never came back). I gave every one of them seated in a circle about me one spoonful of the boiling soup, which, of course, scalded each man's mouth, and made him wince bitterly, yet without telling the next victim. Now they had all partaken of food with their prisoner. How much they relished it, I don't know. All went out, and I took this opportunity to stand near the sheikh, and try to slip the napoleon into his hand. He was quite uncertain what to do when the gold tickled his palm. It was utterly against their code of chief and people for him to take this secret personal gift from a stranger, yet he could not resist the temptation. His hand pushed mine away, but with a very gentle indignation. Soon his fingers played among mine as the yellow coin kept turning about, half held by each of us, unseen behind our backs. Two of the sheikh's fingers were pushing it away, but then the other three fingers were pulling it in. Finally I felt the coin had left me, and I knew now the sheikh was not only bought but *paid for*. Down went his countenance from that moment, and he slunk away abashed. An hour more of palaver was spent by the seniors, during which time I ate my luncheon heartily and read the "Times." Then all came back once more except the chief, and the women were rustling behind the mat screens, and a great bustle seemed to say that the verdict was agreed upon. The "foreman" briefly told it—"You are to go to-morrow."

This will never do—but how to reverse the sentence? I was seated on the ground at the time, and I rose very slowly and gravely, until, standing on a little eminence in the tent, and drawing myself up besides as tall as could be, and stretching up my hand as high as possible (and utterly undetermined what I was going to say, and exceedingly tempted to burst into laughter), I exclaimed with my loudest voice only three words, Bokra?—La!—Ingleez! (To-morrow?—No!—I am English!), and then the orator sunk calmly down and went on reading his paper again. In five minutes more a man came to say I might leave at once. But I was not to be shoved off in this way, so I insisted that they must carry my canoe back to the river. The procession, therefore, formed again, with the Rob Roy in the centre, and her captain walking behind, while boys and girls, and especially the people who had not already seen her on the water, all rushed in a crowd to the bank with the same hoarse shouts they had given before, and which we were now more accustomed to hear. All parties pledged their friendship in deep "salaams" of adieu, and we paddled off, rejoicing.

CHAPTER XVI.

Chase resumed.—A Rascal.—The River.—Buffaloes.—Snakes.—The Barrier. — How to eat. — Prison Fare. — The Rascal again.—Voice of the Night.—Hurrah.—Riding high-horse.—Free.—Duty.—Cheap.

BUT once out of sight of the huts, and when I had just begun a little song of lonely triumph, the crowd came running in pursuit, calling for " bakshish," and very urgent too. I chose out four men of the company, and promised to pay them as a body-guard. In a moment they emerged from their clothes, dashed into the stream, and then ran along the opposite bank. This was to keep me to themselves.

The two parties accompanying me, on different sides of the river, and having different objects, soon quarrelled. The four men on the west bank, who were naked and could swim the numerous lagoons that now branched around the river, called out to me, "Sook! sook!" that is "Pull! pull!" so as to make me go faster on, and thus enable them to return before the sun set. They wished to earn their payment as soon as they could. The others, however, on the east bank, who were delayed by carrying their clothes and clubs and ox-goads—some of them also being girls—commanded me to go slower, by an unceasing cry of "Awash-awash-awashawash!" (no doubt a continuous form of "Shweich." They wished to delay my progress and to extract money the while. This disturbance was an unlooked-for trouble and difficulty. It prevented me from making careful notes of the river's course in this interesting part of its channel, unseen by any other traveller, or, at all events, undescribed.

It was evident, too, that I was still not free, yet I determined to press on, resolved, if I could only get rid of the men, I would cheerfully sleep in the wildest part of the marsh, trusting for better times to-morrow.

The men on the east bank were more angry and insolent

as the current ran swifter. Baroda! again was the cry, and two of them pointed their guns at me as before.

One of these men, whose weapon was as tall as himself, did this at least twenty times in succession, and always called out "Bakshish!" while he brought up his gun to his cheek.

Now my purse was already empty, except of about a shilling, and though they wanted my watch I determined that at any rate for *that* my pistol might fairly be used in defense, because an Arab who would rob a traveller of his watch, would have no scruple about putting "out of the way" the only witness against him, who would be certain to compel the robber to deliver back the booty through the pasha.

The man's repeated menace and pointing of the gun became so common a thing that I speedily got used to the action, and at last, on one occasion, when the muzzle of the long barrel was very close, I moved it aside with my paddle.* After this he stopped, and all on his side with him. Luckily they had come to where a deep lagoon intercepted their progress, and with clothes or guns they could not well swim across this, so I was now more free to observe the river.

Here it was level with the marsh. Much of its volume was lost by flooding aside into branches. The main branch turned and twisted exceedingly, and was now only twenty feet wide at the little group of huts called Zweer,†

---

* It is not very difficult to understand how a soldier becomes used to bullets in the battle. I do not think that *courage* is either increased or diminished by experience, but that it is entirely congenial in kind and degree. Daring or boldness may be called forth by frequent use of them with immunity, or coolness by finding its extreme value, or by desire to sustain reputation, or these may be lessened by experience enforcing caution; but that seems to be because experience enables one man to dare more as he finds the danger less, and forces another to dare less when he finds that the danger is more than he thought at first. A man can learn *what* to fear most, but to fear is born in him. A poodle and a mastiff are different even from their puppyhood.

† This is evidently the last dwelling in the marsh. Thomson states that he had a list of thirty-two villages in the plain, but they were all movable huts, and there was not a "house" in any of them.

LOOLEH HUTS.

out of which another set of men rushed forth, and several of them with guns. However, my four nude aides-de-camp talked to these neighbors, and they allowed us to go on, and half a dozen of the new-comers swam with the others and easily kept pace with the boat.

The swimmers raised a long sharp cry together, calling over and over a word I could not make out, but which was evidently meant as a warning. Yamoos! Yamoos! they shouted, pointing to a dangerous sweep of the stream where six or seven large buffaloes were immersed in the water, and only their heads appeared, and horns and round staring eyes.

In my first canoe voyage, when the Rob Roy and the "Rothion"* began the river Meuse, we met a large herd of bullocks swimming across the stream, and at first sight they looked formidable, but it was soon perceived that they

---

* This canoe is the Earl of Aberdeen's, and she went for a week with the Rob Roy on her voyage to the Danube. The Rothion afterwards crossed the English Channel at night (being the first canoe to perform that feat), under the management of the late Hon. J. Gordon, one of the best oarsmen, best rifle-shots, best canoeists, and best of Christians.

were far more afraid of our canoes than we need be of their horns. Still these were not wild oxen, and we had allowed them room to retreat, whereas the buffaloes in the Jordan were come of a turbulent stock not famed for politeness, and perhaps now they might decline to give way, or they might even attack.

At any rate, the men were unaccountably careful to keep off. I ordered them all to stop perfectly quiet, and then the Rob Roy floated gently through the group of horns and eyes, and not one of the buffaloes did any thing worse than to stare.*

The river forked out now into six different channels. The guides disputed as to which was best, but every one was hopelessly bad, and with all our care—the men working splendidly to help me—the Rob Roy became firmly entangled in a maze of bushes eight feet high. The men bravely pulled us through, but only to get her fixed again in the thickset stumps and reeds and thorny branches which studded the marsh exactly as they had been represented to me so graphically in the tent.

To the utmost possible limit of this I hauled and pushed and punted the Rob Roy, but there was an end to further progress except by getting out. The men standing round, and up to their middles in the water, were amazed to see me also jump into the river.

Immediately there was a sharp twinge at my leg, like the cut of a lancet, and only then I recollected what I had been warned of so often—water-snakes.† But it was mere-

---

* St. Willibald, in the eighth century, speaks of the buffaloes of Hooleh, as "wonderful herds, with long backs, short legs, and large horns; all of them are of one color," and that they immersed themselves in the marshes except their heads (Robinson, vol. iii. p. 342, note).

Thomson ("The Land and the Book," vol. i. pp. 384, 385) seems to consider that the "behemoth" of Job meant the buffalo, and that the land of Uz may be reasonably supposed to be that east of Hooleh, the name of which might be derived from Hul, the brother of Uz.

† May not these be alluded to in the words of Moses—"Dan shall be a serpent by the way, an adder in the path, that biteth the horse heels, so that his rider shall fall backward?" (Gen. xlix. 17). One of the mounds in the morass is called Tell Hay, the "hill of snakes."

ly a leech. There are thousands of these in a pond above Banias, and men catch them for sale by dipping their limbs in the water. It is evident now that there are leeches also in Jordan. Upon a deliberate survey of the little horizon around me, it was perfectly clear that no boat, or even a reed raft, or a plank, could get through the dense barrier before me. I much question whether a duck could, or dare, go far into it, and only a fish would be safe.*

In one sense it was satisfactory to find the obstacle thus definite and beyond attempt. Had it been otherwise, or with the faintest chance for an entrance, I might have spent hours in vain, and the men would have left me as hopeless and mad, and still there would have been before me miles of this impassable, nor can any one say how this would have ended.

Now that their words were proved true, I frankly confessed it was so, saying, "Mafeesh derb!" my Arabic for "No road." So from the point marked N in Map V., we began our journey back. It was a hard fight to retreat against current and snag. The men helped to their utmost, but all of us were already tired. Sometimes they insisted upon towing the boat, but that was soon found to be useless.†

After a tedious travel back, we reached the village banks, and the Rob Roy was carried into another tent—that of the whispering senator, not that of the sheikh. I was wet and weary, and put on more clothes and thick carpets, for I began to shiver. Then a fire was lighted, and the cold night air blew round me rolled up like a ball on the floor.

I noticed a man with a horse, and in secret got a word

---

* This will be confirmed by our knowledge of the other side of this barrier, as explained in the next chapter.

† Towing a light boat in a winding river is one of the most dangerous of aquatic performances. If you tow it down stream, it is nearly sure to run ashore. If you try to tow it up stream, it is most likely to get upset at the corners, when its head is not free, and, in such a case, the contents of the capsized boat float away in a moment, and if you lose hold of your craft, it may be impossible to regain it by swimming.

with him. I promised him good pay if he would start off at once to my dragoman at Mellaha. He said, "To-morrow," but I firmly replied, "To-night much pay—to-morrow no pay at all;" then he asked me for a "writing" to give my dragoman. I knew that Hany could not read English, and that I could not write Arabic, but I sketched upon a bit of paper my canoe fixed in a tree, and this the man put into his pocket. Of course I felt sure that he would not—could not—start over the marsh in the dark.

The tent was soon filled by fifty men sitting closely together. The sheikh came too, but with a face of most hang-dog cheerfulness. He and the host and myself sat cross-legged near the canoe, and on the other side of the bright crackling fire were the visitors. In came a huge wooden bowl of smoking "kusskoosoo," a kind of small bean porridge uncommonly good to eat. Three little black saucers of buffalo cream were set by us, the magnates, and three wooden spoons. Water was brought for our hands, then the chief showed me the manner to eat my supper. Taking a spoonful of the cream he put it in his part of the general bowl and mixed it as he pleased, while I did the same at my side, and the other dark Arab at his. The people in front dipped their hands in the public dish as often as possible, and rolling up a ball of the contents in three fingers, each man cleverly whipped the food into his mouth. When we at the top had finished, the bowl was passed among the rest until every man had his supper. We all drank out of one narrow-necked water-jar. Newcomers dropped in, and each of them bowed to the sheikh and saluted the company. They all behaved with excellent propriety and good-breeding, and yet without any constraint.

Their whole talk was about our day's adventures, especially the lesson in geography—not that in the canoe, but by means of the nutshells—so I had to repeat it, and on a much larger scale. Then I told them a long story about steamboats which I had told to another Arab tribe twenty years before at the Dead Sea. Some old dirty figs were produced as dessert, and I resolved to give them a treat from the "caboose" of the Rob Roy. Roast fowl came forth, therefore, and rice pudding, fine white bread, dates, excellent almonds and raisins, sugar, pepper, eggs, and the best black tea from old England. The raisins they seemed not to know, for they passed them from hand to hand. The tea, too, was quite a novelty, but by far the most prized was the pudding.

Pipes were soon puffing. Every man of them pressed me to smoke his, and a youngster next but one to me* was my greatest favorite from his lively laugh and eyes like diamonds, and his quick perception of all I explained. In a whisper I was told an hour after that this was the identical hero who had aimed at me so often with his gun until I knocked it away with my paddle. I did not now alter my bearing towards him, for it would have been difficult to explain why. Perhaps it would have been difficult for this young rascal to explain why he aimed at me so often, though one can easily understand why the other one had fired the shot before. For consider that, while these people had never seen nor heard of a boat, they had all heard about ghosts and water-sprites, and so when they suddenly saw a thing with a man's face, but all the rest of it unlike a man—a long brown double-ended body joined

---

* He smoked the "sebeel," a curious short pipe from Bagdad, without any stem. An Arab usually carries his chibouque thrust down his back, with the bowl uppermost, near his turban. If he loses his pipe, or forgets to bring it, he is in desperation, almost as bad as a lady who has mislaid her reticule. Once, in Egypt, the man who took us to some caves had left his pipe behind. When we came out, he had rolled up a large thick brown paper, in which we brought the candles, and out of them he made a cigarette twelve inches long and an inch thick. My muleteer, Latoof, was the most inveterate smoker of our party on the tour, and by far the strongest man, but it was the nargilleh he affected, and not the chibouque. At Kerak, on the Sea of Galilee, his nargilleh was lost, and we were too far away from a village to buy another. In this difficult strait, Latoof went mooning about for an hour or two, but to solace his bereavement, he got a glass bottle, and two reeds, and some clay, and long grass, and a bit of wood, and with great ingenuity he managed to construe a new nargilleh, whereat Adoor, our laureate, had to compose a special song, and the old chorus was soon heard again in the gurgling of the hubblebubble.

PRISON FARE IN THE WATERS OF MEROM.

by gray skin to a gray pot-shaped head, and waving about two blue hands (the paddle-blades)—which of them could refrain from taking a shot at such a creature? Would you or I, walking with a loaded gun and a finger on the trigger, and eager for an excuse to fire, if *we* saw for the first time a thing in the air unknown before and yet plainly living, *could* we resist the desire to fire at it instantly? Not I, certainly; so my assailant might well be forgiven.

It was late when I was left with the old Arab only. After one look out on the bright moon, the starry night, and the palm-tree in front of us, I piled wood upon the fire, and carpets upon myself, and matting against the wide-chinked walls of our camel's-hair lodging. Behind a division* in the tent, and within a foot of my ear, was a poor woman groaning all night in the distress of illness. I pitied her sadly in the dark, that she was suffering while I was so happy and well; but I could not speak to her—that would have been felony at the least. The Arab snored beside the dying embers. Fitful thoughts sped dreamily through my brain. I had resolved to slip out unperceived when all were asleep and to cross the river, and then drag my canoe into a hiding-place until morning, and so to scramble somehow over the marsh, and then conceal the canoe and walk on to the camp at Mellaha. But after all attempts to devise a plan, I could not find any method of paying the men who had been my guides, and of course it would never do to leave them unpaid.

In the gentle slumbering of playful dreams that followed, and which are often most pleasant when one is thoroughly tired, a faint far voice seemed to flutter in the midnight. Again I heard it—wakened, and then heard it again distinctly, though so distant, calling out clearly a long-drawn "Rob——Roy——!" The thrill that nerved me in an instant started me up erect, and with the loudest, longest hail I ever gave in my life, I shouted "Rob Roy!"

---

* The expression in Genesis xviii. 10, "And Sarah heard it in the tent door which was behind him," is supposed to mean that she was then on the women's side of the division or screen across the tent.

in return. It was indeed my faithful Hany who was calling to me through the dark morass. Up rose the Arab, and clutched my feet convulsively. He thought I was raving, but it was only joy. I told him, "My dragoman is coming, hurrah!" but we listened long again, and yet no answer came to my hails, for Hany was now fording the Jordan, and he had quite enough to do. My messenger had, in fact, reached the camp at Mellaha, and had found Hany just arriving after eleven hours on horseback. Yet not for a moment did Hany hesitate what to do—to rest, or to rescue the Rob Roy. The messenger then told him he had brought a letter from me, but searching for it, no letter could be found.* Hany then suspected some plot of the Arabs to capture both dragoman and master. Yet the brave fellow started, and traversed this desolate wold.

And now the sound of near hoofs reached me, and a loud long hail, which was answered by the Englishman's authorized formula, "All right!" Up trotted Hany on his tight little Arab quite as game yet as it had been at sunrise. Latoof came on my horse, and Adoor on the horse for the canoe.

All was changed round us in a moment by this arrival. The news spread fast, and the sleepers were roused in the huts. "Leave it all now to me, sir," said Hany; so I sank into a mere spectator of a real drama in life, and the play of character seen for the next half-hour was far beyond the fancies of the hired fictitious stage. Hany stirred up the old host to extreme activity, and then piled up a blazing fire, sent for the Arabs all round, and rated them soundly with caustic effrontery. One Arab dared to half mutter a protest, but Hany spurned him to the floor; he launched out thus against even our friends, and abused Latoof for not quickly cleaning my boots—saying (aside) to me, in English, "Don't mind, sir! Latoof and I have arranged all this before." Hany was abject to me in manner—respectful is not the word—but contemptuous to the wild

---

* He had lost it in the marsh, and I have got it now (all stained by his red sash), having found the letter myself in the water.

Hoolehites, and all this was as much as to say to them, "See how you are like grasshoppers before *me*—yet I am but the slave of Howaja, and *his* height above you how measureless—him you have dared to insult!"

I ventured to suggest, though timidly, "Hany, all this is but humbug." His answer was instant and final, "Without humbug, master, we could never manage these men." Candles, and a sumptuous feast, and a brilliant teapot, came quickly out of his saddle-bags. I had to sit in state, and to eat with feigned hunger, while the Arabs could only gaze with awe.

It was difficult not to smile at their altered bearing, but I paid all of them well that had worked for me, and managed to get a few compass-bearings by the pale light of dawn. Amid the loud rebukes and feeble answers at our parting, there was an amusing conversation in an undertone, and which we may render thus, wherein *H.* is my indignant dragoman, and *A.* is the Arab least abashed in reply:

H. Who was it fired on my master?

A. He was a Druse—a stranger.

H. When did he come, and where did he go?

A. He came two hours before, and left at once.

H. Why did you not catch him? Why did he fire?

A. Because the boat was so low the Howaja was sure to be drowned, and because, if he went on, he was sure to lose his way.

H. And so to save him from drowning, or being lost, you thought it best to shoot him? Ah! dogs, brutes, pigs, Jews!*

---

* Here, as well as some twenty years before, I heard men in Palestine call their fellows "Jew," as the very lowest of all possible words of abuse. When we recollect that the Jews in this very land, their own, were once the choice people of the world; that now, through the whole earth, among the richest, the bravest, the cleverest, the fairest, the best at music and song, at poetry and painting, at art, and science, and literature, at education, philanthropy, statesmanship, war, commerce, and finance, in every sphere of life, are Jews—we may well remember the word of prophecy which told us long ago that the name of Jew would be a "by-word and a reproach," even in the Jews' own land.

S

H. After Howaja paid you, why did one of your own men aim at him?

A. Only to frighten Howaja.

H. Did it frighten him?

A. Why—no.

H. Do you think a great English prince will be frightened by *your* wretched guns? (Hany had his double-barrelled English rifle and his Colt's revolver dangling about most ostentatiously all this time.) Did you ever hear of Abyssinia?

A. Oh yes! we know all about the Ingleez at "Habash."

And so on.

We soon forded the Jordan—the Rob Roy carrying me. The journey over the plain, in a direction N. W., was difficult; but what must it have been last night for Hany and the jaded horses? Often the Rob Roy had to be carried by hand, or floated on the pools, while the horses scrambled through. Once the sturdy Latoof went down completely overhead in a treacherous hole.

At another place the canoe-horse sunk down until his head was buried in soft mud, even above his eyes, yet he flinched not at all. I never saw so steady a nag. Other parts of this journey, or voyage, were so much of land and water* mixed that I towed the Rob Roy along the surface by tying her painter to my waist in the saddle. The two guides who accompanied us from Salhyeh being handsomely paid, we trudged along easily under the mountains for the rest of our road, but Hany, still furious at the whole transaction of these two days, was urgent that I should write upon it to the English Consul at Damascus.

It is a traveller's duty to think of the others that may follow his route, and to remedy abuses, and to punish extortions, and to abstain from doubtful actions, lest others may suffer, even if he is not injured. No person can be

---

* One of three larger streams we forded was called by the Arabs "Ain Messieh," the "spring of Christ." Another was Ain Bellatu, "fountain of big stones." Our route along these is marked on Map V.

more sensible of this duty than one who has been so much benefited by the good conduct of other travellers as I have been; and it would not be from carelessness or a forgetful content with my own good-fortune that I should by weakness, or lavish giving, or by niggard pay, or winking at wrong, do any thing to spoil a good road for future tourists. But, after mature reflection on this incident in Hooleh marsh, I felt it was not one to complain of to our consul. The custom, well settled over all the East, is that the traveller must either come guarded by the local ruling power with an escort of adequate force; or he must contract with an Arab tribe, in which case the "ghufr," or protection payment, makes the receiver of it responsible; or, thirdly, the traveller may go at his own risk, but then he must abide the usual consequences, and can not fairly complain either to his own Government at home or to that of the Sultan.*

Now, the canoe could not have a Turkish guard, for it paddled where even Arabs could scarcely swim. Then its crew could not contract for "ghufr," because no tribe would answer for a man's safety unless their sheikh or his soldiers could go with him. Having chosen the third of these plans—that of travelling alone—I had to deal with the Hooleh Arabs only as between individuals; and, after all, they had done me no harm, and had not injured the boat. They extorted money, indeed, but that is not uncommon in Europe. They fired at me point-blank, but then it was because the thing they fired at was unlike any thing they had ever seen before, with a voice coming out of it singing in an outlandish tongue.

Nor were these Arabs very rapacious when they found that the ghost was a man. The Arabs of Hooleh do

---

* A Yankee sailor once shared my tent for some days, and being impatient of the slow travel, he took one of our muleteers, and set off by himself. He wore a "chimney-pot" hat and black coat, just as if he was in a European town. In a week he was robbed of all but his hat and coat. He got fitted out again by his consul, and in ten days more all his money was stolen again. Meanwhile I plodded on, and saw far more, and spent far less.

not go to the great centres of Eastern commerce, such as Damascus, Aleppo, or Jerusalem, where they would meet Europeans. Their trade is carried on by wandering Druses, who act as middlemen, while the natives stick fast in their primitive mud. Again, travellers do not stray to the suburbs of Zweer, and therefore, happily, the natives did not know what a ransom they might have demanded —at least £100—as the proper price for an Englishman; and I really can not complain of their terms of compromise, when I had a feast, and a lodging, and porters, and protection, and excellent fun, and all for the very reduced tariff of 16s. 4d. sterling.

The whole transaction was harmless, after all, and it was an interesting comment upon the prediction of what Ishmael was to be—"his hand shall be against every man and every man's hand against him."

CHAPTER XVII.

Mellaha. — Waters of Merom. — The Lake. — Raft of Bulrushes. — From above. — Puzzle. — Kedesh. — Start. — Arabs again. — Pelican-hunt. — Grand Discovery. — New Mouth. — Thunder. — Inner Lake. — Lilies. — Royal Salute. — Breadth of Barrier. — Sixteen Swans. — Papyrus. — Its Use. — How it grows. — Bent by Current.

RIDING on in front, my gray helmet was seen over the hill by our men at the camp near Mellaha, and shouts soon told how glad they were. After a little paddle on the lake and a bath, the remainder of the day was not too long to spend in rest upon my own comfortable sofa-bed. The change from prison to freedom, from uncouth strangers to my own contented, well-behaved retinue, with the Rob Roy now released and sleeping all safe in the sun, and Hany recounting his story, and melodious Adoor singing it all over again, while a dim picture of its best scenes kept ever moving past me in day-dream—this was an enjoyment which only the lone traveller can feel.

This great morass of Hooleh, or the lake at the end of it is spoken of once in the Bible as "the waters of Merom" (Joshua xi. 5). It is called by Josephus and later writers Samachonitis; and the name of Hooleh, as applied to the vicinity, is at least as old as the Christian era. Some of the Arabs in the neighborhood call it the lake of El-Mellahah, and others Bahr Banias, or Bahr Hait.*

---

* The name Merom is from the Hebrew, "high lake." "This explanation of Merom is undoubted" (Stanley, "S. and P." 391, note); and the place is also called "Kaldayeh," "the high."

The name Samachon (Josephus, "Jewish War," book iii. ch. x. sec. vii.; and book iv. ch. i. sec. i.) has three explanations:

(1.) From the Arabic Samak, "high."

(2.) From the Chaldaic Samak, "red;" which may well allude to the red clay banks of the Jordan, already noticed, or to the very dark water in the lake itself.

The name of Hooleh, as applied to the lake, is as old as the Crusades. This may be derived from Hul, or Chul, one of the sons of Aram (Gen. x. 23).*

The name "Melcha" ("the salt") is applied by William of Tyre to the whole of the lake ("Will. Tyre," xviii. 13), "circa lacum Melcha." Burkhardt says (vol. i. p. 316): "The south-west shore bears the name of Mellaha, from the ground being covered with a saline crust;" but I did not observe any thing of a deposit except a grayish clay where the water of the lake is deep, quite close to the bank. The Arabs give the name "Ain Mellaha" to the spring running in at the north-west angle of the lake. Schwartz speaks of it as Ain Malka (p. 29), "Spring of the King," which may allude to Joshua's battle; for we find Neby Yusha (Tomb of Joshua) on the hill to the west of the centre of the marsh, and on the east is said to be the Tell Farash (the Arab name of Joshua).†

The wide level tract on the south-west verge of the lake is called "Ard el-Hait," or "Belad el-Hait." This level ground is richly cultivated,‡ justifying the name, for "hait"

(3.) From the Arabic Samach, "a fish." It is called Samac in the Jerusalem Talmud. The name Sabac, "a thorn," given to it in the Babylonian Talmud, it is said, "may allude to the thorny jungle round it," but I saw no "thorns" in any part.

* We may compare the tomb of Sitteh Hooleh, the "Lady Hooleh," near Baalbec. Robinson (vol. iii. Appendix, pp. 135, 137) speaks of the other Hooleh in the government of Hanes; and Finn mentions a village of the name east of Tibneen ("Byeways of Palestine," pp. 257, 386). In Smith's Dictionary ("Merom"), it is said that the word Hooleh seems in Arabic and in Hebrew to mean "depression." This may well explain how the term Hooleh is first applied to the district "Ard Hooleh," as a "hollow" among the hills, while "Merom" indicates the lake, as "high" among the waters. Burkhardt says: "The lake of Houleh or Samachonitis is inhabited only on the eastern borders" (vol. i. p. 316). I have used the spelling "Hooleh" instead of the usual one "Huleh," as the latter is apt to be pronounced "Heuleh."

† Stanley, "S. and P." p. 393, note. The "Wady Farash" is also marked in Vandevelde's map (as I have inserted it in mine), but though I asked the Arabs for it frequently, they never seemed to agree as to the exact spot; nevertheless the name was evidently known.

‡ Pococke places Harosheth here ("Pinkerton's Voyages," x. 463), and many authors consider that Joshua's battle with Jabin was on this plain.

means "wheat." A beautiful lily flourishes here, and is renowned as the "Lily of Hooleh.*

From Map VI. it will be seen that Mellaha, where we are resting for Sunday, is at the north-west corner of the lake of Hooleh, on the pleasant sward beside a quiet lagoon. On this, in the shallows, I found a man afloat on a bundle of reeds, which he punted along, while his spear was stuck up like a mast. His delight and surprise when

REED RAFT.

the Rob Roy glided alongside, and then darted away to the depths where he could not follow, amused me much. From this, as head-quarters, it was my purpose to thoroughly examine these curious upland waters, because the few references to them in travellers' books are exceedingly meagre; and yet great decisive battles had been fought upon these shores, and the steps of our blessed Lord had hallowed their eastern verge.

It is impossible to examine the upper part of this lake except from a boat, for the boundary there is entirely com-

* Thomson thinks that this is the plant referred to by our Saviour when He compares Solomon with the lilies (Luke xii. 27).

posed of tall papyrus plant,* perfectly inaccessible to man on account of its extremely close growth, and therefore this has never before been visited by any one who has told us what is there. And great additional interest was imparted to this voyage by the fact I had just proved, that the Jordan can not be followed all the way from its source; but that it eludes our sight by diving into jungle, where it defies all search from the north side as to where its waters roll into this lake of Merom. Therefore it became important to go from the lake itself upward along any channel containing the river, and then to go as far as the barrier which had stopped us in descending, so as to see how broad that barrier is. The result of the next few days' work upon the problem was an ample reward for all the trouble incurred in the complete and novel discovery of the hitherto unknown channel, as will speedily be seen.

First, in order to scan the district from above, I ascended the hills nearest Mellaha. There were ruins upon each of them, but we can not stop to consider these now when our eye is fixed upon the wider features of the plain.

From this height the lake is seen just below us, bounded on the east by the hills of Bashan, which form a high plateau, behind which one sees the tops of another distant range. Westward of the lake, on the wide green level, a few tells rise by the water's side, and little groups of dwellings.† The dwellers here must be hardened to fever and frogs, wild boars, snakes, and ague half the year. They have many buffaloes and horses, but their trade is done by oth-

---

* This is explained in detail (*post*, p. 294).

† Stanley's description of this is not so accurate as his other pictures in words of what he saw himself. "In the centre of this plain, half morass, half tarn, lies the uppermost lake of the Jordan, about seven miles long, and in its greatest width six miles broad, the mountains slightly compressing it at either extremity, surrounded by an almost impenetrable jungle of reeds, abounding in wild fowl" ("S. and P." p. 390). According to my observation the size of the lake is not one-fourth of the area given here, the reeds are thin and easily entered, and in the jungle of papyrus, which is impenetrable, there are very few waterfowl, while the "lake," whether that means the whole morass, or the open water, is not by any means in the centre of the plain. Finn says that there is a Wady Meleh, or Salt Vale, near Carmel.

ers, for the natives seem to revel in their marshy home and rear their red rice,* while the big world outside them is left to roll on as it can.

In different seasons and in different years the whole appearance of this lake and its shores must be altogether different. Thus, thirty years ago, Mr. Smith, twice travelling here, "had been able to get from the road only one or two glimpses of the water."† But when I saw it, the banks of the lake were quite bare except on the north side, where stands, as a savage border to the open water, the densest jungle ever man can see. This is nearly three miles across and perfectly flat, with a sombre color, and is marked with shading on Map VI. The outline of the lake is irregular, but distinct. The marsh above it has a few still darker lines winding through the level, evidently the deeper shades of narrow hollows like canals, bounded by the jungle which hems in these silent, stagnant streams. Farther to the north are patches of water,‡ with islets plainly visible, and then the prospect shades away to greener hues until the eye rests on the trees of Dan, far off, and lofty heights of Banias.

Dr. Thomson speaks of this lake as a peculiar "pet" of his, and says it is of "unrivalled beauty." One is allowed to say this about a "pet lake," but I do not yet feel that enthusiasm.

Between the marsh itself and the western shore—which we had skirted by the path under the hills—an irregular edging of water lies in disjointed shreds. This water is

---

* Schwartz says (p. 47): "Many canes also grow here, among which wild beasts, etc., find shelter, especially serpents and wild boars. Not far from the village Malcha, situated on its northern shore, the Jordan enters this lake. The inhabitants of the village just named cultivate the rice plant in this vicinity, which is the only place in Palestine where this plant grows. This rice, which is sent to the other towns, is quite singular in its color and flavor; it is red in appearance, and swells in cooking to an unusual degree."

† Robinson, vol. iii. sec. xv. p. 341, note.

‡ The largest of these, near the centre, and which we visited afterwards, may have been that alluded to by Buckingham, as another lake north of Hooleh. See Robinson, vol. iii. sec. xv. p. 340, note.

often several feet deep,* and I had paddled my canoe upon it in various places; nor would it be difficult, I think, to come all the way by water from the upper plain quite down to the lake. But in this bordering edge there is no perceptible current, though it receives a few rills from springs near the margin. At any rate, to take a boat along this fringe of puddles would not be to follow the Jordan.

Then where does the Jordan run to when it hides its dark stream after Zweer? Vandevelde's map boldly marks it on the east of the marsh, and most other maps do the same. Dr. Tristram, the traveller who has written of it after dwelling longest here, says that Jordan's course can be clearly distinguished on the east.† More cautious myself, perhaps, in tracing rivers than those who have not to get a boat through the imagined channel, I could not discern any sign of a stream on the east part of Hooleh, and for the good reason, as was afterwards proved, that no river at all goes there.

The ruins of Kedes (Kedesh Nephtali) are in a valley to the west of the lake; and although I saw them from above, and they would be very interesting to describe, yet I must not depart so far from our actual log.

Having made careful plans of the marsh by bird's-eye views of it from several hills, I started from Mellaha, ardent and rejoicing, to begin this most interesting voyage of discovery. The weather was very propitious for such an occasion: a cloudy day, with no wind, and a general mildness. I had, of course, arranged a regular plan of investigation, so as to measure the distances by counting my paddle-strokes, checked by the time on my watch; to take the angles by my compass; and to sound the depth by a 20-fathom line. To do these four different things accurately,

---

* I agree with Robinson, who says this is an artificial canal. He also states that it is led off from the Hasbany (vol. iii. sec. xv. p. 342), which is now known to be the case. Thomson describes the fountains of this side in detail.

† Smith's "Dictionary of the Bible" also tells us the Jordan "enters the lake close to the eastern end of the upper side."

and to note the results in my log-book, gave full employment to mind and body, while any thing to spare of energy was devoted to look out for curious sights, birds, fishes, animals, plants, and stones, to scan the shores for hostile Arabs, and to note the character of the hills aloft and the beaches by the waterside.

The first "course" for the canoe was to be straight across the lake at the northern end, where the water is widest, and then to inspect the supposed mouth of the Jordan in the east. Next I intended to embark a stone from the Bashan shore, wherewith to commence soundings at regular intervals on the return voyage. But after 800 double paddle-strokes, that is, about two miles and a half due east, I could see an Arab with a gun descending the slope of the rugged mountains straight in front of me. I turned to the right, and he followed. I went the other way, until the Rob Roy was hid behind the jungle, but standing up in the boat I could see through the reed-tops that the man was lying under a shady tree on a beautiful green tell close by the waterside. Now, whether the man had shooting intentions or not, it would evidently have been unwise for me to turn up a channel (if one was found there), leaving him in command of the mouth of it to intercept my return. Therefore, as he would not depart or come out of his hiding-place, I turned south along the eastern shore, and he followed running, and half a dozen more soon clambered down from the rocks shouting all in chorus. But in open water I could laugh at their humble efforts to keep up with the Rob Roy as they struggled through thickets and round deep bays, while I had a smooth lake to paddle on, and in any direction I chose. However, it being absolutely necessary for me to land that I might get a stone for sounding, I made a feint as if to reach a point jutting out, and when they were all in full cry for this to reach it also, I coolly turned to another promontory, leaving a bay between us, and ran the Rob Roy into the bank below some shady trees. Very soon I could hear the Arabs splashing through the shallow edge of the bight, and breaking down the jungle canes in an eager rush to my new landing-place. But after choosing and taking on board three stones, we slipped away in good time, and when they arrived, all hot and hasty, the Rob Roy was quietly floating in deep water 250 yards from the shore. This was the distance Hany told me would be safe, as an Arab would not risk his bullet for a longer shot. All their efforts to persuade me to land were futile. I am afraid I "chaffed" them rather unceremoniously, but then they roared at me till they were hoarse.

The process of sounding now proceeded methodically, and the entries of time, distance, depth, etc., soon occupied all my attention. Some beautiful Arab horses were grazing under the trees. Little coveys of wild ducks bobbed about on the sunny wavelets, or the shy ones dived, or the wary took wing. Now and then pelicans sailed by on the air in solemn silence, and seagulls skimmed the edges of scattered isles. But after the myriads of ducks at Hijaneh, and the clouds of pink flamingoes, and swans and pelicans, on Lake Menzaleh, one is "spoiled" for any wonderment at a few hundred birds anywhere else. However, at one pretty bay on the deep green papyrus margin I came upon a group of six pelicans together, swimming very near me. The desire to bring back a pelican from Hooleh seized me irresistibly, but how to do it, with only a small pocket-pistol? I cautiously "stalked" them round reeds and tiny islands, until I could fire with good hopes of hitting. At the shot five birds rose majestically, but the sixth remained floating there. His struggles to rise were vigorous, but in vain, for he had only one wing to beat the air, so he always fell sideways again on the water. Quickly my pistol was reloaded, but with my last bullet, and I must not throw this away. I knew it would be a difficult piece of business to kill this powerful bird. His struggles with me might overset the Rob Roy, or with his strong beak he might smash her cedar deck or her captain's face. Then what to do with him when dead? He was far too large and awkward as a cargo to carry two miles in comfort, and cutting off his head would be a troublesome operation. So I resolved to make him carry his own big body all the way to the camp by chasing him towards it while he swam. We both prepared for the chase. He began by disgorging a volley of small fish from his beak, but I took a different plan, for, as it was now full time for luncheon, I put my usual lunch on the deck before me and ate luxuriously at intervals while I chased the poor pelican for an hour and a half. He soon saw what were my tactics, and he swerved right and left to get back into the coverts; but I headed him always like a greyhound coursing a hare, and yet never came within a few feet of his beak, lest he might be driven to attack my boat in desperation.

Our camp had been moved down to Almanyeh, and our men there wondered to see the Rob Roy coming slowly from afar and very crooked in her course, with a white something in front of her bow, which seemed in the distance to be a foaming wave. When near the camp, I rushed in quickly to get the double-barrel, and then went off again to the pelican, who meantime was far on his way to some reedy home. There was only small shot in the gun, and that could not penetrate his feathers; but at length I chased him ashore, and he was soon enveloped in an Arab cloak, fighting bravely all the time. His wing measured four feet six inches, which (allowing for the body) would give about ten feet of stretch between the two tips. His head I brought home, but the great black feet, which it was thought would dry into a sort of imperishable leather, were soon dissolved into a mass of black meaningless jelly.*

---

* The Arabs call the pelican "mjah," and sometimes "jemel el bahr," that is, "sea-camel," which well describes its manner of carrying the head with the neck in a double arch. Besides those that fly by the sea, and the Nile, and the lake Merom, the pelican is found upon other lonely ponds. Finn states that one was killed in Solomon's Pools, near Jerusalem.

The captured head, which has curly feathers, was shown (with other curiosities of this voyage) at the exhibition held in summer by the Palestine Exploration Fund, as remarkable on account of its size, the manner of its capture, and the place where it was taken.

Next day was devoted to a strict examination of the northern side of Merom, and very soon on turning into one of the deep bays in the papyrus, I noticed a sensible current in the water. In a moment every sense was on the *qui vive*, and with quick-beating heart and earnest paddle-strokes I entered what proved to be *the mouth of Jordan*. At this place the papyrus is of the richest green, and upright as two walls on either hand, and so close in its forest of stems and dark recurving hair-like tops above that no bird can fly into it, and the very few ducks that I found had wandered in by swimming through chinks below, were powerless to get wing for rising, and while their flappings agitated the jungle, and their cackling shrieks told loudly how much they wished to escape from the intruder, the birds themselves were entirely invisible, though only a few yards from me all the time. But they were safe enough from me or any other stranger, for in no part could I ever get the point of the Rob Roy to enter three feet into the dense hedge of this curious floating forest.

The Jordan's mouth here is hundred feet wide, and it is entirely concealed from both shores by a bend it makes to the east. The river thus enters the lake at the *end* of a promontory of papyrus, and one can understand that this projection is caused by the plants growing better where the water runs than in the still parts, so that the walls or banks of green are prolonged by the current itself. Once round the corner, and entering the actual river, it is a wonderful sight indeed. The graceful channel winds in ample sweeps or long straight reaches in perfect repose and loneliness with a soft beauty of its own. Recovering from the first excitement of this important discovery, I set about recording all its features in a methodical way. First, of course, by counting paddle-strokes, as I slowly mounted the stream, then by noting the bends right and left in my book, and the few tributaries that entered on this side and that. On the west, one joined which I might have easily mistaken for the true channel, but happily recollecting my sketch made from the mountains, I knew that this

THE NEW FOUND MOUTH OF THE JORDAN.

arm from the west ends in nothing, so I went steadily up the other. Presently a strange noise came out of the foliage, and approaching cautiously, I found two great falcons or water-eagles feeding on something in their nest on an islet. The Rob Roy at once "beat to quarters," but when her crew attempted to "board," out rushed the male bird, and screamed and whirled about me so defiant that "discretion was the better part of valor," and the nest was left alone.

A few tiny sparrow-like birds hovered here and there on the papyrus tops, and two or three divers swam a yard or so in the open, and then rose and went out of sight; but the solitary silence of the place was almost painful, and it begot a feeling of awe when nothing but green jungle was present on every side, and yet I was glad no other man was there—not from churlish jealousy, but for his own sake too, who might wish to enjoy this scene—let him come also, but free from me, and at some other time. The paddle in new places is best enjoyed alone, just as the fishing-rod or the exciting tale.

The channel narrowed, and the current sharpened, too, at 800 double strokes (about 4000 yards), and I confess that here I was almost about to return, from some vague unaccountable fear, or weariness, or presentiment that I was to be lost in the maze of green; it seemed then so far to have gone away from life and light outside, and in so short a time. Very often since have I rejoiced that more bravery came, and I determined at least to rest and think, before returning. The Rob Roy clung to the shady side of the channel, and then a long and glorious peal of thunder rolled athwart the sky.

I have listened to that deep-toned voice when standing on a volcano's crater—when gazing at night on the Falls of Niagara—and when sailing alone in the hurtlings of a midnight storm on the breakers at Beachy Head. These were, indeed, splendid times and places for hearing in the depths of one's mind the loud speaking that comes out of the unseen. But none of them was so perfectly new and

T

strange as this one single roar from heaven, shaking the vast quiet of Hooleh.

An immediate effect of it was to awaken energy and to nerve me to go on, so as at least to accomplish the round sum of 1000 double paddle-strokes. But before doing so, an old newspaper I had cast on the river, and which now floated along, suggested the idea of measuring the speed of the current. For this I cut a long papyrus-stem into pieces of a few inches, and carefully scattered them across the channel and marked the time by my watch, so as to see how long would elapse before they were overtaken afterwards in our descent of the stream. This plan, however, though carefully worked, was futile, for I never saw one of my floats again.*

At 960 strokes, suddenly rounding a corner, I entered a beautiful little lake, just one you would picture in fancy. The general contour of it was round, but the edges were curved into deep bays, with dark alleys and bright projecting corners, and islets dotted the middle. Every single part of the boundary about me was green papyrus— not ragged and straggling, but upright and sharply defined. The breadth of this east and west was estimated at half a mile.† Extreme caution was instantly prescribed by this novel scene, for without coolness and clear noting of the course, it might be difficult or impossible to find again the narrow entrance which I must pass through for my return. Therefore, I bent down some of the tall green stems and tied them together, and placed upon them for a warning-flag large slips of "the Supplement." Then carefully noting the compass-bearings, I advanced to the next group of islands, and did the same again, always placing the beacons upon the right hand, so as to show the way out in re-

---

* After much consideration, and as it was better to overrate the current than to overstate my advance into the papyrus, it appeared right to estimate the distance traversed by each double stroke of the paddle here at four yards instead of five and a half, and this part of the map, therefore, is constructed upon that reduced scale.

† Seen from the mountain, it appears certainly wider than this, but I have followed the MS. notes, entered at the time in my log.

turning. The lake was *perfectly* still—not "calm as a mill-pond," which expression often includes a shivering ruffle on the water, but with a smoothness like glass itself, and the water below was clear and without the slightest current. The lake was shallowed to five feet, but all the bottom was a soft mass of delicate water-moss, patterned in pretty green net-work. Large yellow lilies floated on the surface in gay-colored bouquets. I had seen many of these lilies along the north shore of the lake, but their stems were very thick and multitudinous below, so that, whenever I tried to drag up the very roots of them—if, indeed, they have any roots in the earth at all—the weight became so great that it was quite unmanageable. However, I cut and brought home some portions of the complicated mass. In the very centre of the lake, the canoe "hove to" for compass-bearings.

The sun was now very hot, but the air was cleared by the thunder. The view, so much contracted before by the high papyrus-walls, now opened on all sides, for there was space about me.

To the north was the rounded head of splendid glittering Hermon, and to its left the far-off snow on the sharp indented Sunnin, chief of the Lebanon range. High on a lonely crag to the west was Neby Yusha, "Joshua's Tomb,"* and the eastern shore was girt by the "hill of Bashan."†

---

* Thomson seems to consider this to be the site of Hazor. Finn well reminds us that the relics may often be intended to honor Moslem "saints," who had Scripture names.

† In our sketch at p. 287, the two snow mountains are depicted. This sight of Senir and Lebanon, and the hills of Bashan, all at one time, and from a boat, reminds one of the beautiful verses in Ezekiel (ch. xxvii.), where the rich grandeur of Tyre is painted in language so magnificent, and the mountains now before us have a place:

"Thus saith the Lord God; O Tyrus, thou hast said, I am of perfect beauty.

"'Thy borders are in the midst of the seas, thy builders have perfected thy beauty.

"They have made all thy ship boards of fir trees of Senir: they have taken cedars from Lebanon to make masts for thee.

In the middle of all, and evidently as yet unconscious of my nearness, was one of the most graceful of living objects—a pure-white swan, floating upon the lovely lake, that mirrored his image again below. It never entered into my head to shoot him, pretty creature—that would have been sheer sacrilege : his tameness was quite shocking. But, just to waken up the echoes around us, and to give vent to the emotions of my mind, so long pent up in absolute silence, I fired a volley, and gave three cheers. It was a very difficult thing to make quite sure that this little lake was a termination of the journey upward ; that it was not merely an enlargement of a stream which I had now resolved to follow up, *coûte que coûte*, to the end. But a careful circuit of its labyrinthine borders satisfied me that this is *the earliest flow of Jordan as one river* after it dives into the barrier whither I had traced it some days before. The north end of this lake was at 1130 double paddle-strokes from the mouth of the channel : that is, 6000 yards, or less than three miles and a half; and, allowing for current, it may be well averred that the Jordan aggregates its waters in this inner lake at the head of a channel which winds along nearly three miles before it enters the larger lake of Hooleh.

The interesting question as to the breadth of the impassable barrier could be settled only after my return, and by a comparison between the observations made in my journey down the river in Map V. and those made now in this central lake, the northern end of which is marked P in

---

"Of the oaks of Bashan have they made thine oars ; the company of the Ashurites have made thy benches of ivory, brought out of the isles of Chittim.

"Fine linen with broidered work from Egypt was that which thou spreadest forth to be thy sail ; blue and purple from the isles of Elishah was that which covered thee.

"The inhabitants of Zidon and Arvad were thy mariners : thy wise men, O Tyrus, that were in thee, were thy pilots.

"The ancients of Gebal and the wise men thereof were in thee thy calkers : all the ships of the sea with their mariners were in thee to occupy thy merchandise."

Map VI.* This was done with the advantage of the MS. survey of Captain Wilson, already noticed; and it will be seen that the interval between N and P—that is, the breadth of the barrier—is about half a mile.

The journey back along the new channel was pleasant and easy, and lasted less than an hour. My various beacons all were spied, and, to guide the next canoeist, I left them there; but with the keenest look-out, I could not discover any one of the current-floats which had been so carefully strewn for the purpose, and only the floating newspaper could be discerned on the gliding stream.†

At the mouth again, all safe, the Rob Roy was moored for luncheon in the shade, and never was a roast fowl eaten with a heartier relish than after such a delightful morning's work.

Next she entered a bay farther eastward, but this quickly narrowed and ran up into a *cul-de-sac* at 2000 yards, until I could pass only through a narrow gap into deep gloomy waterways, without any stream, and where the tall papyrus-stems were tangled over my head. Still I followed this up to its positive termination, and with all the precautions (as to beacons and guide-marks) so useful before: and again the canoe came back into the light, where, in the green circuit of the bay, once more I found, in one group of graceful elegance, sixteen wild swans swimming together. Beautiful as they were, I was glad to have seen that one swan first before meeting so many. Again a salute from the pistol stunned the air. All the white beauties rose in terror or high dudgeon; their wavy circlings above me cleft the sky with bright gleaming tracks for a moment, and they passed away like a vision.

As the Rob Roy again neared the lake, I felt that the

---

* For observations as to latitude, I was dependent entirely on one bearing of Neby Yusha, seen from point P, but the distance estimate from paddle-strokes may well be considered to transfer the measurement to the mouth of the river in the lake, and so to connect it with the survey of the lake itself.

† This, however, did not help me to estimate the current, because the time and place of its starting had not been noted. As a rough guess, I should say that Jordan's current here is, at the most, about a mile in an hour.

wind had risen very suddenly, and this soon explained a most curious hissing, grinding, bustling sound, that was heard like waves upon a shingly beach. For, to my surprise and delight, I found that the margin of the lake about me was waving up and down, and the papyrus-stems were rubbing against each other as they nodded out and in. It was plain in a moment that the whole jungle of papyrus was *floating upon the water*, and so the waves raised by the breeze were rocking the green curtain to and fro.

My soundings had shown the depth in Jordan's channel to be almost uniform, at from twelve to ten feet, all the way up; and at first it seemed strange that there should be any special current in one part, when the water had apparently a wide way to run through underneath the floating field. But the reason of this is soon apparent when we know how the papyrus grows; and as the vast area of it now before us is believed to be the largest mass of papyrus in the world, it may be a proper time to look at this strange plant here.

The papyrus plant (in Hebrew "gôme," and in Arabic "berdi") is called "babir" by the Arabs of Hooleh, which is as near the Latin word as can be, considering that the Arabs use b for p. Its stem is three-cornered; in this feature it is one of a limited number of plants. The thicker and taller stems are not at the edge, but about five or six feet inward; therefore I was unable to get at them without incurring great danger. Also, as I meant to bring out the largest possible specimen, I kept putting off the endeavor until finally the opportunity had passed. The following sketch shows the manner of growth of this plant. There is first a lateral trunk, A, lying on the water, and half-submerged.* This is sometimes as thick as a man's

---

* The woodcut in Smith's "Dictionary of the Bible" represents the *stalks* as under water, but the natural free growth of the plant seems to me from a floating trunk, and this would only be submerged exceptionally. The small flowerets on the hairy threads of the *thyrsus* top in Smith's sketch are not seen in winter. The sketch of papyrus given by Dr. Thomson does not show its multitude of tall stems. The papyrus represented by a steel engraving in "Bruce's Travels" is very accurate.

body, and from its lower side hang innumerable string-like roots from three to five feet long and of a deep purple color. It is these pendent roots that retard so much of the surface-current where the papyrus grows, as noticed above for explanation. On the upper surface of the trunks the stems grow alternately in oblique rows; their thickness at the junction is often four inches, and their height fifteen feet, gracefully tapering until at the top is a little round knob, with long, thin, brown, wire-like hairs eighteen inches long, which rise, and then, recurving, hang about it in a thyrsus-shaped head. The stem, when dead, becomes dark brown in color, and when dry, it is extremely light; indeed, for its strength and texture, it is the lightest substance I know of.

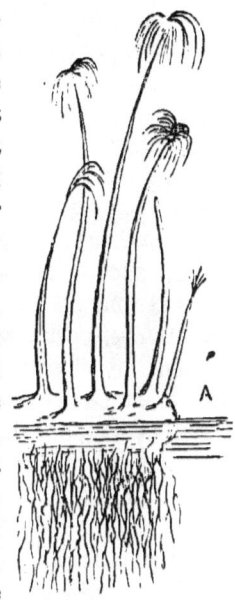

PAPYRUS STEMS AND ROOTS.

The papyrus was used for writing upon by the Egyptians, and was prepared for this purpose by cutting it into thin slips. These were laid side by side, and upon them others in a cross direction, and both were joined by cement and then pressed into a continuous sheet. It is obvious that by this means the length, and to a certain extent the breadth, of a papyrus roll might be made according to pleasure. The name *papyrus* (*babir*) still survives in the English name of the material upon which these words are printed. Smith's Dictionary tells us that the Hebrew word for the papyrus, gôme, is used four times in the Bible.*
The Ethiopians made boats of it; Ludolf says that these boats are used in the Tzamic Lake, and Moses was hid in a vessel made of this.† I have mentioned above that I

---

* In the Septuagint the word $\pi a \pi \nu \rho o \varsigma$ is used. See also *ante*, pp. 86, 87, note. For reeds in general the Hebrew term is kaneh.

† Dr. Thomson ("The Land and the Book," vol. i. p. 337) says the process described in Genesis ii. 3, may mean that the ark was "bitumed" by the

saw a man on an "ark of bulrushes" at Hooleh, and I have often seen a woman put her baby on a bundle of reeds and swim across the Nile while she pushed it along. The plant is mentioned in a beautiful passage of Isaiah (chap. xxxv. 7), and in Job it is asked, "Can the papyrus grow up without mire?" (chap. viii. 11). Herodotus says that the papyrus was eaten after being stewed. This *Papyrus antiquorum* is not now found in Egypt, nor anywhere in Asia except in Syria. But it grows 7° from the equator in Nubia, on the White Nile. The marsh of Hooleh is, therefore, perhaps the largest collection of papyrus to be seen anywhere. It is traced along the Jordan only a short distance (as is noticed hereafter), and then re-appears at Ain et Tin, on the Sea of Galilee, and is also said to be found on the River Aujeh, near Jaffa; but I did not observe it in the part I examined of that river. Another kind (*Papyrus syriacus*) is cultivated in our botanical gardens, and is found wild on the plain of Sharon.*

It is not difficult to understand how the papyrus grove is so very thick just at its boundary edge, whereas reeds, or rushes, or other aquatic plants, usually get sparse and stunted or broken down all round the borders of a marsh, or where it merges into open water.

This peculiarity, which gives to the papyrus plain of Hooleh its most remarkable feature of upright wall-like sides—and that, too, on deep water—is caused, I think, by the manner of the plant's growth. Such of the lateral stems as shoot out into open water become bent or broken by waves, and so they bind in the rest, and the outer stems have too much wind and rough weather to flourish as well as the others do inside, being well protected. This may be noticed even more distinctly when the papyrus grows in running water, as in this part of the marsh through which

---

mixture, so as to resemble a coffin, and thereby to enable the mother to take her child out of the house.

* Dr. Tristram, in the "Leisure Hour," 1866, p. 553. Thomson probably alludes to the latter kind when he mentions papyrus in the river Fulej, near the Aujeh ("The Land and the Book," vol. ii. p. 268).

the Jordan flows. While we remark that the plant seems to thrive best where the water is not stagnant, and so the largest stems are near the channel of the river, yet it may be asked how it is that they do not spread across the channel itself. The sketch below will explain this at once. It is a bird's-eye view of several of the lateral trunks, which are represented as being turned by the force of the current all in one direction—that of the arrow, S—and so gradually bending round to the positions R, T, U, they at last fold upon, encircle, and strangle their neighbors, and seriously hinder their growth. The width of the clear channel is therefore kept at a uniform relation to the speed of the current; for if that is slow, it allows the trunks to spread and to cover the surface, and with their roots to narrow the channel until the speed of the stream is thereby increased, and the trunks are by it curved stunted, and worn off, and so a just balance is regained.

The amount of water exhaled by the evaporation from millions of these stems, presenting so large an area of surface above, must be prodigious, although, on the other hand, the shade of their thick darkness keeps the direct rays of the sun from striking into the water itself. So much for the papyrus.

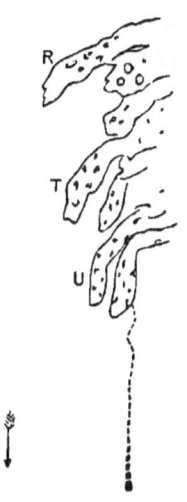

GROWTH OF PAPYRUS.

The Rob Roy then entered every little bight along the indented edge, to make perfectly sure that no other open channel was to be discovered, until at length she came to the eastern coast of the lake. Here I peeped round the cape, but no Arab was in sight at the moment: yet I was too tired with work and the excitement of discovery to venture upon a longer journey here, and I slowly paddled across the open water to the hovels of Mataryeh, whither our camp had been ordered to move.

CHAPTER XVIII.

On Hooleh. — Cutting a Cape. — Canoe Chase. — Hooleh Lake. — Jacob's Bridge. — Who crossed it. — Templars' Keep. — Grand View. — Jew's Lament. — Ten Miles of Torrent. — Hard Times. — A Set of Ruffians. — The Worst. — At last. — All right. — Note on the Rivers.

The Rob Roy was eager next morning for one more day of search, and to scan especially the eastern border of the lake. To aid the fishing venture on Lake Hooleh, a boat had actually been built of boards carried there from Tiberias. I went to see this wreck, which foundered at her launch, they said, and was now lying under water in a deep bend of the western shore.*

It was not entirely without misgivings that I once more paddled to that same mysterious corner at the north-east end of the laké, where the Arab, like a spider in his web, had full command of the approaches, and might wait in ambush for his prey. But this point had to be examined before our survey could be called complete; and, as it must be done, we had best do it at once, and thoroughly. I did not steer a straight course to the spot, but first across the lake to the wall of papyrus, and then along that, entirely hidden, until I came close to its eastern end.

Here a new plan of action was devised, namely, to cut the cape in two, instead of "doubling" it, and thus I might stealthily come out opposite the little tell, and so spy out the land while invisible myself. A break in the boundary favored this design, for there were only canes here, and thick white reeds, and not papyrus. Storing my

---

* For travellers, however, and especially for those who wish to visit the charming central lake we have spoken of, or to gather the ferns, and papyrus, and lilies on the water, or to fish, it is well to know of this sunken craft, which a few nails would doubtless soon make quite seaworthy, but oars must be brought, for there were none, and no wood to make them of.

paddle below deck, then I dragged my boat in by hauling on these canes with a hand on each side.

But the water shallowed, and if an Arab saw me, he could wade out and catch the Rob Roy fixed in this dense jungle. After much reflection, therefore, I returned to open water, and then went into the jungle of reeds again, but this time *stern foremost*, so that in the event of an alarm I might be in the most favorable position for running away! Yes, there *is* a time to prepare for a safe retreat as well as one to get ready for a bold attack. The Rob Roy now "advanced backward" through the reeds, and soon came at last into open water, having cut across the isthmus, and so entered the bay of the east side, where the maps indicate the Jordan as issuing from the marsh. It was a fine open bay, and the green tell and the large shady tree were there on the land, but no human being was visible, nor even a horse. The dashing of an unseen cascade was the only sound.*

With hurried strokes the Rob Roy ran up northward, impatient to finish the problem which could be considered only half solved until it had been proved that here no stream comes forth. The regular river had been met and followed up for three miles in its new-found course on the west. Still there *might* possibly be another or a branch of it here. Well, there *is* no stream at all in this eastern bay, which has distinct bounds all about its circuit. And now being fully satisfied of this important fact, I thought it wise to get out of the *cul-de-sac*, and set off at a good pace, happy with the work we had accomplished. It was quite easy then to paddle along the eastern shore, and to sound the depth of water as I went. But though the Arabs were high up in the hills with their tents and flocks, they very soon noticed the little boat, the only speck on the lake below them. The clear air which they looked through, with the clear eye that only an Arab or an English sailor possesses, also carried to my ear the shouts from the shepherds standing amazed on the rocky peaks, "Shaktoorah! shak-

* None of the maps mark a stream here, and I forgot to ask its name.

toorah!" as they rushed down, impetuous to get near. It was no use, of course, for they could not catch the canoe either by running through the dense jungle on shore or by swimming in the water, and I only laughed at them gayly, and waved the paddle in defiance.

The lake lies quite close to the hills on the Bashan side, but, strangely enough, the water is not so deep there as on the west, near the plain of Mellaha. To test this, I ran in oblique lines and sounded every fifty strokes (and sometimes twice as often), though it was a tiresome process, because the canoe had always to be stopped, but then the result was satisfactory. Though done for the first time, it was done thoroughly, and the depth of the "waters of Merom" is now ascertained forever. The result may be stated generally that Hooleh Lake has an average depth (in the winter time) of about eleven feet. By Jordan's mouth, on the northern edge, it is twelve feet, and for some way up the channel. In a few places (and these principally close to the west bank) the depth is fifteen feet, once it is seventeen feet deep, but in no part of the whole lake did I find three fathoms of water.*

Near the south end there is a bay with fine trees on the banks and steep rocks above, among which upon the slope is a ruin, and here the canoe paused a long time, carefully scrutinizing the square strong building, which we were assured afterwards is only a mill, but the ruin looks very different from that.

For luncheon the Rob Roy landed at the west side below Tuleil, where the bank was of grayish clay, very cohesive. Then we carefully sounded and "compassed" the narrowing end of the pear-shaped lake, until between islets of papyrus and tall canes the water closed into a regular channel once more, which, by graceful winding, narrowed to a hundred feet across, with a good current going, for it was now a decided river. This is the first unquestionable

* On Map VI. (page 303), drawn (like Map V.) to the scale of half an inch to the mile, the soundings of principal places are marked in feet. But there were many other soundings taken besides these.

BRIDGE OF JACOB'S SONS.

Jordan that can be approached from shore, and is formed of all its three wonderful streams that are born from the rock, gush out at Hasbeya, Dan, and Banias, pour down into the marsh of Hooleh, there combine, and thence rush on to the Sea of Galilee; and through that onward, winding fast, they hurry into the Dead Sea.* The course of this part of Jordan is given in Map VI., as it passes with a broad sweep round the Tell Beit Yacob; and after this place (at the point marked in the map) I recorded in my note-book "last papyrus here." It was interesting to observe afterwards, while reading Bruce's narrative (written some eighty years ago), that he in his journey had remarked the papyrus at this identical spot.† This great traveller seems to have always had his wits about him, and almost all the observations of his that have been reviewed since are found to be accurate, even when he said that in Abyssinia men cut beefsteaks out of their living oxen as they travel, though the doubts cast upon this statement by his contemporaries went far to break his honest but sensitive heart. Our camp was near the bridge of black basalt depicted in the sketch at the corner of the map, and which is the first bridge over the complete Jordan. From the end of the lake this bridge was distant 650 paddle-strokes, that is, 3523 yards, or three yards over two miles, which is the measure on shore given in Murray. Thomson gives a sketch of this bridge as seen from the north. Schwartz calls it "Jisr Abni Jacob," Bridge of Jacob's Sons. The bridge is about sixty feet long, has three arches, and no parapet.‡ At the west end is an

---

* I think that by a cutting 400 yards long, and twenty feet deep, at the end of Hooleh Lake, the whole of the marsh and lake would be made dry in a year, and an enormous tract of land would become productive and salubrious.

† "Bruce's Travels," A.D. 1790, vol. v. Appendix, p. 3. The river Hendaj is marked as running into Jordan from the west, above this bridge (in Vandevelde and in Petermann), and near Almanyeh in Porter's map. I did not observe any river enter as thus represented.

‡ Robinson states that it "has four pointed arches, and is sixty *paces* long" (vol. iii. p. 363); but he does not appear to have visited it.

ugly round tower, and a khan is over the river. The current is very trifling until quite close to the bridge. A few unkempt soldiers were in mat huts near the bridge, and their horses dreadfully dirty, but good nevertheless. These men take toll from passengers.* The bridge itself has been most likely built since the Crusades (Schwartz says in 1112, by Baldwin IV.), but the spot selected at once suggests that a ford was here, for it is just where the deep water ends, and before the high banks of the torrent begin; and no other place would be suitable for twelve miles north or eight miles south of this ford.

Robinson† states that the writers before and in the Crusade era mention this only as a ford of Jacob. Abulfeda calls the ford "El Ajran," and the spot Beit Yacob (House of Jacob), as others did, probably referring to the tell with ruins on it a little farther north, and shown in our sketch. As to the name which seems to connect this place with "Jacob's daughters," it seems almost clear that Jacob himself did not cross to meet Esau here, but "passed over the ford Jabbok,"‡ on the occasion which is marked by his wrestling with "a man," when he called the place Penuel. Naaman, the prince of a pagan race, may have gone this way to the prophet; and the zealous Saul may have crossed here, "breathing out slaughter," going to Damascus, or the Apostle Paul coming back. Our Saviour himself may have passed over this to Cæsarea.

Much against all advice, I now determined to follow the river close by its verge all the way to Galilee; not, of course, in the channel, for that was utterly impossible, as

* Gumpenberg, in A.D. 1450, seems to have paid toll here, but the usual route for caravans before that was to cross the Jordan below Tiberias.

† Vol. iii. p. 362.

‡ Gen. xxxii. 3-22. The subsequent route of Jacob, as described in this and the following chapters, it is not easy to follow, unless the words "passed over" refers sometimes to fording the Jordan and sometimes to the Jabbok or Zerka River; and it may be that the name "Bridge of Jacob's Daughters" means the ford used by them, or with regard to them, separate from the particular journey of their father. Thomson says that the oaks of Hazury, near Banias, are said to be inhabited by "Benat Yacoub," or "Jan," a genus of spirits ("The Land and the Book," vol. i. p. 372).

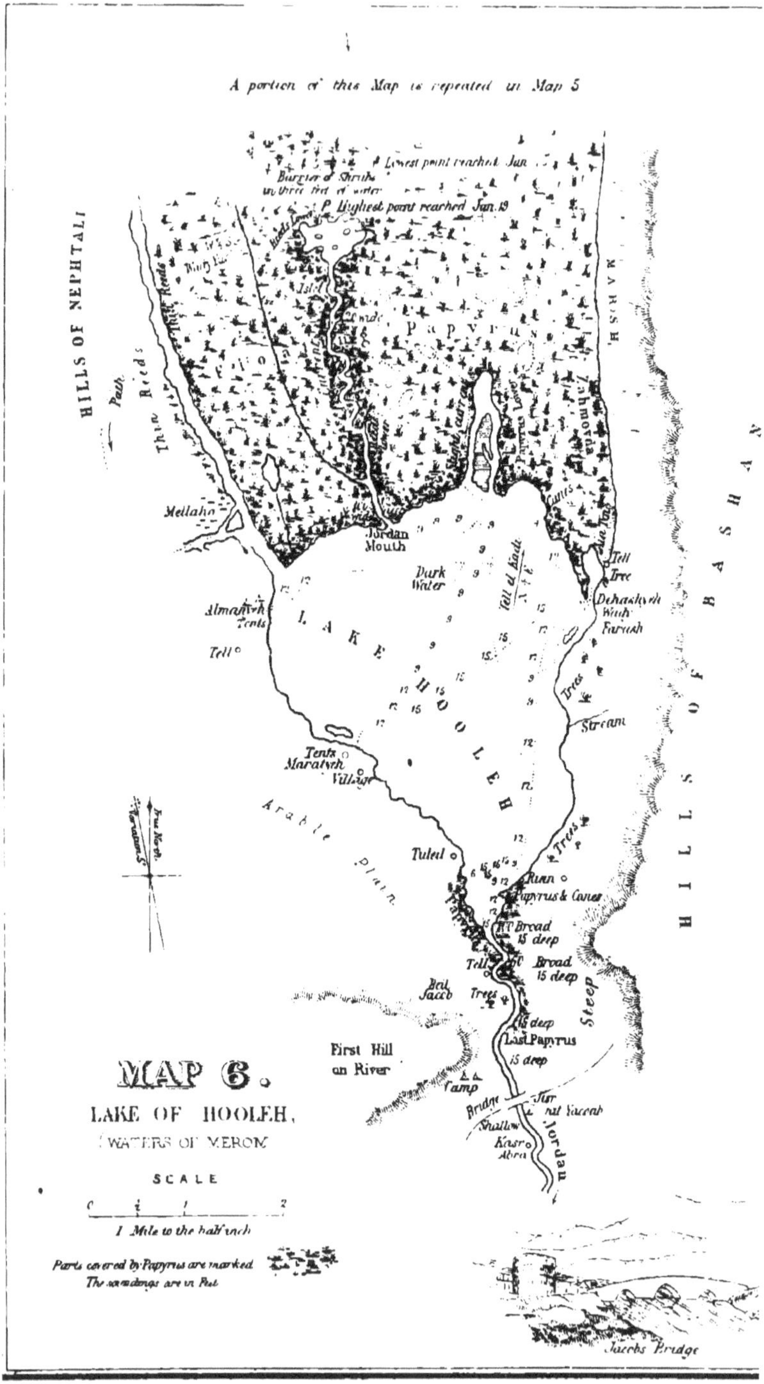

MAP 6.

LAKE OF HOOLEH,
(WATERS OF MEROM)

SCALE

1 Mile to the half inch

Parts covered by Papyrus are marked.
The soundings are in Feet.

HARPER & BROTHERS, NEW YORK

it soon becomes a mere torrent-bed, and a white-foamed bursting rush of water hurries between rocks thick set with oleanders, which often meet across the stream not a dozen feet in width. Before the river settles down into a thorough-going mill-race speed, it makes a sweep or two to right and left, as if with a struggle to get free, and its stream is divided by islands and large rocks. About a mile below the bridge are some imposing ruins. Their position settles at once that the building was put here to command this important ford. It was, in fact, a castle built 700 years ago,* and was given to the Templars, who then held this road. But Saladin took the fortress, and razed its proud battlements. Now it is only a disappointing ruin. Our evening was spent until dark in a long ride by this channel and over the stony hills to see if it were possible to carry the canoe on these dizzy precipices, where not one single inhabitant is found for miles, and not even an Arab's tent was to be seen all day.

Few travellers have had the same strong reason for going by this route—the desire to continue what had been as yet adhered to as a rule—that I should actually *see* the bed of the Jordan from its very beginning right on to its end. Hany was against the plan, though he had learned to doubt his own doubts as to what could be done with a canoe. He never once, however, opposed himself entirely to any distinct resolve of his master. In this important point of his character, and in many others, he is undoubtedly the best dragoman in Syria. Therefore we rode on, my horse being frisky enough for any mountain climbing, until a most interesting point was reached, and there is only one such place, I suppose, in this curious gorge, from whence you can see both the lake Hooleh with the Jordan coming out, and the lake of Genesareth, into which the river flows. The distance between these lakes is not more than ten miles in a straight line and the river has few long bends between them; so it probably does not add more than three miles to its course by winding. Yet the

* Robinson, vol. iii. p. 363.

U

descent of "the Descender" is very rapid here, for it falls in these ten miles about 700 feet.* During the whole course of the Jordan from source to end there does not seem to be one notable cascade or regular "fall."

The point we have reached is a good one to pause at, for several boundaries meet here, and the passage from one to another of these is sudden and distinct. Behind us are the threefold springs of the river's birth. In front we have the bright lake whose shores and waters had teemed with life all fed from Jordan; beyond that lake, and dim to the eye far off, is the river dead in Sodom's Sea.

The bridge behind us marks a new chapter in the history of our Lord. Already we have lingered where Christ had visited a high mountain, and the Law and the Prophets had met the Gospel each by its noblest representative, to discourse of the great event which is the centre of God's dealings with mankind, the offering of his Son. But now we are looking to where He lived most among men. On that mount that is now behind us, Peter would have made a tabernacle to dwell in, but he is not to abide in the cloud, however glorious. The fisherman is to return to his nets in that sea below.

Behold here the front of that grand stage upon which so great a drama was enacted, where the Teacher taught longest, the Healer cured most, the Prophet first gave warning, the Saviour gathered his people, the Light of the world shone brightest, "Galilee of the Gentiles." While thoughts of Jordan recall past wonders to the Christian, and a glorious future too, there is sadness in the reverie upon this river penned by an Israelite† thus:

"My God! how is my soul bowed down within me, when I remember thee in this land of Jordan (Psalm xlii. 7). Is not this whole district of the Jordan abundantly watered,

---

* In the first five days of the Danube from its source, the canoe had descended about 1,500 feet, but then there was more water to float in, several weirs, and a few cascades, and yet the current was at any rate as fast as one would wish to see, and that was nothing compared with the speed of the Jordan here. † Rabbi Schwartz (p. 81).

fruitful, and blessed, like a garden of the Lord? (Gen. xiii. 10). And still it is scarcely trod by the foot of a traveller, it is not inhabited, and the Arab pitches not there his tents, and the shepherds do not cause the flocks to lie down there (Isaiah xiii. 20). Still, thus speaketh the Lord Zebaoth, There shall yet be in this place, which is waste, without man and cattle, again a dwelling for shepherds, causing their flocks to lie down. In those days shall Judah be redeemed, and Jerusalem shall be inhabited in security. And this is the name it shall be called, THE LORD our Righteousness (Jer. xxxiii. 12, 16)."

The annexed sketch is an outline, north and south, from the hill we have mentioned. Before us we see the lower end of Hooleh Lake, with the Jordan running out of it *towards* us. If we now turn the book round, and look from the same central mount, but now facing southward, we see the Jordan running *from* us, until it enters the Sea of Tiberias.

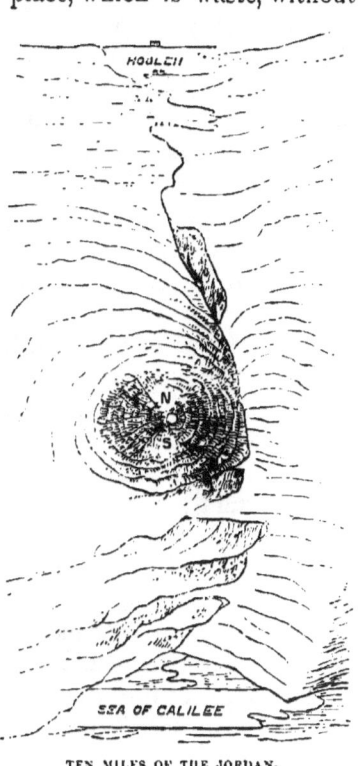

TEN MILES OF THE JORDAN.

The two projecting points to the left in this view are the Wady Semakh and Wady Fik,* while the southern shore at Kerak is seen to bound the lake in the far distance about twenty miles from our point of view. An intervening hill on the right hides the land of Genesareth; and the actual entrance of Jordan into that lake is

---

* Both of these are shown at page 413.

not visible, I think, from our present stand-point, being shut out by a hill to the right. How great the descent of Jordan is, we can see pretty plainly here by a glance first at Hooleh above and then at Tiberias below, comparing their levels by the eye, while the loud noise of the river foaming at our feet tells also to the ear how fast the Jordan flows.

Our camp was astir early to follow the route we had thus reconnoitred. For horses and mules there was nothing to make the way difficult, but the danger we feared most for the canoe was that which came from the wind. In the high gusts of a breeze it was always found necessary to put two men behind the Rob Roy to prevent the little horse that bore her from being actually capsized when the wind pressed hard against the long flat side of the boat perched high upon the cautious creature's back. Now the path was much too narrow here to allow even one man to keep near so as to help the Rob Roy thus, and especially in the most awkward places of the road, where it wound along the edges of deep precipices, and where the footing was worst and the wind was strongest. In such places an upset, or even a false step in staggering against the blasts, would instantly hurl the horse and its burden into the torrent below.

Often we had to dismount the canoe, and to carry her by hand past sloping edges or crooked rocks. Sometimes even to carry her by hand was difficult, when the mountain gusts blew strong, and when one man could not hear the other's voice for direction. Patience and perseverance triumphed here once more, and the route began to descend rapidly, with a full view of the splendid Sea of Galilee ever cheering us on.

I had now such full confidence in Hany (like that which a mother feels in a well-tried nurse) that I could leave him alone to take care of "the young lady;"* and indeed he

---

*   Not decked in dead folks' hair is she,
        Her ribs not cramped in steel,
      No draggle-tail, for you and me
        To tread on, dangling at distorted heel.

begged me to go out of sight at the worst places, so that he might have only one anxiety at a time. To stifle anxiety by hard exercise, I climbed the heights about us, and always had some new beauties to see from the top. At last, having gone far ahead, riding alone, I selected a place for luncheon where a crystal stream rushed past in headlong race for the Jordan, and lovely anemones spangled the turf under shady trees.

The instant I dismounted, a man's head appeared over a rock beside me, and then another opposite, and a third behind. In such a case, alone and outnumbered, one has only to be cool and stand firm. Presently seven or eight men, all armed with guns, closed in upon me.

A half-policy here would be of no use, so I quietly slipped off my horse's bridle, loosened his girths, and spread my large cloak under the tree, and, having haltered my horse's leg, laid myself down in the most confiding way that traveller could behave. My visitors were not Arabs: they were the veriest set of ruffians to look at that any one could set eyes upon. They stood round and nodded, and I had a free chat with them all ; but they began it. "Who are you?" "Ingleez." "Where are you going?" "Tiberya." "What have you to sell?" "Nothing." "Are you here alone?" "Oh, no! there is a shaktoor coming soon, and you will see it." "A shaktoor? Did you say a boat?" So I told them of the canoe on the Nile, and the Red Sea, and the Barada, and the Hasbany ; but when I spoke of sailing her upon Lake Hooleh, they burst out into derisive jeers. One of them seemed to be a Greek, but the leader was more like the men one meets in the Balearic Islands ; so I tried him with a few words of the peculiar Spanish *patois* there, and, sure enough, he turned out to be a renegade from the mild sway of the motherly Isabella, Father Claret, and the Bleeding Nun. He was amazed at such a *rencontre*, and so was I. All the others were silent, but soon they retired for consultation and came again for "backshish," when, just at the proper moment, the bow of the Rob Roy appeared over a distant hill, nodding, nodding, as the horse stepped carefully bearing it. I pointed to that. The men were bewildered at such a sight. The mule-bells tinkled in our approaching caravan, and they saw I was not quite a lone wayfarer fit for these cowards to rob.

Soon my men were near. Hany saw it all at a glance. The only time I ever saw him frightened was then. "Get away, sir! get away from this place as fast as possible! Cross the stream! These are a pack of regular robbers. We can not stop here for one moment."

So the palaver was put an end to, and my friend from Majorca moved off, saying they were "only looking out for game to shoot;" and, indeed, just before they came up, I had noticed two otters (as I thought), or they may have been conies, wandering among the rocky clefts of the stream, and observing my movements with great keenness and sagacity. The view a little farther on from our bivouac was truly magnificent, as the whole lake of Genesareth opened wide beneath us. Twenty years before I had gazed on these waters, but not from this end of the lake, and with only that tantalizing look which a limited hour's visit to such a scene causes to be a mixed joy to see it so pretty and sorrow to leave it so soon.

But now I gazed upon this lake as the haven of a long voyage, the chiefest purpose of a charming journey, the delightful waters where I was to stop, to see, to see thoroughly, to have unbounded enjoyment upon for many days, if only I could get my boat safely there; and it was so.

But the part of the road now to be done was by far the most trying of the whole travel. Hany had predicted this, and I had alternately confuted his logic, and rallied him on his fears. They were not causeless, however; and how we ever got a canoe through that last mile of stones and marsh and sliding precipice, I can only wonder still; and most earnestly would I warn any other person against it who intends to come here with a boat.

Marsh we had learned to plunge through, stones and rocks we knew how to manage, for at the worst the canoe could be carried by hand. But here the deep morass was full of large round boulders, so that the horse's feet might be ever so sure in their hold, and just at the critical moment the stone he was standing upon gave way. The mules—those clever and amusing companions, if you will but learn their fun—were completely puzzled here. Wandering right and left, and refusing for once to follow the little black donkeys who could lead best of all, they staggered and fell, with a loud crash of crockery and the shouts of the men who were wading over the bog. Hany and Latoof carried the Rob Roy for a quarter of a mile at a time. I admired their pluck and patience, while I mourned for their falls and bruises. It was hard enough to get on without any load, and I was quite wet through while leading my puzzled horse and jumping from island to island among the pools. But that mattered nothing, of course. Indeed, we all felt that no one must spare himself this time. It was the very last time we had to be anxious about, for once the Rob Roy was in the Sea of Galilee, I knew she would be well able to meet any dangers there. Water we can deal with in a boat, or if she founders, it is a legitimate end; but to perish by a fall in a quagmire, *that* would indeed be inglorious for a travelled canoe. After about eight hours spent over as many miles of journey, the bottom of the hill was reached at last.*

The Jordan has come down the narrow gorge much faster than we have scrambled through it; and now the river, tired with its foaming, spreads as if resting on a sort of delta, which is gradually wider to the shores of the lake. This fertile land is beautifully green, with bushy trees and level sward. Numerous side-currents from the main stream meander here, and flocks of buffaloes, horses, and goats, are scattered over the plain. Other parts of it are cultivated, and the tents of an Arab tribe dot the green

---

* It must be remembered that this was midwinter, and that we were directing our course to an unusual point, where the canoe could be again launched upon the river. The road is a bad one, but for usual travelling it is tolerable, and the scenery along it is a full reward for any trouble.

landscape with their quaint black hamlets. I had ridden among these very slowly, until the mule-bells sounded near behind me coming on, yet for a long, long time there was no sign of Hany, and none of the canoe.

The Arab horses, browsing free and frisky, trotted up to gaze upon us. The Arabs themselves must have wondered why the Howaja kept riding on while his face was always turned behind in anxious expectation. At length, through the copse of brushwood, the well-known bows of the Rob Roy were seen aloft, and a hail from Hany shouted aloud, "All right!"

Glad hour, that ends our fears and ushers in bright happy days of life upon the Lake of Galilee!

And here, before launching on the most interesting water in the world, we may give a parting glance to the rivers we have left.

NOTE ON THE COURSE AND FALL OF THE JORDAN.

As we are leaving Jordan here, it seems a fit time for a brief general survey of some of its principal features.

From the Hasbeya source to the Dead Sea, the direct distance is about 120 miles. I estimate the addition to be made for winding of the channel from the source to the end of the Sea of Galilee as 20 per cent., and for the rest as 100 per cent. (judging from Warren's outline of that part).

This would make the water in the first part to be 60 miles long, and in the second part 140 miles, or in all 200 miles of channel, from the source to the Dead Sea.

The Hasbeya source is 1700 feet above the Mediterranean, and the Dead Sea is 1300 feet below the Mediterranean, so that the total fall of Jordan is 3000 feet, which would be 15 feet per mile of its channel, or 25 feet per mile of its direct distance.

If we subtract the lake of Genesareth, and the lake and marsh of Hooleh—20 miles together—the fall in the remaining 100 miles of direct distance is 30 feet per mile.

The level of Hooleh morass is estimated at 150 feet above

the Mediterranean, so that about 1500 feet, or half the total fall of Jordan, is descended before the river reaches the barrier in Hooleh,* and the Jordan comes to the level of the Mediterranean about two miles below Jacob's Bridge. Thence it pours down its waters into the heart of the earth, and if the Mediterranean Sea were to be admitted to the interior of Palestine, it would rise nearly to the ruin of the Templars' keep at Jacob's Bridge.

The surface of the lake of Tiberias is 653 feet below the ordinary sea-level (its greatest depth is 165 feet).

From Kerak, at its southern end, the river descends about 650 feet into the Dead Sea. As a general outline, then, it may be said that the Jordan runs 20 miles, falling 1400 feet, into a basin 12 miles long; then runs 10 miles, falling 700 feet, into another basin 14 miles long; then runs 65 miles, falling 700 feet, into a basin 50 miles long and 1800 feet deep. Here, the waters of Jordan being fresh, and therefore lighter than the highly saturated salt water of the Dead Sea, the river stream most probably disperses over the upper surface only, and so, being evaporated before they mingle much with the brine that lies heavy and deep below, they are wafted by the south wind in clouds once more to Hermon, and, condensed into snow-flakes, with water from the Abana and Pharpar, also borne up to Hermon, they trickle down again to run along old Jordan's bed, their endless round.†

---

* The fall from Hooleh Lake to the Jisr Benat Yacob is given at ninety feet (Wildenbrach), but I consider this estimate to be at least seventy feet too much. .

† In the "Journal of the Geographical Society," vol. xviii., are two papers by Dr. E. Robinson, of New York, and by Petermann, the well-known geographer, from which the following notes may be inserted upon the comparative "fall" of rivers; but the value of these for comparison depends upon the degree of accuracy with which the "lengths" are measured along the general course, or the actual windings of all the channel.

The Dee, of Aberdeenshire, ranks in size with the Jordan. From the Linn of Dee (after its cascades as a torrent) to the sea, it runs 72·2 miles, and descends 1190 feet, or 16·5 feet per mile.

The Tweed runs 96·4 miles, and falls 1500 feet; average about 16 feet per mile.

The descent for the Severn is 26½ inches, and for the Shannon 9 inches, per mile.

The Clyde runs 98 miles, and falls 1400 feet, about 14 feet per mile.

The Abana falls 1442 feet from the mill five miles below Zebedany to Damascus, about 20 miles, or 70 feet per mile; but the fall afterwards, until it is lost in the lake, is trifling —say, 100 feet, or 5 feet per mile. The Pharpar seems to fall about 25 feet per mile at first, and 5 feet afterwards.

Thus we have reviewed some of the principal characteristics of the chiefest of those "waters of Israel" which Naaman would not compare with the "Abana and Pharpar rivers of Damascus." True, these Syrian streams gave more fertility than the deep-cut Jordan, but they could not wash away his blot of leprosy. God had appointed for that the river He chose to bless as a means; and for *our* hearts, sick with sin, He has also pointed out a healing stream. Morality is good, but powerless for this deadly stain, "There is a fountain filled with blood."

The Thames runs 215 miles, and descends 376 feet, or about a foot and a half per mile.

The mighty Amazon falls only 12 feet in the last 700 miles of its course, or only one-fifth of an inch per mile.

Robinson makes Jordan fall 14·3 feet per statute mile, and says the Rhine in its most rapid portion, and including the fall of Schaffhausen, has but one-half the average descent of the Jordan, which in the 984 feet of its descent in 60 miles has room for three cataracts, each equal in height to Niagara, and still leaving an average fall equal to the swiftest portion of the Rhine, including the cataract at Schaffhausen.

Baalbec is 3726 feet above the sea (Vandevelde). Dr. E. Robinson says the Litany runs 55 miles to the sea. This would give a fall of 67 feet per mile, or if we take the latter part of the river, after it has cut through the rock, 50 feet per mile.

CHAPTER XIX.

"On deep Galilee."—Bank.—Names of the Lake.—Shores.—Submerged Ruin.—Naked Stranger.—Lagoons.—Ports.—Bethsaida Julias.—Oozing Streams.—River Semakh.—Gergesa.—A Pause.—Tell Hoom.—Kerascli. —Fête.— Search for Piers.— Submerged Remains.— Breeze.—Storm.— Searching below.—Curious Stones.—No Port.—Tabiga.—Bethsaida Bay. —Flocks and Shoals.—Genesareth.

NEXT morning opened gloriously with sunshine on the lake. Thick grass, browsed short by the flocks, was a carpet for the Arabs squatting in a circle about our tents, the occupation they so dearly love and will always work so hard at—looking on. Merriness filled our camp. Our perils were done. Nobody could be anxious now. The horses neighed, the mules even gambolled, and Adoor sung out his blithest lay. Climbing behind the hills of Bashan, the sun poured over their edges into the deep bosom of the lake, and the shadowy mists of the night gat them in haste away. The Rob Roy's deck was still glistening with dew-drops as we carried her before the sight-seers straight to the banks of Jordan.

The river is noisy here, but with a pleasant harmless, chatty sound, and sweeping in wide bends among white boulders and clean gravel. Then it enters a quieter channel, skirted by stiff banks of clay, well clothed by grass and the red branches of oleander. A few strokes in such an onward current soon took us away from the Arabs, who stood on a point in a wondering group, and their deeptoned " Ullah!" was scarcely heard. Now she was to enter the Sea of Galilee, and in the most enlivening of all ways, entirely alone. By gentle curves the Jordan softly closes here to the western shore, and passes two large flat buildings near its mouth. For the last two hundred yards the river enlarges suddenly, and for twice that distance back the current is almost nothing, which shows that the level of the lake extends some way up the river's channel, and this being so when the water was low, no doubt, when the lake is full, the current must nearly cease a long way back from the present mouth.

The actual junction of Jordan with the lake is remarkable. A long point of fine black gravel, almost like sand, and full of shells, juts out westward from the eastern bank, and in the bay formed by this I rested to survey the lovely scene, while buffaloes gradually assemble to gaze, with their necks outstretched. This peculiar form of bank (nearly crossing the river's mouth from one side) is a marked feature of the streams at the north of the lake, and the same elegance of curve, regularity of slope, and neatness and purity of the gravel on the bank, were also invariably seen all round the shores, and more easily now, because the water was low. This curved neck of fine black grit and white shells mingled, narrows the mouth of Jordan to seventy feet, the stream being chiefly on the west, as may be seen from the soundings given in feet in the sketch, which represents the mouth of Jordan as the point shown in Map VII., at Chap. XXI., which is reduced from part of a photograph of the unpublished Ordnance Survey Map, made by Captain Wilson, R.E., and Lieutenant Anderson, R.E., in 1866, and which was kindly presented to me for use on the voyage. It is now inserted in my log as the first correct map yet published of the Sea of Galilee. The soundings are in feet from Vandevelde, taken from Lynch.

This lake or sea has had four names, Chinnereth, Genesareth, Galilee, Tiberias.* All these are inserted together in the old map of W. Wey (see *post*, p. 377, note).

The lake is called "Chinneroth"† in the Old Testament, either from "Chinnereth," one of the fenced cities, or from the district, or perhaps from the oval, harp-like form of its

---

* The name "Tarichion" (from Tarichea, now Kerak) was sometimes given (Pliny, lib. v. ch. xv.).

† Stanley ("S. and P." pp. 373, 4), referring to Numbers xxxiv. ii; Josh. xii. 3; xiii. 27; xix. 35. The Talmud says it was called Cinnereth because its fruits were sweet, like the sound of a harp (Neubauer, "Geog. Talm." p. 215).

basin. Now that the real shape of the lake can be seen in our map, the word "oval" does not apply, but the form is more than ever seen to be harp-like. De Saulcy* says that in Joshua xi. 2, the Hebrew text has "south of Chinnereth," and the Chaldaic text has "south of Gennesar." It

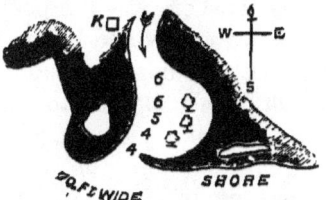

MOUTH OF JORDAN, SEA OF GALILEE.

was called Genesareth from a town or district on the shore. When the lake is called by John (vi. 1) "the Sea of Galilee,† which is *the Sea* of Tiberias" (the Sea of Galilee, of Tiberias), it may be to distinguish this lake from that other sea of Galilee, Lake Hooleh. The earlier Evangelists call it the Lake of Genesareth, for Tiberias was then a new and unimportant town; but John, who wrote later, calls the lake by the name of the town, which had by that time become important.

Soon after the river has emerged, it forms a "bar," the usual outwork of a swift stream when suddenly arrested by the water of a lake or sea, for the matter in suspension then subsides. High short waves bristled here, but not caused by wind, and after a splash or two from these as a welcome to the Rob Roy, she floated in peace on the Lake of Genesareth. In low lake the water is fordable at the bar, and the depth is about three feet, except for a short interval, but the more usual ford is nearly a mile and a half up the stream, where I saw men wading over in four feet of water, while each of them carried his clothes on the top of his head.‡

* "Journey to the Dead Sea," etc., vol. ii. p. 431.

† The name Galilee in Joshua xx. 7, is in Hebrew *Galil*, and in 2 Kings xv. 29, it is Na-Galilah. It came to signify an entrance or bound (as in architecture now "the Galilee" or porch of the cathedral). Twenty of the cities of the district were annexed by Solomon to the kingdom of Tyre, and formed the "boundary" or "offscouring" ("Gebul," or "Cabul"), afterwards the "coasts," of Tyre (see "S. and P." p. 363).

‡ Fords in some rivers shift suddenly, but not such an one as this, so that it is likely that the people crossed here when they followed our Lord, who went over the lake in a ship.

To make a complete examination of the Holy Lake along its shore was the purpose of my voyage during the next two weeks, and by method and system we at once began with the northern shore. On the west of the river the beach of this lake has the appearance of tan-dust or peat, very soft and yielding, nearly black at the water's edge, and brown where it is dry. A fine tree here at Abu Zany grows just by the lake, the only one close to the water all round the western side. It is 500 yards west of Jordan mouth. Turning east again, we soon come to a few palm-trees* about fifty yards inland, and near them is a small shapeless ruin. Here is a wall of hewn stone five feet under water, and about ten feet long, extending to twenty feet from shore. The beach there is of black gritty basalt particles mingled with sand and multitudes of shells. The shore shelves rapidly, so that at twenty feet from the edge there is seven feet of water. The land is flat and swampy, in a level plain called Butaiah, as marked on Map VII.

The canoe had skirted slowly along this shore, keeping just far enough from the edge to enable my eye to see any thing like large stones or buildings under water between me and the bank, and this was the general course pursued all round the lake. For seven hours a day during seven days my sight was half below and half above the surface, scanning every object with eager interest, and few searches are more exhaustive of time, patience, and energy, than this, if it be done carefully. On five other days I kept to land work only, so as to be refreshed by variety. To do this in any other lake might be wearisome enough, but here on these blessed shores it was indeed a labor of love. Thus eying the deep, I began to examine the ruined wall, and to probe with my paddle. Now, at least thought

---

* These palm-trees are often spoken of as if they were exactly at Jordan's mouth, by writers who have not actually seen the place closely. Vandevelde marks this as Bethsaida el Mesadyeh. Thomson seems to regard it as the eastern part of Bethsaida, built, as he supposes, on both sides of Jordan. The three sets of palm-trees on the north-eastern shore are depicted in our outline sketch (*post*, p. 349).

we, no robber can be near, and the sight below can be scanned in peace. Certainly the shores for some way inland were perfectly clear when the search began; yet just as my eye was close to the calm water, and every sound was hushed that I might drink in the pleasures of sight, a loud shout was heard close beside me, " Ya walud!" (Holloah! you there!) and I looked up just in time to see the dark-brown body of a naked man in the very act of "taking a header" as he dashed in from the shore towards me. But my paddle was instantly in action, and when his wet head came up at my bows, the Rob Roy was backing astern full speed, and my new friend was full half a moment too late to catch hold of her, while he received an ample splashing of water from my blade in his eyes. Splendidly the fellow swam, but I merely played with him and laughed at his frantic efforts and wild shouts. He paused and stared—quite at home in deep water—spouting at me a loud and voluble, indignant address, and then he retired in defeat, while I neared the shore again. There he stood erect and gleaming with moisture, and redundant life playing through his brawny muscles, a most strange object to behold. Now that man must have been not a little brave to dash in thus, in order that he might seize the "sheitan" at once and unarmed; but invincible is the desire of man to get hold of what is unknown. Waiting did not get rid of him, so to lose no more time, I had to proceed without a proper examination of the ruin below water, and this, I think, is the only subaqueous novelty all round the lake that I did not investigate well. The entrance of the crooked lagoon near this on the map is twelve feet deep, and no doubt there was a port inside, but I did not enter there on account of the naked Arab.

The margin soon afterwards had small bushes growing on it, some of them oleander. There the sand predominates, and large round boulders are in the deeper parts. We are still coasting along the level plain, which curves round the north-east edge of the lake. Several travellers have ridden across parts of this, but the notices of its nature and contents are extremely meagre. Yet here must have been many villages, if not towns, in the days of our Lord, for the tells and other signs of former habitation are thickly scattered. Several inlets from the lake run through the shore to the level country behind.*

We next paddled on to a lagoon near *C* in the map, and shown in our sketch. Near the mouth is one hewn stone

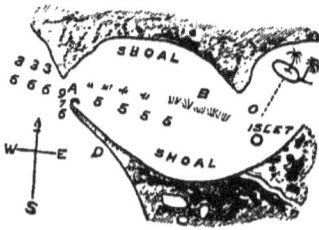
LAGOON AND PORT, BUTAIA PLAIN.

under three feet of water, and a wooden stake one foot long, under two feet of water. This is an inch and a half thick, and is round and upright, and in a line with the submerged causeway. The post was too firmly fixed to be pulled up, though I tried hard for a long time, yet it looked very old. The entrance of this lagoon is between two low narrow points of fine black sand, one of them curiously turned round (see another of this kind at W. Semakh). The part at *D* is only three inches above water, and twenty feet wide. The channel (entrance seventy feet wide) runs in E.S.E. From point *B* the palm-tree near Jordan bears N.W. by N. The channel, after 400 yards, turns at right angles towards a tell with ruins, and here is the second clump of palms.

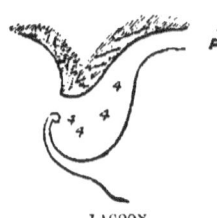
LAGOON.

At *B* the boundary is above water. On the north side of the channel is a row of rush-turfs, half submerged with two or three feet water, and close alongside them all the way it is five and six feet deep. A channel, six feet deep, runs out fifty yards into the lake.

Farther on, near *D* on the map, there is another gap in

---

* When the Ordnance Survey of the lake was made, a long storm of rain had filled the lake, but my visit, though at the same time of the year (in January), was after a long drought had made its level low, and the contour of the lake was, therefore, slightly different from that in the map.

the beach. The channel is four feet deep, and winds up to a palm-tree. Farther east there is a port with a channel to another palm-tree, but the bar is closed. At D on the map there are oleanders, and from this the large terebinth in the plain bears N.E. Going still south, we come to Kefr Argib* or Argob. In the bays about this, there are very large boulders under water, and it is a dangerous place for ships. The bottom is stony for some distance northward, but the stones are not so large. The same character prevails southward, until we reach the delta of Wady Samakh, where the bottom is of stiff clay.

No Arabs approached within sight during my cruise about these latter places, and I landed and walked right and left, but always within a run of the boat. Yet the survey was not so leisurely effected as it might have been had we hired a guard to ride on the bank while the Rob Roy pored over the water. Nor have the Arabs of this plain a bad repute, but they are inquisitive, and might injure the boat without intending harm. On the shores of Bashan they might have captured us for a ransom, and that would have caused a loss of precious time. The hills after Kefr Argib and the Wady Shukayah come so near the sea-shore, and the coast seems to be so little adapted for a port (and without appearance outside of any channel inward), that we may well suppose the usual point of embarkation from the north-eastern coasts must have been one of the ports along the strip of beach already described.

This is an interesting reflection; for our Saviour often crossed to this side, and when He came over to Bethsaida Julias to feed the five thousand, and before he walked upon the sea at night, it must have been at one of these ports he landed, and from one of them the apostles embarked.†

---

* In Vandevelde's map this is called Duka. There is a rocky tell projecting, and a few huts upon it, and large stones of ruins. On going near, I found none but women there. The ruins upon it, when examined by Wilson, did not reveal any thing of importance.

† It has even been urged by able writers that the plain of Butaia is the land of Genesareth (Stanley, "S. and P." p. 386, note). As to the special bearing

X

The sensation of being in such a neighborhood — and that, too, in one's own little boat and all alone—was peculiarly impressive. In other places, once made holy by His presence, it was the ground, and not the water, that claimed regard. But now a new element attracts our interest, and not the less so because the water itself had changed: for the precise position of an event on sea, or lake, or river seems to be unmoved by the shifting of the actual tide or current.

Our course still trended south, and the terebinth marked in the map under the letter A of the word Butaia, and which had long seemed to be close to the water's edge, was now left behind in the plain.

A respectable-looking Arab came to the door of a neat little tent here, and his wife took leave of him affectionately as he mounted his well-fed donkey and went along the path with a friend. The Rob Roy approached, and we had a most pleasant talk about things in general. It was very remarkable how distinctly every word was heard, though our voices were not raised, even at 300 yards off; and it was very easy to comprehend how, in this clear air, a preacher sitting in a boat could address a vast multitude standing upon the shore.

Bethsaida Julias was behind, if it stood where that green mound (Et Tell in our map) shines fertile in the sun.* The Bashan hills are on our left, but still the water is not much deeper near that side. At only one spot of the shore all round it, from this to near Tiberias (by the south), do the cliffs approach the water, and then it is not abruptly. My present inspection of this shore in front, and the hills overhanging it, was chiefly to find where—for it is supposed to have been near this—the herd of swine ran into the sea, as related in the eighth chapter of St. Matthew. After most

of some of the features of this shore in relation to the site of Capernaum, we shall return to the subject farther on.

* It will be observed that this tell in Vandevelde is far too distant from the shore. Wilson does not consider that Et Tell is proved to be Julias. Josephus clearly places Julias on the east side ("Jewish War," book iv. ch. viii. sec. ii.), and marks the other eastern boundary of Palestine on the south at Somorrhon (Gomorrha?).

scrutinizing search I could not perceive any one locality which might be pointed to as the "steep place" in question; and at this there was no small disappointment, though all difficulty about the matter was entirely removed on a subsequent occasion at another part of the coast.

The underwood now thickens on the verge of the sea. The gravel bank is redder in color, and of larger pebbles and fewer shells. The streams flowing in here are numerous, but nearly all of them enter the lake in a remarkable way by forming a narrow strip of lagoon along the *land* side of the high gravel beach, and inside of this the water from the rivulet would filter silently and invisibly through the clean pebbly barrier without any break in the shore.* From a wide glen on our left there projects into the lake a tongue-shaped promontory about half a mile broad at its eastern base, and covered with thick bushes of many different kinds. Some of these are twenty and thirty feet high, and the flood-mark is distinct upon them all from three to four feet above the present level of the lake, while the roots of many dip into the water, and their thin polished branches wave over the surface. Several palm-trees were growing here, with their roots in five feet of water, which seemed a very unusual position.† To skim along in the calm silence under the trees was delicious. The towers of Tiberias, on the other side of the lake, had long white reflections on the water, and the smooth slopes rose behind it where once was poured forth to refresh the whole world that sermon of texts, beginning with "Blessed are the poor in spirit, for theirs is the kingdom of heaven." The cleft in the chain of hills above me was the Wady Semakh, and, according to the marking in the map, I expected to reach the mouth of the river before arriving at the end of its gravel tongue.‡

* Wady Sulam, Wady Tellahych, and Wady Jermaiah, or (if Vandevelde be right) Jernaiah, all enter the lake in this way, being quite invisible from the water.

† There are palm-trees at the north, south, east, and west sides of the lake.

‡ From this point west to the shore near Magdala is the greatest breadth of the lake, 6¾ miles.

It was with some surprise, then, that this mouth was found to be not at one side of the tongue, but precisely at its end. This deviation of the map from the present coast-line was, however, readily explained by perceiving that the ground near the river is lower on the north shore than on the south, and that this part was submerged at the time the map was made.

The mouth of this river, Semakh, is about sixty feet wide, and the curious scroll of sand at the extremity of the southern bank of it (like what we have remarked upon for the other inlets) is here intensified in a remarkable manner, and has a second interior scroll slightly less regular. These scrolls are shown in our sketch. The gravel here is minute and absolutely clean. The water gurgles with the tiniest ripples in the delicate angles of the mathematical figure at the end, the top of which is not two inches above the surface; and the wonder is how so fragile an ornament can stand the wash of a single wave, and as to what becomes of the whole when the lake swells deeper, some four feet over its present verge.

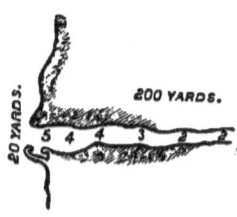
SEMAKH RIVER, NEAR GERGESA.

We paddled up the river eastward until, at about two hundred yards, it was only two and three feet deep, with thick undergrowth on both sides, and numerous boulders in the channel. Pushing farther in, there was only four inches of water, and beyond this the canoe could not well float, being heavy with the materials for camping out and four days' food. Here I could see the ruins described by former travellers as the ancient Gergesa,* now called Khersa, and some of which are on each side of the river, and are close to the water.

If Arabs had come at this time, they could have caught the Ingleez very readily; but I had made up my mind to risk it, being now thoroughly interested in the voyage, and determined not to forego any important investigation at

* As to this name, see *post*, chapter xxiii.

such a point.* Therefore I landed and penetrated the thick jungle of canes, a wild and savage lair for any beast to live in. Some of these canes had evidently been cut down for thatching, or some other use, by the Arabs. One of the tallest that I cut with my knife was exactly thirty-two feet high.

It was now time to cross the lake, steering for Tell Hoom,† whither the camp had been ordered to go. The water was perfectly calm, and I could see no sign of the Jordan flowing in the mid-lake, as has been sometimes reported; but this will be noticed when we go farther south. The lake water was clear, but not very clear—not nearly so translucent as that of the Red Sea; in fact, the bottom was never visible in depths beyond thirty feet.‡

A few—that is, a few hundred—waterfowl were in the middle of the lake—ducks, grebes, and gulls; also a bird like a cormorant, and one or two very shy pelicans. Halfway across to the land of Genesareth, the Rob Roy paused for one of those luscious draughts of pleasure which such a panorama yielded every time it was seen. On such occasions I could recline at ease in the boat—you would no more roll out of the canoe than out of a comfortable sofa—and then my little pocket copy of St. John's Gospel was always the most vivid hand-book of the scenery around. Open the sixth chapter, and as you read verse by verse, the very places mentioned in them are on all sides in view.

From that pure strand He "went over the sea," and

---

* The inhabitants of the place we are now describing attacked and seized Lieutenant Anderson when he was found alone.

† As it is pronounced thus, I see no good reason why it should be spelt "Tell Hum," which is so likely to be called "Tell Humm."

‡ The water of the Jordan from three miles above the mouth is dull in color, not exactly muddy, but with very fine matter in suspension. This color it had also from below the first bridge on the Hasbany, being varied in the north part of the Hoolch by a redder tinge of the Banias River, and a color nearly black in Hoolch Lake, and then again purifying itself in its rapid run over rock after Jacob's Bridge, but again absorbing earthy matter in the Butaia plain.

along that plain "a great multitude followed Him." Among those hills He "went up into a mountain, and there he sat with his disciples," and fed the faint thousands with miraculous bread, and gave forth words of life for the millions of all hearers to the end of time. It was upon those heights He lingered on "a mountain himself, alone," till in the dark and in the storm, and somewhere close to the spot where I am now reading, they saw the same "Jesus walking on the sea." Faith is not, indeed, begotten by this vividness of places. Faith is of loftier birth than sight; but faith may be nourished, if not engendered, by things seen, and a verse of the Bible which you have traced out thus is graven anew in the memory, with the earth and water round it for a visible framing to the nobler spiritual picture. The setting can never be worthy of the gem, still it may help our clumsy hands to hold the jewel.

Christ's is a religion that came from heaven, but is meant for all places in the world, and for all people; not for temples only, or shrines, or priests, or hermits, but for the breezy hill-side, and the work-day town, and the collier in the mine, and the sailor in the boat. All these need his love; and until this is got, the richest man is needy, while the poorest who has pardon and peace has a wealth laid up of glory.

The ensign at our camp was waving languidly in the sun, and the white tents stood out in contrast on the green grass by the deep black shore at Tell Hoom. The beach here is all of basalt stones, rounded by tumbling waves, but never smoothed. A fringe of oleanders, growing in the water, screens the shore for fifty feet outward. In no part about this point is there any proper place for boats. The land is too rocky to beach them; the water is too shallow to moor them; the bottom is too stony to anchor them. There is no protection here from the worst winds, no pier, no harbor; and where you can neither beach, nor moor, nor anchor a boat in safety, how can that be the port of a large town?

The shore of Tell Hoom Cape slopes steep to a height of twenty feet. Behind that is flatter ground, all strewed with rough black stones. These are often grouped in mounds, as if once they had been walls; but, after a diligent examination of them, the conclusion we arrived at was that most of these grouped stones were mere inclosure-dikes, exactly like those near the cities of Bashan, and where flocks and produce were kept, and are now kept in Brak, as we have before described.* Even if these rounded stones were once in the walls of houses, the thickness of such walls would be very great, else the stones would' not stand, and thus a small house might leave large ruins. The fertile ground behind Tell Hoom would need many folds and store-places; and though there are small ruins of hewn stone here and there among the vast masses of shapeless boulders, their number and position and dimensions do not (I think) indicate that any large village or town was here. But excavation has unearthed at this place the splendid sculptured stones of what is supposed to be a synagogue.† One would wish that this place *may* prove to be Capernaum, and that the synagogue is the one where our Lord so often taught; but the evidence against this particular site (to be adduced farther on) seems too strong to leave any such hope; while we find once more how much easier it is to marshal the objections against each suggested site than to produce direct evidence in favor of any one of them.

A deep-set ravine from the mountains west of the sea winds down here, inclosing a considerable stream, which rolls the round boulders when the torrent is in flood. By this I mounted on and on, until the crags aloft were seen to be crowned by massive ruins, and at length I climbed to those of Keraseh. Captain Wilson and Lieutenant An-

---

* *Ante*, chap. xi.

† Careful and minute descriptions of these and photographs are published by the Palestine Exploration Fund. The building is not yet proved to be ancient. The wood-cut at p. 344 of "Buckingham's Travels" represents an octagonal building, which is not now to be seen, nor does he describe it.

derson first described this place; and if this be Chorazin, it must surely be by a stretch of expression that we can say that town was "upon the lake."*

From Keraseh a great part of the lake is hidden. Its distance from the lake is at least two miles and a half by the present path, and only a mile less if measured in a straight line. The beautiful relics at Keraseh are shown in the photographs of the Palestine Exploration Fund (query, *Society*), and they include some beautiful niches, delicately chiselled out of the rough black basalt.†

Gushing streams water these high-perched precipices, and under one of the few trees was a camel resting, and an Arab. Farther down, the tents of other Ishmaelites nestled in sheltered nooks, and men and women ran out to inspect the lonely visitor with loud but not rude pressure for the hateful "backshish." Thence I rambled long upon the hills, but as these may be described by land travellers, we shall hasten back to the shore, and there we find our tents all gay with special decorations, festoons of oleander, hedges of bright yellow shrubs new-planted at the doors, huge bouquets of wild flowers grouped upon the table, singing, shouting, firing of guns, and a general hubbub of fête and gala, all improvised since my departure in the morning, because it happened to be the voyager's birthday, January 24. A huge roast turkey and plum-pudding graced the board, and opposite the door at night was a frame, supported on two poles, with forty-four wax tapers burning when the sun sank, and the muleteers whined their unmeasurable song until night enveloped the "fantasia," and the sea too went asleep.

The bays and shore-line north of Tell Hoom had next to be examined up to the mouth of Jordan. It is difficult

---

* De Sauley says that St. Jerome tells us Chorazin was two miles from Capernaum, but "in littore maris." Wey's map, in 1442, puts it east of Jordan, and so does Hondius's in 1624. Cruden says "Chorazin" means "the secret," or "here is a mystery."

† Thomson does not appear to have seen these beautiful sculptured ruins, but only some boulders in the neighborhood, which he styles "the shapeless heaps of Chorazin" ("The Land and the Book," vol. ii. p. 8).

to estimate the relative breadth and the indentation of a bay when viewed from either of its projecting boundaries or from a height in-shore.* Perhaps it is on this account that the bays all round this lake appeared to me deeper in their indentation than they are marked on the Ordnance Map, but in one or two instances I found by actual bearings that the coast is more indented than is shown. A very careful search was made for any semblance of a pier or breakwater near Tell Hoom. To use the place for boats, it can scarcely be supposed that some sort of pier was not absolutely necessary, and it could have been made very easily, for the stones are near at hand, and so many of them are round that they might easily be rolled down into the water, though they would form but a clumsy wall on land. Once submerged, they would never have been displaced. They could not be raised again from eight or ten feet under water. Their shape binding them between the rounded rocks at the bottom would prevent the waves from dislodging them, and if they are not to be seen there now, it is most probably because they never have been there. The search was somewhat difficult, because the wind was south, and the swell made it dangerous to lean much over the side of the canoe to put my eye close to the surface. However, the care bestowed was enough, I believe, to insure that no ruins near the edge under water were unnoticed. Clear indications of a pier were found at the promontory marked B in the rough diagram of coast (*post*, p. 333) bearing E.N.E. $\frac{1}{4}$ E. from our camp (near C),

* If you look along the course of a river, the bend seems to be more sudden than when you look across, for the divergence right and left from the medium line of the stream is seen in full breadth by looking endways, whereas the length of the curves is foreshortened, and the farther half, at any rate, is sure to seem more sharply crooked than it is in truth. When you look at Westminster Bridge from Southwark Bridge, the bend of the Thames appears twice as sudden as it does when viewed from the bridge at Charing Cross, and one can generally tell whether a traveller has judged of a lake's size from its side or its end, by observing whether he makes it too long or too broad. The sketch of the Sea of Galilee, seen from the north (and given *ante*, p. 307), represents how much the size is foreshortened from north to south.

SEA OF GALILEE
UNDER WATER, NEAR TELL HOOM.

and N. of Wady Kerazeh. These relics are shown alongside on a larger scale. The soundings are in feet. The quay begins on shore, and part of it is above water, though in the lake. Beyond that the dotted part is submerged two or three feet, and ten feet broad. At *A* in the middle of the wall (which is about four feet thick) there is one large stone reaching within six inches of the surface, and inside of this the water was calm, being sheltered.*

For a time the search was suspended, as a brisk breeze from Bashan had freshened while we paddled along these bays, and the short "choppy" waves at Jordan's mouth were angry enough to require attention while crossing there. I ascended the Jordan again to wait for the wind's pleasure if it might calm down, but instead of that, the sea rose more and more, and at last heavy clouds in the east burst into a regular gale. Fortunately my canoe was in her lightest trim to-day, but the waves on the lee-shore were exactly upon her beam, which is always the most awkward direction when the wind catches the tiny craft just on the thin crest of a breaker. For some time I hesitated to start, knowing well that, once in the middle of it, there would be no place to take shelter at until we could reach Tell Hoom, about two miles away, and then it would be very doubtful how one could land upon that rough shore with such a sea. Hunger (the only plague of strong health) forced me at last to the journey, and having tightly braced up every thing to the task, the Rob Roy launched on the Jordan and dashed over the bar, having there received one good ducking to start with, so that no fear remained that any thing up to my shoulders could get more wet than it was. It was well known that the waves far out from land are longer and more regular than in shore, so our course was in oblique lines, giving a very wide

* Farther on we shall notice a few more traces.

berth to each headland; and as this was the first occasion on which our present canoe had to stem a really high sea (for in the Red Sea we had been running before the breeze), it was

STORM ON THE SEA OF GALILEE.

with great satisfaction I found that her full floor near each end made her extremely buoyant and safe in her plunges.*

* One of the numerous advantages which a canoe has beyond what can ever be had in a rowing-boat, is the power of using the paddle just at the critical moment on the top of a wave, when two entirely opposite dangers have to be encountered. For, on the one hand, if, when rising on a billow, you incline the deck to windward too soon, a drenching sea from the wave-crest will, of course, be received heavily, and stagger the whole fabric for several seconds. On the other hand, if, to avoid that danger, you delay to lean up to the wind as you mount the sloping side of a wave, the full force of the crest-water is thrown against the bottom of the boat on the weather side, and just at the moment when the wind also catches the hull (and your own body) with its greatest force, so as to make every possible provision for a complete capsize. In an open boat, of course, both these two pleasant alternatives may come together, for while the bow of the boat is pressed by the wind, just as it tops the wave-crest, the full body of curving green water descends into the stern, and rushes at once to the lee side, to help the poor vessel to roll over.

The canoe-man meets this double danger with the enormous advantage of looking it in the face, and with the addition of a long and powerful hand, the

The wind whistled now, and sea-gulls screamed as they were borne on the scud. Thick and ragged clouds drifted fast over the water, which became almost green in color, as if it were on the salt sea, and the illusion was heightened by the complete obscurity of the distance, for the other side of the lake was quite invisible.

The wind shifted about as the Rob Roy came to the offing at Tell Hoom, and she " hove to," for it was not safe to turn her in such a cross-sea. The tents were flapping and fluttering, and straining at their strong cords. The ensign crackled sharply in the gusts that drove its free end upward, as the wind-current was deflected aloft by the sloping shore below. Hany and his men stood picturesquely on high points, shouting all sorts of excellent advice, only it was quite unheard, and the waves burst in upon the oleanders, and broke high and noisy against the rugged rocks. After consideration, it seemed to be a clear case for the last resort in landing at such a place, so I jumped out and we floated safe ashore, the boat being all right, of course, the moment my feet found the bottom, when I could drag the Rob Roy light upon the beach to be grasped by Hany, who said he had been at this place a hundred times, but never saw so severe a storm upon the lake.

The storm lasted next day, and I spent the hours on shore, but on January 26th it was calm, and again I returned to the bays north of Tell Hoom, because although nothing had seemed to indicate there any harbor in water deep enough for a port, yet the waves had prevented careful sounding, and sometimes even made it dangerous to approach the shore, where rocks just concealed by the water, when at rest, were bared in the trough of each wave, and showed their pointed tops quite hard enough to stave in a boat if cast upon them. Besides the pier described at p. 330, and which is at *B* on the sketch here given, there is

broad end of his paddle, to which he can apply the entire force of both his arms, while he reaches the blade deep down on the lee side of his quivering craft, and so applies from forty to fifty pounds of pressure only for a second or two, but just long enough to lift her gallantly over the foam.

CURIOUS STONES.   333

a line of big stones forming a sort of wall about twenty feet long and ten feet broad at *C*, projecting N.E., also fainter relics at *A*. Going south-west past Tell Hoom again, we find at *D* some traces of several large dressed stones in three and four feet water near the old tower at E, but they are not laid regular-

COAST AT TELL HOOM.

ly, and there are many smaller ones on shore just on the verge, so that it seems as if all are from the ruins above. One stone, a cube of two feet, looks a little like part of a pier, and two others not far off resemble it. None of these structures, however, all the way hither from Jordan mouth, could protect even one fishing-boat in wind. A remarkable stone pictured below was noticed at *F*. It was on the verge of the water, and half submerged. In times of full lake it would be unnoticed, but a wave receding happened to reveal it as we passed. The shape is an oval, about four feet long and two feet broad (not so smooth as in this drawing). In the middle is a deep cut, a foot broad, and from two to six inches

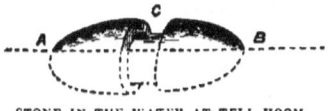
STONE IN THE WATER AT TELL HOOM.

deep, leaving a sort of neck between two bulging ends. At first this seemed to be a stone for an anchor, but I think it would be too heavy for that. For a mooring it would be too light, and the sharply defined indentation would not be required for either of these purposes. The waves were too high to allow me to examine it better. It remains for the *next* land traveller to bring this relic to No. 9 Pall Mall East. Not far off and south of it is another stone hammer-faced, and both of them are of black basalt like the rest.

Farther west there are several small capes or natural piers, but not one artificial group longer than twenty feet, and these usually with only four or five feet of water alongside. Some of the small bays that seem best for boats here are quite shallow, and studded with dangerous rocks only two feet under water. The islet past the old tower, which looks like the remains of a landing-place, has very little water round it. Two curious clumps or bunches of thick canes stand out in bold relief in this bay as islets. The first had five feet and the second six feet of water alongside. It appeared to me not unlikely that these may have originally grown out of the wrecks of boats, and they would thus accumulate earth about their roots for a permanent hold. I have never observed any thing like these before in any lake.

Pococke speaks of seeing (most probably here) "a round port for small boats."* Other persons have noticed the same appearance, and undoubtedly the semblance of a little harbor is presented by the points of rocks and detached stone projecting above water when the lake is low. But my visit to this spot entirely dispelled any such illusion. The points belong to a few of the highest of a thousand enormous rocks and detached boulders dotted over the whole surface below. There is no room whatever for boats to pass in here, much less to lie at peace protected. These rocks are of all irregular shapes, but very many have sharp edges, and not a few are whitish in color. They are in water of all depths, even to twenty feet, and their summits rise to a few inches above the surface, and to every less height, without any appearance of regular design, except what may perchance seem formal in shape when a few are associated by accident together. Thus, what might be called a "port" from the shore is, in fact, a most treacherous reef, and the whole of the area about it for a quarter of a mile square is, perhaps, the most dangerous part of the lake—and certainly is "*statio malefida carinis.*"

The first beach of sand and gravel west from Tell Hoom seems to be a good one, but that bay is full of sunken rocks most awkwardly placed.

In the next much smaller bay is the first soft strand where fishing-boats could venture to beach, and it is pro-

* Vol. ii. p. 72 (fol.).

tected from wind by a natural breakwater.* The beach itself is a pretty bit of strand, with whiter pebbles and shells, and the shore was perfectly clean from drift-wood or debris, although a whole day's gale had been blowing right into it until this morning. Rain and mist came mildly down now, and I drifted along with my white umbrella hoisted in a most lubberly fashion, but very comfortable.

Rounding again the next point close upon Tabiga (Bethsaida), we find great rocks projecting from the shore into the waves, while verdure most profuse teems over them, and long streamers of "maiden's hair," and richest grasses, and ferns, briers, and moss, wave in the breeze and pendent trail upon the water. This part of the coast is entirely different from any other round the lake. The water is five and six feet deep right up to the rocks. The rocks are thickly incrusted with a moist trickling petrified gray substance, and this stalagmite projects so far over the edge that the Rob Roy easily went beneath the rocks, where the clear water had hollowed out caverns, and was sounding within a deep-toned note as every swell of the sea beat upward in the dark recesses. Gray steam-like vapor rises from the surface here, and exhales from the streaming rocks above us, for the water is hot, and bursts from the ground a little way off, and bears in solution to the lake a saturated current of limestone, which deposits its crust as the stream is cooled, and irrigates the rich vegetation with a tepid gush, a powerful stimulant to the rank tangled herbage. The rocks thus *grow* horizontally by accretions from this stream, and roots, leaves and stalks stand out petrified, while their neighbors sprout above, being forced into excessive life. One can readily understand how the warm waves of the lake wear away the lower parts of these rocks, while the upper edges are growing sideways, so that I could thrust in my paddle its full length of seven feet under these table-like structures, while above water some three or four feet thickness of a

* Vandevelde was evidently ignorant of this beach and others near it ("Syria and Palestine," vol. ii. p. 399).

calcareous plateau was supported by thin pillars, and just lapped by the wavelets beneath.

Here it was well to stop, and no more charming spot could be chosen for our well-earned luncheon. This surely is Bethsaida, the " house of food, or hunters, or snares," according to Cruden's derivation, and in all three renderings plainly meaning the "fisherman's home."

Tabiga is the Arab name for the mills and the few houses and huts that mark the spot. We are not in view of these just now, but the sound of rivulets and cascades, and the musical dripping of water from the long-pointed stalactites in the caverns beside us, and the low rumbling, splashing, tremulous beat of the mill-wheels working unseen, blend a mixed harmony round the sunny little cove where the Rob Roy rests on the rushes, while her captain reclines at ease with limbs outstretched on deck and every muscle lax. One or two quiet-looking natives soon found out the canoe, and sat in silence, smiling through the long grass at our floating feast. It gave them pleasure to look on, and it did no harm to me.

The place soon asserted its right to the name Bethsaida by the exceeding abundance of the fish we saw tumbling in the water.* The hot springs flowing in here over these rocks, and a little farther on in larger volume over a clean brown sand, warm all the ambient shallows for a hundred feet from shore, and, as much vegetable matter is brought down by the springs, and probably also insects which have fallen in, all these dainties are half cooked when they enter the lake. Evidently the fish agree to dine on these hot joints, and, therefore, in a large semicircle, they crowd the water by myriads round the warm river-mouth. Their backs are above the surface as they bask or tumble and

---

* Vandevelde, however, considers that Bethsaida lies at Khan Minyeh (vol. ii. p. 395), but he is almost unsupported in this; and Thomson places it on the Jordan mouth. The latter supposition I find to be so entirely irreconcilable with the directions and distances of the apostles' voyages (considered afterwards) that I have omitted it altogether. He derives Tabiga from "Dabbaga," the Arabic for "tannery," and says the water is "precisely the kind best adapted for that business."

jostle crowded in the water. They gambol and splash, and the calm sea, fringed by a reeking cloud of vapor, has beyond this belt of living fish a long row of cormorants feeding on the half-boiled fish as the fish have fed on insects underdone. White gulls poise in flocks behind the grebes or cormorants, and beyond these again ducks bustle about on the water or whirl in the air. The whole is a most curious scene, and probably it has been thus from day to day for many thousand years. I paddled along the curved line of fishes' backs and flashing tails. Some leaped into the air, others struck my boat or my paddle. Dense shoals moved in brigades as if by concert or command. But the hubbub around in the water, and the feathered mob in the sky, were all unheeded now, for we had come in full view of the land of Genesareth.*

* Stanley says that the name "Gennesar" may be from *Gani*, "garden," and *Sar*, "prince," the "Gardens of Princes," alluding, as the Rabbis allege, to the princes of Nephtali ("S. and P." p. 375, quoting Lightfoot). Neubauer (p. 215), besides this derivation, cites, "rich garden" as a meaning. In the Midrasch, Chinnereth is identified with Seunabris and Beth Yerah.

Y

CHAPTER XX.

Bethsaida Beach.—Of old.—Evidence.—Bias.—Sermon afloat.—Stones.—Fishermen.—Ships and Boats.—Distinction.—An Explanation.—Present Boats.—The "Pillow."—Sailing-boat.—Fish.—Nets.—Hooks.—Cliff.—"Scorpion Rock."—"Capharnaoum" Ain et Tin.—Other Streams.—The Coracinus.—Other Fish.—The hot Springs.—The Aqueduct.—Josephus's Fountain.—At Tabiga.

It may be irksome to those who can not imagine something of the inward thrill of a voyager at such a time to hear from another how fast his heart beat then, but for those who can even a little realize a delight like this, perhaps the mere outward picture of the scene will be enough.

Bethsaida beach recalled bright pictures of our Saviour's life. For here it was, as seems to me, that the first and shortest sermon of Christianity was preached, "Behold the Lamb of God." The hearers were but two, and both of them heard to purpose (John i.); and of these Andrew found next day his "own brother Simon," whom Jesus christened Cephas (a "stone"—not "the Rock"); and after him He "findeth Philip," who "was of Bethsaida the city of Andrew and Peter;" and Philip "findeth Nathanael," and brought him with the invitation "Come and see." Here was the cradle of Christianity, and years afterwards here again was "the third time that Jesus showed himself to his disciples after that he was risen from the dead."[*]

Almost the same persons are this time on the shore again: Peter, and Thomas, and Nathanael, and James, and John; but only "that disciple whom Jesus loved" could at first recognize his Lord. Peter, who had before cast himself into the same sea to go to Jesus, now did so again; but the Lord now thrice called him "Simon," as if the unstable one had by his threefold denial lost his better title. On

[*] John xxi. It is only by this Evangelist, who was present, that the scene is related.

the shore were coals, and food thereon. "The banquet is prepared. Shall He issue the invitation, 'Come, all things are ready?' Nay, something still is wanting! The Almighty Provider has yet some element of bliss to add ere the feast is complete. 'Bring,' he says, 'of the fish *ye* have caught.'"*

The central figure of this group was a new one in history—the *risen Saviour*. Do we believe that He rose again? The rest of the Gospel seems to follow with our answer, Yes, or No.

If indeed He rose, the narrative of his life becomes consistent and credible, and the sanction of his teaching is from on high; but "if Christ be not raised, your faith is vain."†

The evidence for the resurrection is more tangible, general, and distinct, than that for any other miracle, and it was a belief in this cardinal fact of history that was written upon and preached most constantly and most urgently by the apostles.‡

The evidence for the resurrection of Christ was precisely that which common men could best know at the time as witnesses, and common men now can best understand as testimony. Did Christ evidently die? Did Christ evidently live again? Surely no questions could be more plain for those who knew Him to decide. In an argument on this subject with an unbeliever, after other evidence had been discussed, a Christian read as follows: "He was seen of above five hundred brethren at once, of whom some remain unto this present; but the greater part are fallen

---

* "Memories of Gennesaret," by the Rev. Dr. Macduff, p. 255—a book full of beautiful descriptions of the Gospel scenes upon this lake and its shores.

† 1 Cor. xv. 14, and again 17.

‡ Though a regular attendant at church, the writer has heard only one sermon upon this subject. This was a powerful sermon by the Dean of Canterbury, in the cathedral, to a very large congregation, chiefly of Volunteers assembling for the Dover review. If barristers omitted their best evidence in addressing a jury, as clergymen do in addressing their people, they would get few clients and no verdicts.

asleep." The unbeliever quickly interposed — "Yes, it was very convenient that most of the alleged witnesses were dead. If it had been stated publicly that most of them were then *alive*, the evidence of the fact would have been very powerful." Then the Christian read the words correctly, as Paul wrote them (1 Cor. xv. 6)—" After that he was seen by above five hundred brethren at once, of whom the *greater part remain unto this present*, but some are fallen asleep."

This truth before the world for so many hundred years, how little it has spread! Yes; but the truth that "honesty is the best policy" has been much longer asserted; and it has progressed just as little, though no one denies the maxim on logical grounds. A score of sanitary maxims are made perfectly evident to our reason, but pleasure for the moment keeps the will from abiding by what the reason is convinced of.*

The Holy Spirit of God must do *this* work.

"Neither would they be *persuaded*, though one rose from the dead."

In an age or community where many profess to be "believers," there is at least distinction to be gained, if not satisfaction, by believing little and distrusting much. There is dignity in asserting independence, and you can be piquant if you are not orthodox. On the other hand, it is a pleasant excitement to believe in unseen facts, if we are thereby associated with the unseen, the mysterious, and the unknown, which may be, and probably is, so much more sublime than every-day life. An emotional bias warps our reason when we try to use that upon propositions which must affect our whole standard of life and determine the

---

* It is well said in the "Spectator" (Oct. 16, 1869): "It seems to us that the *constraint* to believe which the study of Christ's life produces is hardly an intellectual constraint, even where it is most strongly felt—that, judging by the intellectual state of the argument solely, if that were possible, men may be strictly *reasonable* who pronounce the evidence insufficient as well as those who pronounce it adequate, and that the real force of the belief depends upon an undefinable personal impression produced by Christ on the spirit which can never be adequately translated into an intellectual form."

centre of gravity of our system. If the devout man forgets to allow that this bias may warp him towards credulity and superstition, he will soon be reminded of the fact by his skeptical friend, and he ought not to ignore the tendency. But may we not also tell the cold schoolman that he too has a most powerful emotion warping his deductions when his logic deals with arguments that may convict him of pride, foolishness, and ingratitude, and would force him to submit his will to a Being whom he has always put far off? Feeling this want of some *cultus*—if not some Pope—he has set up for worship that impalpable thing called Truth, which is the pretty name given to the idol that clever men have been carving at (or paring away) for thousands of years, and which is shapeless still; nor can they ever agree as to how many heads it has, though the noise of their work goes on—the noise of the crow-bar and the pickaxe, rather than of the hammer and the trowel. In short, the religious man confesses that he must beware of believing in what he wishes may be true, but the philosopher somehow forgets to confess that *he* has the prejudice of pride, the superstition that kneels before human intellect, and a carnal heart, which persuades us to doubt what it dislikes.

Another scene in the Holy Life which probably happened on this beach is related by Luke (chap. v.) where, when the multitude pressed upon the Great Preacher "to hear the word of God," He entered into one of "two ships standing by the lake." This ship, we are told, "was Simon's," and Christ "prayed him that he would thrust out a little from the land, and he sat down and taught the people out of the ship." Then followed the miraculous draught of fishes. As the ship was Simon's, and his house was at Bethsaida, and as his partners were gone out of the ships, "and were washing their nets," we are at once brought close to this very spot where the fishermen now do the very same thing; and only a few yards away are the shoals of fish we have seen by the hot springs.* Just here, too.

---

* The fishermen told me that, though fish are in other parts of the lake, they are always most plentiful here.

the beach rises rapidly, and there is deep water within a few yards of the shore, while at the same time a multitude of hearers could place themselves so as to see the Saviour in the boat, and there is no such natural church along the other coast by Genesareth. On another occasion the Lord again taught the people out of a ship, while "the whole multitude stood on the shore;"* and often in other ways did He manifest forth his glory when floating on the water both in storm and calm.

Continuing my voyage, I could discern just in front, and under a looming cliff (almost the only one all round the lake which rises sheer out of the water) my tents now pitched at Genesareth, and the ensign drooping with no wind. But we need not hasten to our camp, so let us linger on the way.

The beautiful white beach of Bethsaida is gracefully bent round its pretty little cove in a gentle slope of gravel, shells, and purest sand. No footstep this morning has marked the tender surface smoothed and 'laved once more by yesterday's waves. "The beach on which the limpid waters still gently ripple retains the same pearly margin on which was spent the childhood of the young fishermen of Bethsaida."† The bay is admirably suited for boats. It shelves gradually; the anchorage is good, and boats can be safely beached. Rocks project at the south-west end about fifty yards beyond those seen above water. These would form a good protection to the harbor. There appears to be no jetty. The water is deep, and nearly free from boulders until near the south-west end. Evidently the Jews and Romans, who successively owned these coasts for many years, thought more about building palaces on shore than about removing rocks from the water. Here also we noticed a few large stones, arranged as in the sketch. These are in two feet of water (even when the lake is low), and though arranged in the manner of "fish-traps," they could

* Matt. xiii.; Mark iv. In this sermon were the parables, beginning with that of the sower. See note upon the size of ship used, *post*, p. 345.
† "Memories of Gennesaret," Preface.

scarcely be used for these unless the water was much lower.

On the east edge of Bethsaida bay, and close to the water, upon a smooth hard bank of grass, very near

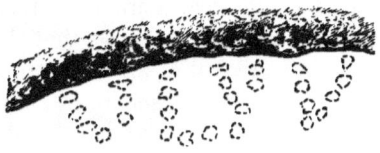
UNDER WATER, NEAR BETHSAIDA.

the gushings of the clear hot stream, a fishing-boat was drawn up on land beside two fishers' huts, made entirely of reed matting, and not unlike the huts in Hooleh, but smaller, neater, and more clean. About a dozen fishermen instantly came out. Their delight and amazement as to what this canoe could be, and what was I, had a spice of superstitious doubt in their stare, yet we speedily became good friends, and I invited them to visit me at the camp in the evening.

The subject of fishing and fishers' boats was, of course, of great interest in connection with this beautiful lake, where, in old times, among the fishers, were those men whose faithful pens have written what goes to our hearts and gives us the marrow of life.

When the Sea of Galilee was fringed by towns and villas, trees and cornfields, then the water was covered by little vessels sailing about in hundreds.* It is not easy to ascertain what was the size of the largest of these vessels; but probably, as the distances were short, and the ports were shallow, the boats were not larger than they are now, say about thirty feet long and seven feet beam. The number of them employed then on the lake will be shown very well from the following curious narrative related by Josephus, of what occurred when he was occupied busily in keeping quiet the district along the lake. At that time Tarichea and Tiberias were in frequent contention, and one of the revolts of the latter city was quelled by a stratagem of Josephus. He was then at Tarichea, and without soldiers; but he ordered a large fleet of ships, 230 in num-

---

* It was then a very populous district, and, as Stanley says, might be regarded as the "manufacturing districts" are spoken of by us in England.

ber, to sail, each with four men for a crew.* These he kept so far from Tiberias that the people there thought the vessels were full of armed men, and so they surrendered to him all their 600 senators, who were sent over the lake, while Josephus demanded the chief instigator of the revolt, one Clitus. He commanded his own lieutenant, Levius, to cut off this man's hand; and, as he hesitated to do this alone, Josephus, enraged, prepared to go ashore himself to do it, and only relented so far as to leave the poor fellow his right hand if with that he would cut off his left, which feat of arms he did at once with his own sword, and the people were thus awed into obedience.

When Tarichea was besieged by land, the inhabitants retired aboard ships, by which also they were able to attack from the sea the Romans then on the shore. Finally, the ships fled, and Josephus† tells us that Titus quickly got ready vessels wherein to pursue, "because there was great plenty of materials and a great number of artificers also;" and the description of the battle on the lake is then given, which colored the water with blood, and strewed the shore with corpses.

With respect to the size of vessels formerly used in the lake, two words are employed in the New Testament, πλοιον (*ploion*) for the "ship," or larger vessel, and πλοιάριον (*ploiarion*) for the smaller one, or "boat." Thus the "ship" from which Christ taught the people on shore (Mark iv. 1) was πλοιον; and, evidently referring to the same vessel,

---

* Josephus, "Jewish War," book ii. ch. xxi. sec. viii. Whiston remarks that these vessels are constantly called "νηες, πλοια, and σκαφη, i. e., plainly ships" ("Life of Josephus," sect. xxxiv., note). In another place Josephus quotes Menander as relating an expedition at sea, when the Phœnicians supplied sixty ships (ναῦς), and 800 men to row them, or about ten oars for each ("Antiq. of the Jews," book ix. ch. xiv. sec. ii.), so that even on the salt sea mere barges were employed as fleets of war.

† "Jewish War," book iii. ch. ix. and x. It seems to be stated that Titus and Trajan, Vespasian and Agrippa, were present at this fight; and Clarke says Vespasian was on board the fleet, but I do not gather that from Josephus. However, this naval fight was prolonged for some time, and was probably the last great display of ships upon this lake. Nowadays one single Armstrong gun at Gamala would command the whole Sea of Tiberias.

verse 36 says, "and they took him even as he was in the ship" (πλοιον); "and there were also with him other little ships" (πλοιάριον).*

Again, when (Mark iii. 9) "He spake to his disciples that a small ship should wait on him," it was πλοιάριον; and after his resurrection, when the disciples "entered into a ship" (John xxi. 3) πλοιον is used; but those who dragged the full net to shore "came in a little ship" (verse 8), πλοιάριον.

In the several accounts of the voyage in which our Lord was seen walking on the sea, the ship used by the apostles is called πλοιον fourteen times;† but in John, vi. 22‡ we read, "The day following, when the people which stood on the other side of the sea saw that there was none other boat there save that one whereunto the disciples were entered, and that Jesus went not with his disciples into the boat, but that his disciples were gone away alone," here the word πλοιάριον is twice used for the "boat" into which the disciples had entered.

At first sight there thus appears to be a confusion between the words for "boat" and "ship;" and if it could not be otherwise explained,§ we might suggest that the application of both words to the same vessel does not show that their technical meanings were not distinct; for among ourselves, even in so nautical a country as England, landfolk use the words a "ship," a "barque," and even a "cutter" and a "boat," for the same thing seen upon the water,

---

* Griesbach, however, seems to retain here the term πλοιον in both instances. As the pronunciation of these words may interest some readers, it has been given in common letters, following the good example set by the present Premier in his last book.

† Matthew xiv. 13, 22, 24, 32, 33; Mark vi. 32, 45, 47, 51, 54. John vi. 17, 19, 21. Luke, who was an accurate writer about ship matters (see note. p. 362) uses πλοιον for the general word always, except in Acts xxvii. 41, when he uses ναῦς (naus). The ship's boat (ver. 36), he calls σκάφη (skaffe).

‡ The other incidents of the Apostles' voyage are discussed in our next chapter.

§ Stanley ("S. and P." p. 379, note) seems to consider this double use of the words shows they were not so different in meaning, remarking that it is the tendency of modern Greek to substitute diminutives everywhere.

while each of these words, used technically, has a distinct meaning to the sailor, who, if he desires to speak of the floating thing in general, will call it a "vessel," or "sail," or "craft," but never a "sloop" or a "barque."

But I venture to suggest an explanation which may not only clear up the difficulty but throw light also upon other parts of the narrative, and vindicate once more the extreme accuracy of the New Testament even in minute particulars. In John's account of the transaction, he says the disciples went down unto the sea, and entered into a "ship," and went over the sea towards Capernaum; "and it was now dark, and Jesus was not come to them" (verse 17). Now, this last expression seems to show that they expected Jesus to *come to them;* probably, therefore, they waited in their "ship" before or even after they had weighed anchor, expecting their Master to come; and for this He would be expected to use a small "boat," whereby to reach the "ship," as in a rising sea the ship could not easily come to shore.

Entirely consistent with this is the expression that next day* "the people saw that there was no *boat* there save that one whereunto his disciples were entered, and that Jesus went not with his disciples into the *boat;*" for this tells us that the disciples themselves used a "boat," no doubt, to go out to the "ship" (which would be more likely left at anchor than on shore, or even in port, for they had all left it), while it says that the people saw that Christ did *not* go into the "boat" with them, and that "none other boat"† was there by which He could have gone on board the ship unperceived. Still further, this use of both boat and ship on the occasion shows the reason why the Evangelist considered it necessary to state afterwards that "other boats" (πλοιάρια) came from Tiberias (probably running into shelter before the same gale which was for the apostles' ship "contrary"), to show how it was that enough

---

* For if by the "boat" was meant the "ship" that had gone away the day before, the people could not see "*that one*" the "next day."

† Griesbach reads πλοιον here.

"boats" were now there to put the people on board when "they took shipping" (ships, πλοια), then still* at anchor off the shore.†

Turning now to the lake and its boats, as seen in the present days, how great is the falling off in the number, when for a long time there was not even one boat on the lake!‡ From inspection, I came to the conclusion that in 1869 there are three fishing-boats and two at the ferry, or five in all, besides the ferry-boat at Semakh. It is the absurdly prohibitive tax upon boats which alone prevents these from multiplying. Nominally, the rent the fishers pay for the right to fish at Bethsaida is £100 per annum.

* For it is not said that the apostles' was the only "ship" there, but that the boat they used was the only "boat" then available, and it does not mention the arrival of "ships," but of "boats," from Tiberias.

† The recent publication of Tauchnitz's 1000th volume, the New Testament in our authorized version, with the readings of the three MSS., more ancient than those available to our translators, is a very great boon to all readers of the Bible, and it is enhanced by the excellent preface of Tischendorf. Applying this new comment to our text, we find that the passage John vi. 22–24, is given by the Sinai MS. as follows: "The day following, when the people which stood on the other side of the sea saw that there was none other boat there save that whereunto the disciples of Jesus were entered, and that Jesus went not with them into the boat, but that his disciples were gone away alone. When therefore the boats came from Tiberias, which was nigh unto where they did also eat bread, after that the Lord had given thanks, and when they saw that Jesus was not there, neither his disciples, they also took shipping, and came to Capernaum, seeking for Jesus."

[The Alexandrine MS. omits the first "when" of our version, and the Vatican and Alexandrine MSS. have "save one" instead of "save that one," and omit the words "whereunto . . . entered."]

This reading does not render our explanation of the word "boat," as used in both versions, less probable, although it seems to point to another place, if not to another time, for a miraculous feeding of a multitude.

‡ The following shows the state of the navy of this sea in various years, according to travellers' statements :

In A.D. 1738, Pococke found one boat on the lake of Genesareth. In A.D. 1806, Seetzen saw one boat, but it was useless ; 1812, Burkhardt, the only boat had fallen to pieces in 1811 ; 1817, Richardson, two boats ; 1818, Irby and Mangles, "no boat whatever ;" 1822, Berggren, no boat ; 1822, Buckingham, "not a boat nor a raft large nor small ;" 1829, Prokesch, no boat ; 1834, 1835, Smith, one boat ; 1838, Robinson, one boat ; 1852, Vandevelde, one ; 1856, Newbold, one ; 1857, Thomson, no boat, once only in his other visits he saw a sail ; 1869, Macgregor, six boats besides the Rob Roy.

The revenue guard I noticed in a tent on a wild cliff, with a little flag, like a colored rag, hanging over it. His rapacious hands carry away 20, 40, even 60 per cent. of the fishers' hard-earned gains; and who can bear up against such extortion?

The boats now used in the lake by the fishers are all about the same size, rowing five oars, but very clumsy ones, and with a very slow stroke. Generally only three oars were in use, and I much regret that I failed to remark whether there was a rudder, but I think there was none. Their build is not on bad lines, and rather "ship-shape," with a flat floor, likely to be a good sea-boat, sharp and rising at both ends, somewhat resembling the Maltese. The timbers are close and in short pieces, the planks "carvel built," and daubed with plenty of bitumen, for that is readily obtained here.* The upper streak of the boat is covered with coarse canvas, which adheres to the bitumen, and keeps it from sticking to the crew when they lean upon it. The waist is deep, and there are no stern sheets, but a sort of stage aft. As there appears to be no reason to suppose that the Turks should have altered, or at any rate improved, the Jewish boat on the lake, it is impossible not to regard the modern fishers' boat of Galilee with great interest, and to people it at once with an apostolic crew. But the part of the boat on the stern has a special and sacred attraction to our gaze, for the Bible tells us that He who "never slumbers nor sleeps" was once in a ship on this lake "asleep on a pillow."† The raised platform already mentioned would most probably

---

* The wicker boats on the Euphrates are mere baskets, an inch thick with pitch. Noah's ark was probably made of interwoven trees cased thus with bitumen "within and without," and a most serviceable plan this is when mere flotation is the purpose, without the strain from masts or engines, or heavy seas, and when the vessel is to be grounded only once after being launched by the rising of the water around it.

† Mark iv. 38, ἐπὶ τὸ προσκεφάλαιον (proskephalaion), evidently a regular part of the boat's equipment, from the use of the definite article "*the* pillow." Smith's "Dictionary" mentions another term used, but that this was its equivalent, and renders it "boatmen's cushion."

be the place where our Lord in the weakness and weariness of his humanity was thus resting, and the word "pillow"* was perhaps the best one available for the translators when they sought to describe that his rest was settled, not accidental, and that, when He was on the water, some softer thing was found for the repose of Him who, when on the land, though all his own, had not "where to lay his head."

During twelve days of constant gazing upon this Lake of Galilee, I never saw a fishing-boat moving upon it by

GALILEE FISHING-BOAT.

daylight, except one morning, when a boat sailed past, and perhaps her crew had "toiled all the night." The sketch represents this boat, and the outlines of the back-ground as seen from Tell Hoom. These comprise the whole of the Butaia plain in front, with the large tree on the right as a boundary, the two clumps of palm-trees and the hills of Bashan behind. This and the picture of Bashan (Chap. XXIII.) exhibit nearly the whole eastern shore. The boat carries the ordinary lateen of the Mediterranean, not that of the Nile, or the Levant, or the Lake of Geneva. Nothing could be more miserable to the eye of a sailor than to behold this sad distortion of the sailor's art. Nev-

---

* All the versions in Bagster's "Hexapla" use this word "pillow." The stern in ancient ships was much higher than the prow, and this form continued even to the last century in England, while it is still the fashion in Egypt. It was on this account that they could anchor from the stern (as in the case of Paul's shipwreck), and the high stern made a safe and sloping place, where our Saviour slept in the storm.

ertheless he made the sketch of her abominable rig, and as he put his pocket-book away, the sketching sailor sighed.

I can not find any thing in Josephus about the fish in the lake except in the two following passages:* "Now this lake of Genesareth is so called from the country adjoining to it. Its breadth is forty furlongs, and its length one hundred and forty; its waters are sweet, and very agreeable for drinking, for they are finer than the thick waters of other fens; the lake is also pure, and on every side ends directly at the shores, and at the sand; it is also of a temperate nature when you draw it up, and of a more gentle nature than river or fountain water, and yet always cooler than one could expect in so diffuse a place as this is; now when this water is kept in the open air, it is as cold as that snow which the country people are accustomed to make by night in the summer. There are several kinds of fish in it, different both to the taste and the sight from those elsewhere. It is divided into two parts by the river Jordan.

"The country also that lies over against this lake hath the same name of Genesareth; its nature is wonderful, as well as its beauty; its soil is so fruitful that all sorts of trees can grow upon it, and the inhabitants accordingly plant all sorts of trees there; for the temper of the air is so well mixed that it agrees very well with those several sorts, particularly walnuts, which require the coldest air, flourish there in vast plenty; there are palm-trees also, which grow best in hot air; fig-trees also, and olives also, grow near them, which yet require an air that is more temperate. One may call this place the ambition of nature, where it forces those plants that are naturally enemies to one another to agree together; it is a happy contention of the seasons, as if every one of them laid claim to this country, for it not only nourishes different sorts of autumnal fruit beyond men's expectation but preserves them a great while; it supplies men with the principal fruits, with grapes and figs continually, during

* "Jewish War," book iii. ch. x. secs. vii. and viii.

ten months of the year, and the rest of the fruits, as they become ripe together, through the whole year; for besides the whole temperature of the air, it is also watered from a most fertile fountain. The people of the country call it Capharnaoum; some have thought it to be a vein of the Nile, because it produces the Coracin fish, as well as that lake does which is near to Alexandria. The length of this country extends itself along the banks of this lake that bears the same name, for thirty furlongs, and is in breadth twenty, and this is the nature of that place."

Josephus does not appear to tell us any thing as to the regulations of the fishing in this lake, though these must have been very distinct when so large and valuable a commerce had to be provided for. Nor does he seem to mention any of the particular modes of fishing which were used. The Talmud says that Joshua enacted that the fishing with a hook on the sea of Galilee should be open to all the world (Neubauer, p. 25), and once our Lord bid Peter use a hook. The most usual method of catching fish was by the casting net, δίκτυον (*dictuon*), Matt. iv. 20, 21; Mark i. 18, 19; Luke v. 2; John xxi. 6: the ἀμφλίβηστρόν (*amphlibcestron*), Matt. iv. 18; Mark i. 16;* probably like that used in Egypt: also σαγηνή (*sageench*), Matt. xiii. 47, which was larger, and required a boat with men on shore to haul it in. Probably our word "seine" for a net of this kind may be derived from the Greek. The use of a weir or fence of reeds within which the fish were caught was forbidden on the Sea of Galilee, because the stakes of it damaged the boats, but the small traps of stones I have noticed at p. 342 may be an old mode of fishing, and the plan is used at present. The hook was called by a Hebrew word showing that it resembled a thorn, Amos iv. 2; ἄγκιστρον (*ankistron*), Matt. xvii. 27. The rod is not mentioned in the Bible. Another mode was by the "barbed iron" or trident, or the spear, as practised in Egypt for the crocodile, Job xli.

* The Sinai and the Vatican MSS. have it "casting *nets* here and there into the sea;" the Alexandrine, "casting a net here and there into the sea;" and in verse 18, the Sinai and the Vatican MSS. have it "forsook the nets."

.7, or hippopotamus. The hook referred to in Job xli. 2, refers to the practice of putting a ring or "thorn" into a fish's gills to tether him to a stake by a rope of reeds (A. V. "hook") that he might be kept alive.

Having thus examined the boats and nets, we may resume the paddle in our own trim craft, and skirt the pretty white strand which lies north of Genesareth. The water is a perfect glassy calm, and it is easy therefore to make a careful examination of all the little bights and coves, which show in this part of the shore more variety of outline and character than is met with elsewhere. Although I willingly gave to this the most thorough exploration under water, so far as it could be done by peering down and by sounding and probing with the paddle, yet the place where we might have expected that something worth looking for was sure to be found did not contain one single evidence of building or of hewn stone, either placed in the water designedly or fallen from the cliff hanging over us from above.* Notwithstanding this dearth of visible remains, it is upon that cliff which surmounts Khan Minyeh, and is the sudden barrier of the land of Genesareth on the north, that Capernaum may have stood, and was thence into that deep below "thrust down." The cliff is vertical for about fifty feet at one place, and round it the rocks are bold, scarped, bare, and jagged, of various bright tints by weather blasts, and from their clefts spring weird-looking trees, which dangle their farthest branches in the water, so that it is even difficult to approach the actual verge, and the trees and underwood almost conceal the junction of rock with water in some parts.† Large fragments of many hundred tons in weight have evidently fallen into the lake from above, and some stick out as islets, others lurk just

---

* Wilson says the only shaft of a column seen in this neighborhood was a small basaltic one five inches in diameter, standing in the lake near the point where the Ain et Tin flows in.

† The rock descends here in some places into the lake without a beach between. It does this also south of Magdala, and south of Tiberias, as well as at Bethsaida. It is, therefore, not strictly accurate to say that there is a beach all round the lake.

below as breakers. The water about them is clearer than that north of Tell Hoom, both because the Jordan does not sully it in these quieter bays, and because the rock and gravel here yield less for suspension. Perhaps also the warm solutions at Bethsaida combine with ingredients from other fountains, or from Jordan and those of the lake, and so precipitate what would be again stirred up only by powerful gales. Of the several rocks appearing above the surface close to this cliff, one is particularly remarkable, which is at A in our sketch and is depicted in two views below. This consists of a level flat summit, seven feet long by four feet wide, and about two feet thick, of which three-fourths were above the surface of the lake. This upper portion is supported by a stalk, very thin compared with the head above, and divided into three parallel columns with vertical slits between them. One of these subordinate pillars has been thinned and broken near the bottom, where also the other two are attenuated for a space, but they thicken again below and spread into a solid foot at a depth of seven feet from the surface. The form will be understood by the end and side views in the sketch. When the lake is full, this rock is doubtless entirely covered, but situated as it is between Bethsaida and the fountain at Khan Minyeh called "Ain et Tin," a curiosity

A, ROCK IN THE WATER.

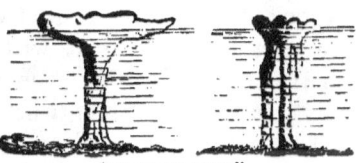

"SCORPION ROCK."

of this striking character would surely be well known in ancient times. Now Josephus mentions somewhere* the "Scorpion Rock" as known in the lake, and as this re-

---

* An index to Josephus would be a great luxury to those who use his work. Various fancies suggest themselves as to why it may be called a scorpion, but none are at present satisfactory to me, unless it be considered that the head and lobster-like claws of the scorpion resemble the upper part of the rock, while the body is like the narrower stalk below, and the tail is like the root.

markable perforated stone which we have described seems to be the only one of abnormal appearance all round the shores of this sea, perhaps he alludes to that.

Gliding over the sea, we now touch the placid shore of Genesareth,[*] where our Saviour dwelt so long.

The beach is very low and sloping gently, with a thick fringe of oleanders skirting the deep brown sand. Our tents are almost hid in the foliage, and the soft carpet of grass is patterned bright with wild flowers.

With such a simple boundary curving inward to the land, the plain is bent into a crescent form, just three miles long by one in breadth, and rising gradually inland to the west. About this amphitheatre the mountains close. Streams and rills from these, and two fine fountains in the plain, bless this favored region with lasting fertility. Surely, this is one of the memorial places of the past to be kept for the return of Israel.

Now the fountain mentioned by Josephus as called "Capharnaoum" is evidently of great importance with relation to the site of Capernaum, concerning which so much controversy has arisen; and with diffidence we shall venture to have a word on the subject, because a look at the question from a sailor's eye has not yet been noted. At first our interest in the respective claims of the three localities asserted by different writers to be Capernaum was less than languid. But, even as a problem, the question rapidly became absorbing when the places themselves had each been examined. They are all so near together, and in such well-traversed ground—certainty as to which is the true site would impart such new attractions to the spot, and the idea seems so strange that a place could be entirely forgotten where Christ did more of his works than in any other village—that we gradually become enlisted in

---

[*] It is stated that Christ "left Nazareth and dwelt at Capernaum," and thus the frequent expression afterwards, "the house," in relation to this place, meant, no doubt, the dwelling in which He resided there, during intervals long and short, between his numerous visits to other parts of the country.

the debate, though the point in dispute is not of vital moment.

Three principal places are maintained by different groups of authors to be the site of Capernaum. A few others are advanced by isolated authorities, but they may with fairness be left aside as unsupported.

The usual but not very ancient tradition is that Capernaum was at Khan Minyeh, and, as our camp is now within a few yards of this place, we can give it a brief description. Under the high cliff already mentioned as at the northern end of the land of Genesareth, is the ruin of an old khan, or resting-house, frequented by pilgrims and caravans passing by this way from Jerusalem on the regular route to Damascus. The building is not very old, and excavations close to it, and even within a somewhat wide range of the place, have failed to bring evidence out of the ground.

A few yards from it, and near the bottom of the cliff, a clear perennial fountain pours out from the rock, about eight feet higher than the lake; and, as it is shaded by an old fig-tree, the name it goes by is "Ain et Tin," the "Fount of the Fig-tree."* The water descends into a long marshy lagoon, half choked by flags and reeds and papyrus.† From the lake I paddled the Rob Roy through the channel into this jungled pool, and carefully searched

---

* The name is by no means distinctive, for many fountains in this and other districts rise under fig-trees. Wilson says that Ain et Tin has two heads, a large and a small one. From old water-marks on the cliff, it appears that the lake at times rises into the fountain. The water is slightly brackish, though less so than at the Tabiga fountain. The inmates of the khan always use the lake water, and say the water of the fountain is unhealthy. The volume was estimated at one-eighth or one-tenth that of Banias. The temperature on January 25, 1866, he gives as follows:

		Degrees.	
Temperature of the air		62·78	Fahrenheit.
"	lake	60·44	"
"	small spring	72·32	"
"	large spring	77·36	"

† Stanley ("S. and P." p. 375) says the papyrus is also "found on the shores of the lake, between the plain of Genesareth and Tiberias." This I did not see, though passing along the place.

every nook and cranny in it which could be reached in my canoe or on horseback, but with not the least trace detected of any sort of building.

Most of the land of Genesareth is above the level of this fountain's head, and though the amount of water in it now may be less than before (by the action of the earthquake thirty years ago), it is evident that "Ain et Tin" could not water the plain, as is described by Josephus to be a feature of the fountain called "Capernaum." Much of the plain is at present well cultivated, and the water for its irrigation comes from several streams (marked in Map VII.) entering on the west, and which would seem to be capable of use over at least twice as much area when the land was fully tilled. One of these, Ain el Amud, comes from the south along the "Wady Hamam," or "Vale of Doves;" and after being diverted at a high level, and pouring a genial rivulet through many a fruitful acre of good soil, it falls into the lake. Up this stream the Rob Roy penetrated a long way, but without any discovery of art employed, or even of much masonry, and on horseback I followed it closely for several miles.

Another stream, called Wady Rubbadyeh, flows into the lake more northerly; and I paddled also upon that, ascending in like manner from the shore, but with a precisely similar absence of result. Between these two, and near the base of a projecting hill, is a fountain proper, called "Ain Mudawara," which quietly mounts from the earth below into a large round reservoir, and, escaping thence, the portion of it not used for irrigation (very little at present) finds its way to the lake.* On horseback I examined the interior and neighborhood of this fountain, and entering the walled inclosure, which is about 100 feet wide, and in depth from three feet to a few inches, I traversed it in all directions, and at different times.† This

---

* By the channel the Rob Roy entered again, though scarcely floating, and then for a short distance worked her way into the marshy plain.

† Wilson estimates the volume of water at about the same as at Ain et Tin. It is sweet and good. Temperature 73° Fahr., when the air was 64°.

careful search was made to see whether I could observe in it a specimen of the *coracinus*, or "cat-fish," which Dr. Tristram had found plentifully in this fountain a few years ago (but not in winter), and which seemed to be evidence that this was the fountain indicated by Josephus.

Various ruins are found not far from the fountain, and, though not distinct, these might be the remains of Capernaum. However, the town need not have been quite close to the fountain; although, if both had the same name, it is likely, either that they were close together, or that, if apart, the town was of considerable size. In default of any other proper claimant, and if possessed of the fish as an exclusive feature, the round reservoir at Mudawara would undoubtedly be entitled to the highest probability of being the fountain which Josephus alludes to. But (1.) its peculiar claim in respect of the fish is no longer tenable as exclusive; and (2.) another claimant, formidable on other grounds, is also asserted to possess the fish.

The question as to what fish[*] inhabit the lake has assumed special interest because of the fish "Coracinus."

Haselquist the naturalist says: "We afterwards went out to the shore of the sea Tiberias, and had some fish brought us by the fishermen. I thought it remarkable that the same kind of fish should here be met with as in the Nile, Charmuth, Silurus, Bænni, Mulfil, and Sparus Galilæus. The water in the river is sweet, but not very cold, though wholesome.[†] This was in May, 1751, and the last clause seems to refer to a stream, but its name is omitted.

Burkhardt[‡] says that the most common species of fish

More water flows down Wady Rubbadyeh and Wady Amud than in Wady Hamam.

[*] Dr. Tristram, in his "Land of Israel," gives recent information as to the various fish of Palestine, and a complete list of them is given by Gnuther, in the "Student" for July, 1869 (Groombridge). A vertebra from a very large fish, picked up on the shore of the Dead Sea, by Mr. Sandbach, this year, was shown to me at Liverpool, on October 4.

[†] Haselquist, "Travels in the East" (London, 1766), p. 158. Petherick's narrative (1869) gives Harmouth as the name of a Siluroid fish in the Nile.

[‡] "Travels in Syria and the Holy Land" (1822), p. 316.

are the *Binni*, or carp, and the *Mesht*, which is about a foot long and five inches broad, with a flat body, and like the sole. What is here called the *Mesht*, and by Haselquist, *Charmuth*, is probably what was called *Barboot* or *Burboot*[*] to me by the fishermen themselves, and meant the cat-fish or Coracinus, which they and my dragoman alleged was found plentifully in the lake, and was exported by thousands to Damascus and Beyrout. A dead one was said to be on the ground near our camp.

After a diligent search in all the streams and fountains of Genesareth, and a total failure to discover any of the *coracinus* fish there, I made particular inquiries from the five fishermen who came to my camp in their boat by invitation, and were most courteous and intelligent in their talk.[†] These men told me—and not in reply to any leading questions, but to the most formal and strict examination which a Templar could give to such witnesses—that the *coracinus* fish is found in summer time (after the month of April) in the fountain of Mudawara, but *also* in that of Ain et Tin; and that it ascends to both of these from the lake, where it is *always* found, but in the colder months only beside the hot springs of Bethsaida. Thither I rode at once to see further into this matter, and spent some hours on horseback, splashing among the tepid streams; and at last in the lake itself, and just at the spot the men indicated—that is, where the waters are warmed by the heated rivulet—I noticed one of the fish in question darting out of the shallows of the warm sand, and a few yards off burrowing until its body and even its long tail were hidden again. Now, as this fish was seen in the lake, and as the Rob Roy floated from the lake both up the stream of Ain et Tin and

---

[*] Rabbi Schwartz thus alludes to this (p. 302): "There is found also in the Sea of Chinnereth a very fat fish, 'al Barbud,' which has no scales, wherefore it is not eaten by Jews; I consider it to be a species of the eel."

[†] All wore the same kind of dress, a cloak, or scarf (the "fisher's coat"), and below it a short kilt. When a man had only this latter garment on, he was said to be "naked." This explains the expression used when Peter went into the sea to go to Christ—he girt his short loose dress about him with his zummar (girdle).

of Mudawara, it is plain that the *coracinus* could also ascend to these fountains; and though only seen as yet in one of them by a tourist who could record it, the fish may very likely be found in both fountains, as the fishermen assert is the case; and so the feature noticed by Josephus need not be peculiar to one fountain more than to another.

But now that we are again at Bethsaida and on shore, let us see whence the gushing brooks arise which we have dipped our hands in by the fishers' huts, and have seen from afar dimmed by a beautiful white cloud like finest smoke, as their vapor cooled in the evening air while the mill-wheel splashed their waters.

Behind these mills,* and far higher above the lake than Ain et Tin and Mudawara, a perennial stream at Bethsaida comes from a great round fountain, also girded by walls which are at least twenty feet high. Some part of the masonry is very ancient, and fig-trees, bursting though it, clamber down the sides, and hang their white-barked hoary limbs over a hot sullen pool below. Steps reach partly down to this, but I could not find a practicable way by

* There are buildings for five mills, but only one was in use. Captain Wilson says there are five springs; the water is more or less brackish. The main spring issues west of the foot of the octagonal reservoir, and has a volume a little more than half of that of Banias fountain. This turns the mill (on a vertical shaft). The octagon reservoir is of irregular shape, part of it on the east is cut in the rock. By this the spring would be raised to a height of about twenty feet, and was then carried by the aqueduct to the Ghuweir (Genesareth). The Arabs called the fountain Ain Dhabur, and the wady running into the plain Wady Jamoos. At Tabiga the limestone crops out through the basalt (dip 20°, strike 315°). The temperature of the main spring was 86° Fahr., and apparently increased inside the rubbish. This is the hottest fountain on the lake. The aqueduct had already been observed by Thomson ("The Land and the Book," vol. i. p. 545). De Berton speaks of "some ancient aqueducts from under the hill (at Khan Minyeh) carrying the water which supplies the mills at Taibiga," which seems a dim notion of their purpose, though in a wrong direction. De Saulcy suggests that Josephus did not mean that the name of the fountain was Capharnaum (for Kefr would not be inserted in a town's name), but that it was named from Capharnaum, and may have had another title. He mentions also having passed a stream, Tabrah, in going north-east from Nahr Rubadyeh; may this have been a lingering of the name of Tabiga aqueduct when that had gone to decay?

which to descend without a rope, and though I do not mind a ducking, I object, on the whole, to be boiled.

Now, why has this fountain, so near the sea, been walled so high and at great expense? Not to supply drinking water to any town at Bethsaida—a much smaller reservoir would suffice for that. Not to drive the mills, for there is plenty of fall to do that without so much artificial elevation. Then where did the water run to from so high a head? This is what has been most satisfactorily answered by the happy keenness of an intelligent observer, Captain Wilson, who traced the remains of an ancient aqueduct leading from this round fountain at Tabiga by a sure but winding route all the way to the rocky cliff we have so often mentioned at the edge of the land of Genesareth. We easily trace it thither. Then we ride up the cliff, and find the level water-way has come there too. But to take it over that cliff was impossible, and to tunnel through it would be needless; so the channel is cut round the rocky slope, and we go inside the old dry aqueduct, long used as a riding-path, but now plainly seen to be a way for water by its section like an inverted horseshoe: the very least convenient form for a road, and the very best for a channel.* Can this fountain at Tabiga be that named in Josephus? Fish could come to it from the lake.† Water brought from it to the cliff might well be said to come from a fountain named after the most considerable village upon its course; and if Capernaum was near this hill—or, as I think, partly at least upon the cliff itself—then the fountain, little more than half a mile distant, might well be called by the same name as the town. From this elevation it could readily irrigate all the plain, and the aqueduct leading it for this purpose by the north-west horn of the crescent gar-

---

* A photograph of this, published by the Palestine Exploration Fund, shows very clearly to the eye the facts mentioned here in words.

† Perhaps not at present *into* the reservoir, but to the mill-dam, where the miller said they are found, and then, when the water in the reservoir was low, they could go to that. As this fish lives at the bottom, it might not be noticed in the reservoir unless the water was shallow.

den has also been traced by Wilson quite far enough to show that this was done. Thus the description of Josephus would be entirely explained as to the fish in the fountain and the fountain watering the plain.

It may well be supposed that, as the very existence of this aqueduct has been only lately ascertained, no record has been found of when its functions ceased. However, it appears to me that this may have been the "channel of Jordan" alluded to in an old but distinct account* of what was once at Khan Minyeh. Coming from so high a level, the stream might readily be mistaken for a canalette from the river, like those we have described in connection with the Abana, and indeed quite similar to these both in purpose and in construction, cutting through the rock, while to any other stream in Galilee the description seems to be inapplicable.

* This is what Saunderson says, writing A.D. 1601: "After leaving Tiberias, we came to Almenia" (the sound of the word very much resembling that of Khan Minyeh), "which hath been a great citie, also 7 or 8 miles off, close built by the sea side, along through which runneth a channel of Jordan, this undoubtedly is Capernaum, for that is over the point of land;" but with respect to the name, he allows that "the Jewes, neither the Turkes, could directly advise me which it was" (Purchas's "Pilgrims," vol. ii. p. 1635).

CHAPTER XXI.

The Apostles' Voyage.—The "Desert Place."—The Embarkation.—Direction.—Position of the Ship.—The Weather and Waves.—Approach of Christ.—Action of Peter.—Arrival of the Ship.—Other Incidents.—Other Evidence.—"Exalted to Heaven."—Josephus.—Wounded.—Dimensions. —Testimony.—Thanks.—Maps.

WE propose to devote this chapter to a look at the site of Capernaum from a sailor's point of view. The city is mentioned in the New Testament on one occasion, which seems to deserve our attention here, as the sole instance where the position of the place is indicated in relation to other places, and a distance on the water is given. These are found in the narrative of the dark and stormy voyage of the twelve apostles, related by three of the Evangelists, and each of them records features or incidents which must all be considered together if we would view the description as a whole. Let us endeavor to combine in consecutive narration the three separate accounts* of this voyage contained in Matt. xiv. 13-34; Mark vi. 30-53; and John vi. 1-25.

Our Lord having been told of the death of John the Baptist, the twelve apostles "gathered themselves together" unto Him, and " he took them" and "departed thence by ship," "and went aside privately" "into a desert place." So far the authorized versions of the four Evangelists agree with the versions in Tauchnitz's. But in Luke ix. 10, after the word "privately," whereas our version reads "into a desert place belonging to the city called Bethsaida," the

---

* St. Luke (ix. 10-17) narrates only the first portion of the events of that day. The "beloved physician" who here recounts the cure of the sick could have well described the voyage afterwards, for there is great distinctness and power in his account of Paul's voyage to Rome, and especially of the shipwreck, wherein he gives more information about the ships of the time than is found in any other author, or, perhaps, in all other authors together.

Vatican MS. reads "into the city called Bethsaida," while the Sinai MS., being without these words originally, has them inserted in correction. The name Bethsaida here is mentioned by only one Gospel, and being styled "the city called Bethsaida" (not *a* city), we might suppose that the Bethsaida on the west of the lake, "the city of Andrew and Peter," is meant. But it is generally considered that the other Bethsaida (called Julias), and on the east of Jordan (at Et Tell), is the place indicated, because after the miracle Christ directed the apostles to get into a ship "and to go to the other side, before unto Bethsaida" (Mark vi. 45). This was the Bethsaida on the west, which is always styled simply "Bethsaida,"* as if it was well known, while the other on the east is "the city called Bethsaida."

"The people saw them departing, and many knew him, and ran afoot thither out of all cities, and outwent them and came together unto him;" "and he received them, and spake unto them of the kingdom of God, and healed them that had need of healing." That the people were able to come

---

* Dr. Thomson supposes that there was one Bethsaida which was built on both sides of the Jordan. While deference may be paid to this opinion of a scholar, long resident in Palestine, and acquainted with the locality, we may remark that his description of the voyage of the apostles is by no means satisfactory to a sailor. He supposes the boat to "set sail" from a point in the Butaia plain, and to be "driven past" Tell Hoom, to near the plain of Genesareth. Now this presumes that the wind was at least north of west, and in such a case (1.) there would be few waves at first, and much less as they went on; (2.) they could easily keep close to shore, as their proper course; and (3.) they would not be "in the midst of the sea;" and after rowing "25 or 30 furlongs" they would not be "toiling in rowing," but in calm, and, indeed, would then be actually on shore. Thomson also says: "I do not believe that another instance can be found of two cities of the *same* name close together on the same part of a small lake" ("The Land and the Book," vol. ii. p. 31). Yet he himself mentions the Wady Semak above Khersa, and the village Semak, farther south, on the same eastern shore of the lake (but nearer to the other than the two Bethsaidas were). These places have the same modern name, because it was applicable to them both (meaning "fish"): and, for the same reason, two cities may have been called "Bethsaida," "the fisherman's home." It may be also observed that a city placed some way up the river's channel would be a very inconvenient place for fishers boats plying on the lake, although it might well be a place for catching the fish that ascended the river.

"afoot" to the place before the boat, shows probably that there was not a favorable wind, or that the boat went slowly. The greater the distance between the starting-point and the place they came to the less easy would it be for people to walk round to it faster than the boat went across the curve, and this makes it less likely that the boat went far south on the Butaia plain. The 5000 were then fed, and twelve baskets were filled with the fragments.*
"And straightway he constrained the disciples to get into the ship,† and to go to the other side‡ before unto Bethsaida," πρὸς Βηθσαϊδάν, "over against Bethsaida" (Griesbach). While the apostles went to obey the directions of Christ, He sent the multitude away, and departed into a mountain "to pray." The day had passed, and two things are next mentioned, each with the same time noted. "When the evening was come, he was there alone" (Matthew). "When even was now come, his disciples went down unto the sea" (John).

There is no indication of the exact spot from which this embarkation was made. We have already described several ports and channels on the north-east shore, at any one of which the apostles may have left "the ship," and it appears to have been the same vessel that they now embarked in. For the sake of clearness, therefore, it will be necessary to consider the midnight voyage both on the hypothesis

* Sitting in 50 ranks, of 100 in each rank, the men would exactly number 5000. Baskets were carried by the Jews when travelling in the Passover time, for their food and other things, lest they should be defiled.

† Mark vi. 45. The Sinai MS. has "a ship." In Matt. xiv. 22, where it is "a ship," the Sinai MS. reads "the ship."

‡ The words εἰς τὸ πέραν, translated "to the other side," need not, perhaps, mean to the opposite side of the lake, east or west of the Jordan. Josephus, departing from Tiberias, says he "sailed over to Tarichea," διεπεραιώθεν ("Life," sec. lix.), while Tiberias and Tarichea were on the same, western, side of Jordan, and without any deeply indented bay between them. Several of the more notable texts involving this subject are cited by Robinson, and it may be unwise to disturb the general understanding as to the word πέραν. Many questions would have to be opened anew if the meaning does not always involve a passage over the lake east or west, yet possibly some difficulties now unexplained would yield to better inquiry on this point. The name of the district Peræa comes from πέραν.

that it began from the north end of the Butaia plain near the point A on Map VII., and on the hypothesis that it began near the south-east end of the plain at the point E on the map. The intermediate cases of embarkation from some port between A and E may be worked out by those who are sufficiently interested in the question.

They embarked, however, "and went over the sea towards Capernaum," ἤρχοντο πέραν τῆς θαλάσσης εἰς Καπερναούμ, "were going," we might say [Sinai MS. "and came over the sea towards Capharnaum"]. But Mark has told us that the Lord bid them go "unto Bethsaida," and we may well suppose that they went in the direction He had ordered. Matthew says, "and when they were gone over, they came into the land of Genesareth" [Sinai and Vatican MSS., "they came to land unto Gennesaret"]. Mark says the same, adding "and drew to the shore," while John tells us that, when they had received Him into the ship, "immediately the ship was at the land whither they went" [Sinai MS., "whither it went"], and that next day "the people came to Capernaum seeking for Jesus." We may surely deduce from these specific statements that the place to which Christ bid the apostles go (Bethsaida), the place the apostles were going to, and which next day the people went to in search of Him (Capernaum), and the place they arrived at (Genesareth), were all in the same direction.

We have now to apply the foregoing conclusions to test some of the claims of the two rival sites, the one at Tell Hoom (which we shall call T), and the other at Khan Minyeh (which we shall call K), and we shall do this by following what would happen in the voyage as if it began at A or at E separately.

I. As to the *direction* or bearings of the course laid down at starting.

(1.) If the ship started from A, the direction would be the same for T, for K, for Bethsaida, and for the land of Genesareth. Nothing, then, can be decided from this case.

(2.) If the ship started from E. Now Bethsaida bears W. by N. from E, and the land of Genesareth W. $\frac{1}{2}$ N.

And as T bears W.N.W., while K bears W. ½ N., it is plain that the bearings would have only half a point difference if the ship was going to Khan Minyeh, but would have three times as much if she was going to Tell Hoom, so that this is in favor of Khan Minyeh. We shall now consider the evidence to be gathered from what happened during the voyage itself.

II. As to the *position* of the ship. The ship had started, and Matthew says it was now "in the midst of the sea" [Vatican MS., "many furlongs distant from the land"]. Mark says the same.

(3.) If she started from A, whether for K or T, the ship's course would never be five furlongs from the land, for if the wind was from anywhere in W.N.W. to W.S.W., she would "hug the shore," and if it were from W.S.W. to S.S.E., she would not be driven from the land. This, therefore, is against the supposition that the start was made from A.

(4.) If she started from E, and rowed the distance mentioned (in our next section), then, if going to T, she would not now be four furlongs from land, but if going to K, she would still be double that distance—which is in favor of Khan Minyeh.

III. As to the *weather* and *waves*. Matthew says the ship was "tossed with waves, for the wind was contrary." Mark says that the men were "toiling with rowing, for the wind was contrary unto them." John says, "the sea arose (ἐπηγείρετο, 'was rising') by reason of a great wind that blew. So when they had rowed about five and twenty or thirty furlongs,"* the great event occurred which all of them recount. We may reckon the furlong or stadion (by the best authorized computation) at 202 yards, so that twenty-seven furlongs and a half, the mean of the distances

---

* He says also, "And it was now dark, and Jesus was not come to them" [Sinai MS., "'And the darkness overtook them, and Jesus was not yet come to them"]. This remark, showing that Christ was probably expected, and therefore waited for, is considered in another place (*ante*, p. 346), but it does not bear upon the reasoning as to the claims of K or T to Capernaum.

given, would be about three miles. Applying this and the other new particulars, we observe:

(5.) If the ship started from A to go to T, the distance rowed would bring her on the shore, for Tell Hoom is only two miles from A; but if she was going to K, she would still be nine furlongs distant. This again is in favor of Khan Minyeh. The contrary wind might be the same in both cases.

(6.) If she started from E for T, she would now be five furlongs distant. In this case the wind, to be "contrary," must be from north-east, round by west to south-west: and if it blew from north of their course (W.N.W.), the sea would be almost calm near the spot the ship has now come to. Again, if it blew from south of their course, the ship could not be drifted to the land of Genesareth. But if she started from E going to K, she would now be nearly twenty furlongs distant from K (almost midway on her voyage), and the wind, being contrary (from the west), would come out of the high gorge of the Vale of Doves and across the land of Genesareth, with a sweep of nearly eight miles, without shelter from the hills; so that not only would the sea be high at starting, but the force of the wind would be felt to the very end of the voyage, because there the beach is low and the hills recede; whereas at T the land is quite different in this respect. This is strongly in favor of Khan Minyeh.

We have thus used the narrative of the apostles' voyage to test the claims of Tell Hoom and Khan Minyeh, by supposing one and then the other of them to be Capernaum, and have regarded it under the heads of—I. The direction or bearings at starting; II. The position of the ship in the lake; III. The weather and waves. Three wonderful events next signalize this voyage; IV. The approach of Christ: V. The action of Peter; VI. The arrival of the ship; after which there is, VII. The search next day. These we shall consider solely with relation to the question of the site of Capernaum. For other purposes, the minds of the most profound and devout men have studied the subject, and the ablest pens have written.

IV. *The Approach of Christ.*—It was at the "fourth watch of the night" that this happened—not earlier than three o'clock of the succeeding morn; and the apostles had left Him on land at least six hours before. Now they saw Him "walking on the sea."* Mark says of the apostles, "they all saw him." In Matthew it is written, "he went to them." Mark says, "he cometh unto them;" and John describes Him as "drawing nigh unto the ship;" so that He was not standing, but moving, and the direction of his progress seems to be indicated by Mark, when he adds that "the Lord would have passed by them." There is no room left to suppose that He who "plants his footsteps in the sea" was standing upon some point of land, or went along some shallow, which, at all events now, does not, I am certain, exist in or near either place, K or T. It states distinctly that He went on the sea after them, came from behind to them, but on one side, and so overtook the ship while it was in deep water, and before it "drew to the land."

V. Peter is now forward to be called into danger. He requests, he is bidden to "come;" he walks, doubts ("If it be thou"), fears, sinks, calls for help, and this is given, and with it the title "thou of little faith," in presence of them all. This Peter, who at another time leaped into the water to go to Jesus, would have done so now without fear, had the wind been calm, or the waves less boisterous, or the water shallow, or the land near.

(7.) All these features in the incidents of Christ's approach and Peter's conduct seem to harmonize well with the supposition that the ship was away from the shore, and that the sea was yet rough; and thus they favor the view that the ship had not gone towards Tell Hoom.

Still more is this shown by the next words, "And he

---

* ἐπὶ τῆς θαλάσσης. Alford considers that this expression clearly means "upon the sea." Matthew, after using the word like the others (ver. 25), uses also ἐπὶ τὴν θάλασσαν (ver. 26), which form is used by John (ver. 16), when stating the embarkation of the apostles. When Peter "walked on the water," it is ἐπὶ τὰ ὕδατα (Matt. xiv. 28, 29).

went up unto them into the ship;" "Then they willingly received [Sinai MS., 'came to receive'] him into the ship;" for we can see no reason why He should then go on board, and take Peter there also, if the ship was already at its destination, or if it was even near to the place.

VI. Quickly, however, there follows the remarkable expression, "the wind ceased," both in Matthew and Mark; while John tells us, "and immediately ($εὐθέως$) the ship was at the land whither they went" [Sinai MS., "it went"].

(8.) Now, Bethsaida was "whither they went;" and whether this was (as Thomson places it) at Jordan's mouth, or was near K (and no other position for Bethsaida seems suggested), it was in each case several miles from T. This last consideration seems sufficient to dispose of the claims of Tell Hoom as the site of Capernaum.

But we are told distinctly by John that, "when they were gone over, they came into the land of Gennesaret" [the Sinai and the Vatican MSS. even more definitely read, "they came unto land to Gennesaret"]. This land is more than forty furlongs distant from any part of the north-east plain, except that just near the Jordan, from which it is about thirty-nine furlongs. The apostles' estimate of twenty-five or thirty furlongs from the point of their embarkation is not likely to be incorrect or hap-hazard, for they were fishermen in their own boat, and homeward bound. We may, therefore, believe that the vessel was now at least a mile from the shore.

A distinguished expositor of the New Testament seems to intimate, in his note on this subject, that the speedy arrival of the ship was not necessarily miraculous. Doubtless, the question turns a good deal upon whether the word " immediately " does or does not allow sufficient interval of time to bring the ship from " the midst of the sea," and one mile over the water, to the land itself, say at the least a quarter of an hour. But as we have had already in the narrative a succession of miracles—Christ walking on the sea, Peter walking on the water, the calming of the wind—so now, perhaps, we have another—the quick arrival of the ship.

A 2

Some persons feel it difficult to believe that any miracle has ever occurred, because, they say, it would be a "breach of the laws of Nature." I do not believe that any "breach of the laws of Nature" has ever occurred, but that these laws have been always observed, and that one of the laws He ordained (though we did not know it, being ignorant) is that He can do, has done, and will do, whatever is his will and pleasure, at all times, in all places.

VII. *The Action of the People next day.*—They "took shipping, and came to Capernaum, seeking for Jesus."

(9.) Insomuch as this indicates that Capernaum was distant enough to make it advisable to go by sea, it is in favor of K as the site rather than T. (The difficult passage, [John vi. 22–25], we have considered already, at p. 346, and it does not affect our present question.)

We have thus endeavored fairly to apply the whole narrative of this voyage as a test of the rival sites of Capernaum. The difficulty of doing so satisfactorily is enhanced by the fact that, while *direction* and *distance* are given, the starting-point is uncertain from which our direction is indicated, and from which our distance is measured. The starting-point has, therefore, been regarded in its two extreme positions on the plain. Doubtless, it may have been between these, and not either at A or E; and an attentive consideration of the preceding argument will probably convince the reader that the starting point was nearer to E than to A. He will also perceive that, while the site at Tell Hoom would be violently inconsistent with the narrative in one or another group of important particulars, *wherever* the starting-point really was, the site of Khan Minyeh for Capernaum fulfills easily every one of the conditions under the seven heads we have considered, and supports the whole narrative as to the direction, distance, weather, the transactions on the sea, and the conduct of the people on the shore.

Some remarks may be added upon other passages of the New Testament where Capernaum is mentioned, applying the reliable information now first available as to the contour of the shore, the distances between the several points, and the form of the hills and valleys on land, and our knowledge, in addition, of the bays, beaches, harbors, and the winds.

(10.) After our Lord had called his disciples from their nets and Zebedee's ship, it is stated (Mark i. 21), "And they went into Capernaum, and straightway on the Sabbath day he entered into the synagogue and taught" (probably at the beginning of the Sabbath in the evening, for the fishermen would not be employed at their nets on the Sabbath); "And forthwith when they were come out of the synagogue, they entered into the house of Simon and Andrew with James and John." This and Luke iv. 38, as well as numerous other passages, show that Capernaum was near to Bethsaida, so that whatever force there is in our arguments from the sea and the shore in favor of Bethsaida being at Tabiga will apply to show that Capernaum was at Khan Minyeh.

(11.) "And in the morning, rising up a great while before day, he went out and departed into a solitary place and there prayed." The rough hills behind Khan Minyeh, but not far off, seem to provide more naturally for this than the cultivated ground about Tell Hoom.

(12.) In Matt. v. we are told that Christ "went up into a mountain." After the long Sermon on the Mount related in that and the next two chapters,* he came down, the leper was cured, "And when Jesus was entered into Capernaum" (Matt. viii. 5, and Luke vii. 1), the centurion came about his servant, and then the cure of "the great fever" of Simon's wife's mother is related.† So that, whether this was done immediately after the calling of the fishermen, or after the Sermon on the Mount, the position of Capernaum

---

* The floor of a boat-house in Ireland appeared to me so remarkably good that I asked of what it was made, and the reply was "of refuse salt." This illustrates verse 13 in the sermon, where the salt is "trodden under foot of men."

† It is remarked that the plain of Genesareth and the parts adjacent are now very subject to fever, and probably were so of old, but I think that this, though corroborative of a detail, is not an important fact in the evidence.

as close to Bethsaida seems implied; and as in the former case we bring Bethsaida near to Tabiga, because of the shore, and the sea, and the fish, so in the latter case we are led to place Capernaum on the way to Bethsaida from the "Mount," otherwise the route of our Lord on this occasion, and after such long proceedings, would be very circuitous; and as the "Mount" has usually been placed south of Genesareth, we shall find Capernaum south of Bethsaida, *i. e.*, at Khan Minyeh.

(13.) In Luke x. 15, Christ uses the expression "exalted to heaven" in relation to Capernaum. Whether this refers to the actual situation of the buildings, or is only metaphorical, it deserves to be noticed. No other city all round the lake had a hill on the shore so high* as that at Khan Minyeh which could be built upon. If the houses were on this hill (as well as below) the couch of the paralytic (Mark ii. 4) could more readily be carried to the roof from the terrace above than by the usual outside stairs to the roof, which would have their entrance on a level with the floor, and therefore be less accessible on account of the crowd.

(14.) We may also ask how it was that, if Capernaum

* The cliff projecting into the sea is Tell Lareyne. Wilson estimates the height of the hill as from 200 to 300 feet.

De Sauley (vol. ii. p. 428) cites a remarkable passage from Adamnan, in the seventh century, who says ("De Locis Sanctis," lib. ii.), writing of Capernaum—"quæ ut Arculfus refert qui eam de monte vicino prospexit murum non habens angusto inter montem et stagnum coartata spatio, per illam maritimam oram longo tramite protenditur, montem ab aquilonali plaga, locum vero ab australi habens, ab occasu in ortum extensa dirigitur."

(De Sauley, indeed, to force this to agree with him, turns all the bearings through an angle of about 45°; but, if needful to support his own theory, this lively French traveller turned maps, and pictures, and testimony through even 180° without any ceremony.)

Benjamin of Tudela says:—"Caphar Nahhum is foure leagues distant from thence (Carmel), retayning the ancient name, a very high place, which exceedeth Carmel in prospect" (Purchas's "Pilgrims," vol. ii. p. 1444). Tabor, if that was meant by "Carmel," is about four leagues from Khan Minyeh. This extract is cited, not as to the geographical position, but the elevation of the town. Saunderson also, in A.D. 1601, may allude to this elevation of the place when he says it "is over the point of land" (see the passage, *ante*, p. 361).

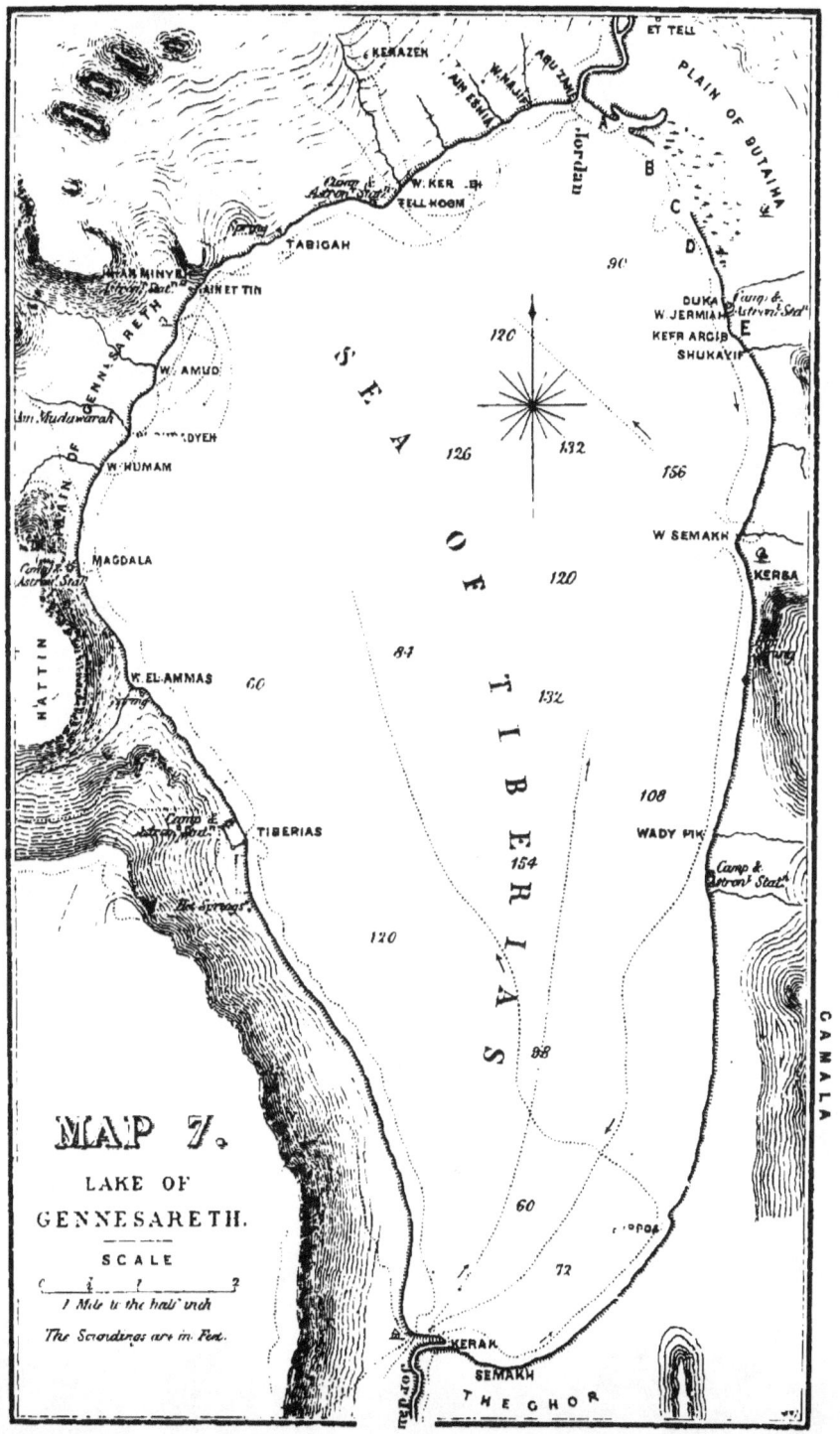

was not there, no other city or building seems to have been placed on this cliff, the most commanding site of any round the lake, with a good harbor below, with water accessible in the aqueduct above, and with the richest ground alongside. That no name should have lingered here, and no relics, is explained if we consider this was the place to which Christ's words applied, "And thou, Capernaum, which art exalted to heaven, shalt be thrust down to hell"

RUINS AT TELL HOOM.

(Luke x. 15).* With such a fate denounced upon Capernaum, we may wonder that, if Tell Hoom be the city, not only has the name survived, but chief amongst the ruins there—the best-preserved of any round the lake, and the finest of their kind in Palestine—should be those of the

* In the Sinai and Vatican MSS., "And thou, Capernaum, shalt thou be exalted to heaven? Thou shalt be thrust down to hell."

very synagogue where our Lord was most rejected, and which would incur the deepest woe.*

(15.) There are three passages in Josephus wherein Capernaum is mentioned. In one of these he speaks of the fountain, and this we have already discussed. Another is in the narrative of his own life (sec. lxxii.), where he relates several skirmishes and battles in the Butaia plain,† and close to Julias, after one of which he says:—"And I had performed great things that day if a certain fate had not been my hindrance, for the horse on which I rode, and upon whose back I fought, fell into a quagmire and threw me on the ground, and I was bruised on my wrist and carried into a village named Capharnome.‡ . . . I therefore sent for the physicians, and while I was under their hand, I continued feverish that day, and as the physicians directed, I was that night removed to Tarichcæ." From this "quagmire," wherever it was,§ the wounded general was carried (ἐκομίσθην) to Capernaum. Now Josephus had at this time two hundred ships at Taricheæ. His party had complete command of the water, for next day, after another fight, "when they (the Romans) heard that some armed men were sailed from Taricheæ to Julias they were afraid and retired" (sec. lxxiii.), so that no doubt Josephus had boats near the battle-field, and to go by water would be the most natural, the most easy, and the safest, shortest, and

* The name "Keraseh" and the ruins there are subject to the same remark if that place can be considered to represent Chorazin. Bethsaida, however, has not preserved its name, and no ruins remain *in situ*.

† In sec. lxxiii. it is distinctly said that Sylla's ambush was "beyond Jordan." The details given in sec. lxxi. appear to be equally applicable to either side of Jordan, and not to determine the position of Julias, which, however, from other notices, we may conclude was on the east.

‡ In Whiston's translation is inserted here, "or Capernaum," but this is not in the Greek of Dindorf's version (Paris, 1845), which has only the words εἰς κώμην Κεφαρνώμην λεγομένην, and it may be noticed here that this is not exactly the same word as that used by Josephus when speaking of the fountain, καφαρναουμ ("Jewish War," book iii. ch. x. sec. viii.).

§ It may have been upon either side of Jordan, so far as the nature of the ground indicates. For on the east side is the marshy Butaia, and on the west is the treacherous morass described already as most difficult to ride over (see *ante*, p. 311).

surest for a wounded man. The port they reached on their way to his home at Tarichew would be Capernaum. There the physicians consulted, and as he was feverish, and as the fight, the wound, the sending for the doctors, and the time under their hands were all in one day, it must have been late when he set out again for Taricheæ, to which he was taken ("carried over," μετεκομίσθην) that night. Now if he was taken by land from Tell Hoom to Tarichew (Kerak), it would be over fifteen miles of road, occupying at least eight hours (a sick man travelling at night), but if he went by water from Khan Minyeh to Taricheæ, which is about ten miles and a half, he could be rowed as fast as possible, at all events, in three hours. It is, therefore, most probable that Josephus embarked for Taricheæ at once when he was wounded, that he stopped at Capernaum to consult the physicians of his army (then in that neighborhood), and that there is nothing here to show that Capernaum was close to Jordan.

(16.) One more passage in Josephus seems to bear upon the site of Capernaum, although with only negative evidence against the claim of Tell Hoom. He says ("Jewish War," book iii. ch. iii. sec. i.) of Lower Galilee—"Its breadth* is also from Meroth to Thella, a village nearest to Jordan," where the name Thella has much the sound of Tell Hoom,† but Josephus mentions it without any reference to Capernaum.‡

* μηκίνεται, *latitudo* (Dindorf); but Whiston translates it "length;" and ; εἴτονος, *proximo* (Dindorf), he translates "near."

† "Thella is undoubtedly the ancient Tellum, now Cherbath Tillum, situated on the north-west shore of the lake of Tiberias" (Schwartz, p. 70).

‡ The accuracy of Josephus in his descriptions seems to be more clearly brought out in proportion as recent researches have uncovered the evidence long buried under ruins. While we read this author's books for information as to the places made notable in the Bible, it may be allowed, perhaps, to mention the following allusions made by him to some of the principal persons of the New Testament.

In his "Antiq. of the Jews" (book xviii. ch. iii. sec. iii.) he says: "Now there was about this time Jesus, a wise man, if it be lawful to call him a man, for he was a doer of wonderful works, a teacher of such men as receive the truth with pleasure. He drew over to him both many of the Jews

The question as to whether Khan Minyeh or Tell Hoom has most right to be regarded as the site of Capernaum from what has been written since the Bible and after Josephus, and from the opinions of modern travellers, opens a very large and interesting discussion quite beyond the limits of the Rob Roy's cruise. My opinion on this general question has no particular weight, but the new and special *data* here supplied from the water and the map may be useful to those who have the ability, diligence, and scholarship necessary to give importance to their decisions. Such men have already investigated the question with the knowledge available when each one wrote. To them for their facts, and their arguments, their reflections, or their

and many of the Gentiles. He was [the] Christ. And when Pilate, at the suggestion of the principal men amongst us, had condemned him to the cross, those that loved him at the first did not forsake him; for he appeared to them alive again on the third day; as the divine prophets had foretold these and ten thousand other wonderful things concerning him. And the tribe of Christians, so named from him, are not extinct at this day." (See also a note to "Jewish War," book ii. ch. ix. sec. i.)

Pontius Pilate is mentioned in "Antiq. of the Jews" (book xviii. ch. ii. sec. ii.); and Josephus mentions that "John that was called the Baptist" was slain by Herod at Macherus ("Antiq. of the Jews," book xviii. ch. v. sec. ii.), and that "the brother of Jesus, who was called Christ, whose name was James," was stoned (book xx. ch. ix. sec. i.).

An interesting comment is also supplied by another fact which Josephus relates. When the appeal of Paul forced King Agrippa to say, "Almost thou persuadest me to be a Christian," the prisoner answered that he wished all who heard him were not only almost but altogether as himself, "except these bonds," and he raised up his hands fettered by a chain. The king must have felt this gesture specially above all, for he himself had been bound at Rome with an iron chain, and when he was pardoned, the emperor "changed his iron chain for a golden one of equal weight," which Agrippa afterwards brought to Jerusalem, and "hung it up within the limits of the Temple over the Treasury, that it might be a memorial of the severe fate he had lain under, and a testimony of his change for the better" (Josephus, "Antiq. of the Jews," book xviii. ch. vi. sec. x.; and book xix. ch. vi. sec. i.).

Such notices of the leading personages in Christian history will be received by some readers not only with interest, but with special attention, because the author occupied the peculiar position of apparent neutrality. If a pagan writer tells distinctly the same facts as the Bible, people are sure to ask, "Why did he not believe them?"—and yet, if he *did* believe them, and so became a professed Christian, they immediately exclaim, "He is a partial witness."

stirring words, or their bright descriptions, each new traveller owes a debt that can not be paid, and is only imperfectly acknowledged by scrupulously citing each name when its special authority is used. This willing tribute is given in these pages to Robinson, Stanley, Tristram, Thomson, Porter, Wilson, Alford, Finn, Schwartz, Newbold, Smith, etc., besides the classic authors who are now beyond our thanks.

The argument in favor of Tell Hoom as the site of Capernaum appears to me to rest chiefly upon its name, which is supposed to have been altered from Kefr Nabum (the village of Nahum) to Tell Nahum (the hill or ruin of Nahum) when the place had become deserted. But while we find the name Kefr Nahum applied by authors to various other places, I do not see it applied to the place now called Tell Hoom in any ancient writer, and though Wey's map*

---

* As we have inserted in this chapter the newest map of the Sea of Galilee, it may be interesting to notice some of the older maps. The oldest map relating to Palestine we have been able to find is that called "Mappa Mundi," in Hereford Cathedral, a MS. of the date about A.D. 1310, very elaborate in its outlines, being symbolical and almost romantic. It shows the Abana and "Farfar" running into the Euphrates. Jordan has three streams—"Fons Jor." "Fons Dan," and "Fons Torrens." On the east of where is now Port Said, there is marked "Sirbonis" (the "Sirbonian bog"), and other curious points are noted. Another and more useful map of Palestine, 400 years old, is in the library of the Royal Geographical Society. It is about seven feet long, and carefully made, but probably without visiting all the localities. Distances between important places are given in a list, and in the book of which the title is "The Itineraries of Wiliam Wey, Fellow of Eton College, to Jerusalem, A.D. 1458, and A.D. 1462."

From the original manuscript in the Bodleian Library, printed for the Roxburgh Club (London, 1857), at p. 138, is the following list of distances in Roman miles :

Milliario 4° a Bethsayda est Coroazym.
" 2° a Coroazim est Cedar.
" 2° a Capharnaum est descensus montis in quo dominus predicabat turbis.[1]
" 2° a Genesaret est Magdalum castrum.[2]
" 2° a Magdalo Castro est Tyberiadis.[3]
" 16° a Nazareth contra Mare Galilee est Genazareth vicus in quo Christus misit legionem demonum in porcos.

[1] After this entry is inserted in the similar list on the map—Milliario p° a descensu est locus in quo dominus pavit V millia hominum ex V panibus et duobus piscibus.
[2] In the map list this is " oppidum," but on the face of the map it is " castrum."
[3] In the map this is—Milliario I° a Magdalo Cenereth vel Tiberias ; (and then follows this) Milliario 4° a Tyberiade Bethuliaci.

(A.D. 1462) places it near Jordan, yet the definite distances he gives in his list do not favor this position. On the whole, then, the evidence seems to be much in favor of Khan Minyeh from (1.) Scripture, (2.) Josephus, (3.) old authors, (4.) modern travellers. So, having now delivered the verdict of her crew, the Rob Roy may be hauled ashore, and safe among the bushes, tired, but not weary, we welcome the sweet rest of night, that link of peace in the chain of pleasant days.

From Dan to Beersheba, 160 milliaria. From Joppa to Jordan 60 milliaria.

The map represents the Sea of Galilee as a long narrow lake, with large fish in it. (In the Dead Sea several buildings are depicted under water), and among other features we notice that on the east of Jordan are Chorazin, *Godera*, and *Gedarennes*. Capharnaum is at the north-west, and Magdala close to it, with a stream between. Bethsaida is farther west up this stream, and on the same side as Capernaum. To the south of Magdala is Bethsaida, and then Genereth, and west of that is Tabor. Kades is at the southwest of the lake, and west of that is Carmel; to the north of which is Caipha, on a stream. The relative apparent distances between the towns on the map do not at all correspond with those stated in the list.

In "Hondins his Map of Terra Sancta," printed in A.D. 1624 (Purchas's "Pilgrims," vol. v. p. 91), the position of the towns is as follows: West of Jordan we have Capernaum at the north end, then a stream, and south of that Bethsaida, Magdala, Tarichex, a stream, Tiberias, and then Jordan; east of Jordan we have Chorazin, and Julias at the north end; then Gadara (in the centre of the east shore), a stream, Hippos, and Jordan.

In D'Amville's map (A.D. 1794), Capernaum is on the north-west shore of the lake. From Gilboa the Kishon flows, and a river running to the Sea of Galilee. Mageda is marked south of Phiale, Gadera on the east of the lake at Khersa. In the Talmud, Kefr Ahim is noticed with Chorazin, also Tanhoum, Tanhoumin, Tchoumin (Neubauer, "Geog. Talm.," 221).

LAKE OF TIBERIAS, FROM THE BATHS.

CHAPTER XXII.

Sea of Galilee.—Magdala.—Dalmanutha.—Ain Bareideh.—Tiberias.—The Jews.—Fast Travellers.—American Confessions.—How to see England.—A rainy Day.—Earthquake.—Shore south of Tiberias.—Hot Swimmers.—South-west Shore.—Night.—Joyous.—Size of the Lake.—Kerak.—Ruins.—Exit of Jordan.—Down Stream.—Molyneux and Lynch.—Farewell.

> "As when in heaven the stars about the moon
> Look beautiful, when all the winds are laid,
> And every height comes out and jutting peak
> And valley, and the immeasurable heavens
> Break open to the highest, and the stars
> Shine, and the shepherd gladdens in his heart."

THE silence on this shore of Genesareth is perfect—almost startling, but in the dark stillness there comes a muffled sound, with regular beat, yet as from afar. Let us look through this chink in the tent on the beautiful picture of the night, seen by old Homer, and told in Greek, which the Laureate of England has rendered as we give it above. The sound we hear is the plash of oars in that little fishing-boat gliding past like a vision. She is coming back after a night of toil, and the chant of her crew gives the time to their oars, and then it floats over the lake to the Rob Roy, listening in her oleander-bed.

Next day our camp moved to Tiberias.* We have already described what we saw in the canoe and on horseback along the shore until Magdala is reached at the southern end. The place is called Mijdel now, and is only a poor village, without beauty or cleanliness, at once the only pollution of the lake by its slovenly disorder, and the only town all round the shores retaining the name it had before.

In Mark xiv. we are told how Christ was anointed by "the woman that was a sinner," and the promise of our

* Tiberias is mentioned only once (John vi. 23), except as part of the name of the lake.

Lord that, "Wheresoever this gospel shall be preached throughout the whole world, this also that she hath done shall be spoken of for a memorial of her." It is remarkable that, while the deed is thus embalmed in universal memory, the name of the woman is not mentioned here, but if it was indeed the Mary of Magdala then the name of her town has been for some good reason still preserved by the Arabs of Asia, and was assumed for the great fortress of Theodore by the Abyssinians of Africa.* Here it is interesting to read what an Israelite has written about Magdala. Citing Jewish authorities for details, the Rabbi Schwartz says (p. 189) that Migdal is the village Medjdl. "This town is also called by the Christians Magdelenia," and is alluded to in the Talmud. "Migdal Nunia† is one mile from Tiberias." The identity of this Mijdel and Magdala is also stated by Quaresmius. In Mark viii. 10, the place called Magdala by Matthew is styled "the parts of Dalmanutha,"‡ and if the word in Mark means Magada, which may have been on the east side of the lake, then Dalmanutha may be the Dalhamia (or Dalmamia) mentioned by Thomson as on the Jordan below Kerak,§ and which would accord well with Christ's route "from the coasts of

---

* Magdala may be the Migdal-el of Joshua xix. 38 (Stanley). In Matt xv. 21, is stated the incident of the woman in the coasts of Tyre, to whom the Saviour said, "O woman, great is thy faith." After this He came "nigh unto the Sea of Galilee," and fed the four thousand upon "a mountain." Then "he took ship, and came unto the coasts of Magdala."

This name has long been supposed to be inserted for some other name. The Sinai and the Vatican MSS. read "Magadan" instead of "Magdala," and Magedan may have been on the eastern side. It is so marked in Hondius's map in 1624. All the MSS. read "the ship" here, and the Sinai and Vatican do so also in Mark viii. 10 (the parallel passage), showing, perhaps, that it was the vessel regularly employed, as would be consistent with the rest of the story.

† It will be seen from Map VII. that Magdala is three miles from Tiberias on a straight course by water, and a little farther going by the path on shore. Neubauer ("Geog. Talm." p. 217) mentions Migdal Nunia (tower of fishers) as a different place from Magdala, and the Talmud says this latter was destroyed because of the wickedness of its inhabitants.

‡ In the Vatican MS. "Dalmanuntha" (Tauchnitz).

§ "The Land and the Book," vol. ii. p. 60.

MEJDEL, AND PLAIN OF GENNESARETH.

Tyre and Sidon unto the Sea of Galilee through the coasts of Decapolis."* This explanation would appear to place the miracle of the "four thousand" on the east shore,† and thus the Bethsaida they came to afterwards (Mark viii. 22) would be, that on, the west coast, which would be a likely place for them to go to for the bread which they had forgotten.

Just behind Magdala the hills again rise abruptly to the height, as Wilson estimates, of one thousand feet. From this point, all the way to Tiberias, I found an inhospitable shore bristling with breakers, sunken rocks, and treacherous reefs. Some few of these look like islands. One is only about an inch under water, though a hundred yards from shore, and on the whole we may regard this to be the most dangerous coast of the whole circuit. The Wady el Ammas sends a hot spring into the cool water about a mile from Magdala. The little triangular plain at Fuliyeh (just overhanging the lake) corresponds to the particulars given in Matthew xv., as Wilson also considers, who describes three springs here giving together a little more water than the round fountain at Ain et Tin. The centre spring is open, and the water runs down to the lake. The two others are inclosed, probably for mill purposes, and the structures may be the circular Roman baths noticed by Irby and Mangles. Though warm, the water of these fountains is sweet to the taste. They are called "Ain Bareideh," "cold fountain."‡ The stream from these (and I think also from another lower fountain) gushes into

STRUCTURE IN WATER NEAR BAREIDEH.

---

* Mark vii. 31. Or as the Sinai and Vatican MSS. have it, "from the coasts of Tyre, he came through Sidon unto the Sea of Galilee."

† See also Robinson (vol. iii. p. 278).

‡ Thomson says that the Arabs do not apply this name to them. Possibly the temperature may have been altered by the earthquake. On January 29, 1866, Wilson found the temperature of these as follows.

		Degrees.	
Temperature of the air		64·76	Fahrenheit.
"	north spring	84·76	"
"	central spring	80·6	"
"	south spring	85·46	"

the lake, where the heated water remains so distinct from the rest that you can put one hand on each side of the boat with about 20° difference in the warmth of the water. To the south of the two buildings over the hot springs, there are remains of a building in the water not likely to be remarked from the land. The sketch shows a plan of this, which stands in four feet water, and has walls of rubble masonry four feet thick, and much eaten away by the waves. These walls appear to have encircled a pool, in which there is now a hot spring. The cliff seems to cut it off from the nearer of the two others. The detached part has at B, between it and the rest, a passage from three to four feet deep, about a foot broad, and covered by hammered stones, as represented in the sketch. Where the dotted line shows the water-level, several of the stones are *in situ*, but others have fallen down. The passage looks like a water-channel, and the inclosure resembles a bath rather than part of a mill.

COVERED PASSAGE IN SEA-WALL.

The Rob Roy next arrived at Tiberias, and a crowd gathered soon on the shore, and pressed so close upon me that it was with more difficulty than usual the canoe could be shouldered and carried through the narrow lanes to the *locanda*, a guest-house, doing half duty for a hotel, when occasionally travellers are unwise enough to leave canvas homes for stone prisons. In the great arched room, whose walls were ten feet thick and scarcely lighted, the canoe lay stretched upon the floor, and her captain on a divan. Part of my tent was hung across the room to screen it a little from the women-folks who came in and out, night and day, and who could now see the boat to far better advantage by peeping over and under the very feeble barrier we had placed to guard our privacy. Poor bodies! they did their best in civility and activity, and so did their other *permanent* lodgers, whose diminutive size was made up for by their myriads of numbers, so that long before midnight I had pronounced all houses to be wretched every-

TIBERIAS AND THE LAKE, LOOKING TO THE NORTH-EAST.

where, and this one detestable, in comparison with the cleanly comfort of a tent. When *Toorieh*, the pretty girl of this hospice, brought the "Visitors' Book" for my name to be inscribed, she evidently was in happy ignorance of the comments made in every page of it by each traveller who had survived his stay. In charity and truth combined, I could only write that the Rob Roy and myself had stopped there two nights, and that the canoe was not devoured. The town of Tiberias is chiefly remarkable for the exceeding filthiness of most of its streets, and especially in the Jews' quarter. How any civilized European Jew can see his people degraded as they are in Tiberias, and then come back to his own gilded home in the west, and leave his brethren to wallow in such a mess beside that lovely lake, is beyond conception. Jews amongst us Gentiles in England have refinement, cleanliness, luxury, and elegance—why don't they send to the Rabbis of Galilee, at any rate, besoms and soap.*

Our attack upon the people's nastiness in this city is not too severe, nor is it made by an enemy, but by a friend of the " nation scattered and peeled "—one who reveres their name, their past and their future; who admires their patience and pluck, their learning, science, and art, their musical talent, their military prowess, their schools and asylums, their fitness for every post, premier, banker, and senior wrangler, any thing perhaps that men can be (except a sailor); but who wonders how with all their love of their people and their land they leave it to us Christians to scarh for their records among the rubbish—how they never ask the world for what the world would give them free, their own beloved Palestine, while they still with obstinate persistence cling to a hopeless hope.

Let us leave this filthy town, and hie to the mountain brow. The climb up slopes of smiling green mid sweet perfumes of the flowery grass, and painted glittering flies that dance in warm sunlight and buzz their short hour of

* In Tiberias I read the "Times," telling of millions of gold left by Rothschild's will.

life, brings us to the highest hill from which the lake is seen outspread below. It is a precious hour, the contemplation of so grand a scene, grand, I mean, not by bigness of mass in mountains, or by other mere earthly features, but because each snowy peak, each jutting point, each swelling mound, each trickling stream before us, is the centre of a hundred thoughts within about things that are grandest of all in the universe—the deeds of God made man, the message of the Ambassador of Peace to a rebel world, the promises of the King of Heaven to the poor lost sinners of earth. Surely it does not need a fanciful or even an imaginative mind to feel that there can be character and almost soul in scenery. The face of a hero we gaze upon with admiration, though his eye is only a lens, and his brain is but phosphorus, and his bones are lime. Palestine is the visible embodiment of the most wonderful and holy deeds and thoughts that have lived upon this world. The lineaments of what is noble and righteous and wise are shining here, though the lake is only water, and the hills are only stone.

We are rhapsodizing on this mountain; let us get down again to the mud. On the slope below, we found an American in his tent. Next morning he was gone. These cousins of ours do do their sight-seeing *so* uncommon quick. About thirty of them I met at various times in this voyage, but not a word or look from any one that meant appreciation or enjoyment of the wondrous land they had scurried through. If this vice of foolish swiftness in a country which you can not "skim" (for the cream of it is not at the top) were incurable as well as inherent in these people, it would be cruel to notice it; but it is the vice of a few, and it is curable. Yet all Americans incur the blame for it. They are sensitive to public outcry against their countrymen, though they are far more meek under censure than John Bull, and, no doubt, once sufficiently stirred up by friendly plainness upon this point, the Americans will surely organize a "caucus" on such a national stigma and will rub it off, or hold a "convention" and put it down. At any rate, now it is the most rabid nuisance in the East.* Some of the very best Oriental travellers are Americans; need we cite Dr. Robinson's name, or Dr. Thomson's? But nine out of ten of those who come from " the States " to see the world, pass through it, and over it, and see almost nothing. This is partly because they allow, say, a year for the grand tour, and few minds can travel for a year in different countries with any proper zest and purpose all the time. Partly, too, it is owing to the fact that in America you can see nearly all as you move by rail or steamer over the wide continent. The towns there are uninteresting, architecturally. Partly, it is because men, badly educated, but rapidly rich, often try to cram knowledge by running after it over the world. Partly, again, it is because the love of ancient things needs to be fostered young, and Americans, therefore, do not and can not appreciate ruins or antiquities; and, lastly, the unfortunate lack of sentiment, romance, or quiet enjoyment of the dreamy past, is made stronger, if not perpetuated, by the speed of affairs, the unhappy " dollarism," the unceasing bustle, change, and excitement of an American's daily life in the dreary crowds of a huge hotel—the climate of his country being too *vif* for rest and peace, and the food he lives upon and the habits of his life heating body and mind to impatient hurry, even in the most captivating scenes, which can not be grasped in a glance, and which refuse to yield their precious sweets to a passing squeeze.

* Here, for instance, is the conversation, almost verbatim, of two tourists at a hotel. The words can be written down, but the suffering and pity which other travellers feel for the hapless wights who are such slaves of speed, and whose gloomy careworn restlessness tells of their dreary task, can never be described.

" Been to Jurden, sir?
" Yes, sir; come back 4 35 this afternoon.
" Road—how's that?
" Wal, sir, its rough, that's so—nothin' particular to see but scalded hills. Came back by Marsaba, and Neby—(Jane, what do they call it?) You goin' to Jurden? take my word the Dead Sea is only a dull-like place, sir."

And this man had been looking on the most sacred river in the world, and into the deepest hollow to be seen on earth.

The better travellers from America deplore this sad defect in many of their countrymen, and it is to support these in protesting against this absurd sort of travelling, and to remedy the evil, that I venture to dwell upon the subject here, because our cousins know full well that our mutual criticisms are useful to both countries—whether they touch yachts, or boat crews, or travellers' ways—and that both Englishmen and Americans are sensible enough to bear even a sharp word or two upon our special frailties.

Once an American traveller entered Nazareth with me at eight o'clock in the evening. At half past four next morning he had left. In America he could *say* he had seen Nazareth. Another, who had journeyed in Syria, had omitted to visit Damascus. He could not bear this when talking with others, and he came back all the way to Beyrout with me, and rode to Damascus and back and embarked again. Another, being in quarantine with me, confessed that whole pages from "Murray" were sent home as her journal, and that she inserted in the "towns visited" all the stations on the London and Brighton Railway, which she had traversed once by train. Such a traveller can not really enjoy any one place, but is always speaking of the next place to be "done," and of the shortest time to do it in.

The great mistake they make is to go to many spots, and over many miles, rather than to see some places well. Above all, the East must be seen deliberately. To run over it is exactly like looking at bright pictures in a book without reading a page of its print. The man who stops two days in one neighborhood, and who thus imbibes the air of the place, knows more of the whole land of Israel than if he had passed through five other places in the same day without resting, thinking, and pondering over what is around him. A young American told me lately he intended *not* to go to Palestine. He said, "All our Yankee tourists 'do' the Holy Land. One of our cleverest girls in New York said to a learned minister who had just returned from his foreign tour, 'Well, did you go to Palestine?' He replied (half ashamed), 'No, I did not.' 'Ah!' she said, 'I am *so* glad; for I have been so much bored lately by all my friends who have come back from Palestine, and have been *at* Samaria, and *at* Bethlehem and *up* Mount Tabor, and *down* to Jordan, and not one of them seems to know as much of the realities of the Holy Land as I can read in a school-book; so I am quite delighted to meet a traveller who has *not* been to Palestine.'" An American who had come to see Europe asked me in London, after having bestowed two days upon seeing the largest city in the world, "Can you tell me if I can go and see Birmingham, and Warwick Castle, and Kenilworth, and then Oxford, and go on to Southampton, all in one day?" I answered that he could *see* a great deal more than that in one day, and it was a pity not to do as much as possible in the time; and, as for his method of travelling, daylight was of no consequence—the best way would be to take a return ticket to Edinburgh, and start by the night mail, for then he could say that he had seen York Minster, and a whole host of English towns.

Enough has been said about this class of travellers. They have little time to spend. This is their misfortune, and for that no blame attaches: but we complain that, having little time, they waste it by trying to stretch it over what it will not cover; and thus they lose the benefits of a proper tour, they get little profit or pleasure themselves, and they are bores to other travellers here; they are unworthy representatives of their great and wonderful people, and thus they do wrong to themselves, to their nation, and to us. Against such I most earnestly protest, at least for Palestine and Egypt. If a man has only half an hour to read Longfellow's poems, he had far better read one or two of the best pieces right through than read a half-line on every page.

At length there is a rainy day for the Rob Roy, and all day too. This was the only day in the tour that I could not walk, or ride, or boat; but every hour of it was agreeably filled up, and not a moment hung heavy on my hands.

Murray's "Handbook for Syria" is, of itself, a most interesting work to peruse. In my opinion, it is the best of all Murray's Guide for Travellers. It gives just what you want to know, and in plain but pleasant style, with full explanation of Scripture allusions, and a devout spirit pervading the whole, as ought surely to be the case when it tells of the Holy Land.*

When the Rob Roy launched again from Tiberias, all the walls and house-roofs were covered with people come out to see; so she turned about also to look at the sight on shore. The town juts out into deep water. Ugly circular towers, built lately and badly, lean here and there, with huge cracks through their toppling sides. The earthquake which occurred on New-year's Day in 1837 had its centre at Jish, but, in its wide revelry, it shook these bastions of Tiberias, and one would wish it had levelled them entirely.

One relic of the more solid past remains—a wall of blackened bevelled stone, that just tops the water for a hundred yards, and still proudly testifies to the better masons of better days gone by. The south end of this wall seemed to be a little lower than the other. This might be because more stone was left upon the north; but a nearer examination showed me that three courses of stones were above the water at the north end, and only two at the south, while the line of the bevel course was inclined; so that the whole wall, unbroken, almost unshaken, had sunk down in one grand mass obliquely towards the south; while the other rude white towers built yesterday—only a few hundred years ago—have staggered, jostling one against the other, broken into melancholy wreck. Until my arrival in England, the importance of this observation had not occurred to me, otherwise the exact length of the base, and the depth of the depression at one end,

---

* No doubt Dr. Porter will take care that in future editions his letter-press is accompanied by a better map.

would have been easily measured. This can, of course, be done by any traveller, for there is usually a fishing-boat at Tiberias.*

On the shore, at the north end of the sea-wall, are numerous squared stones, detached and in the water, but nothing attracting particular attention until we reach the southern end of the wall. Open arches yawn above this place; under one of these I thrust in the canoe, and so inspected a fishing-boat therein beached. The remarkable sinking down of the south end of Tiberias is soon explained when we paddle farther south along the shore. For there, about a mile only from the town, is the famous warm bath, always supplied from the heat of Vulcan's forges, deep in the earth, and from whence has flowed for ages a hot sulphurous stream. We must recollect that the Sea of Galilee itself is a great hollow, and at the bottom it is about 800 feet depressed into the crust of the earth. The surface of the water is so low that, if St. Paul's Cathedral were set upon the shore, and the lofty spire of Salisbury on the top of that, the summit of this pile would still be lower than the Mediterranean Sea.

But the earth's cuticle seems also to be constitutionally thin in Galilee; and hence it is that, when you stand upon one of the flat-roofed houses that overhang the lake, you can see to the left hot vapors rising from the boiling stream of Tabiga; while again, close on your right, the self-acting, self-heated warm bath of Emmaus is ready always for the weary traveller, or the soft idler, or the dirty public in general, to soothe and to please and to cleanse them under its dark dome. Hot water pouring out thus for thousands of years has, no doubt, still further thinned the skin of earth at this place; so, when the earthquake came, probably the crazy arch of rock gave way, and giants' halls be-

---

* Our Lord does not appear to have entered Tiberias on any occasion. The reasons suggested for this are that (1.) it was full of foreigners, while He came first " to the lost sheep of the house of Israel;" and (2.) Tiberias was built partly upon ground occupied by ancient sepulchres, and to enter this place would have made Him ceremonially " unclean."

low were crushed together, and the wall of Tiberias sunk towards that side.

Questions suggest themselves by the dozen about this— for the geologist, not for me. Has the wall, indeed, *sunk* at one end, or has it been raised at the other? Has the very shore of the lake sunk too? Has this sinking been to the south, along the rest of the lake? If so, we shall find Jordan issuing there much lower, and therefore deeper now than it was of old; but let us go and see.

Glorious sunny weather now brightened the water as the Rob Roy paddled on this errand, close by the pebbly shore, which here is of beautiful white. My camp was leisurely moving to Kerak, at the south end of the lake, and so there was plenty of time for a slow and careful survey of the coast under water. The ragged ones of Tiberias all rushed out to see the canoe so close; therefore, to shake them off, and to have peace for my pleasant work, I went out to sea, and lolled the time away until their short patience was exhausted; then we came back to the survey. There are numerous ruins farther inland. Pillars stand, or lean, or lie quite flat, in the long grass. Massive walls attest the remains of grand buildings here. The caves hollowed in the cliffs behind were, perhaps, the grottoes of country seats, and the lovely lake was admired from many a Roman villa, and shrined by temples of design most chaste, when here Josephus lived, and Titus led his admirable legions, and the fleet of Vespasian sailed with the sun upon bright Roman shields, and Palestine was just giving up (but with a brave, hopeless struggle) its last shred of liberty; for the day of reproach had come, and desolation for the people. Very much as might have been anticipated, on approaching shore again, we soon found there were pillars and buildings quite visible under the clear waves, and which, before the earth sank here, must have been on the verge, "awash," if not perfectly dry on the beach. There was a little swell, but not too much to prevent me sketching these and measuring their depth under water. From the sketches and notes then made our plan is copied.

SHORE SOUTH OF TIBERIAS. 397

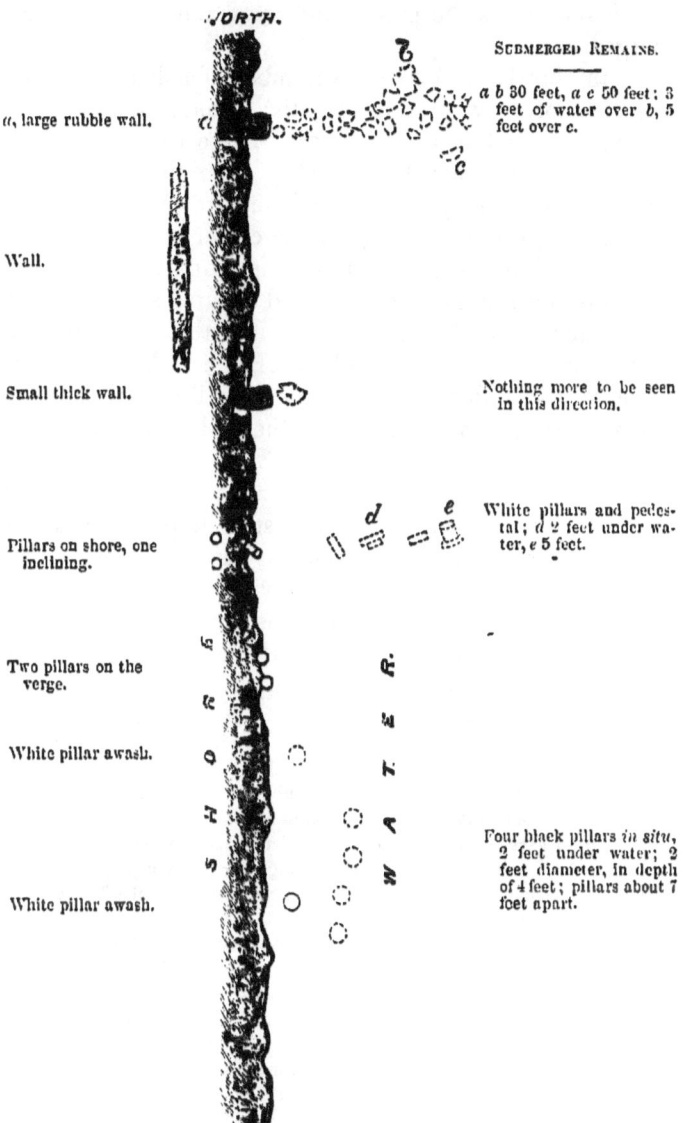

SUBMERGED RUINS ALONG THE SHORE SOUTH OF TIBERIAS.

which represents the part of the coast and the ruins submerged.*

In the hot baths I found a number of naked and moist negroes, not very inviting to bathe among. One of them was playing a flute in the water. These baths have been a hundred times described.† They are rightly within our province, too, for a word or so, being water; but we turn with more pleasant feelings to the cooler sparkling wavelets of the lake itself. Nothing was found under the surface here but a number of detached squared stones. A little farther on, bold cliffs descend into the water, and the road winds over their shoulders. Huge rocks, too, are in the lake just under these, and the Rob Roy had threaded among these; but nothing was there that might not be found in any other lake.

The bays along this part are, therefore, all bad for boats, until the last bay, on the south-west in Map VII., near the mound of Kerak, where an excellent beach shelves quickly to good anchorage in flat sandy gravel. There are remains of a pier, and the north-west wind is powerless in this bay.

The lake narrows at its southern end, and a charming

* The wall marked a will be easily recognized by any traveller, for it is a prominent object on the shore, and the ruins on shore are those indicated in Map VII. The dotted parts are under water. An hour was spent in examining this short piece of coast, going backward and forward several times, so as to have the sun in front and behind, and working in parallel strips; we may, therefore, hope that no object has been unobserved.

† Thomson says the temperature of the baths had varied during twenty years from $136°$ to $140°$ (Fahr.). The springs were more copious for a time during the earthquake. He considers that the word "mules" in Genesis xxxvi. 24, means "warm waters."

Not very far from our own prosaic Temple (that in the City of London, E. C., not in Judea), we have the "Hummums" in Covent Garden, the same Arabic word meaning "Bath;" and in the Strand, close to Somerset House, is a splendid old Roman bath in excellent preservation, and with purest water running into it from the "Holy well," at the corner of a street called (almost in derision) by that name. Such a bath, with water in it, and so preserved, you can not find in Italy. If it were there, all travellers would be ashamed not to have seen it, but being in London, like many other most interesting Roman relics of our great capital, not one man in ten thousand even hears of its existence, though a great notice-board proclaims to all who walk upon the pavement, "To the Old Roman Bath."

slope of green, with gentle knolls enlivening its outlines, shows where the desperate fight took place between the Jews at Tarichex and the heavy-mailed cohorts of Rome. Now the place looks peaceful enough—with the peace of desolation. Bright anemones wave in the evening breeze; red is the most frequent color, but white ones are scattered too. In other localities there are blue anemones; and in one spot by Jordan I noticed a red, a blue, and a white anemone, all three together. This conjunction is regarded as singular.

There is some traffic along the bridle-path by the lake. You meet somebody almost every quarter of an hour. My muleteers had a palaver with each of these wayfarers, and showed off the Rob Roy as part of *their* property, while they praised her exploits in florid story. Then she drew to the shelving beach near Kerak, where we can lie on the shore in the sun for rest and refreshment. Here the lake banks are of red clay, and the water is shallow along a shore of black sand, curved and indented by lagoons; for here again will Jordan once more lay hold of the waters, and hurry them away still down with the "Descender," down to the dull Dead Sea. Our camp grows up in the evening air like mushrooms in the grass, and the canoe reclines among the oleanders, and her crew under the palm-tree by our tent.* This is quite away from all intruders, and no dwelling is in sight but our own; so Kerak is the place for a quiet Sunday, when the beautiful lake is beside the Sacred Book, for now, indeed, we can read a pictorial Bible.

What a relief to be out of that house at Tiberias! What a delightful change to be again in a tent by the sea! Instead of the dark draughty room, with no view, no comfort, no privacy, now I have the fairest green prospect facing me as I recline; the sweetest air around, the light of heaven above, and the sentiment and romance of a wandering life for a quiet undercurrent of enjoyment.

* The Talmud speaks of the fishers in their holidays resting by the lake (Neubauer, p. 213).

That squalling child, too, in that Jews' barrack we have left; how inhuman the mother was to let it cry all day and most of the night! Once I went in and told her so. She stopped it, and the little creature was quite pleased. Instead of this wretched music, we hear now the gentle plash of waves on the clean and sparkling beach, the soft breathing of the evening breeze, the tinkling of the mules' bells as they graze to their full in richest clover, and the merry laugh from the other tent, or the chop of a hatchet as the men gather wood for the fire. The mountains of Bashan have sunk into a sombre outline of deep shade, and the twinkling stars are about us; but just before me they seem to be paler, while the dark of the sky is tinted by a faint unusual light. See, this gets stronger now, and at last, in silent inexpressible beauty, slowly rises the bright full moon, and in a moment the Sea of Galilee is changed into silver, with ten thousand sparkles from the opposite shore in a blazoned path right up to the very waves at my feet. Yes; it is better here than in any house of stone.

Spring had fairly begun, with all its fresh beauties, on this 29th of January. The herbage was profuse about us, and the mules rolled over and over in its soft luxurious coolness. Fancy rolling upon one's food, and eating up one's mattress!

Hany and his men and his beasts were as merry as could be. None of us had a frown or a care, or the least bit of anxiety. Architects, be they never so clever, can not build us a house half so pleasant as the tent. In front is my boat, too, a span from the water, all ready for launching in a moment; while my horse is tugging at his halter, and ready for a ride, if that is better than a sail. The wish and a word is enough to start either of these; but our mountain boots are clamorous for a climb. On with them, then: and in the balmy daybreak we wander away alone, gradually mounting, expanding the prospect, watching the great silent clouds that veil the hot sun, but with no threatening gloom; the far-off patches on the water like roughened glass under the "cat's paws" on the lake; the Jordan, marked for thirty miles, as it pours out upon its last quick journey to the vale of death;* the distant Bethsaida; the green tenantless Genesareth; the dumb shattered towers of Tiberias, only bearable among the beauties of nature, because *any thing* looks pretty when reflected in the lake; the hills of Bashan opposite, with Gamala unbuilt again since its last terrible destruction; the meadows of the Gadarenes in blue distance, scene of the story read so long ago; the hill of the five thousand below; and behind us Mount Tabor, and the groves of Deborah, and that great, wide level, outstretched away, away to dimness on the horizon, the rich mysterious plain of Jezreel. Who would not go to Palestine to see a sight like this, and for such a Sunday walk, which a lifetime of week-days can not wear out from our memory?

A mere speck now is my tent by the shore, but still we feel "it is a home." From this high point we have, on the whole, the best land-view of the lake from the west; but the prettiest view from the water we have yet to see.

From north to south of the lake is $12\frac{1}{2}$ miles long. Across the widest part from Magdala is $6\frac{3}{4}$ miles. Soundings show its depth to be less than 200 feet in any part.†

Kerak is the ancient Taricheæ, a name well known in the writings of Josephus.‡ Its position at the end of the lake is shown by the plan on p. 402, and you can readily see how it was made a strong fortress, and for many ages. It

* The valley of Jordan has been from an early period an almost unproductive desert. "The curse which rests upon it seems to date with the destruction of Sodom" (Newbold, "Journal of the Asiatic Society," xvi. 24).

† The length of the lake given by Josephus is 140 stadia, or sixteen miles, which is much too large, unless he means the distance by land, which would then be nearly correct. He gives the breadth as forty stadia, or about four miles and a half, which, again, is much too small, unless he reckons it from opposite Tiberias, where it is only about four miles and three-quarters.

Abulfeda gives the length as twelve miles, and the breadth six (Buckingham, p. 345). All modern travellers, except Robinson, have erred in their estimates, and usually make them too large, but Buckingham gives eight miles long, and six miles broad, and says the plain above is ten miles square.

If the Jordan could be dammed up at the Hooleh, it would form a lake there of nearly the same size, shape, and depth as the Sea of Galilee.

‡ He places it thirty stadia south of Tiberias ("Jewish War," book iii. ch. x. sec. i.).

was built on a triangular mound, about fifty feet high and four hundred yards in length, which was made into an island by the water led round it. Though bits of masonry, almost hidden in tall grass, were once strong walls about this hill, the Jordan forms a fosse on one side, while the lake guards another, and an artificial lagoon is towards the mainland. The remains of a causeway westward from the mound show how it was approached when insulated. [The Ordnance Map, surveyed, no doubt, when the lake was high, shows water all round. We have ventured to alter

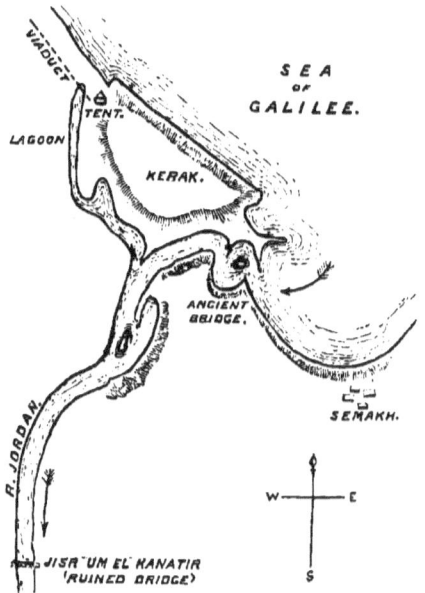

JORDAN'S EXIT FROM THE LAKE.

this because we found it dry. We have also placed the name *Hippos* on Map VII.] When Titus and Vespasian finally subdued other towns of Palestine just before the grand catastrophe of the doomed capital, they came at last to Tarichéæ, and Josephus tells us of the siege.* The des-

* "Jewish War," book iii. ch. ix. sec. x. He speaks of prisoners taken there, and sent to "the Isthmus." Was this to work upon the Roman canal?

olate mound so silent now was once a great city teeming with people and sounding with the shouts of the brave and the din of battering-rams.* The north front has a long beach with oleanders, and the water is very clear and not deep. In paddling over it we could see every object for twenty feet below, yet not one large stone could be detected along this point—only a few flat slabs and soft mossy banks of weed. But on shore it was very different. Kerak has a mine of relics to be dug out when benevolent contributors will pay the diggers, whom our Palestine Exploration Fund would willingly send there to dig. In the steep sides of the clay cliff, and buried by upright masses piled twenty feet above them, are fine Roman pavements with patterns of tesserae, which stick out even now in section on the face of the hill, and you may poke them down by hundreds with your cane, for the debris is soft, and the relics are on a level with the eye of one standing on the beach. This beach, too, is one mass of curiosities, but most of them are much worn by the water and the grinding of the gravel. One relic among many I got here was exhibited lately at the Egyptian Hall and in Liverpool, where it deservedly attracted attention, not from its excellence as a work of art, but from its homely and quaint appearance. It is the figure of a little donkey with waterjars, wrought in *terra cotta* (for which this town was famous), but the waves of twenty centuries have worn the donkey's legs to stumps, have washed off one of the jars from his back, and have scrubbed his long ears so short that they seem only the size of a cat's.† Near it I picked

---

* In front of this beach was fought the only sea-battle between the Jews and the Romans (see *ante*, p. 344). The plain to the west is called Ard el Mellaha by Seetzen.

† The Sultan has recently given strict command that no antiquities shall be removed from Turkey. He is forming a museum at Constantinople. A Greek there, who has a museum, encourages the scheme, because he can thus recruit his own. If this order is carried out, real mummies will rise in price in Egypt. Sham ones are constantly sold. Not long ago the man who made sham idols brought for sale to an Englishman the *brass mould* for casting the counterfeit images!

up some gypsum, and this substance also is mentioned as found near Tarichcæ. Some huts at the end of the great mound are concealed until you come just above them, and here is the ferry-boat, for which the ferrymen live in those little straw mansions among the bushes.

Our next pleasant voyage was along this shore at Kerak, but as it was then too windy and therefore muddy to see well under water, the Rob Roy turned south at the end and went into the Jordan. An able and interesting writer says of this place, "The Jordan leaves the lake in an ordinary manner." Now, the plan of this scene already given was sketched from the high hill above, and corrected from Kerak mound, and again on the water, and we appeal to all dispassionate readers, Can this way of leaving a lake be called an "ordinary manner?" The Jordan, indeed, glides into the Sea of Galilee quietly enough, but its exit is very strange. The east point of Kerak is high, and below it there juts out a promontory, with thick trees growing in the water. The stream runs fast through these, and the canoe cut across this leafy cape and then swept round the bay just in front of the ferrymen, who ran out uproariously shouting, but were soon distanced as the powerful current hurried us along. Here the river is more than a hundred feet wide, and probably about four feet deep. The east bank is twenty feet high and quite steep, except at one place, where some ruins look like the piers of a bridge at first, but not so much when better examined.* Behind Kerak the river bends west and then east under high cliffs, and with canes and reeds through the current is merry enough. So it winds right and left until we reach an Arab camp. From this the people rushed out *en masse*, but the Rob Roy was too fast to be caught, and after a mile or so we came to the ruins of the old bridge, Em el Kanater (mother of arches), of which nine or ten piers still stand in the stream, which is here about a hundred yards broad. My reason for spending a little time

---

* When Kerak was Tarichcæ, there *might* have been a bridge here, but the foundations, I think, would be unsteady.

on this lower Jordan was not with the intention of cruising along that. Twice already it has been descended in a boat, first by an Englishman, Lieutenant Molyneux, in 1847, and then by the American, Lynch, in 1848. All that they saw can be well seen from the shore, and these two difficult and troublesome voyages did not add any thing to our knowledge of Jordan's stream that might not be noticed on horseback. The Rob Roy had gone rather to what could only be seen from a boat, and what no boat had done before, and whether in the Abana, the Pharpar, the lakes of Damascus, Hooleh, and Genesareth, or afterwards also in the Kishon and the Belus, the aim was to hit upon new ground and new water, or to examine the old ways in a new manner, so as to add new facts rather than to reiterate.* But it was interesting to run down this upper end of the lower Jordan, just to see the few first rapids that caused Mr. Lynch so many hours of work, but which, with the canoe, were passed in a few minutes. Lynch had two boats, one of them made of copper, and he had sixteen men. No wonder then that with such a fleet to float he speaks of "twenty-seven dangerous rapids" on the lower Jordan. Molyneux had one boat (a ship's dinghy), and he found the passage easier, though his voyage ended in trouble and in death.† To descend all the way in a canoe would have been easy enough, but *cui bono?* The banks

---

* The Jordan seems never to have been navigable for traffic. If any boat went down the lower part before Molyneux, or the upper part before the Rob Roy, it must have been for exploration. Josephus mentions ships in the Dead Sea ("Jewish War," book iv. ch. viii. sec. iv.), where he tells us the sailors in them used to gather the bitumen floating on the water. He also speaks of the Ammonites as having passed over the Dead Sea to attack Engedi, in Jehoshaphat's time. Yet is it clear that the Greek words "τὴν λίμνην διαβάντες" are rightly translated by "superato lacu," and "passed over the lake," so as to imply the use of boats? (Josephus, "Antiq. of the Jews," book ix. ch. i. sec. ii.)

Newbold says ("Journal of the Asiatic Society," vol. xvi. p. 23) "that we hear no mention of boats or bridges in the different passages of the Israelites." Ferry-boats, however, seem to have been established very early; we hear of one for the Jordan in 2 Samuel xix. 28.

† See a short notice of it in the Appendix.

are high. There is no view to see, and nothing but heat and gravel and Arabs to meet with, wasting much time, muscle, and money, but without even the prospect of any new knowledge to be gained. Therefore, as it was wise to use the convenient portability of the canoe to take her to rivers hitherto untraversed, I resolved to haul up after a few miles* on the Jordan's lower stream, and to take her to untried waters, a resolution amply rewarded, as will be seen farther on. We brought her back to camp on horseback, and the vocal Adoor improvised his (carefully prepared) song of the "Shaktoorah done with Galilee."

Yet in the calm watches of the night, when all was quiet beside, a low sweet murmuring from the river seemed to float as a whisper in my tent.

So had it been for how many thousand years, ever streaming on its fluent story.

Sleep's curtain gently folds us now in dream-land, where the soft music melts into a liquid shadowy picture of great things and people mingled in long procession, and the river tells us over again the wonders of its source, the swiftness of its fall, and the silence of its end—the events that happened by its banks, the miracles wrought upon its waters, the mysteries about its lakes, the glory shining on it from our Saviour at his baptism, his transfiguration, and his appearance after He rose again.

Surely the Jordan is by far the most wonderful stream on the face of the earth, and the memories of its history will not be forgotten in Heaven.

* About six miles from the lake, the Yarmuk enters from the east, having had its sources not far from those of the Pharpar. The Arabs call the Yarmuk and the Jabbok or Zerka "Shereea," meaning a watering-place. They apply this name, too, to Jordan, but adding the title "Great." Below this there is the first bridge now practicable, the Jisr Mejaama, so called because it is at a "meeting of the waters," after another set of islands had divided them.

CHAPTER XXIII.

In the Lake.—Strange Swell.—A Storm.—Submerged Ruins.—The "Herd of Swine."—Semakh Village.—Hippos.—High Sea.—Vale of Doves.—Long last Look.—Cana.—Nazareth.—Old Sights.—Sights unseen.—Plain Words.

> "Full many a glorious morning have I seen
> Flatter the mountain tops with sovereign eye,
> Kissing with glowing face the meadows green,
> Gilding pale streams with heavenly alchemy."

It was just such a morning now as Shakspeare thus describes. The gray veil of hoar frost melted on the face of day, and the crisp air softened into a warm dalliance, gently beguiling the Rob Roy to linger about in a languid laziness. Cease, pleasant dawdling! Our crew is piped to work, and with steady stroke to reach again the farthest point we had touched on our first day's course; for now we must complete our tour of the shore all round the sea.

In traversing the centre of the lake, I came rather suddenly upon a novel sight. The smooth surface of the water was undulated in short sharp swells, without any wind whatever, and none for hours before. These waves were exactly east and west in the ridges, and of the form and size of "steamboat waves" upon the Thames. They had a uniform width of fifteen feet, and my bow often dipped deep in one as my stern left the other. Perhaps the cause of this is some volcanic perturbation either of the water or of its bed below. Molyneux noticed something of the same kind in the Dead Sea, and precisely in the same direction, north and south. On the very deep part of the Rhine also, as it issues from Lake Constance, I observed a similar appearance, but never elsewhere, when afloat.*

---

* Just below the whirlpool at Niagara, the eddies curl like this. All these, however, are in currents, but I could not detect the slightest current here in Genesareth. Neubauer ("Geog. Talm." p. 31) says the Talmud

The wind soon brought the ordinary waves upon the lake, and these confused the previous distinctness of this ground swell. When I was near the middle of the lake, on another occasion, the water was not calm, and so the phenomenon was not observed. It is not unlikely that the assertion is correct that the Jordan does, in fact, run through the lake, without much mingling with the other waters; and I remark that some persons who deny this have passed but few hours upon the Sea of Galilee, but a longer stay is needed for evidence in such a question.

Great heat soon poured down from the fierce sun, and "something," we thought, "must come of this brilliant glare." Gentle zephyrs breathed from behind me; then they lulled; then other little airs fanned my cheek on the right, and then these, too, quite waned away to calm. Patches of the smooth mirror again were ruffled on our left by squalls from the north-west right ahead. But the sun killed them one after the other, and I steadily advanced—yet all the time aware that this sort of weather was not to be trusted.

Just as the Rob Roy passed below Wady Fik, a strange distant hissing sounded ahead, where we could see that a violent storm was raging. Instantly all hands were on the alert to meet it. The waves had not time to rise. The gusts had come down upon calm water, and they whisked up long wreaths of it into the sky. The sea-birds sailed with the roaring blast, which rushed on with foam and fury, but it found the Rob Roy all ataunto. This torrent of heavy cold air was pouring over the mountain crests into the deep caldron of the lake below, a headlong flood of wind, like a waterfall into the hollow; just as is said in Luke (viii. 23)—"there came *down* a storm of wind upon the lake."

The peculiar effects of squalls among mountains are known to all who have boated much on lakes, but on the Sea of Galilee the wind has a singular force and sudden-

mentions the phenomenon on Jordan. But it also says that Jordan runs into the Mediterranean Sea!

ness; and this is, no doubt, because the sea is so deep in the world that the sun rarifies the air in it enormously, and the wind, speeding swift above a long and level *plateau*, gathers much force as it sweeps through flat deserts, until suddenly it meets this huge gap in the way, and it tumbles down here irresistible.

With my best efforts I could scarcely stem the force of this head-wind, though I was in excellent training, and my canoe in her lightest trim. But every moment lost now in getting to the cliffs for shelter would make the work ten times harder afterwards, when the sea had time to rise. By pressing onward, then, with every nerve, and with more exertion than at any time during the cruise, we gained at last the windward shore, and here we could look with safe amazement at the scud of the gale, careering across the lake, and twisting the foam in the air as if tied in knots of spray, which sparkled in the sun like ten thousand diamonds, while the sea-birds still flew helplessly down wind.

The reward of exertion in pure fresh air like this is to find our craft snugly nestling under thick trees in perfect calm, and safe from all the bobbery. This luxurious rest was enjoyed at the very same spot of the Wady Semakh, where the Rob Roy had rested on our first day's cruise, and yet how long a time it seemed since then! So many pleasant things had been thought, and done, and said, and sung, and read, and written. Just so; but now we are entitled to lunch. Swift as the tempest had come down, it vanished away as swiftly, and when we turned our bow to sea again, there was only a fine fresh breeze and common waves to meet.

Just south of the tell, near the mouth of the river, by Khersa, is some heavy rubble masonry, of which part has fallen into deeper water. A few cut stones are submerged, but no other remains of interest were to be seen, for the pile of large stones at the next point seemed to be not artificial, after I had examined them closely. Our gaze was, therefore, directed with eagerness and care to the hills above and the plain below, for much interest must always be felt in looking at this spot as the most likely place for that strange, indeed unique, miracle where the "Legion" entered into the herd of swine.* Other travellers, more or less hurried in their examination of this place, have given their impressions after seeing it from the shore. I shall venture to record what was noticed from the water during some hours of leisure, and from notes written at the time.†

Between Wady Semakh and Wady Fik there are at least four distinct localities where every feature in the Scripture account of this incident may be found in combination.‡ Above there are rocks with caves in them, very suitable for tombs,§ and farther down there is ample space for tombs built on sloping ground—a form of sepulture far more prevalent in Scripture times than we are apt to suppose. A verdant sward is here, with many bulbous roots which swine might feed upon. And on this I observed—what is an unusual sight—a very large herd of oxen, horses, camels, sheep, asses, and goats, all feeding together. It was evident that the pasturage was various, and enough for all—a likely place for "a herd of swine feeding on the mountain." Khersa, near this, in ruins, was probably the Gergesa of old, and, as has been observed repeatedly by authors, this might well be in the "country of the Gadarenes," though a considerable distance from the town of Gadara.‖ We are told that "the whole herd of

---

* Matt. viii.; Mark v.; Luke viii.

† Thomson states incorrectly that "Everywhere along the north-eastern and eastern shores, a smooth beach declines gently down to the water" ("The Land and the Book," vol. ii. p. 36), but his assigned locality for the miracle coincides with one to be mentioned presently.

‡ The place where the herd was feeding is stated to be "a good way off from them," *i. e.* from where the demoniac met our Saviour "immediately" after "he came out of the ship."

§ Wilson appears to have found tombs here, and another traveller states that he saw a mad beggar running about, who lived in a cave.

‖ The incident of the demoniacs is related as having taken place in the "country of the Gergesenes," Matt. viii. 28 [Sinai MS. (corrected) reads *Gazarenes*; Vatican MS. *Gadarenes*]. In Mark v. 1, it is "Gadarenes"

swine ran violently down a steep place." It does not say that it was a "*high*" place, but "steep," κρημνου, and that they "ran" (not, they "fell") down this "into the sea." There are several steeps near the sea here, but only one so close to the water as to make it sure that if a herd "ran violently" down, they would go "into the sea."* But the place which I regard as most likely for the site of this event is at the end of the short plain under some rocks, and near the green *plateau*, where the swine could feed. Here, for a full half-mile, the beach is of a form different from any other round the lake, and from any I have noticed in any lake or sea before. It is flat until close to the edge. There a hedge of oleanders fringes the end of the plain, and immediately below these is a gravel beach, inclined so steep that, when my boat was at the shore, I could not see over the top even by standing up; while the water alongside is so deep that it covered my paddle (seven feet long) when dipped in vertically a few feet from the shore. Now, if the swine rushed along this short plain towards this hedge of underwood (and in the *delta* of Semakh their usual feeding-place would be often among thick brushwood of that kind), they would instantly pass through the shrubs, and then down the steep gravel beyond the deep water, where they would surely be drowned.

[Sinai MS. and Vatican MS. *Gerasenes*, but again corrected in the Sinai MS. to *Gergesenes*]. In Luke viii. 26, it is "Gadarenes" [Sinai MS. *Gergesenes*: Vatican MS. *Gerasenes*]: so that there are four readings, which differ not much in sound. Wey's map (in A.D. 1462) puts Cedar and Godara near this, and "Hondius his Map," in 1624, places Gadara by the river. Damville's map, 1794, has Gadera at Khersa.

The name Wady Fik is derived from the ancient village of Aphek near it (Aphaka is the Phœnician Venus worship). The ruins one sees on the top of the camel-like ridge are those of Gamala, ("gumel" "camel"), perhaps the Gebal and Gammadims of Ezekiel (ch. xxvii). This was the last town taken by the Romans in this direction, and Josephus tells how hard a fight the Jews made there with the brave old legions.

* This is shown on Map VII., at p. 372, by the shaded portion of a cliff touching the shore. It was very satisfactory to me, after making these notes, independently of other travellers' views, to find that Captain Wilson agrees in considering that the coast south of Semakh is the most suitable for the occurrence we are discussing.

The picture here given is a faithful copy of a sketch I made next morning from Kerak. The sun was then just rising behind the hills of Bashan, and therefore each cliff in the mountain had a deep shade, as shown in the picture. The shore under Wady Fik was five miles distant from where I sketched, and, as my eye was near the water-level, the low shore along the base of the hills was beneath the horizon, and therefore invisible; but the extreme clearness of the early morning air made it easy to mark each feature of the picture so illumined. The letter S, near the edge of the picture, is above the south end of the Wady Semakh, and a little to its right below would be the ruins of Khersa. The letter P is above the spot where the large open plain was covered by a flock. Behind this are rocks and caves, and, possibly, tombs. Before it is the curious beach already described as a "steep place." The letter G is over the ruins of Gamala, marked as little spots on the hill. This picture and the outline given at p. 349, *ante*, nearly complete the contour of the east side of the lake.*

The Rob Roy now runs close to shore between two trees in the water, and moors there, with her bows towards land —an attitude the most suitable when visitors may call without sending up their cards. "El asher hadir," "Dinner ready!" and we attack the contents of our bag.

The beach south of Wady Fik is generally steep, and there are some clumps of stones by the water, one of them looking at first like a ruin, but, on close inspection, no remains were visible to indicate ports, piers, or quays, along this part. So our course was homeward bound.

Our camp broke up to return to the land of Genesareth, and by diligent search I discovered a plausible excuse for not leaving the entrancing lake this day, namely, that I had

---

* Here we feel it a pleasing duty to mention that the faithful representation of the original sketches to illustrate this volume has been effected by the artistic skill of Captain May, R.N., under the able and experienced direction of Mr. James Cooper, who has superintended the preparation of the illustrations in this volume, and in the three other records of the Rob Roy's rovings.

COUNTRY OF THE GERGESENES, SEA OF GALILEE.

still to examine one little bit of the southern shore. They left me, therefore, to follow on the lake, and the Rob Roy skimmed away by Kerak; but, although it was clear in the water and calm above, yet not one thing could be seen under the surface worth a word of comment.

The water here is only about twelve feet deep, for fifty yards out, and flat stones are scattered on it even so far from shore. Crossing the Jordan's mouth, we arrive at Semakh village.* This place seemed to be entirely untenanted; it stands, close to the water, upon a cliff of stiff clay, almost indurated into rock, and its appearance is most singular. The houses do not look very decrepit or forlorn. Some of the fifty or sixty dwellings huddled together are of three stories high, and are built of black cut stone, and the roofs are there, and yet nobody is inside.† Then the bareness of the place: no foliage about it, no vale, no mound, no feature of strength or beauty, but just a well-built Arab town, deserted without any seeming cause. A pure and spotless beach is below the cliffs. I landed here, for it was not possible to resist so inviting a shore; and the air was quiet, and the sea, and yet it was sheer waste of time to stop now in these silent shady coves.‡

Reluctantly embarking, and then coasting along, I diligently spied below, but could detect nothing here on the clean level bottom of the lake. When the boats on the Sea of Galilee were counted once by hundreds, surely there must have been numerous wrecks and founderings; and, as the lazy Turks would never remove these, one

---

* The southern village, not the wady we visited yesterday.

† So I was informed. Dr. Thomson speaks of two hundred houses here, and that it was inhabited in 1858. He marks Hippos here in his map. Robinson states the houses at about one-tenth of that number. The name Semakh may be derived from the old name Samaia, mentioned by Josephus ("Jewish War," book i. ch. ii. sec. vi.). In the Talmud the name "Jordan" is not given to the river until it has issued from the lake after passing Beth Yerak and Sennabris, which may be Kerak and Semakh. Susitha (from a word meaning "horse") may be Hippos ("Geog. Talm." pp. 31, 216, 291).

‡ Nevertheless, about six months might well be spent on this lake, with plenty of variety, in place, or weather, or scene, or incident every day, even if no time were devoted merely to quiet reverie.

might well expect to see some relics of them still, but there was nothing until we approached the little tell, now called Sumrah, which is believed to be the ancient Hippos.* If the town was called by this Greek name because of what it means (a "horse"), there is a show of reason for the title, since near it, on the plain, is a splendid pasture for steeds, and not far off I noticed many of them. It is likely, too, their owners noticed me, and, being now on the eastern shore, some caution was advisable, for the tribes there would gladly capture a Feringhee, and they know his proper ransom price. I searched about here with all diligence, but could find only some cut stones in the lake under water near the tell, and south of it a large mass of masonry partly submerged, which seems not only to have tumbled down but to be inverted. The finest view of the lake in panorama is from a point about half a mile west of Hippos. Here we can see snowy Hermon and the white peaks of Antilebanon, closing in the northern end, while Tiberias is visible to the left, and Genesareth beyond. No person who wishes to see the lake of Galilee well should omit to come here for the centre of his panorama.

The wind rose suddenly after I left Hippos to cross the lake. The waves were sharp and high, and in several directions at once, when my course led me into the middle, where the peculiar swell had been noticed before. In ten minutes the sea had risen from sullen calm to anger, and it was necessary to be careful, even in a canoe. Worse it got, and worse, and finally so very bad that I had to "heave to," the only time the Rob Roy was forced to do this during the whole cruise.† In an hour or so the wind had calmed down entirely. The surface of the water became glassy,

---

* Josephus ("Life," sec. lxv.) mentions the country of Justus (evidently Tiberias; sec. lxx.) as being thirty stadia from Hippos, sixty from Gadara, and one hundred and twenty from Scythopolis.

† When a boat is made to "lie to," her bows are turned to the wind and sea, and her progress is moderated, so as to be almost *nil*. By this means the breaking of the waves upon her is harmless, and she rises and falls, and pitches and rolls, with ease, and, indeed, with delight; but much time is lost, and there is the humiliation felt of being thwarted all the time.

but was bent in graceful curves by a long swell. Passing Tiberias about two miles off, I heard every word the people said as they stood on their house-tops in long rows, and shouted all kinds of messages to the canoe, but chiefly ending in "Taly, taly, taly heny!" (Come here!) The Rob Roy insensibly floated once more to Bethsaida, for it was impossible not to pay one parting visit to these pleasant fishermen. The hot steam now rose from the lake itself, outside the thermal fountains, and the fishes' backs,

LAST VIEW OF GENESARETH.

by thousands, roughened the water. After a long day's work, however pleasant, there must come an end, and I paddled for the last time along the strand of Genesareth, and hauled the Rob Roy into the oleanders near Magdala.

Our camp was here, and next morning the regretful feeling assumed sway that now, on this 2d of February, there was no more excuse to linger on the charming lake, and yet with the consolation that to return and have long weeks to spend will be a happy hope.

On *terra firma* now again, it is my turn to carry the Rob Roy, as she has so well and so long carried me. And for the reader, our turn comes to be very brief; for he can find what is seen on the land well told by better scribes who ride and do not paddle. Any one who goes up the rocky gorge of the Vale of Doves, and in winter, will be surprised to hear that we carried the canoe through that rough pass in a heavy storm of wind. Eagles soared about us, circling in the gale. Long years ago, in those dark caves above the upright cliffs, a terrible band of robbers lived, and preyed, and multiplied, until at last bold Herod was sent to deal with them, and Josephus tells us how he managed.*

---

* "Now these caves were in the precipices of craggy mountains, and could not be come at from any side, since they had only some winding pathways, very narrow, by which they got up to them; but the rock that lay on their front had beneath it valleys of a vast depth, and of an almost perpendicular declivity; insomuch that the king was doubtful for a long time what to do, by reason of a kind of impossibility there was of attacking the place. Yet did he at length make use of a contrivance that was subject to the utmost hazard; for he let down the most hardy of his men in chests, and set them at the mouths of the dens. Now these men slew the robbers and their families, and when they made resistance, they sent in fire upon them (and burnt them); and as Herod was desirous of saving some of them, he had proclamation made that they should come and deliver themselves up to him; but not one of them came willingly to him, and of those that were compelled to come, many preferred death to captivity. And here a certain old man, the father of seven children, whose children, together with their mother, desired him to give them leave to go out, upon the assurance and right hand that was offered them, slew them after the following manner: He ordered every one of them to go out, while he stood himself at the cave's mouth, and slew that son of his perpetually who went out. Herod was near enough to see this sight, and his bowels of compassion were moved at it, and

KEFR OANA.

On the plain above this "Vale of Doves," we come to where Saladin routed the Crusaders with terrific slaughter, and finished their long sway in the East. But just before we tread this vast swamp of Hattin, there is one long, last, lingering look behind: a farewell gaze at the loved lake, far below, now left, but not forever. With a melancholy pencil we sketched the scene on page 417, and though only the northern end of the lake is here visible, in a small compass much is seen. Right and left are the rocks of the robbers' caves. In the foreground of the distant lake is the "land of Genesareth." On its left edge is Ain et Tin; then the cliff at Capernaum, and behind that Bethsaida, and farther on, Tell Hoom. The mouth of the Jordan is beyond, and the western end of the Butaia plain. In the far-away background Bashan shows those flat-edged hills which thus close in our little picture.*

Kefr Cana† was our halting-place, and next day the Rob Roy stopped at Nazareth. Twenty years before I had spent ten days here, and then the old doctor-monk, "Fra Joachim," used to come to my bedside and prescribe for me with gravity, and produce homœopathic herbs out of his ample sleeve, while he puffed his cigarette with smiles. We paid a visit to this ancient now. For forty years he has been away from Spain, his native land, so he seemed to care little about "Cosas d'Espagna." His laboratory is like

he stretched out his right hand to the old man, and besought him to spare his children; yet did not he relent at all upon what he said, but over and above reproached Herod on the lowness of his descent, and slew his wife as well as his children; and when he had thrown their dead bodies down the precipice, he at last threw himself down after them" ("Jewish War," book i. ch. xvi. sec. iv.). The story is repeated with variations in "Antiq. of the Jews."

* To obtain this bijou prospect, I went north of the usual road, and tried several points of view, until at last there could be included the largest portion possible of the Sea of Galilee. One of the photographs of the Palestine Exploration Fund represents a part of this scene, but it is taken from a point farther east and south, and, therefore, it has less of the lake itself.

† Full and recent reliable information as to this village, which was the scene of our Lord's first miracle, will be found in an interesting paper by the Rev. J. Zeller, published in the Quarterly Statement No. III. of the Palestine Exploration Fund for October, 1869.

a druggist's shop in a conjuror's cave, and the only draughts he ventured to order this time for my health seemed undoubtedly vinous, and they were speedily drunk off—by him.

Well, he is a worthy fellow; and if all the monks were as little of monks as he is, they would never have been expelled, as they have been almost everywhere, while only England is calling them back to her bosom. The excellent missionary, the Rev. J. Zeller, showed me the Protestant schools of Nazareth, and the new English church now

THE NEW PROTESTANT CHURCH AT NAZARETH.

building here, and of which we present a sketch. It is in a most picturesque position, but to pay for it funds are needed still, and who could refuse to place a stone in the walls of a church at Nazareth? Nazareth is vastly changed in these last twenty years. It is larger, cleaner, more populous, better built, and better taught, for the active catechists are working here with vigor. Things *are* advancing in the East, though the advance is very slow. Mr. Zeller also showed me a very great curiosity, which had an important bearing upon an incident we shall soon have to relate.

VALE OF NAZARETH.

This was the skeleton of a crocodile, about ten feet long, which a person known to Mr. Zeller had killed, three months before, in the river Zerka, which flows into the Mediterranean not far from Cæsarea. Old authors have called that the "Crocodile River," and near it are the ruins of the "City of Crocodiles." Arabs of the vicinity have long persisted in stating that the "timsah" is still found there; and recent authors have written that they had "seen men who had seen crocodiles in the Zerka." But here we had the actual specimen itself, so all doubt is now removed.*

If it is sometimes pleasant to come a second time into a foreign town, when you have already seen all the "stock sights" there, and may therefore now omit them, it is especially agreeable, in a second tour in Palestine, to escape long stories about the Popish paint with which so many grand and solemn holy places have been daubed. In Bethlehem, we had long ago seen the glass case containing "the tongues of the infants slain by Herod;" and we had seen the scandalous impostures in other towns, for which every Romish bishop in England (though he smiles at it) is responsible, for his Church claims to be "one and infallible." We had seen the Saint's blood in Italy, and the pagan crosses for the Indians in Romish America; and the priests, after mass on Sunday in Spain, buying tickets at the lottery, and going off with their whole congregation to the bull-fight. We had seen the "Madiai" imprisoned in Tuscany for teaching the Bible to their servant-girl; and we had visited an English lady in Lucca, imprisoned for giving one tract to a woman. We had seen the "paternal government" that found these writings were "too hard" for the people; while the most stupid nonsense of false saints, with pictures, was publicly sold in their churches,

* Mr. Zeller brought it to England, and it was exhibited in October, 1869, at the Free Museum and Library in Liverpool, and Mr. Zeller kindly promised to present this unique specimen to the Museum of the Palestine Exploration Fund. If other travellers also would keep their faculties alive by collecting articles for the same purpose, they would be doing good service, and would feel too that the fruits of their travels are more widely enjoyed in a public museum than in any private cabinet.

as *easy* to be understood by the people (and exalting the priests). We had read the book of the Romish Bishop of Birmingham, proclaiming the recent miracle of "*La Salette*," in France, where the Virgin appeared to two children, and talked to them *patois* about potatoes; and which tale, he assured us, was approved by the Pope, and therefore he invited us all to visit the place. We had visited the mountain near Grenoble, and had seen the donkeys' panniers bringing down bottles full of water from the holy fountain, while a wily priest at the bottom started a private pump of his own. We had seen the original of the protest against this imposture, signed by fifty priests, who complained that the Virgin came down upon "all the hills around." We had bought, on the spot, the official report of the trial by the highest court, convicting the priests of imposture, and the woman herself who had been dressed as "the Virgin;" and we had seen the "Tablet" newspaper, in England, loudly advancing the trick, and then—silent*—and the Bishop's book withdrawn. But we have never yet seen the retractation by any of these people—Pope, bishop, priests, or editors—of the proved falsehoods they had so freely advocated.

Having seen these things, and many others like them, we placed no faith in what could be shown us now by the monks at Nazareth; and therefore the Rob Roy went past them all, to commune rather with the brooks, and trees, and everlasting hills, which, happily, even the *Syllabus* can not suppress.

It is to be hoped that the plans of the priests will be speedily ripe in England, and that they may open fire along the whole line before our vigor is sapped and our manliness utterly gone. The hard fight—physical fight—that is coming must come soon, or it will find us without heart or sinews. Even if it comes at once, it will find us, poor "swaddlers," half ashamed to be "Protestants," trembling before the sarcasm scribbled in some anonymous gar-

---

* Yet now again, September 25, 1869, warmly espousing another "apparition" in the Pyrenees.

ret, as if it were law and gospel because it is printed. Do we really know what Popery has been of old, what it is even now, what it tells us positively it must and will be here and soon and always—"dominant?" Could you or I be true Papists and yet loyal to England? To the future England that is to serve the Pope we *might* be loyal, but loyal to the England that as yet is free—never. These truths are too true to be told. It is a vast indiscretion to tell them here. But I have seen too much of these things to be ignorant, and I fear too little and too much to be silent. For money, free trade, railways, any thing you please that is earthly, you may hold meetings, write books, fight battles, make any din you like, and be "earnest," and speak plain. But for the free Bible—the right to tell what Popery was, is, and wants to be—you must hush to a whisper any voice you have, and still be reckoned even then a monomaniac. We must be "charitable"—yes, and for whom our charity? Not for our women, our children, our herds of ignorant and weak who are beguiled—but for the army of foreign priests who stream over the land, and raise an alien name above our Queen's. Is it not just possible that our wondrous delicacy in this matter is not from love, but fear? Rather, perhaps, it is because that sort of tone pays best in general popularity—nobody is so sure of approval as the man who is "fiercely moderate." If you want to screen those people here whom the Romish Bishop of Cracow (who ought to know them best) calls "furies, not women," to keep English girls in their prisons under the "moral" restraint of character lost by escape; if you want to justify disloyalty, to hand over to a narrow celibate clique of alien hopes and sympathies the teaching of our nation, to flout the nobles of England cringing to the "Prince" last made by an old bachelor abroad, to stifle free speech, to buy short peace by bribes, ever larger, never enough, to fasten on us again the fangs that sucked England's best blood once, and to shame our nation in presence of the others who have writhed out from under intolerable coils; if you will fear a huge system for its power, and succor it because it is weak—wonder at its wealth, yet pay it because it is poor—bow down to it as divine, yet laugh at it as only a ghost; if you will enthrone error, and put fetters upon truth—bind heavier "them that are fast bound in misery and iron," and set the oppressor free—put priests for our lawgivers and a gigantic imposture for our faith, drown truth in fables and shut our open Bible: if you want to do these things with impunity, nay, to be called "liberal" while you do them—only say it is in the name of "religion" and at the bidding of the "priests," and mind you say "the priests of Rome," for to do these things at the bidding of any others would convict you of "bigotry," or treason, or of craven fear.

CHAPTER XXIV.

Source of Kishon.—Megiddo.— Fords of Kishon.—Kishon's Banks.—Sisera's Steeds.—Launch in a Storm.—Up the Melchi.—Meeting a Crocodile.—What to do.—Feeling a Crocodile.—Flight.—Evidence.—Start on the Belus.—River Aujeh.—Farewell to the Jordan.—Across the Bay of Acre.—"Ariadne."—Praise.

NEXT night, sleeping at Malhoolah, seemed to me the coldest of any in the journey. No doubt this was caused by our "going up" from the deep chasm of Galilee, where the temperature in winter is delicious, to the higher ground on the hills that encircle Nazareth.

Now we are in sight of Mount Carmel, and the Rob Roy is carried over the plain of Esdraelon. Here we come to a river again, and our pen may be set free, for our paddle is to be unloosed.

The source of the Kishon seems to be at Jeneen, the old En-gannim ("fountain of gardens"), given to Issachar by Joshua (xxi. 29). I regret not having examined this fountain during a former visit to Jeneen. But east of this there are earlier streams of Kishon, at least in winter, and Dr. Thomson proves that the watershed of the Jordan and the Kishon is in a line from Ksalis to Endor, and that the Kishon and the Jalud *overlap* one another for several miles.* The Kishon is called Mokatta (ford) by the Arabs, and its valley, *El Kasab*, from the spring, while their name for the plain of Esdraelon is *Merj ibn Amer*. We are here on the regular field of battle for the centre of Palestine, while the Bukaa we had traversed towards Damascus was the battle

---

* "The Land and the Book," vol. ii. p. 140. Schwartz says (p. 166) that the Arabs call the village south-east of Tabor, near which the sources of Kishon are, Sheich Abrik (chief Barak), in allusion to Barak (Judges iv. 6). In 1 Chronicles vi. 37, among the Levitical cities, the village is called Kedesh, and this may be the Kedes marked in Wey's old map.

plain for the north. A hundred other points of interest are round us on Esdraelon, but we must keep to a few that are fairly subjects for our log.

There is euphony in that name for the streams of Kishon, "the waters of Megiddo." This town* was for years left under the power of the Canaanites. Barak and Sisera, "the kings, came and fought" (Judges v. 19), and Deborah sang of the victory. The place was well chosen as a battlefield to contest both the road and the river. The Israelites assembled at Tabor could reach it in six hours if the upper streams of Kishon were dry, but it is not easy to see how Sisera could bring hither his "nine hundred chariots" from Harosheth, if that was near Hazor, "above" the waters of Merom.†

As Barak began the battle, a storm of rain, hail, and wind swept over the plain,‡ "the stars in their courses fought against Sisera," and "the river of Kishon swept them away —that ancient river, the river Kishon."

The treacherous nature of the Kishon exceeds that of

---

* If Megiddo was the Roman station "Legio" (now "Lejun" of the Arab), it is south-east of Carmel on the road to Jenin, and in full view of Jezreel, looking west. Further south, on the same highway, was Taanach, also a Canaanitish town (Judges i. 27), and now called Tannuk. Vandevelde, in his "Syria and Palestine" (1854, vol. i. p. 364), gives an interesting explanation of how it was that Pharoah-necchoh was met here and fought by Josiah (2 Kings xxxiii.).

Rabbi Schwartz (p. 165) thus explains the apparent difficulty in understanding 1 Kings xxxi. 19: "On the spot where the dogs have licked up the blood of Naboth shall the dogs lick up thy blood also;" in conjunction with 1 Kings xxii. 38: "And they washed out the chariot in the pool of Samaria, and the dogs licked up his blood." Naboth was stoned to death in Jezreel, and still it is said, as if in fulfillment of the prophecy, that Ahab's blood was licked up in Samaria. He says that the Hebrew word translated "on the spot" should be rendered "in place of," in punishment for; so the same word in Hosea ii. 1, "And it shall come to pass that *instead* of people's saying of them."

The "Armageddon" in Rev. xvi. 16, may mean either the "fortified city" or the "mountain" of Megiddo (Stanley, "S. and P." p. 338).

† Thomson ("The Land and the Book," vol. ii. p. 143) places Harosheth at the large double mound opposite Carmel, now called Harothieh, and he lucidly explains the incidents of this battle.

‡ Josephus, "Antiq. of the Jews," book v. ch. v. sec. iv.

any river I have seen. Not only are there few fords in the lower part, but they are all difficult of access, even in fine weather, and the depth of water in them varies extremely even without any assignable cause.

As we approached the river, after a long spell of fair weather, Hany was exceedingly anxious to ford it at once, for a few hours' rain might render a passage impossible. On one of the thirty visits he had made to this river, he was kept thus a whole week without being able to pass.

Therefore we pressed on with wearied mules to the upper ford, said then to be the best; but on approaching it I observed about twenty mounted Arabs on the other bank, who tried in vain to cross there, and so we retired and struggled on to the next ford.

To save time I went half a mile in advance, through the reeds; and, descending the steep bank, my horse entered the river, which is there about fifty feet broad; but we had not advanced two yards into the channel before the water came up to my knees sitting in the saddle, and all endeavors to cross there were futile. Our horses, indeed, could have swum, but not the pack-mules.

Again we retreated, and went still down the stream to the last ford (except that at the mouth), and which had the worst reputation of all. To our great astonishment, there was actually not three inches of water at this spot, and the Rob Roy could scarcely float across.

This remarkable uncertainty of the fords is caused by the soft sand and mud at the bottom of the river being moved bodily from one place to another, so that no man can tell where it may be hollowed out one day or heaped up in a bank the next.

It is readily understood, then, how Sisera's army might have easily crossed the Kishon before a storm, and yet be "swept away" in the very same place after rain had flooded the river. This also explains how Elijah told Ahab to hasten lest the rain should stop him.

Another peculiarity of the plain is that, on certain tracts of its surface, there is strong adhesive mud, and this alone enables the banks of the Kishon to maintain their remarkable upright form, even when they are twenty feet high.

Now when horses and mules pass over such places, they are often unable to pull out their feet. The struggles of the mules when they felt this were violent, and the loads of those that stuck fast had to be removed. One of our donkeys, falling into this clay, which is far stiffer than the loam, succumbed without an effort, lying upon his side as if hopeless, deep sunk in the mire, and patiently waiting half an hour until the other animals had been recovered, and he could be released.

I noticed also that the form of the mule's hoof, being sharp and pointed, allows it to sink much deeper than the flat hoof of a horse; but then the mule can, for the same reason, draw his foot out more easily. If a horse's foot is buried in the mud long enough to allow the clay to close over it from above, he finds it extremely difficult to draw his leg out again, and he instantly changes his gait to a series of plunges, with rapid, short, and jerky steps, snorting and groaning the while with terror, and panting and steaming in the wildest excitement.

Therefore it was that in this battle of Megiddo the war-steeds of Sisera were "discomfited," flying before Israel, "so that Sisera lighted down off his chariot," and Deborah could sing in her hymn of triumph, "Then were the horse-hoofs broken by the means of the prancings, the prancings of their mighty ones."

We were now at the foot of Mount Carmel, which is about fifteen miles in length, broad and lofty at the inland end, and narrowing to a lower point that juts out seaward. Having formerly spent a week in the convent here, I was well acquainted with the northern end of Carmel, but now I scaled the heights remote from the sea, to examine and to admire the place where Elijah met the priests of Baal. Stanley well describes this grand theatre, and the sacred tragedy that was enacted there of old. The well whence the water was drawn three times to flood the sacrifice I found quite full to thirteen feet,* and the channel of Kishon bends round close to Carmel just below this spot; and deep in its sands there is buried, no doubt, the golden dust of idols calcined and stamped to pieces by him who was zealous for Jehovah. Then the old river trends away into the marsh again, silently meandering slowly to the sea.

Torrents of rain descended on our camp at night, and the flat morass glistened with rain-drops which warned both man and beast not to traverse it now, and justified our prudent haste in passing it while dry.

At the beginning of our tour I would not have dared to carry the Rob Roy over this terrible bog, but now, fully trusting the horse, we set off to float her again on the Kishon.

The rain beat cold in our faces, and the winter blast was rushing down the crags. It was an anxious time crossing this dreary swamp in such a storm; and as my horse plunged knee-deep, and struggled, he groaned aloud with rage.

"Suppose he sticks here, what shall I do?" was the question, and it seemed to be best then to throw off my broad cloak on the marsh and to jump into it, and lie at full length to prevent sinking; but the next part of the process I never could pre-arrange, and it was just one of those dangers one can not prepare for, and must only be blind to until they occur. After much difficulty the canoe was launched down the deep bank, and once all snug in the Rob Roy, I was sheltered of course from the pitiless rain. Then they left me with a Moslem's blessing, and I was soon out of sight of mankind.

High vertical banks soon shut in the Kishon, which

---

* The depth of water in this well, when noted at all by travellers, is often different, but it is never mentioned as positively dry. Thomson's suggestion that the water was obtained from a fountain near the channel seems to me untenable. He cites an interesting passage from Tacitus, describing the worship on Mount Carmel ("The Land and the Book," vol. ii. p. 223). Just below the sacrifice-place, Moharrakah, which means "burning," is Tell el Kasees (hill of the priests). Finn, however, thinks this name alludes to some hermit of later times ("Byeways of Palestine," p. 233).

flows moodily dark and deep in a bending channel about sixty feet wide. A curious ledge of hard clay projects at each verge about three inches under the surface, and then is steep again to six feet below, within a yard or two from the shore. I tried in vain to find even one single stone with which to sound the middle, and I hesitated to use my pistol for this, not knowing what might be met to require its aid as a firearm.

Rank grass waved on each hand at the top, and wild ducks flew down the wind, and a gray heron and a white one, but neither man nor beast was to be seen. It was evident that the Kishon once begun, we could hope for no landing-place even for a minute's rest, but must go right on to the sea.

Soon there flowed in a tributary stream from the north, and to this I turned off in hopes of adventure or discovery.

This is the stream Nahr el Melchi,* or el Malek, and its mouth is twenty feet wide, with a considerable current, in about six feet in depth. The banks are from twelve to twenty feet high, and very steep, with oleanders on the sides and canes. The course is winding, and the channel soon narrows, while it bends abruptly amid broken islets. Still I pushed upward, being anxious to reach the tell marked in the map, where there might be ruins to reward a search. At length it became impossible to use the paddle, the river was so narrow, and when it was choked by reeds the Rob Roy had to return, stern foremost, for there was not room to turn her round.

Once more in the Kishon, we had open water, and the weather suddenly cleared up with bright sunshine at noon. It was time now to breakfast, so my bag was drawn out, and the viands spread on deck, while the canoe floated gently about twenty feet from the southern bank. Here an event happened which was totally unexpected, and ex-

---

* Schwartz (pp. 191, 192) suggests that this stream, flowing south of Shafa-mer, is named after the ancient Alammelech, which stood on its banks. The plain here may be the "Wady el Melch," for a salt marsh so near the sea is natural enough.

ceedingly interesting. My paddle was at the time across the deck, and I was lolling in the " well " as if on a couch, for it was found quite impossible to land on any part of Kishon's banks. I was dipping a little tin drinking-can, with my hand dabbling in the water, when a strange sound was heard quite near—a measured breathing, gurgling, hissing sound. After this had been repeated, I turned quietly round to look. Within a foot of my paddle, and close to my boat, and just by my hand, I saw the nose and mouth of—a crocodile! For a second or two my eyes were fixed on this extraordinary apparition as if spell-bound by a serpent's gaze. The nose was dark gray in color, smooth and rounded, and it stuck out above water. The mouth was open, and the water gurgled out and in. Not the slightest doubt had I that this was the face of a crocodile, though from its position behind me in the muddy water, and because my head was low, I did not see its eyes. A crocodile's head had long ago been familiar to me, for I had seen, quite near, at least fifty of them on the Upper Nile, and for twenty years the face of one of those I shot has been resting exactly opposite to the seat where this is written. The manner of swimming also, with the nose out of water and the mouth opened towards the flowing stream, was precisely what is so often noticed on the Nile, and the very first crocodile I had met in Egypt was exactly in the same position,* having come to the surface, like this one here, to bask in the sun. Hastily rising from my lounge, I grasped the paddle, but was doubtful what to do with it.

---

* This was just above Minyeh, which was then the limit north for crocodiles. More lately they have been driven far away by the steamboats, so that when the commodore of the Canoe Club ascended the Nile this year, but one crocodile fell to the gun of his royal highness.

But they used to come lower; so when I saw the crocodile near Minyeh, I descended the bank, and held on by one hand to a clump of palm-leaves, while with the other I placed my pistol within a yard of the crocodile's head. Straining then at the trigger to fire it, I found the pistol was only at half-cock, and when I brought it back to the other hand to cock it, the palm-leaves gave way, and I tumbled into the river, but managed to get to land without having lost the pistol, the same weapon used in this canoe cruise.

If I struck the animal, he might lash his tail and injure the boat. If I dipped the paddle gently, it would bring my hand quite close to his mouth, and an unsophisticated crocodile would very probably snap at such a tempting morsel, though those more knowing ones on the Nile are shy, because they learn from experience that men mean guns, and guns mean bullets, and though bullets do not

THE CROCODILE ON THE KISHON.

always mean death, or even wounds to the crocodile, yet they sometimes scratch his sleepy scales.* Cautiously,

* One night in the Nile a crocodile fell from the bank into the middle of my "dahabeeh." He must have been asleep, and the end of the lateen yard may have struck him. Aroused in my cabin, I found all the crew had jumped over, and were clinging to the gunwale, while they screeched most vigorously. At Siout, in 1849, I saw what was said to be the largest crocodile ever killed in the neighborhood. His death was not accomplished until he killed two men by swings of his tail. His body was hung up over the gate of the town, and I estimated its length as twenty-six feet, but others called it thirty feet. One of the crocodiles I killed had a quarter of a pint of pebbles in his stomach, and the bullet of an Arab gun, much corroded.

then, I dipped the blue paddle-blade, and the nose and mouth went down, and the Rob Roy dashed to the middle of the river, for there it would be safer, as the crocodile prefers to attack near the shore.

Then the thought came powerfully, "How important a discovery is this, and yet how indistinct are its details! How wrong it was not to get out my pistol—how culpable now if I do not sift the matter further!" So the canoe came close to the bank to examine the muddy shores. There we found numerous foot-prints, which seemed to be those of crocodiles. The shores were in patches, and in the most favorable condition for inspection, because for a long time there had been no rain until last night, and the river had not yet been swollen much. Many of the foot-marks were in little bights, entirely cut off from the land above by banks quite vertical, so that no ox or other cattle would go there, especially as at the flat mud-banks farther down there are regular places for cattle to drink at. The foot-print of the crocodile is very like the impression made by the human hand if you strike that into mud, with the wrist lowered and the fingers bent. These were what I saw, but to make more sure, I very slowly ran the canoe upon one of the banks, where her bow touched the shore and her stern swung slowly round in the stream. Just as I began to lean over to take a sketch of the foot-prints, I felt something hard under the boat's bottom, which began *behind* me (not floating with the stream), and it went bump, bump, all along, exactly under my seat.

For three years I had been well accustomed to sit on the floor of the canoe (never using a cushion or even a mat), and at once to apprehend the various knocks, and vibrations, and grazings received, which are quite distinguishable as the boat passes over rocks, boulders, shingle, gravel,

---

Fourteen hours after his death, and when his stomach was removed, and the skin was being stripped from his back, he moved his tail so vigorously that we had to place the "pipe-boy" sitting on it, to keep the body still. Warburton, on the Nile, found a lad crying beside a dead crocodile, which had eaten his grandmother. He sold the crocodile for 7s. 6d., with the old lady inside.

sand, mud, or weeds. This *feeling* of the object outside, through the thin oak plank (not an inch from your body), is almost as easy as by the hand itself, and therefore I knew in a moment that some hard, smooth, heavy substance was knocking below against my boat, and moving forward. The most likely of all things was that this was a crocodile, who had seen the large object above him—a total novelty here—and being an animal of curious mind, he had risen underneath it to examine what was shading the light from his eyes. In much less time than has been necessary to put all this on paper the Rob Roy fled from the spot at the top of her speed, and went on until we came in sight of the Mediterranean Sea.

The Kishon widens for the last two miles, and there are large bushes on its banks, but mostly on the north shore. I brought a branch from one of these as a trophy from a point just a little below the Nahr el Melcha. Bustards and hawks were numerous, and I saw one white ibis and one dead fish. The channel* turns suddenly to the north for a quarter of a mile, when its waters reach the sea-sand, and are there a little brackish. Numerous palm-trees are alongside, and a long lagoon of marsh.

Some travellers had come to ford the Kishon at its mouth, and I went up at once and told them I had seen a crocodile, had seen the foot-prints of others, and had felt below my boat what seemed to be one more. One of the party thus met was a foreign consul. He said that none of the people there had ever seen a crocodile in that river. But have they gone up high enough to see one? It will be perfectly easy to take a boat up the Kishon so as to test the discovery, and I only regret that this was not done at the time, and that there is left to some other traveller the satisfaction of bringing home one of the crocodiles I met in the Kishon on February 6, 1869.

It may well be supposed that when this discovery was

---

* It is plain that the mouth of Kishon has been gradually pushed on northward, by the slight but constant current along the coast, which silts up the southern bank of the river. The same is noticed at the mouth of the Belus.

published in a letter to the "Times," a great deal of interest was excited among naturalists in various countries. From Germany I received letters of urgent inquiry, and many from England and America. The Austrian Consul at Jerusalem took much trouble to look up the old writers upon the subject, and the learned Dr. Sandreczki sent me excerpts from different authors. Some of the investigations gave statements as to the crocodile having lived in the Zerka; but it seems quite unnecessary to refer to old writers upon this point, because, as we have narrated, there are now in England the bones of a crocodile killed in that river. But it being indisputable that the crocodile exists in the Zerka, we are more readily prepared to find it in the river Kishon, which is only about twenty miles north of the Zerka;* and indeed the higher tributaries of these two rivers are not five miles apart.

* Dr. Thomson says ("The Land and the Book, vol. ii. p. 244): "I suspect that long ages ago, some Egyptians accustomed to worship this ugly creature settled here (Cæsarea), and brought their gods with them. Once here, they would not easily be exterminated, for no better place could be desired by them than this vast jungle and impracticable swamp. . . . The historians of the Crusades speak of this marsh, which they call a lake, and also say that there were crocodiles in it in their day. If the locality would admit, I should identify this Zerka with the Shihor Libnath of Joshua xix. 26, for 'Shihor' is one of the names of the Nile, the very home of the crocodile; but the river in question was given to Asher, and is probably the Naaman (the Belus of ancient geographers), and the marshes at its source are as suitable for this ugly beast as those of Zoar." It is presumed that this is meant for Zoan, although crocodiles are not found in the Delta of Egypt now. These marshes of the Belus may be what are referred to in the Talmud under the name of Hultha (Neubaner, "Geog. Talm." p. 24). They are only a few miles north of the marshes of the Kishon, which are in every way as suitable for the crocodile to inhabit; and when we find that Kishon is between two rivers, one of them now containing crocodiles, and the other having a name which may indicate its relation or similarity to the Nile, and that the ports at the mouth of all three rivers were visited constantly by ships from Egypt, it appears highly probable that the animal may have been either indigenous in all three streams, or brought by Egyptians for their worship, or by Romans for their games. In "Delitzsch on Job" (Clarke's, ii. p. 366), it is said the crocodile is found near Tantura in the river Damur (N. of Sidon), but, query, meaning the Zerka?

As to the subject generally, see "Jerusalem und das Heilige Land," by Dr. Sepp (Schaffhausen, 1863), vol. ii. p. 476.

The Austrian Consul at Jerusalem made inquiries of the monks at Carmel, and the Rev. J. Zeller inquired of the hunters at Caipha, but none of them knew of a crocodile in the Kishon. The only distinct assertion I can find in modern books of the fact that the crocodile lived in the river Kishon is the following, by Rabbi Schwartz (p. 301): "The crocodile, al buda,* is met with on the shore of the Mediterranean, near Cheifa and Cæsarea, but it is not above two feet in length."† This, of course, refers to the Kishon as well as the Zerka, for Haifa is close to Kishon's mouth.

After a day or two we carried the canoe along the white sand of the bay of Acre to the marsh where the Belus rises. This Shihor Libnath (i. e. "white" or "glass" Shihor, or the "Nile of glass") is the present *Numan* of the Arabs, or the Ramle Abiatz, where, it is said, the manufacture of glass was first discovered accidentally by men who lighted a fire and found glass in the embers. The expression in Deuteronomy (xxxiii. 19), "The treasure hid in the sand," is probably in reference to this, and Josephus mentions the stream.‡

In a strong breeze I launched here and traversed the marshes until it was plain there was nothing to see except water and long reeds, for I did not then know that crocodiles might possibly be here also. There is a strange wild

---

* Dr. Sandreczki, at Jerusalem, said this name is unknown to him.

† The crocodile killed in the Zerka was five times as large.

‡ "Jewish War," book ii. ch. x. sec. ii. "The very small river Belus runs by it [Acre] at the distance of two furlongs; near which there is Memnon's monument, and hath near it a place no larger than a hundred cubits, which deserves admiration; for the place is round and hollow, and affords such sand as glass is made of, which place, when it hath been emptied by the many ships there loaded, it is filled again by the winds, which bring into it, as it were on purpose, the sand which lay remote, and was no more than bare common sand, while this mine presently turns it into glassy sand. And what is to me still more wonderful, that glassy sand which is superfluous, and is once removed out of the place, becomes bare common sand again. And this is the nature of the place we are speaking of."

The sand has been employed for making glass in later times by the Venetians (Kenrick's "Phenicia"); and after riding upon it for several hours, I can testify to its whiteness, purity, and beauty.

HAIFA AND CARMEL.

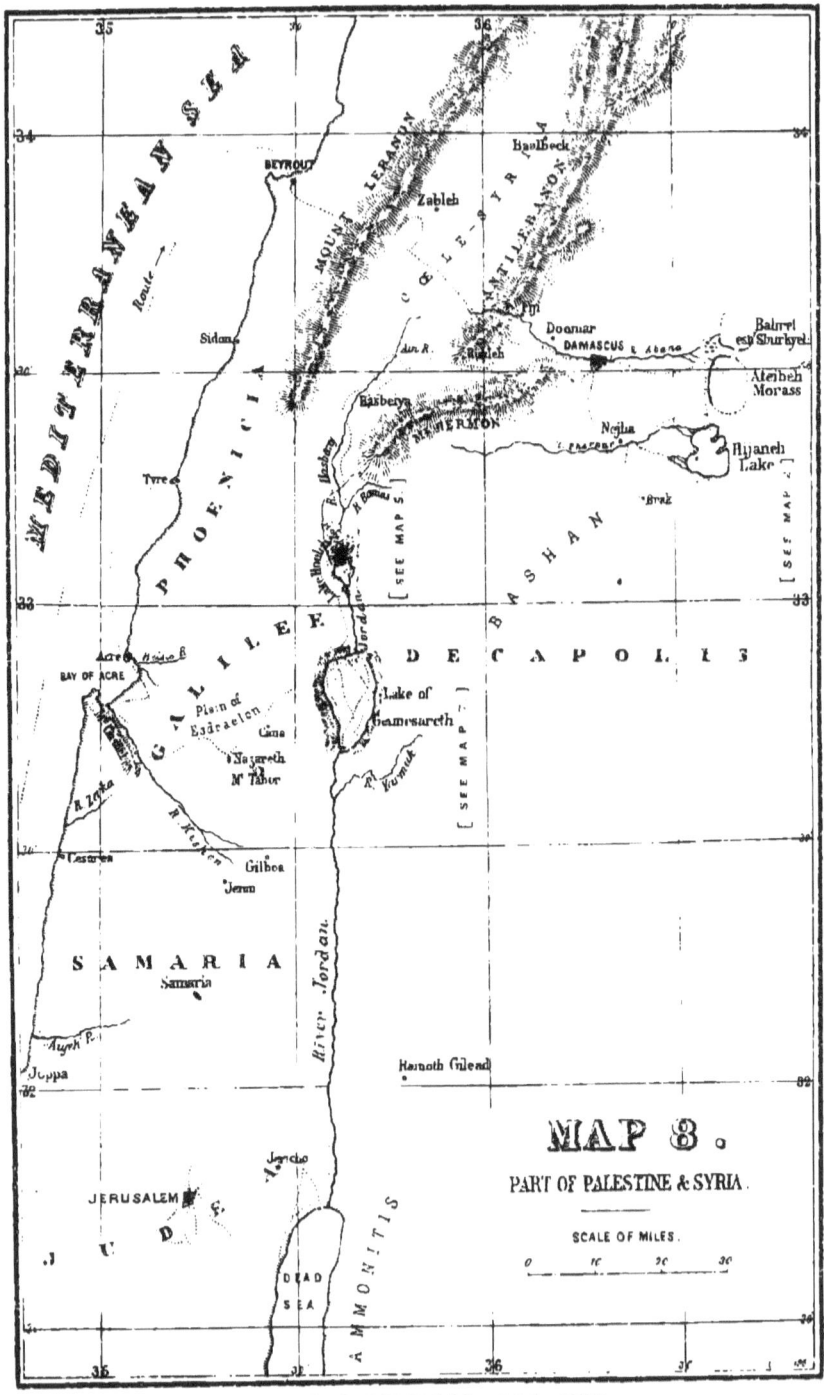

savageness about these marshes of the Belus, while palms grow on the edge, and a few gardens are inclosed. Two beautiful gazelles gave me a long chase on horseback, for it was easy to trace them on the sand.

As no one but Hany was present when we launched on this river, it may well be supposed how astonished the natives were to see the Rob Roy come out at the mouth, and with an air about her all the time that this was the common thing to do. We had found nothing there, but then the wind was so stirring that crocodiles, at least, would not be readily seen in the fens and marshes, though these are just the very places for the "timsah" to rest in; and I commend the Belus to the more diligent search of some future traveller.

Here it may be right to mention—for it could not otherwise come into our log (being only a landlubber's business, and managed without the canoe)—that I made a diligent search along the shores and in the stream of the river Aujeh, which runs into the sea a little north of Jaffa, seeking for evidence of the crocodile there. As this river is between the Zerka and the Nile, and is the longest constant river in Palestine next to Jordan, perhaps it might also have been made happy by the importation of the scaly monster; but though much that was interesting was found in the district around, there was no trace of the crocodile noticed on the Aujeh.* Yet the banks were suitable for its habitat, and one can not rashly pronounce a negative decision in such a case. When the question had been still further pressed upon attention by the kind inquiries of learned men at Jerusalem, it seemed to me not impossible that even in old Jordan, too, there might be a crocodile.

Reports reached me that the animal had actually been seen, long ago, in Jordan, but without much to substantiate their accuracy. Dr. Barclay, the eminent scholar and learned divine, whose pious work as a missionary in Jerusalem is joined with keen interest in all matters of science

* All the rivers along the coast ought to be searched with this purpose in view.

and history, informed me that a few years ago one of his congregation came back from the Jordan mourning the sudden death of a fellow-traveller, who, he said, was carried away before his eyes by some animal in the water. Nor was it easy to banish from one's mind the impression created by the verse in Job xl. 23, which says of "behemoth," "he trusteth that he can draw up Jordan into his mouth," although the explanation of that verse, already given by Stanley, seems to turn its bearing entirely from "the" specific Jordan, and another animal is meant by *behemoth*, the "river ox," buffalo, or hippopotamus.

However, it could do no harm to search even Jordan for the crocodile, and therefore, on a fourth visit to the Dead Sea, I made a close inspection of the last two miles of the river, with only this one object in view. Captain Warren, R.E., also went over the same ground in the opposite direction, and perhaps with less hopeful eye, but neither of us, at the day's end, had discerned the least trace of the crocodile here.*

Yet a day is not lost that is spent by the banks of the Jordan, and we can not have one too many visits to such a stream. How lonely it looked! To think of the millions of people, and thousands of years, that have had this river in their history, and yet not a single house, or tent, or booth, or even hermit's cell, is here to mark where the Son of Man was proclaimed to be the Son of God.

So now, Farewell to Jordan, in ardent hope of coming here again.

Best known of waters in the whole world, you have had

---

* Two things should be noticed as to this inspection; first, that the river was then high, and any foot-prints on the bank would be most likely washed away; and, second, that the Arabs whom we met upon the banks of the Jordan seemed in no way surprised that we were "looking out for a *timsah*." A search may yet be successful even here, if it is made at a time when the water is low, and along the part of the Jordan from the last ford to the Dead Sea—a portion of the river, very difficult to approach closely, quite devoid of any other interest, and, therefore, scarcely ever visited by travellers, while it has at the same time every feature in banks, and weeds, and sandy bays, which would fit it for the habitation of the great reptile of the Nile.

ACRE.

no ports for commerce, no cities on your banks, no green meads watered, no traffic on your waves. But the foot of the patriarch has rested there, and the prophet and the prince have dwelt beside you, and battles have sounded loud, and hosts have crossed your bed dried up by the finger of God. If for ten thousand years your waters had rolled on unused and unseen, there would be reason enough for all their flowing when they at last became the font of our Saviour's baptism, and shone back the light from a Trinity revealed to man.

Smoothly gliding out of the river Belus, the Rob Roy once more floated upon the salt waves of the Mediterranean. Bright sunshine gleamed on them, and a lively breeze curled over each billow-top as it plashed upon the shore. Through the waves we crossed this end of the bay of Acre, and soon reached the outlying ruins in the water, which guarded once this celebrated port of Ptolemais. So strong was the wind that nobody appeared on the walls or at the sally-port seaward, until the canoe had come quite close—certainly the smallest vessel that ever paid a visit to St. Jean d'Acre. But the first man who descried her soon brought the rest by his shouting, and the battlements were speedily crowded, and the shore was lined by a mass of sight-seers. Among the busy group, when I landed, one said to me in good English, "Come and have coffee with me." It was just the very thing I wanted—a cup of hot coffee—so I went, nothing loath, and on the way he said, "I wish to show you my young wife." This seemed odd enough, but I was ready for any thing that might turn up. The lady was a clever Lancashire lass, who had been six years in this funny little town of Acre, and now she prattled Arabic like a Turk, and sat cross-legged on a divan, while her nargilleh gurgled its blue cloud. I staid two days, delighted with this kind Jewish family. Here was a little negro boy, a slave, who had run away from his master, and got safely to the house of the English Consul. And so at once a name was given him, Farraj (free), and with his name a pair of trowsers, and then the broad grin of happiness came on his sable cheeks, all gashed by the slave-stealer's knife. Then the canoe went once more to Beyrout, and plied her azure sail in the harbor as before, and was welcomed by many friends. From this again to Jaffa; and here a long gap occurs in our log, which can not be filled up in these pages, because it was all on dry

A CHEER FROM THE "ARIADNE."

land, or indeed much of it was under the earth, in the shafts at Jerusalem. This was a delightful stay of some weeks at the Holy City. To summarize the proceedings of that happy visit would be merely to tell what can be read elsewhere. To give in detail all the climbs up above, and dives down below, all the rides, and walks, and drives,[*]

[*] Floyd, an American, drove the first carriage seen in Palestine for many

and talks, and sights, and thoughts, of that pleasant month, would need another volume quite as large as this. Farewell to you also, glorious Jerusalem!

At Alexandria once more we launched the Rob Roy to embark her on board the "Delta," bound for home. Farther out, and tossing in a gallant breeze, was the "Ariadne" frigate, the sea-home of our Commodore, and of that fair Princess who has won from all Englishmen the hardest thing to win, our affectionate regard.

The waves tossed angry and boisterous, as the Rob Roy ran out among the sharks to salute the man-of-war.

The crew clustered thick in the rigging of the stately frigate, and cheered the tiny consort with good-will. "Turn round before the wind," they cried, "and show how you can go."

It was a moment both of pride and of fear to me: pride in the craft that could finish such a voyage, fear lest the finish was to be in a capsize.

But the Rob Roy blithely turned upon a wave-top and flew along the foam, and carried safe through all her little flag, and a heart that beat high with grateful praise to Him who had vouchsafed to me thus to enjoy the happiest days of a very happy life.

hundred years, on the new and wretched road from Jaffa to Jerusalem, in June, 1868.

F F

APPENDIX.

I.

THE CANOE.

In "The Rob Roy in the Baltic," a full description is given with wood-cuts of the form of canoe and its fittings which succeeded so well on this cruise. Of course, more improvements were made before the Eastern voyage, but in designing the last Rob Roy a new and difficult problem had to be solved, because this was to be a boat in which one could not only travel but sleep comfortably.

Much consideration was given for months before the design was determined, and we shall now explain minutely the construction of what is in fact a little yacht, in which you can cruise over sea and land for a week, without getting supplies.*

It is always best that for sleeping the boat should be drawn up on shore, and in lawless countries an island or some solitary place should be selected, as you have no guard. It is a question still whether on the whole a light tent is not better than the boat to sleep in. However, we resolved to make the boat itself our comfortable bed, and for this it is absolutely necessary, (1.) to have a clear space of 6 feet 6 inches in length; (2.) to remove enough of the deck to give ample room for the knees in "turning" at night; (3.) to place the timbers of the boat so that they do not gall the shoulders, elbows, hips, knees, or heels; (4.) to have width enough at the end of your bed for the feet inclined sideways with *both* heels on the floor.

This Rob Roy was therefore built round me lying down, as the others had been built about me sitting. Her length on deck is 14 feet. Her floor is made longer by lessening the rake of stem and stern, which are more upright than in the drawing. Her greatest beam, 26 inches, is *not* on deck, but 3 inches below, so that her upper streak "topples in" amidships, but flanges out fore and aft. "Every body" said this would look ugly, but "nobody" now could find out the difference, unless by measurement. The lines thus al-

---

* Although some hundred canoes have been built within the last three years, I do not know one builder who will build a canoe reasonably complete, without constant personal supervision.

tered made the canoe stow more, sail better, and rise to her seas more lively. On the other hand, she is much harder to work in rapids and crooked water, and to drag and to beach on shore. Her garboard-streaks incline *downward*, so that on a flat shore their seams are nearly as low as the keel, which projects less than an inch outside.

The burdens or floor-boards are in four pieces, so made as to form a floor of 6 feet long, and thus support the whole body of the sleeper. They may also be placed above the well, as a round arched cover, exactly filling it up when the canoe has to be carried far. The dotted lines in the wood-cut at p. 139 show the well thus inclosed. The weight of the Rob Roy, with paddle, masts, and sails, is 72 lbs.

To form an open space for sleeping in, I arranged the well so that the beam should be where my body needed most width, and the well is therefore 6 inches longer than is required for sitting in. The fore part of it is half of a hexagon, each side of which is one foot long.

The "apron" is of course the most difficult of all canoe matters to settle satisfactorily.

I tried every feasible plan suggested by others or by myself,* and finally resolved upon the plan which has borne without injury the wear and tear of a whole year's work.

The apron of the Rob Roy is of light white water-proof, a present from a "clerical canoeist," who has lately been paddling with a monkey on board, until jacko went up the mast and upset the canoe and drowned himself.† The apron is fixed on the hexagonal front of the well by a simple and clever device of the builder, and it is kept up by a bit of cane arched over the knees. When this is removed (in two seconds), the apron lies flat—there is no coaming whatever on the sides.

The edges of the apron are fastened at each side by a single button-hole to a round stud 3 inches below deck *outside* the gunwale. This has never cut nor worn out, but it would instantly burst if an upset required all hands to debark.

The after edge of the apron is threaded on an elastic band devised by the Rev. J. Macdonna, of the C. C., and an excellent plan, and thus it lies close to one's chest, and is yet easy and slack, being supported on a breast button of my coat. The painter is fast at each end to the cleat on deck near each knee, and is rove through the stern-

---

* A wooden hatch, after a month's trial in 1867, had been discarded. Certainly, for the Eastern trip, it would have been useless, though for common work it has many recommendations.

† Of the human members of our Canoe Club, more than 200 in number, not one has been drowned in the many long voyages over Europe, Asia, Africa, America, and Australia.

post—not the stem. In heavy weather, by putting the painter under the apron stud, and over the edge of the apron, but lower down than the beading of the upper streak, the apron is bound close to the gunwale, and no water can come in. This plan, invented in the Red Sea, worked admirably ever since. The sails and mast are sufficiently described in our first chapter.* The stretcher is upon a new plan, very simple and successful. Instead of a board across, supported at each side, there are two flat thin boards, one for each foot, which abut on the garboard streak below, and against a carline of the deck above. Thus they have strong support, but are themselves very light, and there is a clear space between them, which can be increased in a moment by removing one of them, when a large bag can be passed in forward, and its neck can always be reached while sitting in the boat. My heels rest on the bare garboard streaks, thus gaining at least an inch more of inclination for the shin-bones, which adds much to comfort when you sit for eight hours at a time.

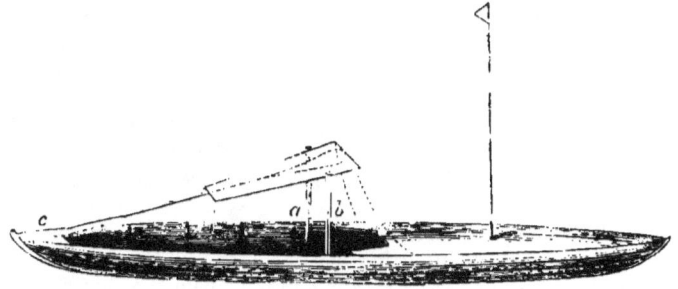

THE ROB ROY CABIN.

Large water-proof pockets are on each side near the knees. The luggage consists of one cylindrical "post-office bag" (Fig. 3. p. 455), 2 feet long, one foot in diameter, very light, with an interior "flap mouth," and so made that, when closed, it may be pitched overboard, and nothing will get damp inside. The bag acts also as buoyant cargo. The other rectangular bag, 12 inches on each side, and 6 inches broad, holds provisions and things less injured by water, and this is stowed just aft of the sitter, so that it can be readily reached. On either side of the well are stowed pistol and ammunition, brandy-bottle and books, large water-proof sheet and coat, the Inverness

---

* The sail is the same in size and shape as in the Baltic Rob Roy. In our last Club sailing-match, a simple lug-sail won the prize from all fancy rigs. The boom goes into a hem as well as the yard. A cord-loop at the end of the boom hooks on a long brass hook at the foot of the mast, so that the sail can be entirely detached, and stowed away without leaving your seat in the well.

cape (weighing 5½ lbs.), a water-bottle of mackintosh (Fig. 4, p. 455), carrying 5¼ lbs., spare shoes, cork seat, topmast (part of fishing-rod), topsail, sponge in tin baler, mosquito-curtain, towel, fishing-net, hooks and lines, sounding-cord, small stores, matches, etc., and the apparatus for the cabin, which we shall next describe.

To open a light boat of this sort for 6 feet 6 inches of its length, and at the part where there is most strain, was a novel proposal, and the builder doubted much, as I did myself, whether she could possibly bear such a mutilation without getting "hogged" or "screwed," or something worse. Careful management, however, overcame the difficulty entirely, and by the following means:

Three feet of the deck aft of the back-board is in a separate piece from the rest, and movable. The fore end of this has on it a strong, curved carline, to receive the whole strain of the back-board, and two other lighter carlines support the rest, and are screwed to this shifting deck, but all those carlines are quite separate from the gunwale.

The fore carline of this movable deck has at its ends strong flat hooks of iron, which go outside the gunwales, and so brace the boat together when the deck is in its place. The surface of the deck is flush with the gunwales, so its edge being inside keeps them in firm.[*] At each side of the well, flat movable boards (forming the bit of deck left there, and about three inches wide) take at each end into recesses in the after deck and against a strong knee near the fore part of the well, flaps of water-proof at each side (made fast outside under a half-inch beading one inch below the level of the gunwale) fold inward and cover the joints.

Now, to rig up our cabin for the night, we haul the Rob Roy on shore, and work her backward and forward in the ground until she is firmly bedded, and this is most important for a good night's rest. Next we remove the two flat pieces last described, and set them upright near the fore part of the well, as shown at $a\,b$ in the drawing, p. 453, which is on the scale of a quarter of an inch to the foot. A light bamboo cane is tied across these near the top. On this we lay the paddle, and its other blade rests on the solid piece of deck astern, and so forms our roof-tree. Next, the movable deck is placed on the paddle, so that its *wider* end projects forward to cover the sleeper's head. Over all, the water-proof sheet is thrown (shown in dotted lines), and tucked in between the canoe and the ground, or is weighted with stones, or tied down on the windward side if the night is not calm.

Aft of the back-board and above the movable deck, when afloat,

---

[*] That this deck should have kept perfectly sound, unwarped, and unbroken, through so many trials, is wonderful, but the piece of cedar was well chosen for its duties, and well seasoned.

there is a loose sheet of water-proof made fast along its edges by the beading below the gunwale outside, and which generally lies folded on the deck and covers it neatly, being kept in shape by the top joint of the fishing-rod that lies along one of its folds. For the night the paddle, being inside of the mackintosh covering, supports it with an inclined roof on each side, represented by dotted lines, while the edges are perfectly secure.*

The mosquito-net has now to be inserted, and then we light the little reading-lamp—which *bijou* it would take too long to describe accurately—and fasten it on the starboard upright, so as to be 6 inches from my left ear when reclining, and thus to throw a good light in front for reading.

The pillow is, of course, our clothes-bag, and for a bed there is an air-cushion, shown in our sketch, 3 feet long and 14 inches broad, with ribs across it so made that it will not collapse. This bed is particularly comfortable, and we have explained in our log that it answers also for several other purposes. Its diminutive size has been ridiculed, but if you try, you will find that, when the shoulders and hips are supported, the rest of the body needs no bed at all, except the head, which has a pillow, and the heels which can rest on a roll of the topsail.

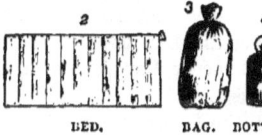

BED.   BAG.   BOTTLE.

Several canoeists have used wheels with much satisfaction where the canoe has to be frequently taken across some beaten path—as when it is kept in a house near a river or lake, and the wheels can be left at an assigned place.

But in my journeys I had found that out of each thousand miles not one mile would have been helped by wheels. However, as the use of them was strongly urged, and possibly it might help on this tour, I made a number of experiments, and finally reduced the size and weight so as to be very small, as represented in the sketch, page 456. These wheels are conical, made of wood, hollowed at the centres, and with light brass tires, and fixed on a steel axle, which turns in a strong brass piece (*b*). Above this is a grooved piece of wood, into which the keel (*a*) will fit, and without any tying or fastening.

---

* This plan may be improved upon. It creates trouble in removing and replacing the deck, and I think that one water-proof sheet would do for the whole roof, while the deck aft might have a projecting ledge above the gunwale, to cover the joint, which, however, at worst, would let in only a little water. The paddle has been often used in two pieces, with a ferrule to unite them. This is convenient, especially for sailing, but I grudge the additional weight even of an ounce. Letters and "patents" about paddle-blades set at right angles have come often to me during the last five years.

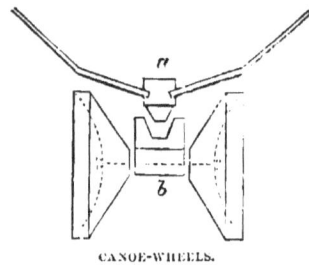

CANOE-WHEELS.

The diameter of the wheels is 4½ inches, and they weigh 2 lbs. The plan answered well on trial, and I carried the wheels all the way round, and never had one single occasion for using them! The fact is, in *real* canoeing, that is, in wild and unknown lands, you find no smooth roads to wheel a boat upon, or if there are roads, you can always get a man to help in carrying the boat; while on rocks, shingle, and jungle, no wheels would help you, and on grass, or earth, or sand, the boat can be dragged along.

Before going to bed in our cabin, our supper has to be cooked by the "canoe-cuisine," which has been fully described, with diagrams, in "The Voyage Alone in the Rob Roy Yawl" (Low, Fleet Street); and as this invaluable "paddler's kitchen" may be had at Hepburn's, 93 Chancery Lane, London, I need not further explain its manifold virtues here.*

In the East one can often manage to get fowls cooked before starting, and even eggs, so that with "Liebig's extract of meat," the essence of beef-soup (Morell's, Piccadilly), and dried fruits, there is always a sumptuous meal, besides tea for breakfast and a tablespoonful of brandy to kill the *animalcula* in the water for dinner. Bread, however, is the important item in travelling, and especially that it should keep well in cold, heat, or damp. I have still some bread that I got in Norway ten years ago, other bread from Africa eight years old, biscuit which was in my Swedish journey in 1866, and neat little loaves (an inch on each side) that I brought from Damascus twenty years ago. This last kind of bread was the best of all for carrying, because it is portable and good. You dip the loaves in water, and they soften and expand. Specimens of these were shown in the Palestine Exhibition, and deservedly excited much interest. It was amusing to find them solemnly denounced by a little evening paper as "remnants of repasts," with lots of other nonsense equally false.

What shall be done with that urchin who cries his news under a gas-jet in Pall Mall, and throws mud at the public because they won't buy his paper, "written by gentlemen," and sold at half-price? Let him be sent to a ragged-school, and, when he has learned "manners," we will give him a blacking-brush in the "red brigade," that he may get his pennies by polishing, not pelting, the public; for politeness pays better than petulance.

* Nor is it possible, I regret, to engage to answer all correspondence on the subject from inquiring strangers.

II.
Dress.

In all canoe cruises it is important to have convenient dress. You are exposed to heat and cold, wind and rain, to sudden chills by the splash of waves and wet of leakage, by working hard and then sitting still for sailing or for rest, or to cook and eat. The dress must be comfortable, light, strong, easily carried, readily donned and doffed, washed, dried, mended, and increased or diminished. Four long voyages in different climates have given some experience in these matters, so a few brief notes are inserted here for the benefit of canoeists who may paddle in hot countries.

A straw hat is quite enough for the sun of France at its hottest, but it is too thin for the more tropical rays of Africa; therefore the straw hat was soon discarded, and I wore the new helmet made by Tress, already described. The neck-shade of this is longer than the peak in front, and so, when the sun is on the face, by reversing the hat, more shade is obtained for the eyes. There is an interval between the hat and the head all round, so as to admit cool air. On some occasions a "puggery" was added. A wet towel falling down on the shoulders and bound over the top of the head answers well in a breeze, but it is close and heating in calm sun. This hat bore every accident well—rain, spray, snow, and heat, and frequent floatings when knocked off in thick jungles. I strongly recommend Tress's hat as an excellent head-dress for riding or boating in the sun, expensive, but not dear.

"Flannel always and everywhere, and all flannel," is the maxim for health. I had two "Norfolk jackets" of fine gray flannel; one can go over the other for a great-coat. They last so well that one of these has been through all four cruises, and it will do again. No wonder the tailors who made it remarked, "That will be good for your business, and bad for ours."

The paddler must put up with wet elbows for his coat; but the inside jersey ought to have short arms, so as to be dry.

A woven sleeveless vest is most useful, as you can slip it on when sailing. When it was desirable to be easily seen at a great distance, I wore a white night-shirt or a red jersey *outside*.

A silk Syrian scarf, of the largest size, was always wrapt about my loins. This is invaluable as preserving the heat of the body. It can be loosened in the boat and in the tent, but it should never be put off out of doors if once it is habitually worn. On the passage home it can be cautiously replaced by flannel, which may be gradually reduced each week.

Trowsers very long at the feet (and turned up usually) allow you to tie them over your shoes when dozing on the shore in midday hours.

and so to puzzle the flies, who think it great fun to bite through socks, however thick.

Gloves are also useful for the same occasions, and a long piece of gauze net, six feet square, tied over the face, made pleasant sleep on the grass or the sand of an island quite enjoyable.

A water-proof white sheet, six feet by five, the cover of my canoe when used to sleep in, was very useful to spread on wet sand for a couch, or tied round the waist to cover the legs on horseback, or stretched inside the tent over my bed in a furious storm of rain.

Boots are well enough for riding (worn outside the trowsers), but are too hot for the canoe. They should be very roomy, and thus they will not do for walking. I used a pair bought at Constantinople in 1849. The pleasant freedom of light easy shoes or slippers, when aboard your boat, amply repays the weight and bother of carrying them. Strong shoes, however, must be carried to be ready for shingle or jungle, or for a long trudge and towing the boat. A pair of the new seamless india-rubber half-boots were found most useful in wet grass or swampy shores.

A nightcap is necessary for sleeping in, as there are draughts in the " state cabin;" for it will not do to close it entirely. My sou'-wester was useful as a bag, and sometimes upon my head in rain and in steamboats, etc.

For rain, either afloat or ashore, I found the best protector was a long white (better stuff than black) india-rubber coat. Yet all such coats with sleeves are too hot to paddle in, unless very slowly, and a better plan was a cape, short near the arms and buttoned before or behind, according as the wind was from aft or ahead. The arms of the canoeist up to the elbow can only be kept dry by water-proof sleeves, but these should not form part of the coat.

At Jerusalem, Damascus, and Cairo, one collar and ribbon was quite enough, and the rest could be left off after the voyage out. At Alexandria you can get all such miserable furniture again for the return voyage.

For warmth I had a large soft thick dark hooded Inverness cape made 18 inches larger than the "largest size," so as to touch my shoes. The comfort and benefit of this could not be overrated. When riding in the cutting breeze over snow, it covered all down to the stirrups; sitting in the raw air of dawn, it kept all draught from one's limbs; lying in the canoe at night, it was sheet, blanket, and coverlet; reclining on sand or grass by day, or sitting to sail in cool evening breezes, it kept out the sun, and dew, and cold; and in the tent it was a comfortable dressing-gown to write in, again reclining, for to sit upright in the East is absurd, and the bed becomes an easy-chair. After all, this useful garment served as an addition to the bed-clothes during sleep, and next morning it was rolled up, like a soldier's great-coat, and strapped on my saddle.

An umbrella, with a white cover to it, may almost be included among " dress," at least for the hot months.* Spectacles of neutral tint (large size the best) give comfort to the eyes in the sun, and when you remove them, say at 4 P.M., the daylight seems to begin again, being about the same as it looked at noon, when seen through the glasses.

The list of "canoe-stores" is given below.

III.

CANOE GEAR AND STORES.

A. *Gear, etc.*—Masts, Sails, Wheels, Canoe-cuisine, Compass, Cork seat, Painter, Air-bed, Mosquito-curtains, Pistol and charges, Lamp, Canoe-bag, Rob Roy bag, Water-proof sheets, Water-bottle, Fishing-things, Net, Rod, Flies, Hooks and lines, Flag, Sponge, Baler, Spare paddle-rings, Plug, Lens, Long knife, Cane, Blocks, Wax-end, Tools, Nails, Screws, Wire, Spare rope and cord, Marine glue, Putty, Filter.

B. *Dress.*—Pith hat, Woven cap, Norfolk jacket (2), Woven vest, Silk scarf, Socks (2), Flannel trowsers (2), Flannel shirts (2), Under vests (2), Cape and hood, Sou'wester, Shoes, Mackintosh coat, Water-proof boots, Slippers, Brushes and comb, Scissors, needle, pins, and thread, Umbrella.

C. *Food, etc.*—Liebig's extract (2), Arrowroot, Tea, Beef-essence, Methylated spirits, James's powder, Insect-powder, Bread, Eggs, Fowls, Pudding, Figs, Oranges, Quinine, Gregory's mixture, Lint, Brandy, Plaster, Wax matches, Fuzees, Chibouque.

D. *Cargo.*—Books, Maps, Papers, Guide-book, Album, Note-book, Ink, Pencils, Penknife, Magnesium wire, Drawing-things, Presents, Money.

IV.

VOYAGE OF MOLYNEUX ON THE JORDAN IN 1847.

Although the Rob Roy is the first traveller's boat recorded as having navigated the Upper Jordan, there were two previous boat expeditions upon the Sea of Galilee and the Lower Jordan and Dead Sea.

---

* The French officers at Port Said had adopted a hat very like a parasol, the top being distant from the head of the wearer several inches all round, and connected by three wires to a leather bag, which goes on the temples.

The first of these was by Lieutenant Molyneux, of H.M.S. "Spartan," in 1847, and the other by Lieutenant Lynch, of the United States Navy, in 1848, who wrote a careful and interesting report, which is published and well known. The voyage of Molyneux was narrated in a paper read before the Geographical Society on March 28, 1848, and printed in their Journal, vol. xviii. p. 104.

This tells us how he transported the ship's "dinghy" (a small boat) from Beyrout to Tiberias by camels, and from thence he started on August 23, 1847, with five men, two of them English. They did not examine the lake, but passed at once southward to begin the Jordan. We have condensed the following brief notes of their voyage:

Molyneux judged the size of the lake to be eighteen miles long and eight or nine wide. He found the hot springs at Tiberias about 130° F. For seven hours after the "broken bridge" (a mile from the lake), they "scarcely ever had sufficient water to swim the boat for a hundred yards together." On the 26th he had to carry the boat on camels alongside the river before reaching the Jisr Mejamia, and after that for a great part of the time he was on the bank and frequently out of sight of the boat, which had four men to pull her and one to steer. On the 30th, just below the junction with the Zerka, she was attacked by fifty Arabs, who fired shots and then captured her, and took the men away.

Two Arabs brought the boat on to Jericho. On the 3d of September Molyneux embarked in her on the Dead Sea with "Toby" (a guide from Tiberias), and a Greek from Jerusalem. He sailed south from 6 P.M. until 2 30 A.M. on the 4th, and, after sailing about continually, landed at noon on the 5th. They shot some birds standing in the water, and saw others flying overhead when in the middle of the sea. They noticed a strip of foam north and south, beginning west of the Jordan's mouth and extending the whole length of the sea, "constantly bubbling and in motion like a stream that runs rapidly through a lake of still water, while nearly over this white track, during both the nights that we were on the water, we observed in the sky a white streak, like a cloud, extending also in a straight line from north to south, and as far as the eye could reach. On the 8th the boat arrived at Jerusalem."

Mr. Finn, then consul at Jerusalem, kindly aided Molyneux, and he tells us the rest of the story in "Under the Crown" for May, 1869. The end of it was as follows: "At my farewell greeting I congratulated him on being so much recovered in health. He answered, 'This is temporary, during the excitement; wait till I get on board, then I shall catch it'—a prophecy, alas! too true. They arrived at Jaffa with the boat, as sound as ever, and the crew set up three cheers on her mounting the deck, and vowed she would never be washed again, but keep her slime of the Dead Sea as a memorial. They rejoined the 'Spartan' on September 8. On reaching the station at Beyrout, fever seized its noble victim, and on the 3d of October Molyneux died."

V.

ALTITUDES ACCORDING TO AUTHORITIES RELIED UPON BY VANDEVELDE.

I.—THOSE IN CONNECTION WITH THE JORDAN.

	Feet above the Sea level
Kefr Kuk (basin north of Wady et Teim)	3,500
Lake Phiale	3,304
Hasbeya town	2,160
(1) Hasbeya source of the Jordan	1,700
Ford below	1,654
Khan below	1,619
(2) Banias source of the Jordan	1,200
(3) Dan source of the Jordan	647
Jisr el Ghujar (Roth)	346
Ain Belata (by estimation)	220
Hooleh marsh	180
Jisr Benat Yacoub	90

	Feet below the Sea-level.
Templars' keep near the Jordan [estimated by J. M.]	0
Lake of Genesareth (Lynch), (greatest depth 160 feet)	653
Dead Sea	1,292
Dead Sea, greatest depth (Lynch, 1308; Moore and Beke, 1800)	3,092

II.—OTHER RIVERS.

Abana River.

	Feet above the sea-level.
Sources near Zebedany (Porter)	3,608
Fall at Suk Barada (Russegger)	3,566
Damascus (mean of 6)	2,400

Pharpar.

Sasa (Schubert)	2,973

Kishon.

Plain of Esdraelon (where drained)	100

III.—MOUNTAINS AND OTHER PLACES MENTIONED IN THE BOOK.

	Feet above the Sea-level.
Lebanon, Jebel el Meskyeh	10,061
Hermon (Mansell)	9,053

III.—MOUNTAINS AND OTHER PLACES MENTIONED IN THE BOOK—*Continued*.

	Feet above the Sea-level
Lebanon, Jebel Sinnin	8,162
Dimes (Allen)	3,825
Zahleh (Russegger)	3,090
Jerusalem	2,642
Damascus	2,400
Highest between Jordan and Litany (De Forest)	2,300
Banias (Subeibeh Castle), by estimation	2,200
Tell et Hara	2,198
Mount Tabor (Mansell)	2,017
Carmel (highest point)	1,861
Nazareth (Roth)	1,265
Kurn Hattin	1,191
Jisr Burghuz	1,186
Gamala ruins	1,170
Kades	500

VI.

SCHOOLS AND MISSIONS.

Besides the institutions referred to already, the following may be noticed:

At Jaffa there is a very interesting little school, conducted by a young lady, aided by friends in England. Several visits to the institution made me admire it more and more each time. The children of Jaffa are in a horrid dirty poky hole of a town, and it must be charming for them to go to a school where bright smiles await them, and the happy teaching of a loving heart. Jews, Turks, and Franks, all partake of this blessing in the very place where Peter was taught that the Gospel was meant for us all. The children are delighted to see a visitor, and as very many travellers pass through Jaffa, it may be a new pleasure to them to look in at the Jaffa school.

The following information has been recently published regarding a most important and extensive educational work:

Society for Promoting Female Education in the East.

For thirty-five years this Society has pursued the special object with valuable results. With an income of about £3000 a year, it has been engaged for thirty-five years in a large field of labor. It supplies £800 in salaries to its own missionary teachers at Hong Kong, Singapore, Calcutta, Cuttack, Piplee, Secundra, Sierra Leone, Shemlan (on Mount Lebanon), Sidon, and Nazareth; also grants and school materials over the field of Protestant missions in the East. The estimated value of ladies' work and clothing sent abroad for sale during the past year is more than £5000. Twenty-one additional schools are needed: twenty-seven additional native teachers are ready for employment. Two ladies are leaving England for Zenana work in India.

Further information will be gladly supplied by Miss Webb, 267 Vauxhall Bridge Road, London.

Extracts from a Speech of the Bishop of Jerusalem at a Meeting in London in July, 1869.

"I first visited Palestine about forty years ago, when there was no Bible to be found either among the Jews or the Christians, or the Mohammedans—the deepest ignorance, darkness, superstition, and vice characterized all the inhabitants of that land at that period. With respect to the Jews, 160 adults have been baptized in Jerusalem, whilst a number of the younger Jews have received the first germs of the truth of the Gospel, and been sent away from Jerusalem by their friends and the rabbis, to remove them from the influence of the missionaries. There are now very few Jewish families in Jerusalem who do not possess a copy of the Old Testament, at least, and a great number have the New Testament, which they read amongst their friends. Whilst forty-two years ago the Jews, taught from the Talmud, believed it to be their duty, whenever the name of the Lord Jesus of Nazareth was mentioned, to curse that name and blaspheme, there are now very few who would do so. We every day meet with some who confess that Jesus was a good and righteous man, and that their forefathers were wrong in persecuting Him. In Jerusalem and the places around, our missionaries in the course of a few weeks dispose of large numbers of copies of the Scriptures. With respect to Roman Catholics, Armenians, Copts, and others, forty-two years ago the priests and laity were ignorant of the Christian religion. There was not a single Christian school belonging to any denomination in the whole of Palestine. We now have twenty-four Protestant schools, containing about 1000 children—Druses, Mohammedans, and Jews—who are taught the Word of God. Of these twenty-four schools, fourteen are under my charge. The people are not able to pay for the education, even were they willing; but they are becoming willing. After the Roman priests had endeavored to prevent the parents from sending their children to our schools, the Greek Patriarch gave us a Bible school. Finding their excommunication unsuccessful, they began to open schools wherever I had succeeded in opening one, so that for every one of our schools there are two others. They do not teach the Bible, yet when the children begin to read, we give them the pure Word of God. When the children repeat passages, their parents often request them to read out of the Word of God. Almost everywhere there are more children in my one school than in the Greek and Roman Catholic schools put together. In Abyssinia about 6000 copies of the Scriptures have been given away; a number of the Jews and others are reading the Bible there. When I first went to Jerusalem, there was only one native Protestant; we have now many congregations of people. They obtain no temporal benefit whatever from becoming Protestants: on the contrary, they have every thing against them."

POSTSCRIPT.—On Sunday, November 14, 1869, Mrs. Bowen Thompson, the foundress of the Syrian schools, died at Blackheath.

VII.

ITINERARY IN SYRIA, PALESTINE, AND EGYPT — FROM OCTOBER, 1868, TO APRIL, 1869.

The dates denote where the Rob Roy stopped each night.

October 9, Southampton; 10-22, "Tanjore" steamer.

EGYPT .... { October 23-26, Alexandria; 27, Steamer "Tage;" 28, 29, Port Said; 30, Ras el Esh; 31, November 1, 2, Kantara; 3, El Guisr; 4, Ismailia; 5, Lake Timsah; 6, Ismailia; 7, 8, Rameses; 9, Serapeion; 10, Zag-a-Zig; 11, Chalouf; 12-15, Suez; 16, 17, Ain Moosa; 18, Suez; 19, 20, Cairo; 21-23, Boulak; 24, Barrage; 25, an island; 26, Benha; 27, Ziftch; 28, 29, Mansourah; 30, Berimbal; December 1, Menzaleh; 2, Mushra; 3, Zoan; 4-7, Port Said; 8, 9, Steamer "Tibre." }

SYRIA .... { December 10-13, Beyrout; 14, Lebanon; 15, Mejdel; 16, El Hameh; 17, 18, Doomar; 19-21, Damascus; 22, Jisrin; 23, El Keisa; 24, 25, Abana mouth; 26-28, Hijaneh; 29, Nejha; 30, Brak; 31, Adalyeh; January 1, Damascus; 2, 3, Dimes; 4, Rukleh; 5, Bekafyeh; 6, Jordan source; 7, 8, Ford; 9, 10, Khan. }

PALESTINE ... { January 11-13, Tell el Kady; 14, Mansourah; 15, Salhyeh tent; 16, 17, Melaha; 18, Almanyeh; 19, Matarieh; 20, Jisr Yacob; 21, Julias plain; 22-25, Tell Hoom; 26, Ain et Tin; 27, 28, Tiberias; 29-31, Kerak; February 1, Magdala; 2, Kefr Kenna; 3, Maloolah; 4, Kishon; 5, Jelami; 6, 7, Haifa; 8, Acre; 9, Russian Steamer; 10, 11, Beyrout; 12, Austrian steamer; 13, 14, Joppa; 15, Ramleh; February 16 to March 17, Jerusalem [four days Dead Sea]; March 18-21, Joppa; 22-24, French steamer. }

EGYPT .... March 25-26, Alexandria.

March 27 to April 8, Steamer "Delta;" 9, Southampton.

THE END.

www.ingramcontent.com/pod-product-compliance
Lightning Source LLC
Chambersburg PA
CBHW022057300426
44117CB00007B/498